Ford Cortina MkIV 2.3 V6 Owners Workshop Manual

by J H Haynes
Member of the Guild of Motoring Writers
and Bruce Gilmour

Models covered
All Ford Cortina MkIV 2.3 V6 Saloon and Estate models; 2294 cc
Includes Cortina 80, often known as Mk V

Covers 'S-pack' and 'Business-pack' suspension options
Does not cover 1300, 1600 or 2000 cc variants

ISBN 1 85010 275 9

Printed in England *(426–4M3)*

ABCDE
FGHI

THE BOOK

Haynes Publishing Group
Sparkford Nr Yeovil
Somerset BA22 7JJ England

Haynes
861 Lawr
N
C

British Library Cataloguing in Publication Data

Gilmour, Bruce
Ford Cortina Mk IV (& 'V') 2.3 V6 owners
workshop manual– (Owners Workshop Manuals)
Haynes)
Cortina automobile
Title II. Series
9.28'722 TL215.C568
IN 1-85010-275-9

Acknowledgements

Special thanks are due to the Ford Motor Company for the supply of technical information and certain illustrations. The Champion Sparking Plug Company supplied the illustrations showing the various spark plug conditions.

The Section of Chapter 10 dealing with the suppression of radio interference was originated by Mr I. P. Davey, and was first published in *Motor* magazine.

Lastly, thanks are due to all those people at Sparkford who helped in the production of this manual.

About this manual   02099952

Its aim

The aim of this manual is to help you get the best value from your car. It can do so in several ways. It can help you decide what work must be done (even should you choose to get it done by a garage), provide information on routine maintenance and servicing, and give a logical course of action and diagnosis when random faults occur. However, it is hoped that you will make full use of the manual by tackling the work yourself. On simpler jobs it may even be quicker than booking the car into a garage, and having to go there twice, to leave and collect it. Perhaps most important, a lot of money can be saved by avoiding the costs the garage must charge to cover its labour and overheads.

The manual has drawings and descriptions to show the function of the various components so that their layout can be understood. Then the tasks are described and photographed in a step-by-step sequence so that even a novice can do the work.

Its arrangement

The manual is divided into thirteen Chapters, each covering a logical sub-division of the vehicle. The Chapters are each divided into consecutively numbered Sections and the Sections into paragraphs (or sub-sections), with decimal numbers following on from the Section they are in, eg 5.1, 5.2, 5.3 etc.

It is freely illustrated, especially in those parts where there is a detailed sequence of operations to be carried out. There are two forms of illustration: figures and photographs. The figures are numbered in sequence with decimal numbers, according to their position in the Chapter: eg, Fig. 6.4 is the 4th drawing/illustration in Chapter 6. Photographs are numbered (either individually or in related groups) the same as the Section or sub-section of the text where the operation they show is described.

There is an alphabetical index at the back of the manual as well as a contents list at the front.

References to the 'left' or 'right' of the vehicle are in the sense of a person in a seat facing towards the front of the vehicle.

Unless otherwise stated nuts and bolts are tightened by turning clockwise and removed by turning anti-clockwise.

Vehicle manufacturers continually make changes to specifications and recommendations, and these when notified are incorporated into our manuals at the earliest opportunity.

Whilst every care is taken to ensure that the information in this manual is correct no liability can be accepted by the authors or publishers for loss, damage or injury caused by any errors in, or omissions from, the information given.

Introduction to the Ford Cortina 2.3 V6

This latest addition to the Cortina range is equipped with a 2300 cc V6 overhead valve pushrod engine. A power assisted steering system is fitted as standard on all models in the range.

There are three four-door saloon models – GL, S and Ghia. The five-door estate car version is available only as a GL or Ghia variant.

Improved suspension and radial ply tyres along with the power assisted steering ensure good handling characteristics, and the standard equipment includes a driver's door mirror, hazard warning flashers, servo assisted brakes and heated rear window.

A wide range of options on the different models includes automatic transmission (not on the S model), reclining front seats, sliding roof, estate car tailgate washers and wipers and a pressure jet headlamp wash system.

Contents

The Ford Cortina 2.3 GL used as the project car for this manual

Ford Cortina 2.3 GL Estate

Buying spare parts
and vehicle identification numbers

Buying spare parts

Spare parts are available from many sources, for example: Ford garages, other garages and accessory shops, and motor factors. Our advice regarding spare part sources is as follows:

Officially appointed Ford garages – This is the best source of parts which are peculiar to your car and are otherwise not generally available (eg; complete cylinder heads, internal gearbox components, badges, interior trim etc). It is also the only place at which you should buy parts if your car is still under warranty – non-Ford components may invalidate the warranty. To be sure of obtaining the correct parts it will always be necessary to give the storeman your car's vehicle identification number, and if possible, to take the 'old' part along for positive identification. Remember that many parts are available on a factory exchange scheme – any parts returned should always be clean! It obviously makes good sense to go straight to the specialists on your car for this type of part for they are best equipped to supply you.

Other garages and accessory shops – These are often very good places to buy materials and components needed for the maintenance of your car (eg; oil filters, spark plugs, bulbs, fan belts, oils and greases, touch-up paint, filler paste, etc). They also sell general accessories, usually have convenient opening hours, charge lower prices and can often be found not far from home.

Motor factors – Good factors will stock all of the more important components which wear out relatively quickly (eg; clutch components, pistons, valves, exhaust systems, brake cylinders/pipes/hoses/seals/shoes and pads etc). Motor factors will often provide new or reconditioned components on a part exchange basis – this can save a considerable amount of money.

Vehicle identification numbers

Although many individual parts, and in some cases sub-assemblies, fit a number of different models it is dangerous to assume that just because they look the same, they are the same. Differences are not always easy to detect except by serial numbers. Make sure therefore, that the appropriate identity number for the model or sub-assembly is known and quoted when a spare part is ordered.

The vehicle identification plate is mounted on the right-hand side of the front body panel and may be seen once the bonnet is open (photo).

The engine number is stamped on the right-hand side of the crankcase (photo).

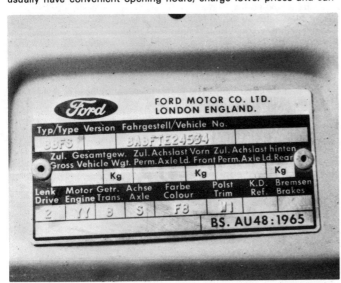

Vehicle identification plate

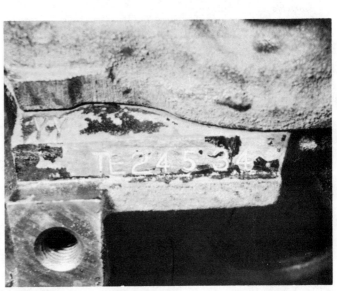

Engine number stamped on crankcase

Tools and working facilities

Introduction

A selection of good tools is a fundamental requirement for anyone contemplating the maintenance and repair of a motor vehicle. For the owner who does not possess any, their purchase will prove a considerable expense, offsetting some of the savings made by doing-it-yourself. However, provided that the tools purchased are of good quality, they will last for many years and prove an extremely worthwhile investment.

To help the average owner to decide which tools are needed to carry out the various tasks detailed in this manual, we have compiled three lists of tools under the following headings: *Maintenance and minor repair, Repair and overhaul,* and *Special.* The newcomer to practical mechanics should start off with the *Maintenance and minor repair* tool kit and confine himself to the simpler jobs around the vehicle. Then, as his confidence and experience grows, he can undertake more difficult tasks, buying extra tools as, and when, they are needed. In this way, a *Maintenance and minor repair* tool kit can be built-up into a *Repair and overhaul* tool kit over a considerable period of time without any major cash outlays. The experienced do-it-yourselfer will have a tool kit good enough for most repair and overhaul procedures and will add tools from the *Special* category when he feels the expense is justified by the amount of use to which these tools will be put.

It is obviously not possible to cover the subject of tools fully here. For those who wish to learn more about tools and their use there is a book entitled *How to Choose and Use Car Tools* available from the publishers of this manual.

Maintenance and minor repair tool kit

The tools given in this list should be considered as a minimum requirement if routine maintenance, servicing and minor repair operations are to be undertaken. We recommend the purchase of combination spanners (ring one end, open-ended the other); although more expensive than open-ended ones, they do give the advantages of both types of spanner.

Combination spanners - 10, 11, 13, 14, 17 mm
Adjustable spanner - 9 inch
Engine sump/gearbox/rear axle drain plug key (where applicable)
Spark plug spanner (with rubber insert)
Spark plug gap adjustment tool
Set of feeler gauges
Brake adjuster spanner (where applicable)
Brake bleed nipple spanner
Screwdriver - 4 in long x $\frac{1}{4}$ in dia (flat blade)
Screwdriver - 4 in long x $\frac{1}{4}$ in dia (cross blade)
Combination pliers - 6 inch
Hacksaw, junior
Tyre pump
Tyre pressure gauge
Grease gun (where applicable)
Oil can
Fine emery cloth (1 sheet)
Wire brush (small)
Funnel (medium size)

Repair and overhaul tool kit

These tools are virtually essential for anyone undertaking any major repairs to a motor vehicle, and are additional to those given in the *Maintenance and minor repair* list. Included in this list is a comprehensive set of sockets. Although these are expensive they will be found invaluable as they are so versatile - particularly if various drives are included in the set. We recommend the $\frac{1}{2}$ in square-drive type, as this can be used with most proprietary torque wrenches. If you cannot afford a socket set, even bought piecemeal, then inexpensive tubular box spanners are a useful alternative.

The tools in this list will occasionally need to be supplemented by tools from the *Special* list.

Sockets (or box spanners) to cover range in previous list
Reversible ratchet drive (for use with sockets)
Extension piece, 10 inch (for use with sockets)
Universal joint (for use with sockets)
Torque wrench (for use with sockets)
'Mole' wrench - 8 inch
Ball pein hammer
Soft-faced hammer, plastic or rubber
Screwdriver - 6 in long x $\frac{5}{16}$ in dia (flat blade)
Screwdriver - 2 in long x $\frac{5}{16}$ in square (flat blade)
Screwdriver - 1$\frac{1}{2}$ in long x $\frac{1}{4}$ in dia (cross blade)
Screwdriver - 3 in long x $\frac{1}{8}$ in dia (electricians)
Pliers - electricians side cutters
Pliers - needle nosed
Pliers - circlip (internal and external)
Cold chisel - $\frac{1}{2}$ inch
Scriber (this can be made by grinding the end of a broken hacksaw blade)
Scraper (this can be made by flattening and sharpening one end of a piece of copper pipe)
Centre punch
Pin punch
Hacksaw
Valve grinding tool
Steel rule/straight edge
Allen keys
Selection of files
Wire brush (large)
Axle-stands
Jack (strong scissor or hydraulic type)

Special tools

The tools in this list are those which are not used regularly, are expensive to buy, or which need to be used in accordance with their manufacturers' instructions. Unless relatively difficult mechanical jobs are undertaken frequently, it will not be economic to buy many of these tools. Where this is the case, you could consider clubbing together with friends (or a motorists' club) to make a joint purchase, or borrowing the tools against a deposit from a local garage or tool hire specialist.

The following list contains only those tools and instruments freely available to the public, and not those special tools produced by the vehicle manufacturer specifically for its dealer network. You will find occasional references to these manufacturers' special tools in the text of this manual. Generally, an alternative method of doing the job without the vehicle manufacturer's special tool is given. However, sometimes, there is no alternative to using them. Where this is the case and the relevant tool cannot be bought or borrowed you will have to entrust the work to a franchised garage

Valve spring compressor
Piston ring compressor
Balljoint separator
Universal hub/bearing puller
Impact screwdriver
Micrometer and/or vernier gauge
Carburettor flow balancing device (where applicable)
Dial gauge
Stroboscopic timing light
Dwell angle meter/tachometer
Universal electrical multi-meter
Cylinder compression gauge
Lifting tackle
Trolley jack
Light with extension lead

Buying tools

For practically all tools, a tool factor is the best source since he will have a very comprehensive range compared with the average garage or accessory shop. Having said that, accessory shops often offer excellent quality tools at discount prices, so it pays to shop around.

Remember, you don't have to buy the most expensive items on the shelf, but it is always advisable to steer clear of the very cheap tools. There are plenty of good tools around at reasonable prices, so ask the proprietor or manager of the shop for advice before making a purchase.

Care and maintenance of tools

Having purchased a reasonable tool kit, it is necessary to keep the tools in a clean serviceable condition. After use, always wipe off any dirt, grease and metal particles using a clean, dry cloth, before putting the tools away. Never leave them lying around after they have been used. A simple tool rack on the garage or workshop wall, for items such as screwdrivers and pliers is a good idea. Store all normal spanners and sockets in a metal box. Any measuring instruments, gauges, meters, etc, must be carefully stored where they cannot be damaged or become rusty.

Take a little care when tools are used. Hammer heads inevitably become marked and screwdrivers lose the keen edge on their blades fom time to time. A little timely attention with emery cloth or a file will soon restore items like this to a good serviceable finish.

Working facilities

Not to be forgotten when discussing tools, is the workshop itself. If anything more than routine maintenance is to be carried out, some form of suitable working area becomes essential.

It is appreciated that many an owner mechanic is forced by circumstances to remove an engine or similar item, without the benefit of a garage or workshop. Having done this, any repairs should always be done under the cover of a roof.

Wherever possible, any dismantling should be done on a clean flat workbench or table at a suitable working height.

Any workbench needs a vice: one with a jaw opening of 4 in (100 mm) is suitable for most jobs. As mentioned previously, some clean dry storage space is also required for tools, as well as the lubricants, cleaning fluids, touch-up paints and so on which become necessary.

Another item which may be required, and which has a much more general usage, is an electric drill with a chuck capacity of at least $\frac{5}{16}$ in (8 mm). This, together with a good range of twist drills, is virtually essential for fitting accessories such as wing mirrors and reversing lights.

Last, but not least, always keep a supply of old newspapers and clean, lint-free rags available, and try to keep any working area as clean as possible.

Spanner jaw gap comparison table

Jaw gap (in)	Spanner size
0.250	$\frac{1}{4}$ in AF
0.276	7 mm
0.313	$\frac{5}{16}$ in AF
0.315	8 mm
0.344	$\frac{11}{32}$ in AF; $\frac{1}{8}$ in Whitworth
0.354	9 mm
0.375	$\frac{3}{8}$ in AF
0.394	10 mm
0.433	11 mm
0.438	$\frac{7}{16}$ in AF
0.445	$\frac{3}{16}$ in Whitworth; $\frac{1}{4}$ in BSF
0.472	12 mm
0.500	$\frac{1}{2}$ in AF
0.512	13 mm
0.525	$\frac{1}{4}$ in Whitworth; $\frac{5}{16}$ in BSF
0.551	14 mm
0.563	$\frac{9}{16}$ in AF
0.591	15 mm
0.600	$\frac{5}{16}$ in Whitworth; $\frac{3}{8}$ in BSF
0.625	$\frac{5}{8}$ in AF
0.630	16 mm
0.669	17 mm
0.686	$\frac{11}{16}$ in AF
0.709	18 mm
0.710	$\frac{3}{8}$ in Whitworth; $\frac{7}{16}$ in BSF
0.748	19 mm
0.750	$\frac{3}{4}$ in AF
0.813	$\frac{13}{16}$ in AF
0.820	$\frac{7}{16}$ in Whitworth; $\frac{1}{2}$ in BSF
0.866	22 mm
0.875	$\frac{7}{8}$ in AF
0.920	$\frac{1}{2}$ in Whitworth; $\frac{9}{16}$ in BSF
0.938	$\frac{15}{16}$ in AF
0.945	24 mm
1.000	1 in AF
1.010	$\frac{9}{16}$ in Whitworth; $\frac{5}{8}$ in BSF
1.024	26 mm
1.063	$1\frac{1}{16}$ in AF; 27 mm
1.100	$\frac{5}{8}$ in Whitworth; $\frac{11}{16}$ in BSF
1.125	$1\frac{1}{8}$ in AF
1.181	30 mm
1.200	$\frac{11}{16}$ in Whitworth; $\frac{3}{4}$ in BSF
1.250	$1\frac{1}{4}$ in AF
1.260	32 mm
1.300	$\frac{3}{4}$ in Whitworth; $\frac{7}{8}$ in BSF
1.313	$1\frac{5}{16}$ in AF
1.390	$\frac{13}{16}$ in Whitworth; $\frac{15}{16}$ in BSF
1.417	36 mm
1.438	$1\frac{7}{16}$ in AF
1.480	$\frac{7}{8}$ in Whitworth; 1 in BSF
1.500	$1\frac{1}{2}$ in AF
1.575	40 mm; $\frac{15}{16}$ in Whitworth
1.614	41 mm
1.625	$1\frac{5}{8}$ in AF
1.670	1 in Whitworth; $1\frac{1}{8}$ in BSF
1.688	$1\frac{11}{16}$ in AF
1.811	46 mm
1.813	$1\frac{13}{16}$ in AF
1.860	$1\frac{1}{8}$ in Whitworth; $1\frac{1}{4}$ in BSF
1.875	$1\frac{7}{8}$ in AF
1.969	50 mm
2.000	2 in AF
2.050	$1\frac{1}{4}$ in Whitworth; $1\frac{3}{8}$ in BSF
2.165	55 mm
2.362	60 mm

Jacking and Towing

Jacking points

To change a wheel in an emergency, use the jack supplied with the car. Ensure that the roadwheel nuts are released before jacking up the car and make sure that the arm of the jack is fully engaged with the body bracket and that the base of the jack is standing on a firm level surface (photos).

The jack supplied with the vehicle is not suitable for use when raising the car for maintenance or repair operations. For this work, use a trolley, hydraulic or screw type jack located under the front crossmember, bodyframe sidemembers or rear axle casing, as illustrated. Always supplement the jack with axle stands or blocks before crawling beneath the car.

Towing points

If your car is being towed, make sure that the tow rope is attached to a towing eye or the front crossmember. If the vehicle is equipped with automatic transmission, the distance towed must not exceed 15 miles (24 km), nor the speed 30 mph (48 km/h), otherwise serious damage to the transmission may result. If these limits are likely to be exceeded, disconnect and remove the propeller shaft.

If you are towing another vehicle, attach the tow rope to the lower suspension arm bracket at the axle tube.

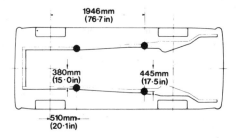

Jacking points (for maintenance and repair operations)

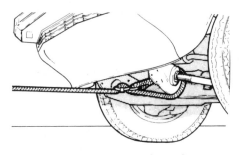

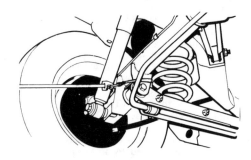

Tow rope attachment to front of car

Tow rope attachment to rear of car

Loosen the wheelnuts before jacking up the car

Car jack in position for raising the car

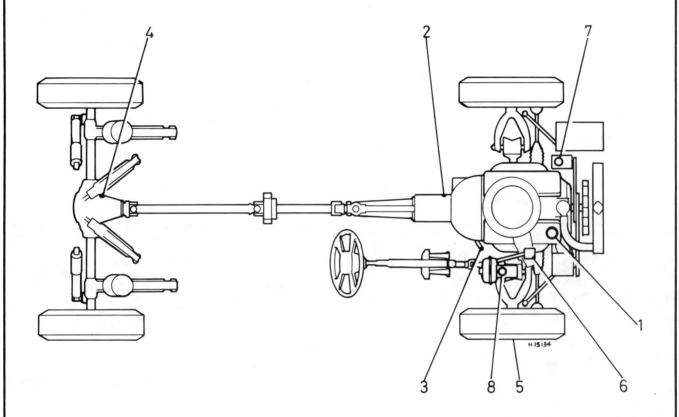

H.15134

Recommended lubricants and fluids

Component or system	Lubricant type or specification
1 Engine	Multigrade engine oil, SAE 10W/40
2 Gearbox (manual)	SAE 80EP Gear oil
3 Gearbox (automatic)	See Chapter 13
4 Rear axle (differential)	SAE 90EP Gear oil
5 Front wheel bearings	General purpose grease
6 Power steering lubricant	SAE 40 engine oil
7 Power steering fluid	SQM-2C-9007-AA
8 Brakes	SAE J1703 hydraulic fluid

Note: *The above are general recommendations for a temperate climate. In other climates, or under severe operation conditions, lubrication requirements may vary. If in doubt consult a Ford dealer.*

Safety first!

Professional motor mechanics are trained in safe working procedures. However enthusiastic you may be about getting on with the job in hand, do take the time to ensure that your safety is not put at risk. A moment's lack of attention can result in an accident, as can failure to observe certain elementary precautions.

There will always be new ways of having accidents, and the following points do not pretend to be a comprehensive list of all dangers; they are intended rather to make you aware of the risks and to encourage a safety-conscious approach to all work you carry out on your vehicle.

Essential DOs and DON'Ts

DON'T rely on a single jack when working underneath the vehicle. Always use reliable additional means of support, such as axle stands, securely placed under a part of the vehicle that you know will not give way.

DON'T attempt to loosen or tighten high-torque nuts (e.g. wheel hub nuts) while the vehicle is on a jack; it may be pulled off.

DON'T start the engine without first ascertaining that the transmission is in neutral (or 'Park' where applicable) and the parking brake applied.

DON'T suddenly remove the filler cap from a hot cooling system – cover it with a cloth and release the pressure gradually first, or you may get scalded by escaping coolant.

DON'T attempt to drain oil until you are sure it has cooled sufficiently to avoid scalding you.

DON'T grasp any part of the engine, exhaust or catalytic converter without first ascertaining that it is sufficiently cool to avoid burning you.

DON'T allow brake fluid or antifreeze to contact vehicle paintwork.

DON'T syphon toxic liquids such as fuel, brake fluid or antifreeze by mouth, or allow them to remain on your skin.

DON'T inhale dust – it may be injurious to health (see *Asbestos* below).

DON'T allow any spilt oil or grease to remain on the floor – wipe it up straight away, before someone slips on it.

DON'T use ill-fitting spanners or other tools which may slip and cause injury.

DON'T attempt to lift a heavy component which may be beyond your capability – get assistance.

DON'T rush to finish a job, or take unverified short cuts.

DON'T allow children or animals in or around an unattended vehicle.

DO wear eye protection when using power tools such as drill, sander, bench grinder etc, and when working under the vehicle.

DO use a barrier cream on your hands prior to undertaking dirty jobs – it will protect your skin from infection as well as making the dirt easier to remove afterwards; but make sure your hands aren't left slippery.

DO keep loose clothing (cuffs, tie etc) and long hair well out of the way of moving mechanical parts.

DO remove rings, wristwatch etc, before working on the vehicle – especially the electrical system.

DO ensure that any lifting tackle used has a safe working load rating adequate for the job.

DO keep your work area tidy – it is only too easy to fall over articles left lying around.

DO get someone to check periodically that all is well, when working alone on the vehicle.

DO carry out work in a logical sequence and check that everything is correctly assembled and tightened afterwards.

DO remember that your vehicle's safety affects that of yourself and others. If in doubt on any point, get specialist advice.

IF, in spite of following these precautions, you are unfortunate enough to injure yourself, seek medical attention as soon as possible.

Asbestos

Certain friction, insulating, sealing, and other products – such as brake linings, brake bands, clutch linings, torque converters, gaskets, etc – contain asbestos. *Extreme care must be taken to avoid inhalation of dust from such products since it is hazardous to health.* If in doubt, assume that they *do* contain asbestos.

Fire

Remember at all times that petrol (gasoline) is highly flammable. Never smoke, or have any kind of naked flame around, when working on the vehicle. But the risk does not end there – a spark caused by an electrical short-circuit, by two metal surfaces contacting each other, by careless use of tools, or even by static electricity built up in your body under certain conditions, can ignite petrol vapour, which in a confined space is highly explosive.

Always disconnect the battery earth (ground) terminal before working on any part of the fuel or electrical system, and never risk spilling fuel on to a hot engine or exhaust.

It is recommended that a fire extinguisher of a type suitable for fuel and electrical fires is kept handy in the garage or workplace at all times. Never try to extinguish a fuel or electrical fire with water.

Fumes

Certain fumes are highly toxic and can quickly cause unconsciousness and even death if inhaled to any extent. Petrol (gasoline) vapour comes into this category, as do the vapours from certain solvents such as trichloroethylene. Any draining or pouring of such volatile fluids should be done in a well ventilated area.

When using cleaning fluids and solvents, read the instructions carefully. Never use materials from unmarked containers – they may give off poisonous vapours.

Never run the engine of a motor vehicle in an enclosed space such as a garage. Exhaust fumes contain carbon monoxide which is extremely poisonous; if you need to run the engine, always do so in the open air or at least have the rear of the vehicle outside the workplace.

If you are fortunate enough to have the use of an inspection pit, never drain or pour petrol, and never run the engine, while the vehicle is standing over it; the fumes, being heavier than air, will concentrate in the pit with possibly lethal results.

The battery

Never cause a spark, or allow a naked light, near the vehicle's battery. It will normally be giving off a certain amount of hydrogen gas, which is highly explosive.

Always disconnect the battery earth (ground) terminal before working on the fuel or electrical systems.

If possible, loosen the filler plugs or cover when charging the battery from an external source. Do not charge at an excessive rate or the battery may burst.

Take care when topping up and when carrying the battery. The acid electrolyte, even when diluted, is very corrosive and should not be allowed to contact the eyes or skin.

If you ever need to prepare electrolyte yourself, always add the acid slowly to the water, and never the other way round. Protect against splashes by wearing rubber gloves and goggles.

When jump starting a car using a booster battery, for negative earth (ground) vehicles, connect the jump leads in the following sequence: First connect one jump lead between the positive (+) terminals of the two batteries. Then connect the other jump lead first to the negative (–) terminal of the booster battery, and then to a good earthing (ground) point on the vehicle to be started, at least 18 in (45 cm) from the battery if possible. Ensure that hands and jump leads are clear of any moving parts, and that the two vehicles do not touch. Disconnect the leads in the reverse order.

Mains electricity

When using an electric power tool, inspection light etc, which works from the mains, always ensure that the appliance is correctly connected to its plug and that, where necessary, it is properly earthed (grounded). Do not use such appliances in damp conditions and, again, beware of creating a spark or applying excessive heat in the vicinity of fuel or fuel vapour.

Ignition HT voltage

A severe electric shock can result from touching certain parts of the ignition system, such as the HT leads, when the engine is running or being cranked, particularly if components are damp or the insulation is defective. Where an electronic ignition system is fitted, the HT voltage is much higher and could prove fatal.

Routine maintenance

Maintenance is essential for ensuring safety and desirable for the purpose of getting the best in terms of performance and economy from your car. Over the years the need for periodic lubrication – oiling, greasing, and so on – has been drastically reduced if not totally eliminated. This has unfortunately tended to lead some owners to think that because no such action is required, components either no longer exist, or will last for ever. This is a serious delusion. It follows therefore that the largest initial element of maintenance is visual examination. This may lead to repairs or renewals.

Every 250 miles (400 km) or weekly

Check tyre pressures and inflate if necessary (photo).
Check and top-up the engine oil.
Check and top-up battery electrolyte level.
Check and top-up windscreen washer fluid level (photo).
Check and top-up coolant level.
Check operation of all lights.

Checking the tyre pressure

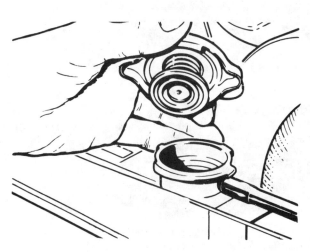

Checking the radiator coolant level

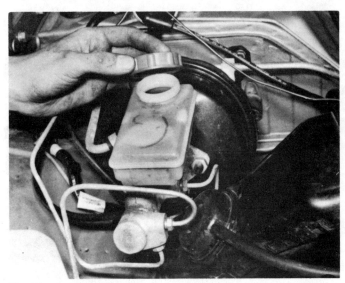

Checking the brake fluid level

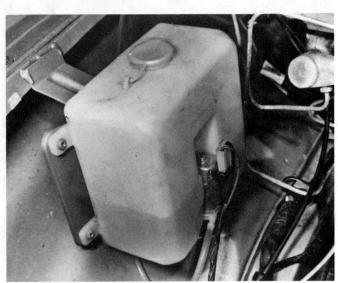

Check the level in the washer reservoir

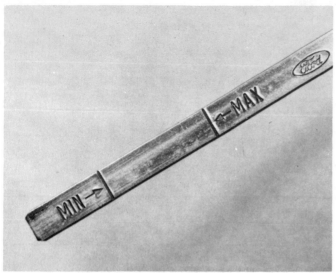

The engine dipstick has MIN and MAX markings

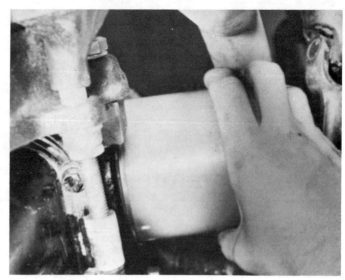

Renewing the engine oil filter

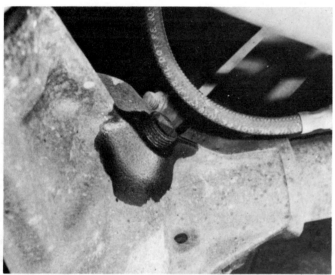

The rear axle filler/level plug

Topping up the power steering fluid reservoir

Remove the plug from the upper swivel balljoint grease point ...

... and from the lower swivel balljoint grease point

Check the brake fluid reservoir (photo).

Every 6000 miles (10 000 km)

Change engine oil and renew filter (photos).
Clean fuel pump filter.
Check carburettor adjustment.
Check drivebelt tension; renew if frayed.
Clean and adjust spark plugs.
Check, adjust or renew distributor contact breaker points.
Check for wear in all steering joints and condition of flexible dust excluders.
Inspect brake fluid lines and hoses for leaks, damage or deterioration.
Inspect front disc pads and rear brake shoe linings for wear.
Check and top-up brake fluid reservoir.
Lubricate door hinges and controls.
Check and top-up gearbox oil level.
Check the fluid level in the power steering reservoir and top-up if necessary (photo).
Check the steering system for leaks.
Check the power steering pump drive belt.
Check and adjust valve clearances.
Check and top-up rear axle oil level (photo).
Check and adjust clutch free movement.
Check and adjust valve clearances.
Move position of roadwheels (balanced off car) to even out tread wear.
Clean crankcase ventilation valve.
Check exhaust system for leaks or broken mountings.

Every 12 000 miles (19 000 km)

Check ignition timing.
Check front wheel alignment.

Every 18 000 miles (29 000 km)

Renew air cleaner element.

Every 24 000 miles (38 000 km) or at two yearly intervals

Drain cooling system and refill with 'long-life' type antifreeze mixture. If other than 'long-life' mixture is used, cooling system should be drained, flushed and refilled every autumn.
Clean, re-lubricate and adjust front hub bearings.

Every 36 000 miles (58 000 km)

Bleed hydraulic system, renew all system seals and refill with clean, fresh fluid.
Remove plugs and grease front suspension upper swivel balljoints (photos).
Renew servo unit filter.

Once a year or more often if the time can be spared

Cleaning

Examination of components requires that they are cleaned. The same applies to the body of the car, inside and out, in order that deterioration due to rust or unknown damage may be detected. Certain parts of the body frame, if rusted badly, can result in the vehicle being declared unsafe and it will not pass the annual test for roadworthiness.

Exhaust system

An exhaust system must be leakproof, and the noise level below a certain maximum. Excessive leaks may cause carbon monoxide fumes to enter the passenger compartment. Excessive noise constitutes a public nuisance. Both these faults may cause the vehicle to be kept off the road. Repair or renew defective sections when symptoms are apparent.

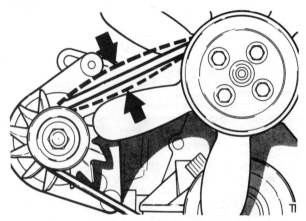

Checking alternator drive belt tension

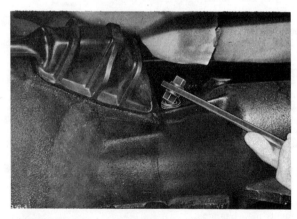

Checking the transmission oil level (manual gearbox)

Chapter 1 Engine

For modifications, and information applicable to later models, see Supplement at end of manual

Contents

Specifications

Engine (general)

Type	6 cylinder ohv in 60° 'V'
Firing order	1–4–2–5–3–6
Bore	3.54 in (90.02 mm)
Stroke	2.37 in (60.14 mm)
Cubic capacity	2294 cc
Compression ratio	8.75 : 1
Maximum engine speed	
Continuous	5700 rev/min
Intermittent	6000 rev/min

Cylinder block

Number of main bearings	4
Bore diameter:	
Standard grade 1	3.5433 to 3.5437 in (90.000 to 90.010 mm)
2	3.5437 to 3.5440 in (90.010 to 90.020 mm)
3	3.5440 to 3.5444 in (90.020 to 90.030 mm)
4	3.5444 to 3.5448 in (90.030 to 90.040 mm)
Undersize grade A	3.5633 to 3.5637 in (90.510 to 90.520 mm)
B	3.5637 to 3.5641 in (90.520 to 90.530 mm)
C	3.5641 to 3.5645 in (90.530 to 90.540 mm)
Standard service	3.5444 to 3.5448 in (90.030 to 90.040 mm)
Oversize 0.5 mm	3.5641 to 3.5645 in (90.530 to 90.540 mm)
Oversize 1.0 mm	3.5838 to 3.5842 in (91.030 to 91.040 mm)
Centre main bearing width	0.848 to 0.850 in (21.560 to 21.610 mm)
Main bearing shell internal diameter (fitted):	
Standard	2.2444 to 2.457 in (57.008 to 57.042 mm)
Undersize 0.254 mm	2.2344 to 2.357 in (56.754 to 56.788 mm)
0.508 mm	2.2244 to 2.2257 in (56.500 to 56.534 mm)
0.762 mm	2.2144 to 2.2157 in (56.246 to 56.280 mm)
1.020 mm	2.2044 to 2.2057 in (55.992 to 56.026 mm)
Main bearing parent bore diameter:	

Standard	2.3866 to 2.3874 in (60.620 to 60.640 mm)
Oversize 0.38 mm	2.4015 to 2.4023 in (61.000 to 61.020 mm)
Camshaft parent bore diameter:	
Front	1.7726 to 1.7740 in (45.025 to 45.060 mm)
Centre 1	1.7576 to 1.7590 in (44.645 to 44.680 mm)
Centre 2	1.7427 to 1.7440 in (44.265 to 44.300 mm)
Rear	1.7277 to 1.7291 in (43.885 to 43.920 mm)

Crankshaft

Endfloat	0.003 to 0.011 in (0.080 to 0.280 mm)
Backlash	0.002 to 0.005 in (0.050 to 0.140 mm)
Main bearing journal diameter:	
Standard	2.2433 to 2.2440 in (56.980 to 57.000 mm)
Undersize 0.254 mm	2.2333 to 2.2340 in (56.726 to 56.746 mm)
0.508 mm	2.2233 to 2.2240 in (56.472 to 56.492 mm)
0.762 mm	2.2133 to 2.2140 in (56.218 to 56.238 mm)
1.020 mm	2.2033 to 2.2040 in (55.964 to 55.984 mm)
Centre main bearing width	1.0389 to 1.0409 in (26.390 to 26.440 mm)
Main bearing clearance	0.0002 to 0.0025 in (0.006 to 0.064 mm)
Big-end journal diameter:	
Standard	2.1251 to 2.1259 in (53.980 to 54.000 mm)
Undersize 0.254 mm	2.1151 to 2.1159 in (53.726 to 53.746 mm)
0.508 mm	2.1051 to 2.1059 in (53.472 to 53.492 mm)
0.762 mm	2.0951 to 2.0959 in (53.218 to 53.238 mm)
1.020 mm	2.0851 to 2.0859 in (52.964 to 52.984 mm)

Camshaft

Number of bearings	4
Drive	Gear driven from crankshaft
Thrust plate thickness:	
Red	0.1559 to 0.1568 in (3.960 to 3.985 mm)
Blue	0.1569 to 0.1579 in (3.986 to 4.011 mm)
Backlash	0.002 to 0.005 in (0.05 to 0.14 mm)
Spacer thickness:	
Red	0.1604 to 0.1614 in (4.075 to 4.100 mm)
Blue	0.1615 to 0.1624 in (4.101 to 4.125 mm)
Cam lift	0.2545 to 0.2565 in (6.465 to 6.516 mm)
Cam length (heel to toe)	1.3385 to 1.3464 in (33.998 to 34.201 mm)
Journal diameter:	
Front	1.6497 to 1.6505 in (41.903 to 41.923 mm)
Centre 1	1.6347 to 1.6355 in (41.522 to 41.542 mm)
Centre 2	1.6197 to 1.6205 in (41.141 to 41.161 mm)
Rear	1.6047 to 1.6055 in (40.760 to 40.780 mm)
Bearing inside diameter:	
Front	1.6514 to 1.6522 in (41.948 to 41.968 mm)
Centre 1	1.6364 to 1.6372 in (41.567 to 41.587 mm)
Centre 2	1.6214 to 1.6222 in (41.186 to 41.206 mm)
Rear	1.6064 to 1.6072 in (40.805 to 40.825 mm)
Endfloat	0.0008 to 0.0040 in (0.02 to 0.10 mm)

Pistons and piston rings

Piston diameter:	
Standard 1	3.5414 to 3.5418 in (89.952 to 89.962 mm)
2	3.5418 to 3.5422 in (89.962 to 89.972 mm)
3	3.5422 to 3.5425 in (89.972 to 89.982 mm)
4	3.5425 to 3.5429 in (89.982 to 89.992 mm)
Service standard	3.5424 to 3.5433 in (89.978 to 90.002 mm)
Service oversize 0.5 mm	3.5621 to 3.5630 in (90.478 to 90.502 mm)
Service oversize 1.0 mm	3.5818 to 3.5827 in (90.978 to 91.002 mm)
Piston clearance in bore	0.0011 to 0.0024 in (0.028 to 0.062 mm)
Ring gap (fitted):	
Top	0.015 to 0.023 in (0.38 to 0.58 mm)
Centre	0.015 to 0.023 in (0.38 to 0.58 mm)
Bottom	0.015 to 0.055 in (0.38 to 1.40 mm)

Gudgeon pins

Diameter:	
Red	0.9446 to 0.9447 in (23.994 to 23.997 mm)
Blue	0.9447 to 0.9448 in (23.997 to 24.000 mm)
Clearance in piston (floating)	0.0002 to 0.0004 in (0.005 to 0.011 mm)
Interference in piston	0.0007 to 0.0015 in (0.018 to 0.042 mm)

Connecting rods

Big-end bearing inside diameter – Aluminium:	
Standard	2.1262 to 2.1276 in (54.008 to 54.042 mm)

Undersize 0.254 mm	2.1162 to 2.1176 in (53.754 to 53.788 mm)
0.508 mm	2.1062 to 2.1076 in (53.500 to 53.534 mm)
0.762 mm	2.0962 to 2.0976 in (53.246 to 53.280 mm)
1.020 mm	2.0862 to 2.0876 in (52.992 to 53.026 mm)
Crankpin/bearing shell clearance	0.0002 to 0.0023 in (0.006 to 0.060 mm)
Big-end bearing inside diameter – Composite:	
Standard	2.1261 to 2.1277 in (54.006 to 54.046 mm)
Undersize 0.254 mm	2.1262 to 2.1177 in (53.752 to 53.792 mm)
0.508 mm	2.1062 to 2.1077 in (53.498 to 53.538 mm)
0.762 mm	2.0962 to 2.0977 in (53.244 to 53.284 mm)
1.020 mm	2.0862 to 2.0877 in (52.990 to 53.030 mm)
Crankpin/bearing shell clearance	0.0002 to 0.0025 in (0.006 to 0.064 mm)
Bore diameter:	
Big-end	2.2370 to 2.2377 in (56.820 to 56.840 mm)
Small-end	0.9432 to 0.9439 in (23.958 to 23.976 mm)

Cylinder head

Cast marking	AN
Valve seat angle	44° 30' to 45°
Valve guide bore	
Standard	0.3174 to 0.3184 in (8.063 to 8.088 mm)
Oversize 0.2 mm	0.3253 to 0.3262 in (8.263 to 8.288 mm)
Oversize 0.4 mm	0.3331 to 0.3341 in (8.463 to 8.488 mm)

Valves

Valve clearance	
Inlet	0.014 in (0.35 mm)
Exhaust	0.016 in (0.40 mm)
Inlet valve	
Opens	20° BTDC
Closes	56° ABDC
Exhaust valve	
Opens	62° BBDC
Closes	14° ATDC
Tappet diameter	0.8736 to 0.8740 in (22.190 to 22.202 mm)
Tappet clearance in housing	0.0009 to 0.0023 in (0.023 to 0.060 mm)
Inlet valve:	
Length	4.133 to 4.181 in (105.000 to 106.200 mm)
Head diameter	1.461 to 1.477 in (37.130 to 37.520 mm)
Stem diameter:	
Standard	0.315 to 0.316 in (8.025 to 8.043 mm)
Oversize 0.2 mm	0.323 to 0.324 in (8.225 to 8.243 mm)
Oversize 0.4 mm	0.331 to 0.332 in (8.425 to 8.443 mm)
Oversize 0.6 mm	0.339 to 0.340 in (8.625 to 8.643 mm)
Oversize 0.8 mm	0.347 to 0.348 in (8.825 to 8.843 mm)
Stem/guide clearance	0.0007 to 0.0024 in (0.020 to 0.063 mm)
Valve lift	0.3574 to 0.3606 in (9.08 to 9.16 mm)
Valve spring free length	1.909 in (48.5 mm)
Exhaust valve:	
Length	4.141 to 4.181 in (105.200 to 106.200 mm)
Head diameter	1.261 to 1.275 in (32.030 to 32.410 mm)
Stem diameter:	
Standard	0.314 to 0.315 in (7.999 to 8.017 mm)
Oversize 0.2 mm	0.322 to 0.323 in (8.199 to 8.217 mm)
Oversize 0.4 mm	0.330 to 0.331 in (8.399 to 8.417 mm)
Oversize 0.6 mm	0.338 to 0.339 in (8.599 to 8.617 mm)
Oversize 0.8 mm	0.346 to 0.347 in (8.799 to 8.817 mm)
Stem/guide clearance	0.0018 to 0.0035 in (0.046 to 0.089 mm)
Valve lift	0.3555 to 0.3586 in (9.03 to 9.11 mm)
Valve spring free length	1.909 in (48.5 mm)

Engine lubrication data

Oil change capacity:	
With filter renewal	7.5 pints (4.25 litres)
Without filter renewal	7.0 pints (4.0 litres)
Minimum oil pressure:	
At 750 rpm	14.5 lbf/in² (1.0 kgf/cm²)
At 2000 rpm	40.6 lbf/in² (2.8 kgf/cm²)
Pressure relief valve opens at	58 to 68 lbf/in² (4.0 to 4.7 kgf/cm²)
Warning light operates at	4.5 to 8.5 lbf/in² (0.3 to 0.6 kgf/cm²)
Oil pump:	
Rotor/casing clearance	0.0059 to 0.0118 in (0.15 to 0.30 mm)
Inner/outer rotor clearance	0.0019 to 0.0078 in (0.05 to 0.20 mm)
Endfloat rotor/casing	0.0011 to 0.0039 in (0.03 to 0.10 mm)

Torque wrench settings

	lbf ft	kgf m
Main bearing caps	70	9.7
Big-end caps	23	3.2
Crankshaft pulley	33	4.6
Camshaft gear	33	4.6
Flywheel	49	6.8
Timing cover	13	1.9
Oil pump	11	1.6
Oil pump cover	7	1.1
Rocker shaft	46	6.4
Oil sump		
First stage	4	0.6
After 15 minutes at 1000 rpm	6	0.9
Oil sump drain plug	17	2.5
Oil pressure switch	10	2.4
Cylinder head bolts		
First stage	36	4.8
Second stage	45	6.3
Third stage (after 10 to 20 minutes wait)	73	10.0
After 15 minutes running at 1000 rpm	73	10.0
Rocker cover	4	0.6
Inlet manifold		
First stage	5	0.6
Second stage	8	1.2
Third stage	13	1.8
Fourth stage	17	2.3
After 15 minutes running at 1000 rpm	17	2.3
Pressure plate to flywheel	13	1.9
Fuel pump	13	1.9
Water pump	6	0.9
Spark plug	26	3.5
Exhaust manifolds:		
Pre February 1978	17	2.5
Post February 1978	20	2.8

1 General description

The engine is a water cooled 60° V6 cylinder four stroke petrol engine. The overhead valves are operated by tappets, pushrods and rocker arms from the camshaft which is gear driven by the crankshaft.

The cylinder heads are of the crossflow design with the inlet manifold located on top of the cylinder block between the two cylinder heads and the exhaust manifolds on the outside of the heads.

The combined crankcase and cylinder block is made of cast iron and houses the pistons, crankshaft and camshaft. Attached to the bottom of the crankcase is a pressed steel sump which acts as a reservoir for the engine oil. The lubrication system is described in Section 23.

Aluminium alloy pistons are connected to the crankshaft by H-section forged steel connecting rods and gudgeon pins. Two compression rings and one oil control ring, all located above the gudgeon pin, are fitted.

The forged crankshaft runs in four main bearings and endfloat is controlled by thrust washers fitted to centre main bearing (No 2 main bearing).

The drive gear for the distributor and oil pump is located in front of the rear camshaft bearing and the fuel pump is operated by an eccentric behind the front camshaft bearing.

2 Major operations with engine in place

1   The following major operations can be carried out without removing the engine from the car:

   a) Removal and refitting of the cylinder heads
   b)* Removal and refitting of the oil sump and oil pump
   c)* Removal and refitting of the timing gears
   d) Renewal of crankshaft front seal
   e) Removal and refitting of the flywheel
   f) Renewal of crankshaft rear seal
   g)* Removal and refitting of the big-end bearings
   h)* Removal and refitting of the connecting rods and pistons

* It will be necessary to raise the engine slightly, place a support under the gearbox and then lower the front crossmember for these operations.

3 Major operations requiring engine removal

1   For the following major operations the engine must be removed from the car:

   a) Removal and refitting of the crankshaft
   b) Removal and refitting of the main bearings

4 Methods of engine removal

1   Although it is possible to remove the engine and gearbox as an assembly it is recommended that the engine is removed as a separate unit. If the engine and gearbox are removed as an assembly it has to be lifted out at a very steep angle and for this a considerable lifting height is required.

2   If the work being undertaken requires the removal of the gearbox as well as the engine it is recommended that the gearbox is removed first, refer to Chapter 6, Section 2 or 10 as appropriate.

5 Engine – removal

1   The do-it-yourself owner should be able to remove the engine in about four hours. It is essential to have a good hoist and two axle-stands if an inspection pit is not available.

2   The sequence of operations listed in this Section is not critical as the position of the person undertaking the work, or the tool in his hand, will determine to a certain extent the order in which the necessary operations are performed. Obviously the engine cannot be removed until everything is disconnected from it and the following sequence will ensure that nothing is forgotten.

3   Remove the battery as described in Chapter 10.

4   Open the bonnet and using a soft pencil mark the outline position of both the hinges at the bonnet to act as a datum for refitting.

5   With the help of a second person to take the weight of the bonnet undo and remove the hinge to bonnet securing bolts with plain and spring washers. There are two bolts to each hinge (photo).

6   Lift away the bonnet and put in a safe place where it will not be scratched (photo).

7   Place a container having a capacity of at least 8 Imp pints (4·5

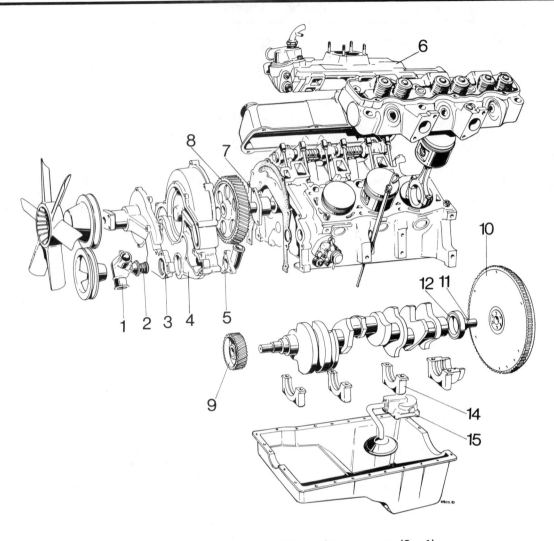

Fig. 1.1 Exploded view of engine main components (Sec 1)

1	Water inlet connection	5	Bypass hose flange	9	Crankshaft timing gear	13	Oil pump drive shaft
2	Thermostat	6	Inlet manifold	10	Flywheel ring gear	14	Crankshaft main bearing
3	Water pump	7	Camshaft thrust plate	11	Crankshaft pilot bearing	15	Oil pump
4	Timing cover	8	Camshaft gear	12	Rear oil seal		

5.5 Remove the hinge to bonnet attaching bolts ...

5.6 ... and lift off the bonnet

litres) under the engine sump and remove the oil drain plug. Allow the oil to drain out and then refit the plug (photo).

8   Refer to Chapter 3, Section 4 and remove the air cleaner assembly from the top of the carburettor.

9   Mark the HT leads, so that they can be identified for refitting in their original positions, and disconnect them from the spark plugs.

10 Disconnect the HT lead from the centre of the ignition coil. Remove the distributor cap and HT leads from the engine compartment (photo).

11 Disconnect the LT lead from the coil at the connection on top of the inlet manifold (photo).

12 Drain the cooling system as described in Chapter 2, Section 2.

13 Disconnect the pressure and return hoses from the power steering reservoir/pump assembly and drain the fluid into a suitable container. Plug the ends of the hoses and the reservoir/pump assembly connectors to prevent the ingress of dirt or water.

14 If the power steering system is not to be dismantled the reservoir/pump assembly can be removed from the engine, without disconnecting the hoses, and placed on the battery tray (photo). To do this slacken the idler pulley bracket securing bolts and remove the power steering pump drivebelt. If the special type wrench is available undo the steering pump to mounting bracket bolts and remove the

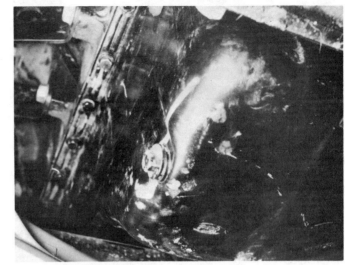

5.7 Engine oil sump drain plug

5.10 Remove the distributor cap

5.11 Disconnect the LT lead from the coil at the resistor on top of the inlet manifold

5.14a Place the power steering pump and bracket on the battery tray

5.14b Removing the power steering pump mounting bracket bolts

5.14c The earth strap is secured by one of the power steering bracket mounting bolts

5.18 The alternator multi-connector is secured with a spring clip

5.25 Disconnect the wiring from the starter motor

5.26 Removing the starter motor

5.28a Pull back the clutch release lever gaiter ...

5.28b ... and disconnect the clutch cable

pump, or alternately, using an ordinary spanner remove the mounting bracket securing bolts and lift away the steering pump complete with mounting bracket. Note the earth strap attached to one of the bracket mounting bolts (photos).

15 Slacken the clips securing the heater hoses to the water pump, automatic choke, intake manifold and heater connections. Pull off the hoses and remove them from the engine compartment.

16 Remove the radiator as described in Chapter 2, Section 5.

17 Remove the exhaust shroud from the right-hand exhaust manifold.

18 Detach the multi-connector from the rear of the alternator (photo).

19 Disconnect the wiring from the temperature sender unit and the oil pressure switch. Disconnect the engine to bulkhead earth strap from the rear of the engine.

20 Disconnect the fuel supply pipe from the fuel pump and plug the pipe to prevent the ingress of dirt or fuel loss due to syphoning. Disconnect the fuel return line from the carburettor.

21 Disconnect the throttle control inner cable from the operating rod.

22 Unscrew the throttle control outer cable securing nut, separate the retaining clip and remove the cable from the mounting bracket.

23 Disconnect the servo vacuum hose from the carburettor intermediate flange.

24 Undo and remove the two nuts securing the exhaust downpipe clamp plate to the exhaust manifold (both sides) and lower the exhaust pipes.

25 Working underneath the car disconnect the main starter motor cable and the two wiring connectors from the starter motor solenoid (photo).

26 Remove the two securing bolts and lift out the starter motor (photo).

27 Undo the two securing bolts and remove the clutch housing lower cover plate.

28 Detach the clutch release lever gaiter from the clutch housing and pull it back. Draw back the clutch cable and disconnect it from the clutch operating arm. Remove the clutch cable assembly through the locating hole in the flange on the clutch housing and tuck the cable out of the way where it will not get caught up as the engine is lifted out (photos).

29 On models equipped with automatic transmission, working through the starter motor opening, remove the torque converter to drive plate bolts.

30 Suitably support the weight of the gearbox by using a jack or other support such as an axle-stand or wooden blocks.

31 Remove the six clutch housing flange-to-engine securing bolts.

32 Attach lifting eyes to the engine and fit a lifting sling (if lifting eyes are not available use a rope passed under the engine mountings) and take the weight of the engine without lifting it.

33 Remove the two nuts securing the engine mounting rubber insulators to the front crossmember (Fig. 1.2).

34 Check that all the relevant parts have been disconnected or removed and that all wiring and control cables are tucked out of the way where they will not get caught up when the engine is being lifted out.

35 Lift the engine slightly to clear the engine mounting studs from

their location in the front crossmember and pull it forward off the gearbox input shaft. Take care not to put any strain on the input shaft.

36 When the engine is withdrawn from the input shaft hoist it high enough to clear the front panel and remove it from the car (photo). Lower the engine and support it so that it will not get damaged.

6 Engine oil sump – removal and refitting (engine in car)

1 Disconnect the battery.

2 Loosen the front wheel nuts. Jack up the front of the car and remove the front wheels.

3 Bend back the tabs of the steering shaft connecting link securing bolts locking plate and loosen the bolts. Remove one bolt and swing the link to one side.

4 Disconnect the brake pipes and hoses at the brackets in both wheel arches.

5 Disconnect the fuel supply pipe at the connecting hose under the right-hand wing (Fig. 1.3) and also at the fuel pump.

6 Remove the starter motor as described in Chapter 10, Section 16.

7 Remove the two nuts securing the engine mounting to the front crossmember.

8 Raise the engine slightly and place an axle-stand or other suitable support under the gearbox.

9 Place a jack under the front crossmember and remove both rear attaching bolts, then loosen the front attaching bolts and carefully lower the front crossmember on the jack.

10 Remove the sump drain plug and drain the engine oil into a suit-

5.36 Lifting out the engine

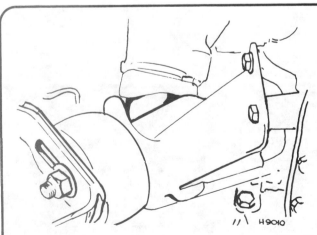
Fig. 1.2 Engine mounting to front crossmember nut (Sec 5)

Fig. 1.3 Fuel line connection under right-hand wing (Sec 6)

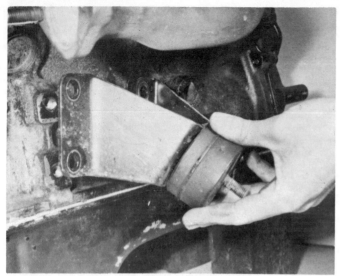

9.2 Removing the engine right-hand mounting bracket and insulator

9.4a Undo the distributor clamp plate bolt ...

9.4b ... and lift out the distributor

9.5 Removing the power steering pump drive belt idler pulley bracket

9.6 Remove the alternator and mounting bracket as an assembly

9.8 Withdraw the vent valve from the rocker cover

able container. Refit the drain plug. Always fit a new washer.
11 Undo the sump securing bolts and remove the sump. If the sump does not come free from the engine block after the bolts are removed, lever it carefully sideways to free it.
12 Refitting the sump is the reverse of the removal procedure. Always use a new set of sump gaskets. Fit the gaskets to the engine block using grease to hold it in position. Ensure that the gaskets and seals are correctly seated, refer to Section 32. Bleed the brake system as described in Chapter 9, Section 2. Don't forget to refill the sump with the specified oil.

7 Engine dismantling – general

1 When the engine is removed from the car, it, and particularly its accessories, are vulnerable to damage. If possible mount the engine on a stand, or failing this, make sure it is supported in such a manner that it will not be damaged whilst undoing tight nuts and bolts.
2 Cleanliness is important when dismantling the engine to prevent exposed parts from contamination. Before starting the dismantling operations, clean the outside of the engine with paraffin, or a good grease solvent if it is very dirty. Carry out this cleaning away from the area in which the dismantling is to take place.
3 If an engine stand is not available carry out the work on a bench or wooden platform. Avoid working with the engine directly on a concrete floor, as grit presents a real source of trouble.
4 As parts are removed, clean them in a paraffin bath. Never immerse parts with internal oilways in paraffin but wipe down carefully with a petrol dampened rag. Clean oilways with nylon pipe cleaners.
5 It is advisable to have suitable containers to hold small items in their groups as this will help when reassembling the engine and also prevent possible loss.
6 Always obtain complete sets of gaskets when the engine is being dismantled. It is a good policy to always fit new gaskets in view of the relatively small cost involved. Retain the old gaskets when dismantling the engine with a view to using them as a pattern to make a replacement gasket if a new one is not available.
7 When possible refit nuts, bolts and washers in their locations as this helps to protect the threads from damage and will also be helpful when the engine is being reassembled, as it establishes their location.
8 Retain unserviceable items until the new parts are obtained, so that the new part can be checked against the old part to ensure that the correct item has been supplied.

8 Engine ancillaries – removal

1 Although the items listed may be removed separately with the engine installed (as described in the relevant Chapters) it is more appropriate to take them off after the engine has been removed from the car when extensive dismantling is being carried out. The items comprise:

Carburettor
Distributor
Fuel pump
Water pump
Alternator
Power steering pump (if disconnected from the power steering system, see Section 5, paragraph 13)

9 Engine – dismantling

1 Unscrew the oil filter with a strap or chain wrench (Fig. 1.4). Remove the dipstick.
2 Remove the clutch assembly as described in Chapter 5, Section 3 (manual gearbox only). Note which way round the clutch disc is fitted. Remove the engine mounting brackets (photo).
3 Remove the power steering pump and drivebelt as described in Chapter 11, Section 33.
4 Undo the distributor clamp plate securing bolt and withdraw the distributor from the cylinder block (photos).
5 Remove the two bolts attaching the power steering pump drivebelt idler pulley bracket to the front cover and lift away the bracket and pulley (photo).
6 Slacken the alternator attaching bolts and lift off the alternator and fan drivebelt. Undo the three bolts securing the alternator mounting bracket to the cylinder block and remove the alternator and bracket assembly (photo).

Fig. 1.4 Unscrew the oil filter (Sec 9)

9.9 Disconnect the choke hoses

9.10 Removing the carburettor intermediate flange

9.16 Lifting off the right-hand cylinder head

9.18 The oil pressure switch is located on the left-hand side of the cylinder block

9.21 Removing the flywheel

9.27 Detach the rear water elbow

9.29 Pull off the camshaft gear (note the alignment marks)

9.39 Remove the bearing shells from the main bearing caps ...

7 Undo the four bolts securing the fan and pulley to the water pump and remove the fan and pulley from the water pump (Fig. 1.6).

8 Disconnect the fuel pipe from the carburettor and withdraw the vent valve from the rocker cover (photo).

9 Slacken the securing clips and disconnect the hose from the choke water outlet connection and the bypass hose at the thermostat housing (photo).

10 Remove the four securing bolts, lift off the carburettor and then the intermediate flange from the inlet manifold (photo).

11 Remove the rocker cover securing bolts and lift off the covers.

12 Undo the rocker shaft securing bolts and remove the rocker shafts and oil splash shields. Note which way the splash shields are fitted. Mark the rocker shafts so that they can be refitted in their original positions.

13 Lift out the pushrods and keep them in their respective positions in relation to the rocker shafts to ensure that they are refitted in their original locations.

14 Remove the inlet and exhaust manifold securing bolts and lift off the manifolds. As sealing compound is used when fitting the inlet manifold it may be necessary to use a screwdriver to lever it free. Do not insert the screwdriver between the mating faces of the inlet manifold and the cylinder block.

15 Remove the cylinder head holding down bolts. Unscrew the bolts in the reverse order of the tightening sequence as shown in Fig. 1.20.

16 The cylinder head can now be lifted upwards (photo). If the head sticks to the cylinder block try to break the seal by rocking it. If this does not free it a soft faced hammer can be used to strike it sharply and break the cylinder head joint seal. Never use a metal hammer directly on the head as this may fracture the casting. Also never try to prise the head free by forcing a screwdriver or chisel between the cylinder head and cylinder block as this will damage the mating surfaces.

17 Undo and remove the two bolts securing the fuel pump to the cylinder block then remove the pump, gasket and operating rod.

18 Unscrew and remove the oil pressure switch (photo).

19 Remove the crankshaft pulley securing bolt and take the pulley off the crankshaft. Restrain the crankshaft from turning by chocking the flywheel.

20 Index mark the position of the flywheel in relation to the crankshaft so that it can be refitted in the same position.

21 Chock the flywheel to restrain it from turning, then remove the six bolts securing the flywheel to the crankshaft and lift off the flywheel (photo).

22 Remove the engine backplate.

23 Position the engine on its side and prise out the valve tappets with a piece of bent brass wire (Fig. 1.5). Place the tappets with their respective pushrods so that they will be refitted in the same tappet bores.

24 Remove the oil sump securing bolts and lift off the sump and sump gasket.

25 Unscrew the two oil pump securing bolts and remove the oil pump complete with suction pipe and oil strainer. Lift out the oil pump driveshaft, taking note of which way round it is fitted.

26 Remove the bolts securing the water pump to the cylinder block timing cover and lift away the water pump.

27 Undo the thermostat housing securing bolts, remove the housing and lift out the thermostat. Detach the rear water elbow (photo).

28 Remove the bolts securing the timing cover to the front of the cylinder block and lift away the timing cover. Discard the O-ring seals.

29 Unscrew the bolt securing the camshaft gear to the camshaft and pull off the gear (photo).

30 Remove the two camshaft thrust plate securing bolts and withdraw the camshaft together with the spacer and then remove the plate spring and spacer.

31 Unscrew the front intermediate plate attaching bolts and remove the intermediate plate (Fig. 1.6).

32 If the crankshaft gear needs to be removed use a standard puller to draw it off the crankshaft.

33 Check that the big-end bearing caps and connecting rods have identification marks. This is to ensure that the correct caps are fitted to the correct connecting rods and at reassembly are fitted in their correct cylinder bores. Note that the pistons have an arrow (or notch) marked on the crown to indicate the forward facing side.

34 Remove the big-end nuts and place to one side in the order in which they are removed.

35 Pull off the big-end caps, taking care to keep them in the right order and the correct way round. Also ensure that the shell bearings are kept with their respective connecting rods unless they are being renewed. If the big-end caps are difficult to remove they can be tapped lightly with a soft faced hammer.

36 To remove the shell bearings, press the bearing on the side opposite the groove in both the connecting rod and the cap, and the bearing will slide out.

37 Withdraw the pistons and connecting rods upwards out of the cylinder bores.

38 Make sure that the identification marks are visible on the main bearing caps so that they can be refitted in their original positions at reassembly.

39 Undo the securing bolts and lift off the main bearing caps and the bottom half of each bearing shell, taking care to keep the bearing shell in the right caps (photo).

40 When removing the rear main bearing cap note that this also retains the crankshaft rear oil seal.

41 When removing the centre main bearing cap, note the position of the two half thrust washers and mark them so that they can be refitted in the same position. It may be necessary to tap the main bearing caps with a soft faced hammer to release them.

42 Lift the crankshaft out of the crankcase and remove the rear oil seal.

43 Remove the upper halves of the main bearing shells and the upper

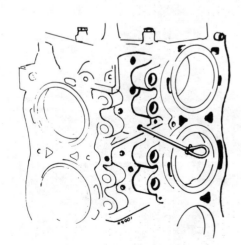

Fig. 1.5 Using a piece of wire to remove the tappets (Sec 9)

Fig. 1.6 Intermediate plate attaching bolts (Sec 9)

9.43 ... and from the crankcase, also the upper halves of the thrust washers

half of the centre bearing thrust washers from the crankcase and place them with the respective main bearing caps (photo).

10 Valve rockers – dismantling, inspection and reassembly

1   Tap out the roll pin from one end of the rocker shaft and remove the spring washer (photo).
2   Slide the rocker arms, rocker supports and springs off the rocker shaft. Keep them in the correct order so that they can be reassembled in the same position. If a rocker support sticks it can be removed by tapping it with a soft faced hammer (Fig. 1.7).
3   Examine the rocker shaft and rocker arms for wear. If the rocker arm surface that contacts the valve stem is considerably worn, renew the rocker arm. If it is worn slightly step-shaped it may be cleaned up with a fine oil stone.
4   Oil the parts and reassemble them on their shafts in the original order. With both rocker shafts fitted the oil holes must face downwards to the cylinder heads. This position is indicated by a notch on one end face of the rocker shaft (Fig. 1.8).

11 Valve tappets and pushrods – inspection

1   Examine the valve tappets for wear and damage. Renew if defec-

10.1 The rocker shaft has a retaining pin at each end

10.2a Compress the valve spring and lift out the collets ...

10.2b ... then remove the spring retainer, spring ...

10.2c ... and valve

tive.

2 Check the pushrods for signs of bending or wear. Correct or renew as necessary.

12 Camshaft and camshaft bearings – inspection and renovation

1 If there is excessive wear in the camshaft bearings they will have to be renewed. As the fitting of new bearings requires special tools this should be left to your local Ford dealer.

2 The camshaft may show signs of wear on the bearing journals or cam lobes. The main decision to take is what degree of wear necessitates renewing the camshaft, which is expensive. Scoring or damage to the bearing journals cannot be removed by regrinding; renewal of the camshaft is the only solution.

3 The cam lobes may show signs of ridging or pitting on the high points. If ridging is slight then it may be possible to remove it with a fine oil stone or emery cloth. The cam lobes however are surface hardened and once the hard skin is penetrated wear will be very rapid.

13 Cylinder heads – dismantling, renovation and reassembly

1 Clean the dirt and oil off the cylinder heads. Remove the carbon deposits from the combustion chamber and valve heads with a scraper or rotary wire brush.

2 Remove the valves by compressing the valve springs with a suitable valve spring compressor and lifting out the collets. Release the valve spring compressor and remove the valve spring retainer, spring and valve (photos). Mark each valve so that they can be refitted in the same location. **Note:** *When removing and refitting the valve spring take care not to damage the valve stem when pressing down the valve spring retainer to remove or refit the collets. If the stem gets damaged the sealing will be ineffective and result in excessive oil consumption and wear of the valve guides. Discard the valve stem seal.*

3 With the valves removed clean out the carbon from the ports.

4 Examine the heads of the valves and the valve seats for pitting and burning. If the pitting on valve and seat is slight it can be removed by grinding the valves and seats together with coarse, and then fine, valve grinding paste. If the pitting is deep the valves will have to be reground on a valve grinding machine and the seats will have to be recut with a valve seat cutter. Both these operations are a job for your local Ford dealer or motor engineering specialist.

5 Check the valve guides for wear by inserting the valve in the guide, the valve stem should move easily in the guide without side play. Renewal of worn guides requires special tools and should be left to your local Ford dealer.

6 When grinding slightly pitted valves and valve seats with carborundum paste proceed as follows: Apply a little coarse grinding paste to the valve seat and using a suction type valve grinding tool, grind the valve into its seat with a semi-rotary movement, lifting the valve from time to time. A light spring under the valve head will assist

in this operation. When a dull matt even surface finish appears on both the valve and the valve seat, clean off the coarse paste and repeat the grinding operation with a fine grinding paste until a continuous ring of light grey matt finish appears on both valve and valve seat. Carefully clean off all traces of grinding paste. Blow through the gas passages with compressed air.

7 Check the valve springs for damage and also check the free length, refer to the Specifications at the beginning of this Chapter. Renew if defective.

8 Lubricate the valve stem with engine oil and insert it in the valve guide. Slide on a new oil seal.

9 Fit the valve spring and valve spring retainer.

10 Use a suitable valve spring compressor to compress the valve spring until the collets can be fitted in position in the slots in the valve stem. Release the valve spring compressor.

11 After fitting all the parts, tap the top of the valve springs lightly with a plastic hammer to ensure correct seating of the collets.

14 Cylinder bores – inspection and renovation

1 A new cylinder is perfectly round and the walls parallel throughout its length. The action of the piston tends to wear the walls at right angles to the gudgeon pin due to side thrust. This wear takes place principally on that section of the cylinder swept by the piston rings.

2 It is possible to get an indication of bore wear by removing the cylinder head with the engine still in the car. With the piston down in the bore first signs of wear can be seen and felt just below the top of the bore where the top piston ring reaches and there will be a noticeable lip. If there is no lip it is fairly reasonable to expect that bore wear is not severe and any lack of compression or excessive oil consumption is due to worn or broken piston rings or pistons (see Section 16).

3 If it is possible to obtain a bore measuring micrometer, measure the bore in the thrust plane below the lip and again at the bottom of the cylinder in the same plane. If the difference is more than 0·003 inch (0·076 mm) then a rebore is necessary. Similarly, a difference of 0·003 inch (0·076 mm) or more between two measurements of the bore diameter taken at right angles to each other is a sign of ovality, calling for a rebore.

4 Any bore which is significantly scratched or scored will need reboring. This symptom usually indicates that the piston or rings are damaged also. In the event of only one cylinder being in need of reboring it will still be necessary for all four to be bored and fitted with new oversize pistons and rings. Your Ford agent or local motor engineering specialist will be able to rebore and obtain the necessary matched pistons. If the crankshaft is undergoing regrinding also, it is a good idea to let the same firm renovate and reassemble the crankshaft and pistons to the block. A reputable firm normally gives a guarantee for such work. In cases where engines have been rebored already to their maximum, new cylinder liners are available which may be fitted. In such cases the same reboring processes have to be followed and the services of a specialist engineering firm are required.

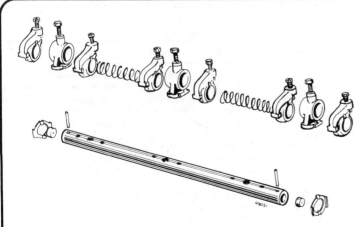

Fig. 1.7 Exploded view of rocker shaft assembly (Sec 10)

Fig. 1.8 Notch indicating position of oil hole (Sec 10)

15 Piston rings – removal

1   To remove the piston rings, slide them carefully over the top of the piston, taking care not to scratch the aluminium alloy; never slide them off the bottom of the piston skirt. It is very easy to break the cast iron piston rings if they are pulled off roughly, so this operation should be done with extreme care. It is helpful to make use of an old 0·020 inch (0·5 mm) feeler gauge.
2   Lift one end of the piston ring to be removed out of its groove and insert under it the end of the feeler gauge.
3   Turn the feeler gauge slowly round the piston and, as the ring comes out of its groove, apply slight upward pressure so that it rests on the land above. It can then be eased off the piston with the feeler gauge stopping it from slipping into an empty groove if it is any but the top piston ring that is being removed.

16 Pistons and piston rings – inspection and checking

1   Worn pistons and rings can usually be diagnosed when the symptoms of excessive oil consumption and lower compression occur and are sometimes, though not always, associated with worn cylinder bores. Compression testers that fit into the spark plug hole are available and these can indicate where low compression is occurring. Wear usually accelerates the more it is left so when the symptoms occur, early action can possibly save the expense of a rebore.
2   Another symptom of piston wear is piston slap – a knocking noise from the crankcase not to be confused with big-end bearing failure. It can be heard clearly at low engine speed when there is no load (idling for example) and is much less audible when the engine speed increases. Piston wear usually occurs in the skirt or lower end of the piston and is indicated by vertical streaks in the worn area which is always on the thrust side. It can also be seen where the skirt thickness is different.
3   Piston ring wear can be checked by first removing the rings from the pistons as described in Section 15. Then place the rings in the cylinder bores from the top, pushing them down about 1½ inches (38·1 mm) with the head of a piston (from which the rings have been removed) so that they rest square in the cylinder. Then measure the gap at the ends of the ring with a feeler gauge. If it exceeds 0·023 inch (0·58 mm) for the two top compression rings, or 0·055 inch (1·4 mm) for the lower oil control ring then they need renewal.
4   The grooves in which the rings locate in the piston can also become enlarged in use. The clearance between ring and piston, in the groove, should not exceed 0·004 inch (0·102 mm) for the top two compression rings and 0·003 inch (0·076 mm) for the lower oil control ring.
5   However, it is rare that a piston is only worn in the ring grooves and the need to renew them for this fault alone is hardly ever encountered. Wherever pistons are renewed the weight of the four piston/connecting rod assemblies should be kept within the limit variations of 8 gms to maintain engine balance.

17 Pistons rings – refitting

1   Check that the piston ring grooves and oilways are thoroughly clean and unblocked. Piston rings must always be fitted over the head of the piston and never from the bottom.
2   The easiest method to use when fitting rings is to wrap a 0·020 in (0·50 mm) feeler gauge round the top of the piston and place the rings one at a time, starting with the bottom oil ring, over the feeler gauge.
3   The feeler gauge, complete with ring, can then be slid down the piston over the other piston ring grooves until the correct groove is reached. The piston ring is then slid gently off the feeler gauge into the groove.
4   An alternative method is to fit the rings by holding them slightly open with the thumbs and both of the index fingers. This method requires a steady hand and great care as it is easy to open the ring too much and break it.

18 Connecting rods, pistons and gudgeon pins – renewal

1   Gudgeon pins are a shrink fit into the connecting rods. Neither of these would normally need renewal unless the pistons were being changed, in which case the new pistons would automatically be supplied with new gudgeon pins.
2   Connecting rods are not subject to wear but in extreme circumstances such as engine seizure they could be distorted. Such conditions may be visually apparent but where doubt exists they should be renewed.
3   As interference fit type gudgeon pins are used it is important that no damage is caused during removal and refitting. For this reason, should it be necessary to fit new pistons, take the parts along to the local Ford garage where the special equipment required for this job will be available.

19 Crankshaft – inspection and renovation

1   Look at the main bearing journals and the crankpins and if there are any scratches or score marks then the shaft will need regrinding. Such conditions will nearly always be accompanied by similar deterioration in the matching bearing shells.
2   Each bearing journal should also be round and can be checked with a micrometer or caliper gauge around the periphery at several points. If there is more than 0·001 in (0·025 mm) of ovality regrinding is necessary.
3   A main Ford agent or motor engineering specialist will be able to decide to what extent regrinding is necessary and also supply the special undersize shell bearing to match whatever may need grinding off.
4   Before taking the crankshaft for regrinding check also the cylinder bore and pistons as it may be advantageous to have the whole engine done at the same time.

20 Main and big-end bearings – inspection and renewal

1   With careful servicing and regular oil and filter changes, bearings will last for a very long time but they can still fail for unforeseen reasons. With big-end bearings an indication is a regular rhythmic loud knocking from the crankcase. The frequency depends on engine speed and is particularly noticeable when the engine is under load. This symptom is accompanied by a drop in oil pressure although this is not normally noticeable unless an oil pressure gauge is fitted. Main bearing failure is usually indicated by serious vibration, particularly at higher engine revolutions, accompanied by a more significant drop in oil pressure and a 'rumbling' noise.
2   Big-end bearings can be removed with the engine still in the car. If the failure is sudden and the engine has a low mileage since new or overhaul this is possibly worth doing. Bearing shells in good condition have bearing surfaces with a smooth, even matt silver/grey colour all over. Worn bearings will show patches of a different colour where the bearing metal has worn away and exposed the underlay. Damaged bearings will be pitted or scored. It is always well worthwhile fitting new shells as their cost is relatively low. If the crankshaft is in good condition, it is merely a question of obtaining another set of standard size shells. A reground crankshaft will need new bearing shells as a matter of course.

21 Oil pump – dismantling, inspection and reassembly

1   If oil pump wear is suspected it is possible to obtain a repair kit. Check for wear first as described later in this Section and if confirmed, obtain an overhaul kit or a new pump. The two rotors are a matched pair and form a single replacement unit. Where the rotor assembly is to be re-used the outer rotor, prior to dismantling, must be marked on its front face in order to ensure correct reassembly.
2   Remove the intake pipe and oil strainer.
3   Note the relative position of the oil pump cover and body and then undo and remove the three bolts and spring washers. Lift away the cover.
4   Carefully remove the rotors from the housing.
5   Using a centre punch tap a hole in the centre of the pressure relief valve sealing plug, (make a note to obtain a new one).
6   Screw in a self tapping screw and, using an open ended spanner, withdraw the sealing plug.
7   Thoroughly clean all parts in petrol or paraffin and wipe dry using a

non-fluffy rag. The necessary clearances may now be checked using a machined straight-edge (a good steel rule) and a set of feeler gauges. The critical clearances are between the lobes of the centre rotor and convex faces of the outer rotor; between the rotor and the pump body; and between both rotors and the end cover plate.

8   The rotor lobe clearance may be checked using feeler gauges and should be within the limits 0·002 – 0·008 in (0·05 – 0·20 mm).

9   The clearance between the outer rotor and pump body should be within the limits 0·006 – 0·012 in (0·15 – 0·30 mm).

10 The endfloat clearance may be measured by placing a steel straight-edge across the end of the pump and measuring the gap between the rotors and the straight-edge. The gap in either rotor should be within the limits 0·0012 – 0·004 in (0·03 – 0·10 mm).

11 If the only excessive clearances are endfloat it is possible to reduce them by removing the rotors and lapping the face of the body on a flat bed until the necessary clearances are obtained. It must be emphasised, however, that the face of the body must remain perfectly flat and square to the axis of the rotor spindle, otherwise the clearances will not be equal and the end cover will not be a pressure tight fit to the body. It is worth trying, of course, if the pump is in need of renewal anyway but unless done properly, it could seriously jeopardise the rest of the overhaul. Any variations in the other two clearances should be overcome with a new unit.

12 With all parts scrupulously clean first refit the relief valve and spring and lightly lubricate with engine oil.

13 Using a suitable diameter drift drive in a new sealing plug, flat side outwards until it is flush with the intake pipe mating face.

14 Lubricate both rotors with engine oil and fit them in the body. Fit the oil pump cover and secure with the three bolts tightened in a diagonal and progressive manner to the torque wrench setting given in the Specifications.

15 Fit the driveshaft into the rotor driveshaft and ensure that the rotor turns freely.

16 Fit the intake pipe and oil strainer to the pump body.

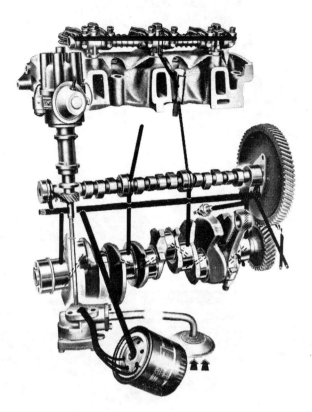

Fig. 1.9 Engine lubrication system (Sec 23)

22 Flywheel ring gear – inspection and renewal

1   If the ring gear is badly worn or has missing teeth it should be renewed. The old ring can be removed from the flywheel by cutting a notch between two teeth with a hacksaw and then splitting it with a cold chisel.

2   To fit a new ring gear requires heating the ring to 400° F (204°C). This can be done by polishing four equal spaced sections of the gear, laying it on a suitable heat resistant surface (such as fire bricks) and heating it evenly with a blow lamp or torch until the polished areas turn a light yellow tinge. Do not overheat or the hard wearing properties will be lost. The gear has a chamfered inner edge which should go against the shoulder when put on the flywheel. When hot enough place the gear in position quickly, tapping it home if necessary and let it cool naturally without quenching.

23 Lubrication system – description

1   The pressed steel oil sump is attached to the underside of the crankcase and acts as a reservoir for the engine oil. The oil pump draws oil from the sump via an oil strainer and intake pipe, then passes it into the full-flow oil filter. The filtered oil flows from the centre of the oil filter element and passes through a short drilling, on the right-hand side, to the oil pressure switch and to the main gallery (on the left-hand side of the crankcase) through a transverse drilling.

2   Four drillings connect the main gallery to the four main bearings and the camshaft bearings in their turn are connected to all the main bearings. The big-end bearings are supplied with oil through diagonal drillings from the nearest main bearing.

3   When the crankshaft is rotating, oil is thrown from the hole in each big-end bearing and ensures splash lubrication of the gudgeon pins and thrust side of the cylinders. The timing gears are also splash lubricated through an oil drilling.

4   The crankshaft second and third bearing journals have a pad at their centres from which oil, under pressure, is intermittently fed to the rocker shafts through a drilling in the cylinder block and cylinder heads. The oil then passes back to the engine sump, via large drillings in the cylinder block and cylinder heads.

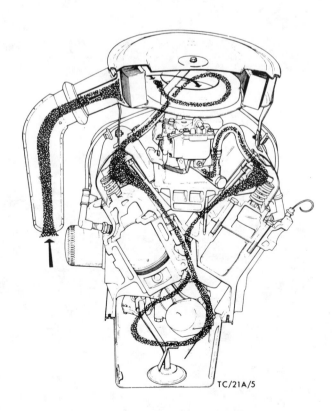

Fig. 1.10 Crankcase ventilation system (Sec 24)

26.1 Fitting the main bearing upper half shells in the crankcase

26.4 Place the upper halves of the thrust washers in position

26.5 Lubricate the main bearing shells

26.7 Fitting the crankshaft in the crankcase

26.10a Fitting the rear main bearing cap

26.10b The arrow on the main bearing caps must point to the front

24 Crankcase ventilation system – description and maintenance

1 The closed crankcase ventilation system is used to control the emission of crankcase vapour. It is controlled by the amount of air drawn in by the engine when it is running and the throughput of the vent valve.

2 The system is known as the PCV system (positive crankcase ventilation) and the advantage of the system is that should the 'blow by' exceed the capacity of the PCV valve, excess fumes are fed into the engine through the air cleaner.

3 At 18 000 miles (30 000 km) pull the valve and hose from the rocker cover on the right-hand side of the engine and wash the valve in a cleaning solvent. Check the valve for freedom of movement. Refit the valve in the rocker cover.

4 Check the security and condition of the system connecting hoses.

25 Engine reassembly – general

1 To ensure maximum life with minimum trouble from an over-hauled engine, not only must every part be correctly assembled but everything must be spotlessly clean, all oilways must be clean, locking washers and spring washers must always be fitted where needed and all bearings and other sliding surfaces must be thoroughly lubricated during assembly.

2 Before assembly, renew any bolts, studs and nuts whose threads are in any way damaged and whenever possible use new spring washers. Obtain a complete set of new gaskets and all new parts as necessary.

3 When refitting parts ensure that they are refitted in their original positions and directions. Oil seal lips should be smeared with grease before fitting. A liquid gasket sealant should be used where specified to prevent leakage.

4 Apart from your normal tools, a supply of clean rags, an oil can filled with clean engine oil and a torque wrench are essential.

26 Crankshaft – refitting

1 Wipe the bearing shell locations in the crankcase with a clean rag and fit the main bearing upper half shells in position (photo).

2 Clean the main bearing caps shell locations and fit the half shells in the caps. If the old bearings are being refitted (although this is a false economy unless they are practically new) make sure they are fitted in their original positions.

3 Apply a little grease to each side of the No 3 main bearing so as to retain the thrust washers.

4 Fit the upper halves of the thrust washers into their grooves each side of the main bearing. The slots must face outwards with the tag located in the groove (photo).

5 Lubricate the crankshaft main bearing journals and the main bearing shells with engine oil (photo).

6 Place the rear main bearing oil seal in position on the end of the crankshaft.

7 Carefully lower the crankshaft into the crankcase (photo).

8 Apply a thin coating of sealing compound to the mating faces of the crankcase and the rear main bearing cap.

9 Apply a smear of grease to both sides of the No 3 main bearing cap so as to retain the thrust washers. Fit the thrust washers with the tag located in the groove and the slots facing outwards.

10 Fit the main bearing caps with the arrows on the caps pointing to the front of the engine (photos).

11 Progressively tighten the main bearing securing bolts to the specified torque (photo), except the No 3 bearing bolts which should only be finger-tight. Now press the crankshaft fully to the rear then slowly press it fully forward, hold it in this position and tighten the No 3 main bearing cap securing bolts to the specified torque. This ensures that the ball thrust washers are correctly located.

12 Press the rear main bearing oil seal firmly against the rear main bearing.

13 Using feeler gauges, check the crankshaft endfloat by inserting the feeler gauge between the crankshaft journal side and the thrust washers. The clearance must not exceed the figure given in the Specifications. Different thicknesses of thrust washers are available (photo).

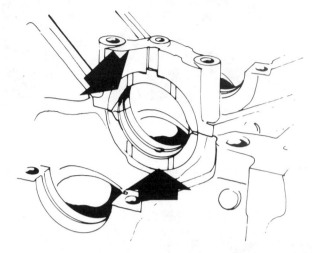

Fig. 1.11 Correct position of No 3 main bearing thrust washers when fitted (Sec 26)

26.11 Tightening the main bearing cap bolts

26.13 Checking the crankshaft endfloat with feeler gauge

27.3a Insert the camshaft from the front ...

27.3b ... then fit the thrust plate ...

27.3c ... and tighten the self-locking bolts

27.4 Fitting the guide sleeve O-ring seal

27.6 Intermediate plate fitted in position

28.1 Piston, piston rings and connecting rod assembly

28.6a Piston with piston ring compressor fitted

28.6b Check the numbers on the connecting rod to ensure it is the correct assembly for the cylinder bore

28.6c The arrow on the piston crown must point to the front of the engine

28.8 Tap the piston into the cylinder bore

28.11 Fit the big-end bearing cap

29.2 Insert the oil pump drive shaft ...

14 Rotate the crankshaft to ensure that it is not binding or sticking. Should it be very stiff to turn or have high spots it must be removed and thoroughly checked.

15 Coat the rear main bearing cap dowel seals with sealing compound and fit in position. Use a blunt screwdriver or similar tool to press them fully in (Fig. 1.12). They should be fitted with the rounded face pointing towards the bearing cap.

27 Camshaft and front intermediate plate – refitting

1 Slide the spacer onto the camshaft with the chamfered side first and fit the plate spring.

2 Lubricate the camshaft bearings, the camshaft and the thrust plate.

3 Carefully insert the camshaft from the front and fit the thrust plate and self-locking securing bolts. Tighten the bolts to the specified torque (photos).

4 Fit the timing cover guide sleeves and O-ring seals onto the crankcase. The chamfered end of the guide sleeves must face outward towards the timing cover (photo).

5 Ensure the mating faces of the crankcase and the front intermediate are clean and then apply sealing compound to both faces. Position the gasket on the crankcase and then fit the intermediate plate.

6 Fit the two centre bolts finger-tight then fit another two bolts temporarily for locating purposes. Tighten the centre securing bolts then remove the temporary fitted locating bolts (photo).

28 Pistons and connecting rods – refitting

1 Wipe clean the connecting rod half of the big-end bearing cap and the underside of the shell bearing and fit the shell bearing in position with its locating tongue engaged with the corresponding cut out in the rod (photo).

2 If the old bearings are nearly new and are being refitted then ensure they are refitted in their correct locations on the correct rods.

3 The pistons, complete with connecting rods, are fitted to their bores from the top of the block.

4 Locate the piston ring gaps in the following manner:

Top: 150° from one side of the helical expander gap
Centre: 150° from the opposite side of the helical expander gap
Bottom: Helical expander: opposite the marked piston front side
Intermediate rings: 1 inch (25 mm) each side of the helical expander gap

5 Well lubricate the piston and rings with engine oil.

6 Fit a universal piston ring compressor and prepare to insert the first piston into the bore. Make sure it is the correct piston-connecting rod assembly for that particular bore, that the connecting rod is the correct way round and that the front of the piston (marked with an arrow or a notch) is to the front of the engine (photos).

7 Again lubricate the piston skirt and insert the connecting rod and piston assembly into the cylinder bore up to the bottom of the piston ring compressor.

8 Gently but firmly tap the piston through the piston ring compressor and into the cylinder bore, using the shaft of a hammer (photo).

9 Generously lubricate the crankpin journals with engine oil and turn the crankshaft so that the crankpin is in the most advantageous position for the connecting rods to be drawn onto it.

10 Wipe clean the connecting rod bearing cap and back of the shell bearing, and fit the shell bearing in position ensuring that the locating tongue at the back of the bearing engages with the locating groove in the connecting rod cap.

11 Generously lubricate the shell bearing and offer up the connecting rod bearing cap to the connecting rod (photo).

12 Refit the connecting rod nuts.

13 Tighten the bolts with a torque wrench to the specified setting.

14 When all the connecting rods have been fitted, rotate the crankshaft to check that everything is free, and that there are no high spots causing binding.

29 Oil pump – refitting

1 Ensure the mating faces of the oil pump and the crankcase are clean.

2 Insert the hexagonal oil pump driveshaft (photo) with the pointed end, see Fig. 1.13, towards the distributor location.

3 Fit the oil pump to the crankcase and secure with two bolts tightened to the specified torque (photos).

29.3a ... then fit the oil pump ...

Fig. 1.12 Fitting the rear main bearing dowel seals (Sec 26)

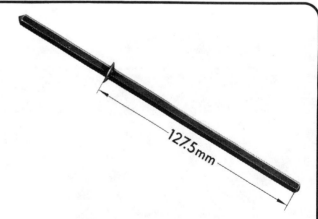

127.5mm

Fig. 1.13 Oil pump hexagonal drive shaft (Sec 29)

29.3b ... and tighten the securing bolts

30.2 Fit the flywheel to the crankshaft

30.4a Chock the flywheel to prevent it from turning

30.4b Tightening the flywheel bolts with a torque wrench

30.5 Fitting the clutch disc and pressure plate assembly

31.1 Renew the seal in the timing cover

31.4 Fit the camshaft gear on the camshaft ...

31.5a ... then the retaining washer and bolt ...

31.5b ... and tighten the bolt using a torque wrench

31.7a Stick a new timing cover gasket in position on the intermediate plate ...

31.7b ... then fit the timing cover

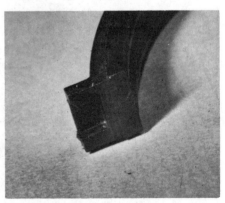

32.3a Cut-out in the rubber seal

30 Flywheel and clutch – refitting

1   Fit the engine backplate on the two locating dowels.
2   Ensure the mating faces of the flywheel and crankshaft are clean and fit the flywheel to the crankshaft, aligning the marks made at dismantling, unless new parts are being fitted (photo).
3   Fit the six flywheel securing bolts and lightly tighten.
4   Chock the flywheel to restrain it from turning, and tighten the securing bolts in a diagonal and progressive manner to the specified torque (photos).
5   Refit the clutch disc and pressure plate assembly to the flywheel making sure the disc is the correct way round (the longer side of the hub to the flywheel) (photo).
6   Secure the pressure plate assembly with the six retaining bolts, centralise the clutch disc using an old gearbox input shaft or suitable mandrel and then tighten the retaining bolts to the specified torque in a diagonal and progressive manner.

31 Timing gears and timing cover – refitting

1   Fit a new oil seal in the timing cover (photo).
2   Check that the keyways in the end of the crankshaft are clean and the keys are free from burrs. Fit the keys into the keyways.
3   If the crankshaft gear was removed refit it to the crankshaft using a suitable diameter tube to drive it fully home.
4   Fit the camshaft gear on the camshaft with the punch mark in alignment with the mark on the crankshaft gear, as shown in Fig. 1.14. Note that there are two punch marks on the crankshaft gear, ensure that the correct mark is aligned (photo).
5   Fit the camshaft gear retaining washer and bolt. Tighten the bolt to the specified torque (photos).
6   Clean the front face of the intermediate plate and the face of the timing cover, then coat both mating faces with sealing compound.
7   Position a new gasket on the intermediate plate and fit the timing cover to the cylinder block (photos).
8   Fit the timing cover securing bolts and tighten them to the specified torque.

32 Engine oil sump, water pump and crankshaft pulley – refitting

1   Clean the mating faces of the crankcase and sump. Ensure that the grooves in the seal carriers are clean.
2   Fit the rubber seals in the grooves of the seal carriers.
3   Apply sealing compound on the crankcase and slide the tabs of the gasket under the cut-outs in the rubber seals (photos).
4   Ensure that the gasket holes line up with the holes in the crankcase and fit the sump. Take care not to dislodge the gasket (photo).
5   Fit the sump securing bolts and tighten them to the correct torque in two stages as specified in Specifications at the beginning of this Chapter.
6   Stick a new gasket on the timing cover and fit the water pump

32.3b Slide the sump gasket into the seal

32.4 Position the sump on the crankcase

Fig. 1.14 Fitting the camshaft gear (Sec 31)

32.6 Fitting the water pump

32.7 Fitting the crankshaft pulley

33.1 Insert the tappets in the cylinder block

33.3 Cylinder head gasket markings

33.4 Fitting the left-hand cylinder head

33.5 Use a torque wrench to tighten the cylinder head holding down bolts

33.6 Insert the pushrods in the cylinder block

33.7a Position the oil splash shields in position ...

33.7b ... and then fit the rocker shaft assemblies

33.10a Place a new inlet manifold gasket in position ...

33.10b ... and then fit the inlet manifold

34.5 Adjusting the valve clearances

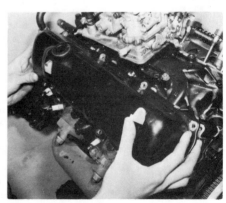

34.8 Fitting the left-hand valve rocker cover

(photo). Fit the thermostat and thermostat housing, refer to Chapter 2, Section 7. Fit the rear water elbow.
7   Coat the crankshaft pulley washer with sealing compound. Fit the pulley, washer and securing bolt. Tighten the bolt to the specified torque (photo).

33 Cylinder heads, rocker shafts and inlet manifold – refitting

1   Lubricate the valve tappets with engine oil and insert them in the cylinder block. Ensure they are fitted in their original locations (photo).
2   Ensure that the mating faces of the cylinder block and the cylinder heads are clean.
3   Position the new cylinder head gaskets over the guide bushes on the cylinder block. Check that they are correctly located. The right and left-hand gaskets are different. The gaskets are marked FRONT TOP (photo).
4   Carefully lower the cylinder heads onto the cylinder block and fit the holding down bolts (photos).
5   Tighten the bolts, in the sequence shown in Fig. 1.15, in three stages as specified in Specifications at the beginning of this Chapter (photo).
6   Lubricate the pushrods with engine oil and insert them in the cylinder block (photo).
7   Place the oil splash shields in position on the cylinder heads and fit the rocker shaft assemblies. Guide the rocker arm adjusting screws into the pushrod sockets (photos).
8   Tighten the rocker shaft securing bolts progressively to the specified torque.
9   Coat the gasket mating face outer edges of the cylinder heads and inlet manifold with sealing compound.
10 Place a new inlet manifold gasket in position and fit the inlet manifold (photos).
11 Insert the inlet manifold securing bolts and tighten them in the sequence shown in Fig. 1.16. Tighten them to the specified torque in four stages, refer to Specifications.
12 Adjust the valve clearances as described in Section 34.

34 Valve clearances – checking and adjustment

1   Adjust the inlet and exhaust valve clearances when the engine is cold, between 20° and 40°C (68° and 104°F). Clearances are important. If the clearance is too great the valves will not open as fully as they should. They will also open late and close early, this will affect the engine performance. If the clearances are too small the valves may not close completely which could result in lack of compression and very soon, burnt out valves and valve seats.
2   When turning the engine during valve clearance adjustments always turn the engine in the direction of normal rotation by means of a wrench on the pulley nut.
3   Turn the engine and align the crankshaft pulley mark with the O-mark on the timing cover.
4   If the crankshaft pulley is rotated backwards and forwards slightly, the valves of No 1 or 5 cylinder will be seen to be rocking (the two rocker arms moving in opposite directions). If the valves of No 1 cylinder are rocking, rotate the crankshaft through 360° so that those on No 5 cylinder are rocking (Fig. 1.17).
5   When the valves of No 5 cylinder are in this position, check the valve clearance of No 1 cylinder by inserting a feeler gauge of the specified thickness between the rocker arm and the valve stem. Adjust the clearance, if necessary, by turning the rocker arm adjusting screw until the specified clearance is obtained (photo).
6   If the engine is now rotated $\frac{1}{3}$ of a turn the valves of No 3 cylinder will be rocking and the valves of No 4 cylinder can be checked and adjusted.
7   Proceed to adjust the clearances according to the firing order as follows. The cylinders are numbered as shown in Fig. 1.18; the valves are listed in their correct order, working from the front of the engine:

Valves rocking	Valves to adjust
No 5 cylinder	No 1 cylinder (in, ex)
No 3 cylinder	No 4 cylinder (in, ex)
No 6 cylinder	No 2 cylinder (in, ex)
No 1 cylinder	No 5 cylinder (ex, in)
No 4 cylinder	No 3 cylinder (ex, in)
No 2 cylinder	No 6 cylinder (ex, in)

Fig. 1.15 Tightening sequence for cylinder head holding down bolts
(Sec 23)

Fig. 1.16 Tightening sequence for inlet manifold securing bolts
(Sec 33)

Fig. 1.17 No 5 cylinder valves rocking (Sec 34)

35.1 Screw in the water temperature switch

35.4 Left-hand engine mounting bracket and insulator

35.5a Insert the fuel pump operating rod ...

35.5b ... and then fit the fuel pump

36.3 Lowering the engine into the engine compartment

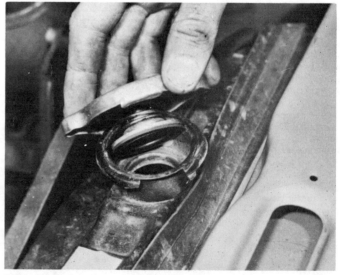

36.5a Check that the cooling system has been filled

8   Fit the rocker cover gaskets and rocker covers. Tighten the securing bolts to the specified torque (photo).

35 Ancillary components – refitting

1   Screw in the water temperature switch and tighten it to the specified torque (photo).
2   Refit the distributor and time the ignition as described in Chapter 4.
3   Clean the oil filter mating face of the cylinder block and apply a film of oil to the oil filter seal. Screw the new oil filter cartridge in until the rubber seal makes contact with the housing, then tighten a further ¾ turn.
4   Screw in the oil pressure switch and tighten it to the specified torque. Fit the engine mounting brackets (photo).
5   Insert the fuel pump operating rod in the side of the cylinder block, fit the insulation washer, fuel pump and securing bolts (photos).
6   Refit the carburettor as described in Chapter 4.
7   Connect the engine breather hose to rocker cover and the fuel line between the fuel pump and carburettor.
8   Fit the automatic choke to water outlet connecting hose and the bypass hose to thermostat housing.
9   Fit the alternator and adjust the drivebelt tension as described in Chapter 10, Section 9.
10 Fit the power steering pump drivebelt idler pulley bracket to the front of the engine and secure with two bolts.
11 Fit the power steering pump and adjust the drivebelt tension as described in Chapter 11.
12 Refit the exhaust manifolds. On models built after February 1978 note the following:

> a) the retaining studs must protrude from the cylinder head by 1·14 ± 0·06 in (29·0 ± 1·5 mm)
> b) use only graphite grease for sealing between the manifold and cylinder head. Gaskets must **not** be used with new manifolds. Gaskets may be used when refitting old manifolds

13 Fit the spark plugs and tighten them to the specified torque. Insert the engine oil level dipstick.

36 Engine – refitting in car

1   Refitting the engine in the car is a reversal of the removal procedure. A little trouble in getting the engine properly slung so that it takes up a suspended attitude similar to its final position will pay off when it comes to locating it on the front engine mountings.
2   Ensure that all loose leads, cables, hoses etc, are tucked out of the way. If not, it is easy to trap one and so cause additional work after the unit is refitted in the car.
3   Carefully lower the engine whilst an assistant guides it into position (photo). If the gearbox is already fitted, it may be necessary to turn the crankshaft slightly to engage the splines of the gearbox input shaft. Take care not to put any undue strain on the input shaft.
4   It is likely that the engine will initially be stiff to turn if new bearings and rings have been fitted and it will save a lot of frustration if the battery is well charged. After a rebore the stiffness may be more than the battery can cope with so be prepared to connect another battery up in parallel with jump leads.
5   The following check list should ensure that the engine starts safely and with the minimum of delay:

> a) Fuel lines connected and tightened
> b) Water hoses connected and secured with clips
> c) Coolant drain plugs fitted and tightened
> d) Cooling system replenished
> e) Sump drain plug fitted and tight
> f) Oil in engine
> g) LT wiring connected to distributor and coil
> h) Spark plugs tight
> j) Valves clearances set correctly
> k) Rotor arm fitted in distributor
> l) HT leads connected correctly to distributor, spark plugs and coil (Fig. 1.18).
> m) Throttle cable connected
> n) Earth straps reconnected
> o) Starter motor leads connected
> p) Alternator leads connected
> q) Battery fully charged and leads connected to clean terminals

37 Engine – initial start up after overhaul or major repair

1   Make sure that the battery is fully charged and that all lubricants, coolant and fuel are replenished.
2   If the fuel system has been dismantled it will require several revolutions of the engine on the starter motor to pump the petrol up to the carburettor. An initial 'prime' of about ⅓ of a cupful of petrol poured down the air intake of the carburettor will help the engine to fire quickly, thus relieving the load on the battery. Do not overdo this however, as flooding may result.
3   As soon as the engine fires and runs, keep it going at a fast tickover only (no faster) and bring it up to normal working temperature.
4   As the engine warms up there will be odd smells and some smoke from parts getting hot and burning off oil deposits. The signs to look for are leaks of water or oil which will be obvious, if serious. Check also

36.5b Refill the sump with the correct grade of oil

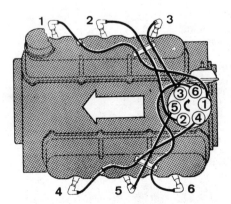

Fig. 1.18 Correct arrangement of HT leads (Sec 36)

the exhaust pipe and manifold connections as these do not always find their exact gas tight position until the warmth and vibration have acted on them and it is almost certain that they will need tightening further. This should be done, of course, with the engine stopped.

5   When normal running temperature has been reached, adjust the engine idle speed as described in Chapter 3.

6   Stop the engine and wait a few minutes to see if any lubricant or coolant is dripping out when the engine is stationary.

7   After the engine has run for 15 minutes remove the rocker covers

and recheck the tightness of the cylinder head bolts. Also check the inlet manifold bolts and the oil sump bolts.

8   When the engine is cold check the valve clearances.

9   Road test the car to check that the timing is correct and that the engine is giving the necessary smoothness and power. Do not race the engine – if new bearings and/or pistons have been fitted it should be treated as a new engine and run in at a reduced speed for the first 1000 miles (2000 km).

38 Fault diagnosis – engine

Symptom	Reason/s
Engine turns over but will not start	Ignition damp or wet
	Ignition leads to spark plugs loose
	Shorted or disconnected low tension leads
	Dirty, incorrectly set or pitted contact breaker points
	Faulty condenser
	Defective ignition switch
	Ignition LT leads connected wrong way round
	Faulty coil
	Contact breaker point spring earthed or broken
	No petrol in petrol tank
	Vapour lock in fuel line (in hot conditions or at high altitude)
	Blocked float chamber needle valve
	Fuel pump filter blocked
	Choked or blocked carburettor jets
	Faulty fuel pump
	Too much choke allowing too rich a mixture to wet plugs
	Float damaged or leaking or needle not seating
	Float lever incorrectly adjusted
Engine stalls and will not start	Ignition failure – sudden
	Ignition failure – misfiring precludes total stoppage
	Ignition failure – in severe rain or after traversing water splash
	No petrol in petrol tank
	Petrol tank breather choked
	Sudden obstruction in carburettor
	Water in fuel system
Engine misfires or idles unevenly	Ignition leads loose
	Battery leads loose on terminals
	Battery earth strap loose on body attachment point
	Engine earth lead loose
	Low tension leads to terminals on coil loose
	Low tension lead from coil to distributor loose
	Dirty, on incorrectly gapped spark plugs
	Dirty, incorrectly set or pitted contact breaker points
	Tracking across distributor cap
	Ignition too retarded
	Faulty coil
	Mixture too weak
	Air leak in carburettor
	Air leak at inlet manifold to cylinder head, or inlet manifold to carburettor
	Incorrect valve clearances
	Burnt out exhaust valves
	Sticking or leaking valves
	Weak or broken valve springs
	Worn valve guides or stems
	Worn pistons and piston rings
Lack of power and poor compression	Burnt out exhaust valves
	Sticking or leaking valves
	Worn valve guides and stems
	Weak or broken valve springs
	Blown cylinder head gasket (accompanied by increase in noise)
	Worn pistons and piston rings
	Worn or scored cylinder bores
	Ignition timing wrongly set. Too advanced or retarded
	Contact breaker points incorrectly gapped
	Incorrect valve clearances

Symptom	Reason/s
	Incorrectly set spark plugs
	Carburettor too rich or too weak
	Dirty contact breaker points
	Fuel filters blocked causing top end fuel starvation
	Distributor automatic balance weights or vacuum advance and retard mechanisms not functioning correctly
	Faulty fuel pump giving top end fuel starvation
Excessive oil consumption	Badly worn, perished or missing valve stem oil seals
	Excessively worn valve stems and valve guides
	Worn piston rings
	Worn pistons and cylinder bores
	Excessive piston ring gap allowing blow-by
	Piston oil return holes choked
Oil being lost due to leaks	Leaking oil filter gasket
	Leaking rocker cover gasket
	Leaking timing cover gasket
	Leaking sump gasket
	Loose sump plug
Unusual noises from engine	Worn valve gear (noisy tapping from rocker covers)
	Worn big-end bearing (regular heavy knocking)
	Worn main bearings (rumbling and vibration)
	Worn crankshaft (knocking, rumbling and vibration)
Engine fails to turn over when starter button operated	Discharged or defective battery
	Dirty or loose battery leads
	Defective starter solenoid or switch
	Engine earth strap disconnected
	Defective starter motor

Chapter 2 Cooling system

For modifications, and information applicable to later models, see Supplement at end of manual

Contents

Specifications

System type . . . .   Pressurised, forced circulation

System capacity (including heater) . . . .   12.1 pints (6.90 litres)

Thermostat
Type . . . .   Wax
*Starts to open . . . .   82 to 92°C (180 to 198°F)
*Fully open . . . .   99 to 102°C (210 to 216°F)
For used thermostats add ± 3°C (6°F)

Radiator
Type . . . .   Corrugated fin
Pressure cap opens . . . .   13 lbf/in² (0.91 kgf/cm²)

Water pump type . . . .   Centrifugal

Torque wrench settings

	lbf ft	kgf m
Fan securing bolts	5 to 7	0.69 to 0.97
Water pump bolts	5 to 7	0.69 to 0.97
Thermostat housing cover bolts	12 to 15	1.66 to 2.07

1 General description

The engine cooling water is circulated by a thermo-syphon, water pump assisted system, and the whole system is pressurised. This is both to prevent the loss of water down the overflow pipe with the radiator cap in position and to prevent premature boiling in adverse conditions. The radiator cap is pressurised to 13 lbf/in² (0.91 kgf/cm²) This has the effect of increasing the boiling point of the coolant. If the water temperature goes above the increased boiling point the extra pressure in the system forces the internal part of the cap off its seat, thus exposing the overflow pipe down which the steam from the boiling water escapes, thereby relieving the pressure. It is, therefore, important to check that the radiator cap is in good condition and that the spring behind the sealing washer has not weakened. The cooling system comprises the radiator, top and bottom water hoses, heater hoses, the impeller water pump (mounted on the front of the engine, it carries the fan blades, and is belt driven from a pulley on the crankshaft) and the thermostat.

The inlet manifold is water heated and the automatic choke is operated by the coolant. On automatic transmission cars a transmission oil cooler is located in the radiator bottom tank.

The system functions in the following manner: cold coolant in the bottom of the radiator circulates up the lower radiator hose to the water pump where it is pushed around the water passages into both banks of the cylinder block. The holes in the cylinder head gaskets are graduated in size so that the coolant flows at an even rate into the cylinder heads and through to the inlet manifold water jacket.

The water then travels down the radiator where it is rapidly cooled by the in-rush of cold air through the radiator core, which is created by both the fan and the motion of the car. The water, now much cooler, reaches the bottom of the radiator when the cycle is repeated.

When the engine is cold the thermostat (which is a valve that opens and closes according to the temperature of the water) maintains the circulation of the same water in the engine. Only when the correct minimum operating temperature has been reached, as shown in the Specifications, does the thermostat begin to open, allowing water to return to the radiator.

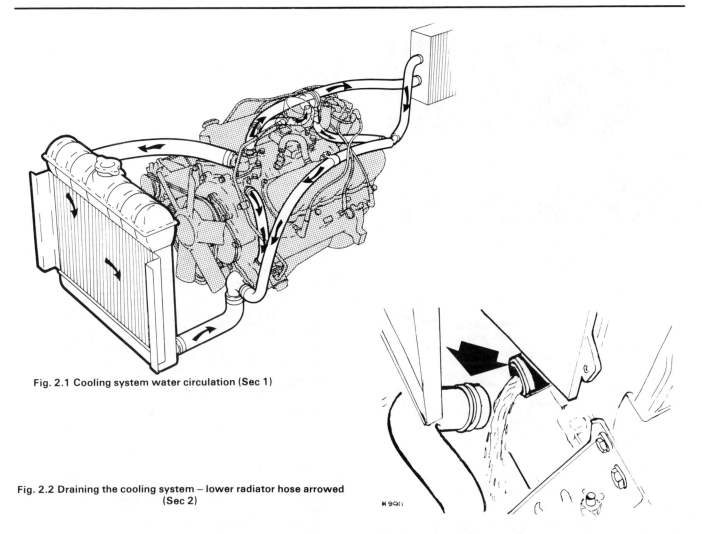

Fig. 2.1 Cooling system water circulation (Sec 1)

Fig. 2.2 Draining the cooling system – lower radiator hose arrowed
(Sec 2)

2   Cooling system – draining

1   If the engine is cold, remove the filler cap from the radiator by turning the cap anti-clockwise. If the engine is hot, then turn the filler cap to the first stop, and leave until the pressure in the system has had time to be released. Use a rag over your hand to protect your hand from escaping steam. If with the engine very hot the cap is released suddenly, the drop in pressure can result in the water boiling. With the pressure released the cap can be removed.

2   If antifreeze is used in the cooling system, drain it into a bowl having a capacity of at least 12 Imp pints (7 litres) for re-use.

3   Disconnect the lower radiator hose and allow to drain. Also remove the engine drain plugs located in each side of the cylinder block (Fig. 2.2).

4   When the water has finished draining, probe the drain plug orifices with a short piece of wire to dislodge any particles of rust or sediment which may be causing a blockage.

5   It is important to note that the heater cannot be drained completely during the cold weather so an antifreeze solution must be used. Always use an antifreeze with an ethylene glycol or glycerine base.

3   Cooling system – filling

1   Refit the cylinder block drain plugs and reconnect the lower radiator hose.

2   Fill the system slowly to ensure that no air lock develops. If a heater is fitted, check that the valve in the heater is open (control at HOT), otherwise an air lock may form in the heater. The best type of water to use in the cooling system is rain water: use this whenever possible.

3   Do not fill the system higher than within a $\frac{1}{2}$ inch (12.7 mm) of the filler neck. Overfilling will merely result in wastage, which is especially to be avoided when antifreeze is in use.

4   It is usually found that air locks develop in the heater radiator so the system should be vented during refilling by detaching the heater supply hose from the elbow connection on the water outlet housing.

5   Pour coolant into the radiator filler neck whilst the end of the heater supply hose is held at the elbow connection height. When a constant stream of water flows from the supply hose quickly refit the hose. If venting is not carried out it is possible for the engine to overheat. Should the engine overheat for no apparent reason then the system should be vented before seeking other causes.

6   Only use antifreeze mixture with a glycerine or ethylene glycol base.

7   Refit the filler cap and turn it firmly clockwise to lock it in position.

4   Cooling system - flushing

1   In time the cooling system will gradually lose its efficiency as the radiator becomes choked with rust, scale deposits from the water and other sediment. To clean the system out, remove the radiator filler cap and engine drain plug and leave a hose running in the filler cap neck for ten to fifteen minutes.

2   In very bad cases the radiator should be reverse flushed. This can be done with the radiator in position. A cylinder block plug is removed and a hose with a suitable tapered adaptor placed in the drain plug hole. Water under pressure is then forced through the radiator and out of the header tank filler cap neck.

3   It is recommended that some polythene sheeting is placed over the engine to stop water finding its way into the electrical system.

4   The hose should now be removed and placed in the radiator cap

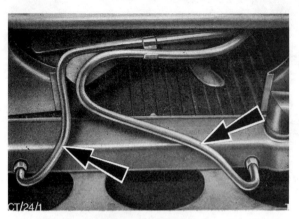

Fig. 2.3 Automatic transmission oil cooler pipes (Sec 5)

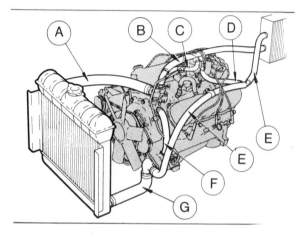

Fig. 2.4 Layout of cooling system hoses (Sec 6)

A Top hose   B Heater inlet hose
C Thermostat to choke hose
D Choke to heater outlet hose
E Heater outlet hose
F Cylinder head to block hose
G Bottom hose

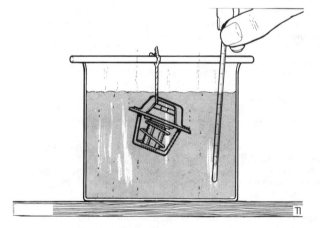

Fig. 2.5 Testing the thermostat (Sec 7)

filler neck, and the radiator washed out in the usual manner.

5 Radiator – removal and refitting

1   Drain the cooling system as described in Section 2.
2   Disconnect the top hose from the radiator.
3   Undo and remove the four bolts securing the radiator shroud to the radiator side panels and lift the shroud over the fan blades.
4   On vehicles equipped with automatic transmission, position a drain tray beneath the radiator, disconnect both oil cooler pipes (Fig. 2.3) and pull them clear of the radiator. Plug the pipes to prevent the ingress of dirt.
5   Remove the four bolts securing the radiator to the front panel, then lift the radiator upwards and out of the engine compartment. Take care not to damage the radiator matrix when lifting the radiator out.
6   Refitting the radiator is the reverse of the removal procedure. Refill the cooling system as described in Section 3. Check and top up the automatic transmission fluid (if applicable) as described in Chapter 6.

6 Radiator – cleaning and servicing

1   Clean the exterior of the radiator by hosing down the matrix with a strong jet of water to remove road dirt, dead flies etc. Clean out the inside of the radiator by flushing, as described in Section 4.
2   Repair leaks by soldering or with a suitable sealing compound.
3   Inspect hoses for cracks, internal and external deterioration, and damage caused by over-tightening of the hose clips. Renew any suspect hoses (Fig. 2.4).
4   Examine the hose clips and renew them if they are rusted or distorted.

7 Thermostat – removal, testing and refitting

1   Position a clean drain tray below the car then disconnect the radiator hose at the thermostat housing and drain the coolant into the tray for re-use.
2   Slacken the heater hose clip at the thermostat housing and pull off the hose.
3   Remove the three retaining bolts and lift away the thermostat housing, sealing ring and thermostat (photos).
4   If the valve is not closed completely at ambient temperature, a new thermostat is required.
5   To test the thermostat, immerse it in a container of water with a thermometer. Increase the water temperature gradually and note the temperature at which the valve begins to open and at which it is fully open. During the test, agitate the water to ensure even temperature distribution (Fig. 2.5).
6   Compare the noted temperatures with those given in the Specifications at the beginning of this Chapter and if they differ considerably the thermostat must be renewed.
7   Usually when the thermostat fails, it remains closed. This results in overheating, and if you are unable to renew it immediately you should remove it and run the car without it, but be sure to renew it as soon as possible as the engine will be operating below its optimum efficiency without it.
8   Refitting the thermostat is the reverse of the removal procedure. Always fit a new sealing ring. Ensure that the thermostat is fitted the correct way round, refer to Fig. 2.6. Don't forget to refill the cooling system, refer to Section 3.

8 Fan belt – removal and refitting

If the fan belt is worn or has stretched unduly, it should be renewed. The most usual reason for renewal is that the belt has broken in service. It is recommended that a spare belt be always carried in the car.
1   Loosen the alternator mounting bolts and move the alternator towards the engine.
2   Slip the old belt over the crankshaft, alternator and water pump pulley wheels and lift it off over the fan blades.
3   Put a new belt onto the three pulleys and adjust it as described in Section 9. Note: After fitting a new belt it will require adjustment after

approximately 250 miles (400 km).

9 Fan belt – adjustment

1   It is important to keep the fan belt correctly adjusted and it is considered that this should be a regular maintenance task every 6000 miles (10 000 km). If the belt is loose it will slip, wear rapidly and cause the alternator and water pump to malfunction. If the belt is too tight the alternator and water pump bearings will wear rapidly causing premature failure of these components.

2   The fan belt tension is correct when there is 0.5 in (12.7 mm) of lateral movement at the mid-point position of the belt run between the alternator pulley and the water pump (Fig. 2.7).

3   Adjust the fan belt, slacken the alternator securing bolts and move the alternator in or out until the correct tension is obtained. It is easier if the alternator bolts are only slackened a little so it requires some effort to remove the alternator. In this way the tension of the belt can be arrived at more quickly than by making frequent adjustment (photo).

4   When the correct adjustment has been obtained fully tighten the alternator mounting bolts.

10 Water pump – removal and refitting

1   Drain the cooling system as described in Section 2.
2   Remove the radiator and shroud as described in Section 5.
3   Slacken the alternator mounting bolts and remove the fan belt.
4   Undo and remove the four bolts and washers securing the fan

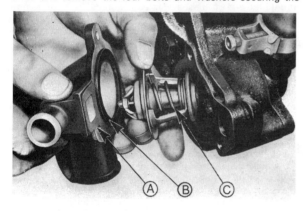

Fig. 2.6 Refitting the thermostat (Sec 7)

A Housing   *B Sealing ring*
C Thermostat

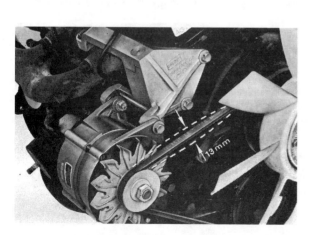

Fig. 2.7 Checking the fan belt tension (Sec 9)

7.3a Remove the thermostat housing ...

7.3b ... and then the thermostat and sealing ring

9.3 Checking the fan belt tension

10.4 Removing the fan securing bolts

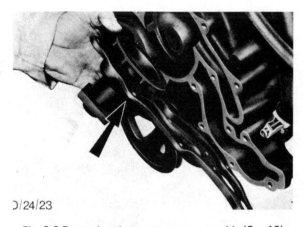

Fig. 2.8 Removing the water pump assembly (Sec 10)

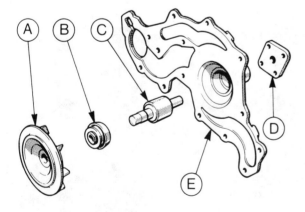

Fig. 2.9 Exploded view of water pump (Sec 11)

A Impeller	D Pulley hub
B Seal	E Pump body
C Bearing shaft	

assembly to the water pump spindle hub. Lift away the fan and pulley (photo).

5   Remove the thermostat housing and thermostat as described in Section 7.

6   Undo the securing bolts and remove the water pump assembly (Fig. 2.8).

7   Refitting the water pump is the reverse of the removal procedure. Ensure the pump and timing cover mating faces are clean. Always use new gaskets and sealing ring. Adjust the fan belt tension as described in Section 9.

11 Water pump – overhaul

1   Before dismantling the water pump check that all the necessary replacement parts are available. You may find it quicker and more economical to obtain an exchange unit.

2   Refer to Fig. 2.9. Using a universal three-leg puller and suitable thrust block remove the pump pulley hub from the shaft.

3   Support the pump body and using a soft faced hammer drive the bearing shaft, seal and impeller as an assembly from the pump body. Take care not to damage the pump body.

4   Remove the impeller from the shaft, using a universal three-leg puller, and then slide the pump seal off the shaft.

5   Clean and inspect all the parts for wear and corrosion. A water pump repair kit is available. Always fit all the items supplied with the repair kit.

6   To reassemble the water pump, suitably support the pump body and press the bearing shaft into the housing.

7   Next press the pump pulley hub on to the front end of the bearing shaft until the end of the shaft projects 0.06 in (1.5 mm) from the end of the hub.

8   Slide a new seal over the shaft and into its housing in the pump body.

9   Press the impeller onto the shaft until a clearance (measured with a feeler gauge) of 0.03 in (0.8 mm) is obtained between the impeller blades and the housing face.

12 Temperature gauge – fault diagnosis

1   If the temperature gauge fails to work, either the gauge, the sender unit, the wiring or the connections are at fault.

2   It is not possible to repair the gauge or the sender unit and they must be replaced by new units if at fault.

3   First check the wiring connections are sound. Check the wiring for breaks using an ohmmeter. The sender unit and gauge should be tested by substitution.

13 Temperature gauge and sender unit – removal and refitting

1   For information on the removal of the temperature gauge refer to

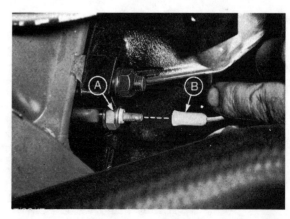

Fig. 2.10 Removing the temperature sender unit (Sec 13)

A Sender unit	B Wiring connector

Chapter 10.

2 Ensure the cooling system is not pressurised by removing and refitting the radiator cap. This will minimise the amount of coolant loss.

3 Disconnect the wiring from the sender unit and unscrew the unit (Fig. 2.10).

4 Refitting is the reverse of the removal procedure. Smear sealant on the threads of the sender unit. Check the coolant level and top-up as necessary.

14 Antifreeze precautions

1 Apart from the protection against freezing conditions which the use of antifreeze provides, its use is essential to minimise corrosion of the cooling system.

2 The cooling system is initially filled with a solution of 45%

antifreeze and it is recommended that this percentage is maintained.

3 With long-life types of antifreeze mixtures, renew the coolant every two years. With other types, drain and refill the system every twelve months. Whichever type is used, it must be of the ethylene glycol type.

4 The following table gives a guide to protection against frost but a mixture of less than 30% concentration will not give protection against corrosion:

Amount of antifreeze	Protection to
45%	−32°C (−26°F)
40%	−25°C (−13°F)
30%	−16°C (+3°F)
25%	−13°C (+9°F)
20%	−9°C (+15°F)
15%	−7°C (+20°F)

15 Fault diagnosis – cooling system

Symptom	Reason/s
Overheating	Insufficient water in cooling system
	Fan belt slipping (accompanied by a shrieking noise on rapid engine acceleration)
	Radiator core blocked or radiator grille restricted
	Bottom water hose collapsed, impeding flow
	Thermostat not opening properly
	Ignition advance and retard incorrectly set (accompanied by loss of power, and perhaps misfiring)
	Carburettor incorrectly adjusted (mixture too weak)
	Exhaust system partially blocked
	Oil level in sump too low
	Blown cylinder head gasket (water/steam being forced down the radiator overflow pipe under pressure)
	Engine not yet run-in
	Brakes binding
Cool running	Thermostat jammed open
	Incorrect thermostat fitted allowing premature opening of valve
	Thermostat missing
Loss of cooling water	Loose clips on water hose
	Top, bottom or by-pass water hoses perished and leaking
	Radiator core leaking
	Thermostat gasket leaking
	Radiator pressure cap spring worn or seal ineffective
	Blown cylinder head gasket (pressure in system forcing water/steam down overflow pipe)
	Cylinder wall or head cracked

Chapter 3 Carburation, fuel and exhaust systems

For modifications, and information applicable to later models, see Supplement at end of manual

Contents

Specifications

Fuel pump
Type	Mechanical, driven by pushrod from eccentric on camshaft
Delivery pressure	4 to 5 lbf/in^2 (0.27 to 0.35 kgf/cm^2)

Fuel tank capacity
12 gallons (54 litres)

Fuel filter type
Nylon mesh

Air cleaner
Type	Thermostatically-controlled
Filter	Disposable paper element

Carburettor
Type	Solex twin choke downdraught
Throttle barrel diameter	1.37/1.37 in (35/35 mm)
Venturi diameter	0.98/0.98 in (25/25 mm)
Main jet	130/130
Idling jet	42.5/42.5
Idling speed	800 rpm
Mixture % CO	1.5%
Basic idle % CO	2.75% at 600 rpm
Fast idle speed	2900 rpm
Float level setting	0.43 $\pm$ 0.02 in (11.0 $\pm$ 0.5 mm)
Pump stroke, direction setting (Refer to text, Sec 20)	0.14 to 0.26 in (3.5 to 6.5 mm)
Choke plate pull down	0.12 in (3.1 mm)
Choke phasing setting	0.012 to 0.024 in (0.3 to 0.6 mm)
Modulator spring gap	0.07 in (1.9 mm)

Torque wrench settings
	lbf ft	kgf m
Fuel pump to cylinder block	12 to 15	1.7 to 2.1
Exhaust pipes to manifold clamp nuts	15 to 20	2.1 to 2.8
Exhaust pipe U-bolt nuts	15 to 20	2.1 to 2.8

1 General description

The fuel system comprises a 12 gallon (54 litre) fuel tank, a mechanically operated fuel pump and a Solex twin carburettor.

The fuel tank is positioned below the luggage compartment and is held in position by two retaining straps. The filler pipe neck is integral with the tank and passes through the right-hand quarter panel.

The combined fuel outlet and sender unit is located in the front face of the tank. Fuel tank ventilation is via the filler cap.

The mechanical fuel pump is connected to the fuel tank by a nylon pipe. It is located on the left-hand side of the engine and is operated by a pushrod driven by an eccentric on the camshaft. Located in the fuel pump is a nylon filter and access is gained via a sediment cap.

The pump draws petrol from the tank and delivers it to the carburettor. The petrol level in the carburettor is controlled by a float operated needle valve. Petrol flows past the needle valve until the float rises to a predetermined level and closes the needle valve. The fuel pump then freewheels under slight back pressure until the petrol level drops in the carburettor float chamber and the needle valve opens again.

The air cleaner is of the disposable paper element type and thermostatically controls the air intake temperature.

2 Air cleaner – description and operation

The thermostatically-controlled air cleaner maintains the intake air at a constant predetermined figure during normal operation and supplies cooler air at full throttle. The air cleaner has two sources of supply, through the normal intake (cool air) or from a heat shroud (hot air) mounted on the right-hand exhaust manifold.

The air flow through the cleaner is controlled by a flap valve, in the air cleaner intake spout, which mixes air from both intake sources to obtain the required air temperature.

The vacuum motor, see Fig. 3.1, operates the flap valve and holds it fully open when the vacuum is above 4.0 in (100 mm) Hg. This allows only hot air to enter the air cleaner (Fig. 3.2). When the vacuum falls the flap valve closes progressively and cooler air flows into the air cleaner. When the vacuum falls to 2.0 in (50 mm) Hg the flap closes and only cool air passes to the air cleaner (Fig. 3.3).

The vacuum motor is operated by vacuum from the inlet manifold and is controlled by a heat sensor located inside the air cleaner.

3 Air cleaner – operating check

1   With the engine stationary check that the flap valve is fully closed. The flap can be seen through the intake spout (use a mirror).
2   With the engine cold (below 25°C (77°F)) start it and check the operation of the flap valve. At idle the flap should be fully open allowing warm air from the exhaust manifold shroud to enter the air cleaner.
3   If the flap valve operates as described above the air cleaner is functioning correctly.
4   If the flap valve remains closed when the engine is started, check the vacuum lines for leaks and renew, if necessary.
5   If the vacuum lines are in order and the flap valve remains closed when the engine is started the vacuum motor and/or heat sensor must be at fault. Testing of these units require a vacuum pump and gauge, so this is a job for your local Ford agent.

4 Air cleaner – removal, servicing and refitting

1   Remove the two screws that secure the air cleaner to the carburettor.
2   Lift the cleaner up off the carburettor and disconnect the vacuum motor pipe from the carburettor.
3   Undo the clips and lift off the lid. Remove the filter element.
4   Fit the new filter element in the cleaner and refit the lid. Ensure that the lid is clipped securely to the cleaner body.
5   Connect the vacuum motor pipe to the carburettor and position the air cleaner assembly on top of the carburettor.
6   Fit the two air cleaner securing screws.

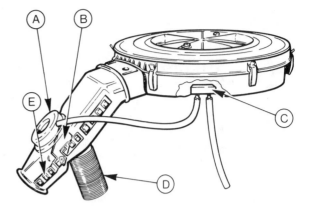

Fig. 3.1 Thermo-controlled air cleaner (Sec 2)

A Vacuum motor   D Warm air inlet
B Flap valve   E Cool air inlet
C Heat sensor

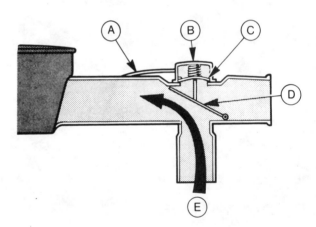

Fig. 3.2 Flap valve open – warm airflow through cleaner (Sec 2)

A Vacuum hose   D Flap valve
B Vacuum motor   E Warm air
C Vacuum diaphragm

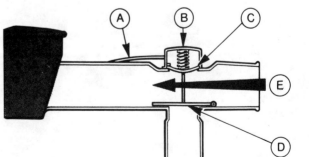

Fig. 3.3 Flap valve closed – cool airflow through cleaner (Sec 2)

A Vacuum hose   D Flap valve
B Vacuum motor   E Cool air
C Vacuum diaphragm

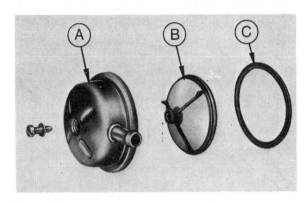

Fig. 3.4 Cleaning the fuel pump filter (Sec 5)

A Cover   B Filter   C Seal

6.1 Location of fuel pump

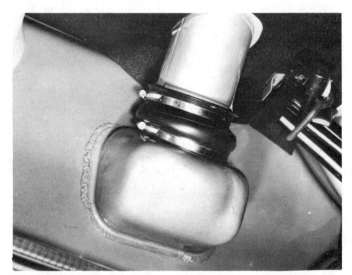

9.3 Remove the tank filler neck rubber connector

5   Fuel pump filter – cleaning

1   At intervals of 6000 miles (10 000 km), undo and pull the fuel pipe from the pump inlet tube.

2   Undo and remove the centre screw and O-ring and lift off the sediment cap, filter and seal (Fig. 3.4).

3   Thoroughly clean the sediment cap, filter and pumping chamber using a paintbrush and clean petrol to remove any sediment.

4   Reassembly is the reverse sequence to dismantling. Do not overtighten the centre screw as it could distort the sediment cap.

6   Fuel pump – description

1   The mechanical fuel pump is mounted on the left-hand side of the cylinder block (photo) and is driven by a pushrod actuated by an eccentric on the camshaft. It is not recommended that this type of pump is dismantled for repair other than cleaning the filter and sediment cap as described in Section 5.

2   Should a fault appear in the system which indicates a defective fuel pump, the pump can be tested and if confirmed, it must be discarded and a new one obtained.

7   Fuel pump – removal and refitting

1   Remove the inlet and outlet pipes at the pump and plug the ends to stop petrol loss or dirt finding its way into the fuel system.

2   Undo and remove two bolts and spring washers that secure the pump to the cylinder block.

3   Lift away the fuel pump and gasket and recover the pushrod.

4   Refitting the fuel pump is the reverse sequence to removal but there are several additional points that should be noted:

    a)   *Do not forget to refit the pushrod*

    b)   *Tighten the pump securing bolts to the specified torque wrench setting*

    c)   *If a crimped type hose clamp was fitted, it will have been damaged on removal, and should be replaced by a suitable screw type clamp*

    d)   *Before reconnecting the pipe from the fuel tank to the pump inlet, move the end to a position lower than the fuel tank so that fuel can syphon out. Quickly connect the pipe to the pump inlet*

    e)   *Disconnect the pipe at the carburettor and turn the engine over until petrol issues from the open end. Quickly connect the pipe to the carburettor union*

8   Fuel pump – testing

Presuming that the fuel lines and unions are in good condition and that there are no leaks anywhere, check the performance of the fuel pump in the following manner. Disconnect the fuel pipe at the carburettor inlet union, and the high tension lead to the coil and, with a suitable container or large rag in position to catch the ejected fuel, turn the engine over. A good spurt of petrol should emerge from the end of the pipe every second revolution.

9   Fuel tank – removal and refitting

The fuel tank is mounted under the floor of the luggage compartment and is supported on two straps.

1   Chock the front wheels, jack up the rear of the car and support it on axle-stands. Disconnect the battery earth terminal.

2   Remove the filler cap and, using a length of rubber hose or plastic pipe approximately 0.25 in (6.35 mm) bore, syphon out as much petrol as possible into a clean container.

3   Loosen the securing clips and remove the filler neck rubber connector (photo).

4   Disconnect the fuel gauge sender unit wiring and the fuel feed and fuel return pipes from the fuel sender unit. Take careful note of the correct pipe connections (Fig. 3.5).

5   Plug the ends of the pipes to prevent ingress of dirt.

6   Using two screwdrivers in the slots in the sender unit retaining ring, unscrew the sender unit from the fuel tank. Lift away the sealing ring and the sender unit noting that the float must hang downwards.

7   Slacken off the tank straps securing nut (photo), detach the straps, then lower the tank and pull it from under the car.

8   Refitting is the reverse of the removal procedure. Ensure that the five rubber insulator pads are securely attached to the tank in the positions shown in Fig. 3.6.

9   Remove the axle-stands and lower the car.

10   Refill the fuel tank and reconnect the battery earth terminal. Test the operation of the fuel gauge sender unit by switching on the ignition and observing the gauge reading.

10 Fuel tank – cleaning

1   With time it is likely that sediment will collect in the bottom of the fuel tank. Condensation, resulting in rust and other impurities will usually be found in the fuel tank of any car more than three or four years old.

2   When the tank is removed it should be vigorously flushed out and turned upside down. If facilities are available at the local garage the tank may be steam cleaned and the exterior repainted with a lead based paint.

3   Never weld or bring a naked light close to an empty fuel tank until it has been steam cleaned out for at least two hours or, washed internally with boiling water and detergent and allowed to stand for at least three hours.

4   Any small holes may be repaired using a special preparation such as Holts Petro-Patch which gives satisfactory results provided that the instructions are rigidly adhered to.

11 Fuel gauge sender unit – removal and refitting

1   The fuel gauge sender unit can be removed with the fuel tank in position. (Refer to Section 9, paragraphs 2 to 6) (photo).

2   If the operation of the sender unit is suspect, check that the rheostat is not damaged and that the wiper contact is bearing against the coil.

3   Refitting is a straightforward reversal of the removal sequence. Always fit a new seal to the recess in the tank to ensure no leaks develop.

4   The float arm should hang downwards. Test the operation of the fuel gauge sender unit by switching on the ignition. Wait 30 seconds and observe the gauge reading.

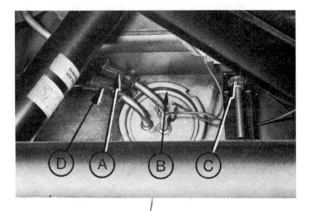

Fig. 3.5 Disconnect the fuel gauge sender unit (Sec 9)

A Fuel feed pipe   C Fuel tank securing strap
B Sender unit   D Fuel return pipe

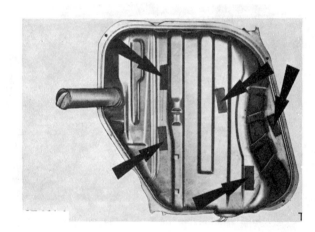

Fig. 3.6 Location of fuel tank insulator pads (Sec 9)

9.7 Fuel tank support straps attachment

11.1 The fuel gauge sender unit is mounted in the front of the fuel tank

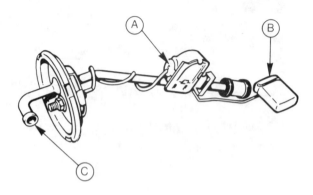

Fig. 3.7 Fuel gauge sender unit (Sec 11)

A Rheostat   B Float   C Outlet connection

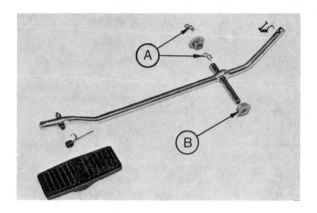

Fig. 3.8 Removal of accelerator pedal and shaft (Sec 12)

A Retaining clips   B Bush

Fig. 3.9 Removing the cable retaining clip (Sec 13)

A Retaining clip   B Accelerator cable

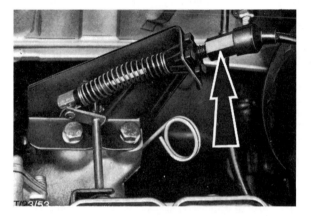

Fig. 3.10 Accelerator cable adjusting nut (Sec 14)

Fig. 3.11 Locknut type accelerator cable adjustment — automatic transmission models (Sec 14)

A Adjusting nut   B Locknut

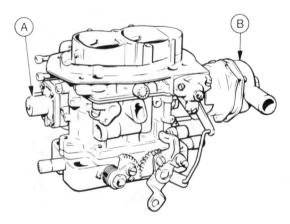

Fig. 3.12 Solex carburettor (Sec 15)

A Anti-stall device   B Choke housing

12 Accelerator pedal and shaft – removal and refitting

1   Remove the screws and take out the lower trim panel.
2   Prise up and remove the spring clip from the top of the accelerator pedal shaft, pull back and remove the throttle cable.
3   Withdraw the two shaft retaining clips and slide out the shaft. It will be found beneficial if one bush is rotated through 90° and with a screwdriver, ease the bush from the bracket (Fig. 3.8).
4   If desired, the pedal may be detached from the pedal shaft spigot by prising the pedal flange out of engagement with a screwdriver. Lift away the pedal spring.
5   Inspect the pedal shaft bushes and if worn they should be renewed.
6   It will now be necessary to check the adjustment as described in Section 14.

13 Accelerator cable – removal and refitting

1   Remove the five screws and take out the lower trim panel.
2   Prise up and remove the spring clip from the top of accelerator pedal shaft, pull back and remove the throttle cable.
3   From under the bonnet, undo and remove the screw, thereby releasing the throttle cable from the engine compartment rear bulkhead panel.
4   Slide the clip from the inner cable socket and the throttle shaft ball so as to disconnect the inner cable.
5   Prise out the cable retaining clip from the bracket on the inlet manifold (Fig. 3.9). Depress the lugs individually with a screwdriver

and twist out the throttle cable retainer.
6   Refitting and reconnecting the accelerator cable is the reverse sequence to removal.
7   It will now be necessary to adjust the linkage, as described in Section 14.

14 Accelerator linkage – adjustment

1   Refer to Section 4, and remove air cleaner.
2   Fully depress the accelerator pedal and wedge with a length of wood between the pedal and front seat.
3   Wind back the adjusting nut until the throttle plate is just fully open, with no slack in the cable and no strain in the linkage (Fig. 3.10).
4   *Automatic transmission vehicles.* Refer to Chapter 6, Section 13, and check downshift cable adjustment to ensure this does not prevent the throttle plate from fully opening.
5   Release the accelerator pedal and refit the air cleaner.

15 Carburettor – general description

The Solex twin choke carburettor incorporates a fully automatic strangler type choke to ensure easy starting whilst the engine is cold. The float chamber is internally vented.

The carburettor body consists of two castings which form the upper and lower bodies. The upper incorporates the float chamber cover, twin air intakes, choke plates and the automatic choke housing.

Incorporated in the lower body is the float chamber, accelerator pump, power valve, float and needle valve, fuel inlet and return unions,

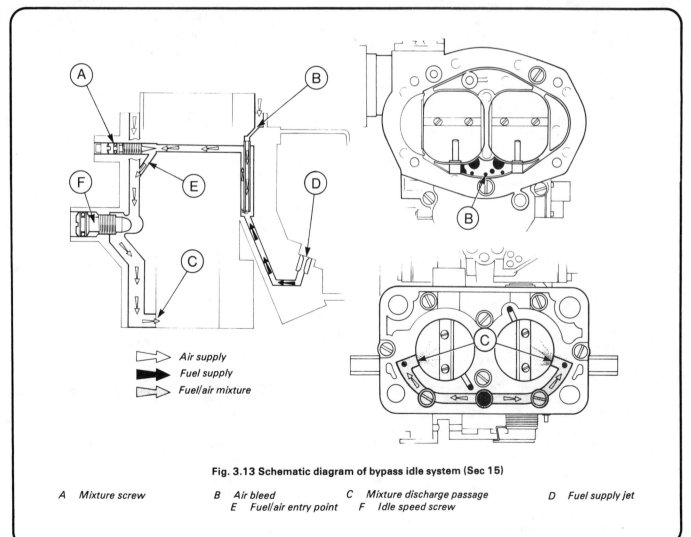

➩ Air supply
➡ Fuel supply
➩ Fuel/air mixture

Fig. 3.13 Schematic diagram of bypass idle system (Sec 15)

A   Mixture screw   B   Air bleed   C   Mixture discharge passage   D   Fuel supply jet
                                     E   Fuel/air entry point   F   Idle speed screw

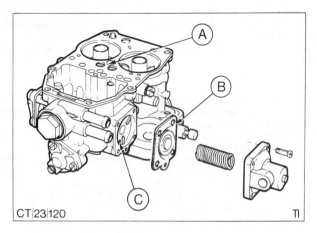

Fig. 3.14 Exploded view of anti-stall device (Sec 15)

A Discharge tube   B Diaphragm
C Fuel inlet

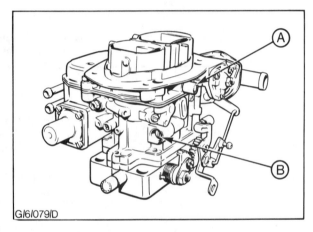

Fig. 3.15 Slow running adjustment (Sec 17)

A Mixture adjusting screw   B Idle speed adjusting screw

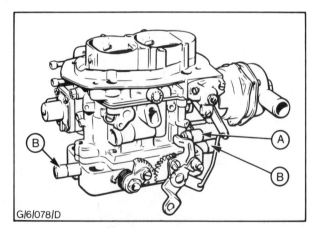

Fig. 3.16 Basic idle setting adjustment (Sec 17)

A Basic idle speed adjusting screw
B Basic mixture adjusting screws

two throttle barrels and integral venturis, throttle plates, spindles and jets. An anti-stall device and fuel return line system are also incorporated.

The carburettor idle system is of the bypass type and the idle mixture adjustment and basic idle adjustment screws are 'tamper-proofed'. (Refer to Section 16).

Refer to Fig. 3.13. Fuel is drawn from the float chamber at D and past an air bleed at B. This air bleed only allows enough air to give a rich fuel/air mixture which passes to the bypass idle mixture screw A. Turning the screw in weakens the mixture, turning it out gives a richer mixture. The mixture is then drawn past the idle speed screw F and passes into the main air flow at C. The idle speed screw regulates the amount of mixture passing through the idle system and therefore controls the idle speed, it does not affect the mixture ratio at idle.

The anti-stall device works in the following way. During normal operating conditions, vacuum from the inlet manifold pulls a diaphragm back against spring tension and this allows fuel to be drawn, through internal drillings, from the float chamber, and into the device at C (Fig. 3.14).

When the engine is about to stall the vacuum drops and the spring operates the diaphragm which pumps the reserve of fuel back through the internal drillings to the discharge tubes to enrich the fuel/air mixture and prevent the engine from stalling. Two non-return valves are fitted, one at the float chamber which allows fuel to be drawn from the chamber but not to return, and the other at the discharge tubes.

16 Carburettor adjustment – general

1   In view of the increasing awareness of the dangers of exhaust pollution and the very low levels of carbon monoxide (CO) emission for which these carburettors are designed, the slow running mixture setting, and the *basic* idle setting should *not* be adjusted without the use of a proper CO meter (exhaust gas analyser).

2   Even if such equipment is available, the plastic 'tamper-proof' caps can only be removed by destroying them. These caps have to be fitted after adjustment, and replacements are only available to authorised workshops.

17 Carburettor – adjustments

Slow running adjustment

1   Warm up the engine to its normal operating temperature.

2   Connect a CO meter and a tachometer, if not fitted to the car.

3   Run the engine at 3000 rpm, then release the throttle and allow the speed to drop back to idle.

4   Check the idle speed and CO level against the specification.

5   Adjust the idle speed screw (Fig. 3.15), if necessary, to obtain the specified idle speed.

6   If the CO level is not within the specified figure the bypass idle mixture screw will have to be adjusted and this will necessitate the removal of the 'tamper-proof' cap, refer to Section 16.

7   The 'tamper-proof' cap can be removed from the idle mixture adjusting screw by compressing it with a pair of pliers to break it and then prising it off.

8   Now both the idle mixture and idle speed screws should be adjusted as required to bring the CO level within the specified figure at the specified idle speed.

Basic idle setting

9   It should not normally be necessary to adjust this setting except after overhaul of the carburettor.

10 Screw in the idle speed control screw (Fig. 3.15) and remove the plastic caps from the throttle stop screws and mixture adjustment screw (Fig. 3.16).

11 With the engine stopped, screw the two mixture adjusting screws fully in and then unscrew them both 5 turns.

12 Start the engine and adjust the throttle stop screw to obtain the specified basic idle speed. Adjust the CO level by turning the two mixture adjusting screws in an equal amount of turns to obtain the specified basic idle CO.

13 Fit new sealing caps on the mixture control screws and the throttle stop screws after setting the basic idle speed.

14 Unscrew the idle speed adjusting screw and adjust the slow

running as described previously in this Section.

15 Fit a new 'tamper-proof' cap on the idle mixture adjusting screw.

16 Disconnect the CO meter and tachometer.

18 Carburettor – removal and refitting

1 Disconnect the battery earth lead.

2 Remove the air cleaner as described in Section 4.

3 Ensure that the cooling system is not pressurised by removing the radiator cap.

4 Disconnect both the water hoses from the choke housing and plug the hose ends to prevent loss of coolant.

5 Disconnect the throttle cable from the carburettor (photo).

6 Disconnect the fuel feed and fuel return pipes. If crimped type clamps are used on the hoses they must be prised open.

7 Disconnect the vacuum hose from the carburettor.

8 Undo and remove the four securing nuts and lift off the carburettor and gasket (photo).

9 Refitting the carburettor is the reverse of the removal procedure, but the following points must be noted:

   a) *Ensure that the mating surfaces are clean and always use a new gasket*

   b) *When connecting the fuel feed and return pipes ensure that they are connected the right way round. Two arrows on the casting indicate the direction of flow, see Fig. 3.17. Fit screw type hose clips as replacements for crimped type clamps*

   c) *Top-up the cooling system before running the engine*

   d) *Check the engine slow running and adjust, if necessary, as described in Section 17*

19 Carburettor dismantling and reassembly – general

1 With time, the component parts of the carburettor will wear and petrol consumption increase. The diameter of drillings and jets may alter, and air and fuel leaks may develop around spindles and other moving parts. Because of the high degree of precision involved it is best to purchase an exchange carburettor. This is one of the few instances where it is better to take the latter course rather than to rebuild the component oneself.

2 It may be necessary to partially dismantle the carburettor to clear a blocked jet. The accelerator pump itself may need attention and gaskets may need renewal and providing care is taken, there is no reason why the carburettor may not be completely reconditioned at home, but ensure a full repair kit can be obtained before you strip the carburettor down. *Never* clean out jets with wire or similar but blow them out with compressed air or air from a car tyre pump.

18.5 Disconnecting the throttle cable

18.8 Lifting off the carburettor

Fig. 3.17 Carburettor fuel pipe connections (Sec 18)

A Fuel return pipe   B Fuel feed pipe

Fig. 3.18 Lifting off the carburettor upper body (Sec 20)

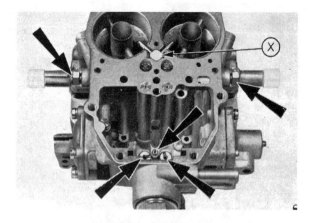

Fig. 3.19 Location of carburettor jets (Sec 20)

X Accelerator pump discharge tubes

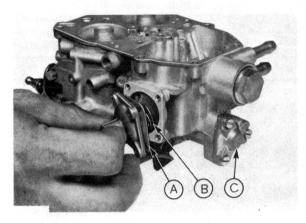

Fig. 3.20 Removing the accelerator pump (Sec 20)

A Pump diaphragm   B Return spring
C Power valve assembly

Fig. 3.21 Dismantling the anti-stall device (Sec 20)

A Diaphragm   B Return spring

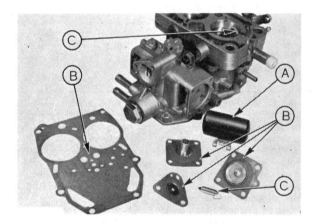

Fig. 3.22 Carburettor dismantled for inspection (Sec 20)

A Check for leaks   B Examine for splits
C Examine for wear and damage

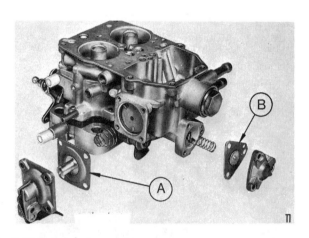

Fig. 3.23 Refitting the accelerator pump and power valve (Sec 20)

A Pump diaphragm   B Power valve diaphragm

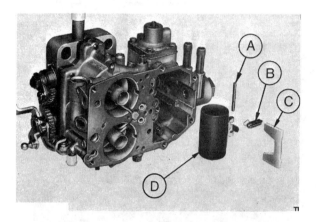

Fig. 3.24 Refitting the needle valve and float assembly (Sec 10)

A Retaining pin   B Needle valve
C Locking tab   D Float

20 Carburettor – cleaning, inspection and adjustment

1   Remove the carburettor from the engine as described in Section 18, and thoroughly clean the exterior.

2   Remove the screws securing the upper body to the lower body then disconnect the choke link and lift off the carburettor upper body (Fig. 3.18).

3   Lever out the nylon float locking tab with a small screwdriver, lift out the float retaining pin, then the float and needle valve.

4   Unscrew the five jets, arrowed in Fig. 3.19, noting the positions in which they are fitted, and then lever out the accelerator supply tubes.

5   Remove the four securing screws and detach the accelerator pump diaphragm assembly, taking care not to lose the spring (Fig. 3.20).

6   Undo the three securing screws and remove the power valve diaphragm assembly.

7   Take off the sealing caps and remove the mixture adjusting screws. **Note**: *The sealing caps are destroyed when being removed, refer to Section 16 and Section 17, paragraph 7.*

8   Remove the four securing screws and remove the anti-stall diaphragm and spring (Fig. 3.21).

9   Clean out the float chamber and the upper body. Clean all the jets and passageways using clean, dry compressed air. Check the float assembly for signs of damage or leaking. Inspect the power valve and pump diaphragms for splits or deterioration. Examine the mixture screws, needle valve and throttle spindle for signs of wear and damage. Renew defective parts as necessary (Fig. 3.22).

10   Refit the two mixture adjusting screws. The new 'tamper-proof' caps are fitted after adjustment of the basic idle speed, refer to Section 17.

11   Fit the accelerator and power valve assemblies with the parts assembled in the order shown in Fig. 3.23.

12   Fit the anti-stall diaphragm assembly, taking care that the diaphragm does not get kinked or twisted.

13   Refit the five jets. Place the accelerator supply tubes in their location and tap them into place in the body.

14   Fit the needle valve, make sure the spring clip is on the valve and then fit the retaining pin to the float. Position the assembly with the float tag behind the needle valve spring and fit the nylon locking tag (Fig. 3.24).

15   To adjust the float level setting slowly fill the float chamber with petrol until the float fully closes the needle valve. Measure the distance between the gasket face and the float. Adjust to the specified setting by bending the float level adjusting tag (Fig. 3.25).

16   To check the pump stroke fuel direction partly fill the float chamber with petrol. Operate the accelerator pump and check the fuel direction in relation to the throttle plates, see Fig. 3.26. Adjust the position of the pump discharge tubes to obtain the specified dimension at A.

17   Reconnect the choke link, position a new gasket on the lower body then fit the upper body and the securing screws.

18   To synchronise the throttle plates unscrew the basic idle speed adjusting screw until it is clear of the throttle mechanism. Loosen the synchronisation adjusting screw (Fig. 3.27). Hold the choke plates open and flick the throttle to close both throttle plates. Press down both plates to ensure that they are fully closed and tighten the synchronising screw. Note that the synchronisation screw has a left-hand thread.

19   Refit the carburettor and adjust the slow running as described in Section 17.

21 Fast idle speed – adjustment

1   Check the slow running as described in Section 17.

2   Remove the air cleaner and without disconnecting the vacuum motor pipe position it clear of the carburettor.

3   Open the throttle partially, hold the choke plates fully closed, then release the throttle so that the choke mechanism is held in the fast idle position.

4   Release the choke plates and check that they return to the fully open position (if not, the assembly is faulty or the engine is not at operating temperature).

5   Without touching the accelerator pedal, start the engine and check the fast idle speed. Adjust by screwing the fast idle screw in or out as

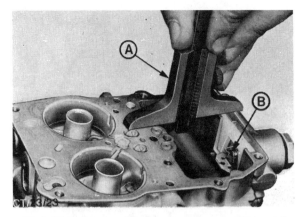

Fig. 3.25 Measuring the carburettor float level (Sec 20)

A   Depth gauge   B   Adjusting tag

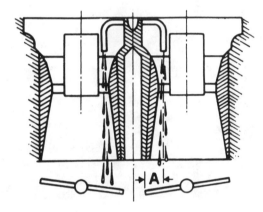

Fig. 3.26 Checking the pump stroke fuel direction (Sec 20)

Dimension A = 0.14 to 0.26 in (3.5 to 6.5 mm)

Fig. 3.27 Synchronising the throttle plates (Sec 20)

A   Basic idle speed adjusting screw
B   Throttle synchronising screw

Fig. 3.28 Adjusting the fast idle speed (Sec 21)

A Choke plates   B Fast idle adjusting screw

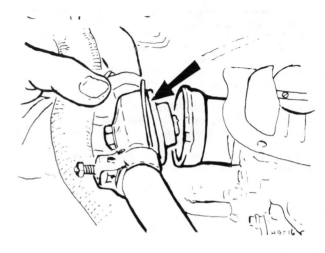

Fig. 3.29 Removing the choke bi-metal spring housing (Sec 22)

Fig. 3.30 Adjusting choke plate pull-down (Sec 22)

A Adjusting screw   B Twist drill
C 'High cam' position (fast idle)

Fig. 3.31 Checking the choke phasing adjustment (Sec 22)

A Fast idle cam   B Adjusting tag
X Operating clearance (see Specifications)

Fig. 3.32 Adjusting the modulator spring gap (Sec 22)

A Choke lever   B Modulator spring

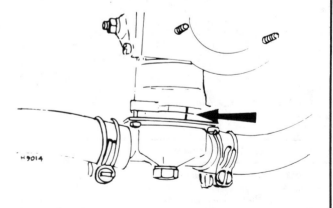

Fig. 3.33 Alignment marks on choke housing (Sec 22)

necessary (Fig. 3.28). To gain access to the screw, stop the engine and partly open the throttle. A $\frac{1}{2}$ turn of the screw alters the speed by approximately 100 rpm.

6   Refit the air cleaner.

22 Automatic choke – adjustment

1   Check and adjust the slow running as described in Section 17.
2   Remove the air cleaner from the top of the carburettor (but do not disconnect the vacuum motor pipe) and position it clear of the carburettor.
3   Remove the securing screws and pull the choke housing and bi-metal spring assembly clear of the carburettor (Fig. 3.29).
4   Detach the internal heat shield.

Vacuum pull-down

5   With the engine at normal operating temperature, partially open the throttle then hold the choke plates fully closed and release the throttle. The choke mechanism will now be held in the high cam position (fast idle), see Fig. 3.30.
6   Release the choke plates and start the engine without touching the accelerator pedal. Carefully close the choke plates until resistance is felt and then hold in this position.
7   Measure the clearance using an unmarked twist drill shank between the edge of the choke plate and the air horn wall, and compare it with the specified figure. Adjust, if necessary, by screwing the diaphragm adjusting screw in or out as required.

Choke phasing

8   With the engine at the normal operating temperature and the choke mechanism at the fast idle position, start the engine without touching the accelerator pedal, then close the choke plates to the pull-down position. Hold the choke plates, partly open the throttle and allow the fast idle cam to return to its normal position.
9   Release the throttle and stop the engine. With the choke plates held in the pull-down position the fast idle screw should locate on the cam next to the high cam stop, leaving a small operating clearance (Fig. 3.31). If necessary, adjust by bending the phasing adjusting tag.

Modulator spring gap

10   Remove the carburettor upper body as described in Section 20 paragraph 2. Measure the clearance between the modulator spring and the choke lever with a twist drill shank. If the clearance is not as specified, adjust by bending the spring to obtain the correct clearance (Fig. 3.32).
11   Refit the internal heat shield.
12   Connect the bi-metal spring to the choke lever, position the choke cover and loosely fit the three retaining screws. Rotate the cover until the marks are aligned then tighten the three screws (Fig. 3.33).
13   Adjust the fast idle as described in Section 21.
14   Refit the air cleaner assembly.

23 Automatic choke – dismantling, inspection and reassembly

1   Remove the air cleaner as described in Section 4.
2   Remove the retaining screws and pull the choke housing and bi-metal assembly away from the carburettor.

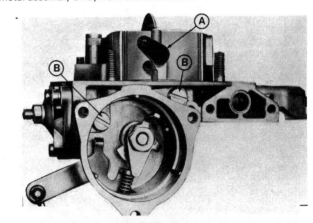

Fig. 3.34 Removing the choke housing from upper body (Sec 23)

A Operating link   B Securing screws

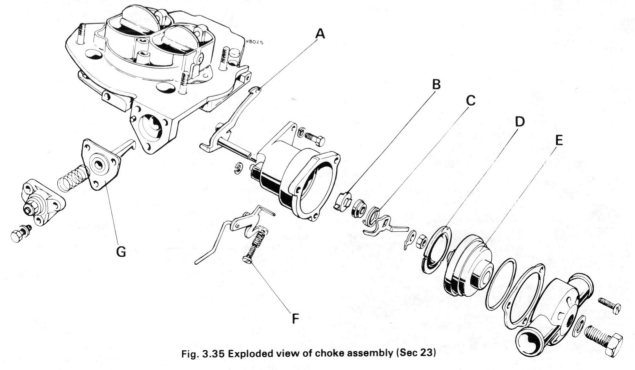

Fig. 3.35 Exploded view of choke assembly (Sec 23)

A Upper link   D Internal heat shield   F Fast idle adjusting screw
B Fast idle cam   E Bi-metal spring assembly   G Vacuum diaphragm
C Cam retaining spring

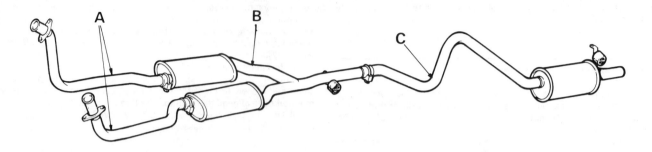

Fig. 3.36 Exhaust system (Sec 24)

A Downpipes   B Front section   C Rear section

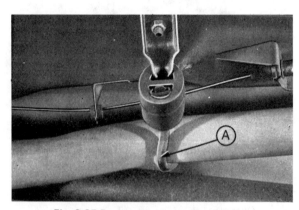

Fig. 3.37 Front rubber insulator (Sec 24)

A Support welded to exhaust pipe

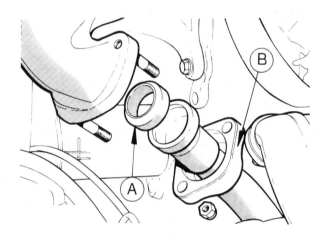

Fig. 3.38 Exhaust down pipe to manifold joint (Sec 25)

A Sealing ring   B Manifold clamp

25.4 Unhook the exhaust pipe from the rubber insulator

3   Detach the internal heat shield.

4   Remove the U-clip and disconnect the choke operating link from the choke plate spindle.

5   Remove the upper body as described in Section 20, paragraph 2.

6   Remove the securing screws and detach the choke assembly from the upper body (Fig. 3.34).

7   Release the locking tab, remove the retaining nut and dismantle the choke assembly.

8   Remove the securing screws and remove the vacuum diaphragm from the upper body, take care not to lose the return spring.

9   Clean all the parts, inspect them for wear and damage and wipe them dry with a clean cloth. Do not use any lubricants during reassembly.

10   Refit the vacuum diaphragm and housing, ensuring that the diaphragm is flat before tightening the securing screws.

11   Reassemble the choke assembly in the order shown in Fig. 3.35, then fit the assembly to the upper body.

12   Reconnect the choke link to the choke spindle, fit the U-clip and the dust cover.

13   Check and, if necessary, adjust the modulator sping gap as described in Section 22.

14   Fit the upper body and connect the choke link.

15   Check and adjust the vacuum pull-down and choke phasing as described in Section 22.

16   Refit the internal heat shield.

17   Connect the bi-metal spring to the choke lever, position the choke and bi-metal housing assembly on the upper body and loosely fit the

retaining screws. Rotate the housing until the marks are aligned, then tighten the screws.

18 Adjust the fast idle speed as described in Section 21.

24 Exhaust system – general description

1 The exhaust system consists of two cast iron exhaust manifolds, two downpipes with separate mufflers at the front which become a single pipe system behind the two mufflers, a rear pipe and resonator. The four sections of the system are joined together by three U-bolt type clamps (Fig. 3.36).

2 The system is flexibly attached to the floor pan by two circular rubber mountings (Fig. 3.37).

3 At regular intervals the system should be checked for corrosion, joint leakage, the condition and security of the flexible mountings and the tightness of the joints.

25 Exhaust system – renewal

1 If possible, raise the car on a ramp or place it over an inspection pit. Alternatively jack up the car and support it, on axle-stands or wooden blocks, to obtain the maximum amount of working height underneath.

2 Slacken the nuts on the U-bolt clamp in front of the rear axle and slide the clamp off the joint.

3 Apply penetrating fluid to the joint and then disconnect the rear

section of pipe from the rear rubber insulator. Now twist the rear section of pipe back and forward to free it at the joint, then withdraw the rear section of pipe over the rear axle.

4 Remove the securing nuts from the left-hand and right-hand manifold clamps, separate the clamps, then unhook the front section of the exhaust from the rubber insulator and remove the downpipes and mufflers from under the car (photo).

5 Remove the two U-bolt clamps in front of the front mufflers and separate the two downpipes from the mufflers.

6 Clean the contacting faces of the sealing rings, manifolds and clamps (Fig. 3.38) with emery cloth. Examine the two rubber insulators for deterioration and renew if necessary.

7 Slide the manifold clamps onto the downpipes, then fit the downpipes to the front mufflers and fit the U-bolt clamps. Do not tighten the U-bolts at this stage.

8 Position the front section of the exhaust system under the car, and suspend it from the front rubber insulator and at the exhaust manifolds by the clamps.

9 Fit the rear section by guiding it over the rear axle and connecting it to the front section with a loosely fitted clamp. Hook the rear section to the rear rubber insulator.

10 Align the exhaust system, ensuring there is a minimum clearance of 0.8 in (20 mm) between any part of the system and the body or body components.

11 Tighten the manifold clamps and the three U-bolt clamps to the specified torque.

12 Run the engine and check for exhaust leaks.

26 Fault diagnosis – fuel and exhaust systems

Symptom	Reason/s
Fuel consumption excessive	Air cleaner choked and dirty giving rich mixture
	Fuel leaking from carburettor, fuel pumps, or fuel lines
	Float chamber flooding
	Generally worn carburettor
	Distributor condenser faulty
	Balance weights or vacuum advance mechanism in distributor faulty
	Carburettor incorrectly adjusted, mixture too rich
	Idling speed too high
	Contact breaker gap incorrect
	Valve clearances incorrect
	Incorrectly set spark plugs
	Tyres under-inflated
	Wrong spark plugs fitted
	Brakes dragging
Insufficient fuel delivery or weak mixture due to air leaks	Petrol tank air vent restricted
	Partially clogged filter in pump
	Fuel pump diaphragm leaking or damaged
	Seal in fuel pump damaged
	Fuel pump valves sticking due to petrol gumming
	Too little fuel in fuel tank (prevalent when climbing steep hills)
	Union joints on pipe connections loose
	Split in fuel pipe on suction side of fuel pump
	Inlet manifold to block or inlet manifold to carburettor gasket leaking

Chapter 4 Ignition system

For modifications, and information applicable to later models, see Supplement at end of manual

Contents

Specifications

Spark plugs
Type .... Motorcraft AGR22
Electrode gap .... 0.025 in (0.60 mm)

Coil
Type .... Low voltage for use with 1.5 ohm ballast resistor wire
Primary resistance .... 0.95 to 1.60 ohms
Secondary resistance .... 5000 to 9300 ohms

Distributor
Type .... Bosch or Motorcraft
Automatic advance .... Mechanical and vacuum
Drive .... Skew gear from camshaft
Rotation (viewed from top) .... Clockwise
Initial (static) advance .... 9° BTDC
Condenser capacity:
    Bosch .... 0.18 to 0.26 mfd
    Motorcraft .... 0.21 to 0.25 mfd
Firing order 1–4–2–5–3–6
Contact points gap .... 0.012 to 0.016 in (0.3 to 0.4 mm)
Dwell angle .... 36° to 40°

HT leads
Resistance .... 30 000 ohms maximum per lead

Torque wrench setting

	lbf ft	kgf m
Spark plugs	26	3.5

1 General description

In order that the engine can run correctly it is necessary for an electrical spark to ignite the fuel/air mixture in the combustion chamber at exactly the right moment in relation to engine speed and load.

The ignition system is divided into two circuits, low tension and high tension.

The low tension (LT), or primary circuit, consists of the battery ignition switch, low tension or primary coil windings, and the contact breaker points and condenser, both located at the distributor.

The high tension (HT), or secondary circuit, consists of the high tension or secondary coil winding, the heavy ignition lead from the centre of the coil to the distributor cap, and the rotor arm and the spark plug leads.

The ignition system is based on feeding low tension voltage from the battery to the coil where it is converted to high tension voltage. The high tension voltage is powerful enough to jump the spark plug gap in the cylinders many times a second under high compression pressures, providing that the system is in good condition and that all adjustments are correct.

The wiring harness includes a high resistance wire in the ignition coil feed circuit and it is very important that only a 'ballast resistor' type ignition coil of the 7 volt type is used. This lead is identified by its white with pink colour tracer colour coding.

During starting this 'ballast resistor' wire is by-passed, allowing the full available battery voltage to be fed to the coil (Fig. 4.1). This ensures that during cold starting, when the starter motor current draw would be high, sufficient voltage is still available at the coil to produce a powerful spark. It is therefore essential that only the correct type of coil is used. Under normal running the 12 volt supply is directed through the ballast resistor before reaching the coil (Fig. 4.2).

The ignition advance is controlled both mechanically and by vacuum, to ensure that the spark occurs at just the right instant for the particular engine load and speed. The mechanical governor comprises two lead weights, which move out from the distributor shaft as the engine speed rises, due to centrifugal force.

The vacuum control consists of a diaphragm, one side of which is connected via a small bore tube to the carburettor, and the other side to the contact breaker plate. Depression in the inlet manifold and carburettor, which varies with engine speed and throttle opening, causes the diaphragm to move, so moving the contact breaker plate, and advancing or retarding the spark (Fig. 4.3).

Two makes of distributor are used, Motorcraft (black cap) and Bosch (red cap). They are similar in design, with the exception of the condenser location, which is external on the Bosch unit.

2 Contact breaker points – adjustment

1 To adjust the contact breaker points to the correct gap, first

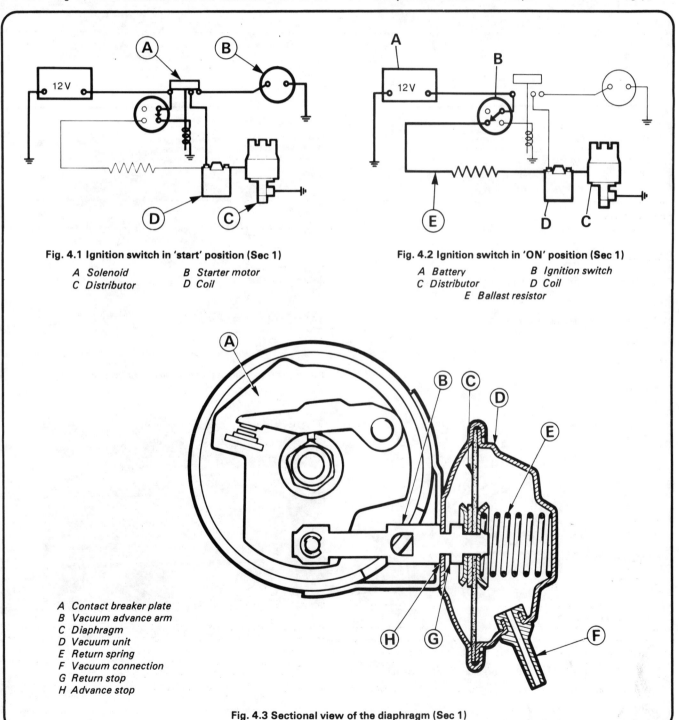

Fig. 4.1 Ignition switch in 'start' position (Sec 1)

A Solenoid   B Starter motor
C Distributor   D Coil

Fig. 4.2 Ignition switch in 'ON' position (Sec 1)

A Battery   B Ignition switch
C Distributor   D Coil
        E Ballast resistor

A Contact breaker plate
B Vacuum advance arm
C Diaphragm
D Vacuum unit
E Return spring
F Vacuum connection
G Return stop
H Advance stop

Fig. 4.3 Sectional view of the diaphragm (Sec 1)

2.7 Recheck the gap after adjusting the points

3.3 Distributor with cap and rotor removed

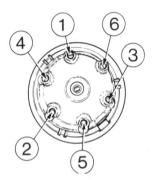
Fig. 4.4 HT leads connections in distributor cap

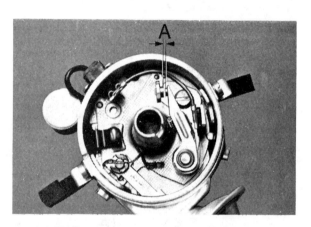
Fig. 4.5 Measuring the contact breaker points gap (Sec 2)

A   Contact breaker point gap (typical)

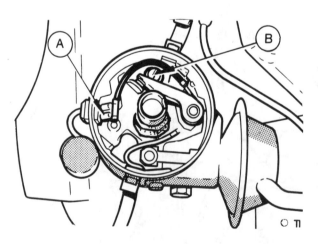
Fig. 4.6 Removing the contact breaker points – Bosch distributor
(Sec 3)

A   LT lead connection   B   Securing screw

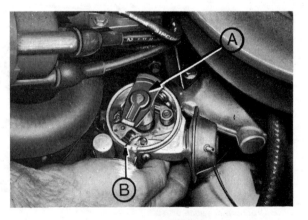
Fig. 4.7 Removing the distributor (Sec 6)

A   Rotor arm   B   Mark on body

release the two clips securing the distributor cap to the distributor body, and lift away the cap. Clean the cap inside and out with a dry cloth. It is unlikely that the segments will be badly burned or scored, but, if they are, the cap will have to be renewed (Fig. 4.4).

2   Inspect the carbon brush contact located in the top of the cap to ensure that it is not broken and stands proud of the plastic surface.

3   Lift away the rotor arm and check the contact spring on the top of the rotor arm. It must be clean and have adequate tension to ensure good contact.

4   Gently prise the contact breaker points open to examine the condition of their faces. If they are rough, pitted or burned it will be necessary to fit new points.

5   Presuming the points are satisfactory, or that they have been renewed, measure the gap between the points with feeler gauges, by turning the crankshaft until the heel of the breaker arm is on a high point of the cam. The gap should be as given in the Specifications (Fig. 4.5).

6   If the gap varies from the amount stated, slacken the contact plate securing screw/s. (Bosch distributor 1 screw. Motorcraft distributor 2 screws).

7   Adjust the contact gap by moving the contact breaker plate. When the gap is correct, tighten the securing screw/s and recheck the gap (photo).

8   Refit the rotor arm and distributor cap. Retain in position with the two clips.

3   Contact breaker points – removal and refitting

1   Disconnect the battery negative terminal.

2   Unplug the spark plug leads, unclip the distributor cap and lift clear.

3   Remove the rotor arm by pulling it straight up from the top of the cam spindle (photo).

4   If the contact breaker points are burned, pitted or badly worn, they must be renewed, since attempting to file or grind them will destroy the special facing.

5   Detach the LT leads at the points:

Bosch   *pull off lead*
Motorcraft   *slacken the screw and slide out the forked ends*

6   Remove the securing screw/s and lift out the contact breaker points (Fig. 4.6).

7   To refit the points is the reverse sequence of removal. Smear a trace of grease onto the cam to lubricate the moving heel, then reset the gap, as described in Section 2.

8   Push the rotor arm onto the cam spindle, ensuring that the locating boss is aligned with the slot.

9   Place the distributor cap squarely on the distributor and retain in position with the two clips.

10 Push the leads onto the plugs, in the correct order, and reconnect the battery.

4   Condenser – removal, testing and refitting

1   The purpose of the condenser (sometimes known as the capacitor) is to ensure that when the contact breaker points open there is no sparking across them which would waste voltage and cause wear.

2   The condenser is fitted in parallel with the contact breaker points. If it develops a short circuit, it will cause ignition failure as the contact breaker points will be prevented from correctly interrupting the low tension circuit.

3   If the engine becomes very difficult to start or begins to miss after several miles of running and the breaker points show signs of excessive burning, then the condition of the condenser must be suspect. One further test can be made by separating the points by hand with the ignition switched on. If this is accompanied by a bright flash, it is indicative that the condenser has failed.

4   Without special test equipment the only safe way to diagnose condenser trouble is to replace a suspected unit with a new one and note if there is any improvement.

5   To remove the condenser from the distributor take off the

distributor cap and rotor arm.

6   *Bosch:* Disconnect the low tension leads from the coil and to the contact breaker points. Release the condenser cable from the side of the distributor body and then undo and remove the screw that secures the condenser to the side of the distributor body. Lift away the condenser.

7   *Motorcraft:* Slacken the self tapping screw holding the condenser lead and low tension lead to the contact breaker points. Slide out the forked terminal on the end of the condenser low tension lead. Undo and remove the condenser retaining screw and remove the condenser from the breaker plate.

8   To refit the condenser, simply reverse the order of removal.

5   Distributor – lubrication

1   It is important that the distributor cam is lubricated with vaseline (petroleum jelly) or grease at 6000 miles (10 000 km) or 6 monthly intervals. Also the automatic timing control weights and cam spindle are lubricated with engine oil.

2   Great care should be taken not to use too much lubricant as any excess that finds its way onto the contact breaker points could cause burning and misfiring.

3   To gain access to the cam spindle, lift away the distributor cap and rotor arm. Apply no more than two drops of engine oil onto the felt pad. This will run down the spindle when the engine is hot and lubricate the bearings.

4   To lubricate the automatic timing control, allow a few drops of oil to pass through the holes in the contact breaker base plate through which the six sided cam emerges. Apply not more than one drop of oil to the pivot post of the moving contact breaker point. Wipe away excess oil and refit the rotor arm and distributor cap.

6   Distributor – removal

1   To remove the distributor from the engine, mark the six spark plug leads so that they may be refitted to the correct plugs and pull off the six spark plug lead connectors.

2   Disconnect the high tension lead from the centre of the distributor cap by gripping the end of the cap and pulling. Also disconnect the low tension lead from the ignition coil.

3   Pull off the rubber union holding the vacuum pipe to the distributor vacuum advance housing.

4   Remove the distributor body clamp bolt which holds the distributor clamp plate to the engine and lift out the distributor. **Note:** *If it is not wished to disturb the timing turn the crankshaft until the timing marks are in line and the rotor arm is pointing to number 1 spark plug segment in the distributor cap (Fig. 4.7). This will facilitate refitting the distributor providing the crankshaft is not moved whilst*

6.4 Mark indicating position of rotor before fitting the distributor

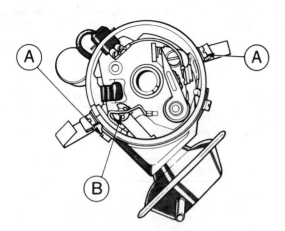

Fig. 4.8 Removing the vacuum unit – Bosch distributor (Sec 7)

A *Securing screws*   B *Pull rod retaining clip*

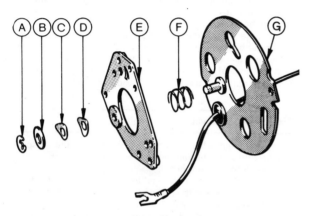

Fig. 4.9 Exploded view of base plate assembly – Motorcraft distributor (Sec 8)

A *Circlip*   B *Plain washer*
C *Wave washer*   D *Wave washer*
E *Upper plate*   F *Spring*
          G *Base plate*

the distributor is away from the engine. Mark the position of the rotor in relation to the distributor body, after it has been lifted clear (photo).

7   Distributor (Bosch) – dismantling

1   With the distributor on the bench, release the two spring clips retaining the cap and lift away the cap.
2   Pull the rotor arm off the distributor cam spindle.
3   Remove the contact breaker points, as described in Section 3.
4   Unscrew and remove the condenser securing screw and lift away the condenser and connector.
5   Next carefully remove the U-shaped clip from the pull rod of the vacuum unit (Fig. 4.8).
6   Undo and remove the two screws that secure the vacuum unit to the side of the distributor body. Lift away the vacuum unit.
7   The distributor cap spring clip retainers may be removed by undoing and removing the screws and lifting away the clips and retainers. **Note**: *This is the limit of the dismantling which should be attempted, since none of the parts beneath the breaker plate, including the drive gear, can be renewed.*

8   Distributor (Motorcraft) – dismantling

1   Refer to Section 7, and follow the instructions given in paragraphs 1 to 3.
2   Next prise off the small circlip from the vacuum unit pivot post.
3   Take out the two screws that hold the breaker plate to the distributor body and lift away.
4   Undo and remove the condenser retaining screw and lift away the condenser.
5   Take off the circlip, flat washer and two wave washers from the pivot post. Separate the two plates. Be careful not to lose the spring now left on the pivot post (Fig. 4.9).
6   Pull the low tension wire and grommet from the lower plate.
7   Undo the two screws holding the vacuum unit to the body. Take off the unit.
8   Make a sketch of the position of the cam plate assembly in relation to the bumpstop, noting the identification letters. Also note which spring – thick or thin – is fitted to which post (Fig. 4.10).
9   Dismantle the spindle by taking out the felt pad in the top. Remove the spring clip using small electrical pliers.
10 Prise off the bumpstop and lift out the cam plate assembly. Remove the thrust washer (Fig. 4.11).
11 It is only necessary to remove the spindle and lower plate if it is excessively worn. If this is the case, with a suitable diameter parallel pin punch tap out the gear lock pin.
12 The gear may now be drawn off the shaft with a universal puller. If

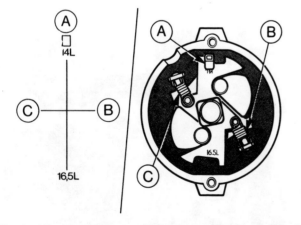

Fig. 4.10 Typical sketch showing location of bump stop (Sec 8)

A *Bump stop*   B *Thin spring*   C *Thick spring*

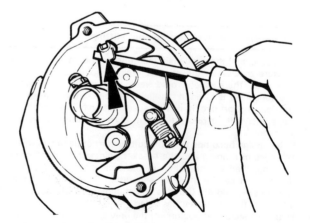

Fig. 4.11 Removing the bump stop (Sec 8)

Measuring plug gap. A feeler gauge of the correct size (see ignition system specifications) should have a slight 'drag' when slid between the electrodes. Adjust gap if necessary

Adjusting plug gap. The plug gap is adjusted by bending the earth electrode inwards, or outwards, as necessary until the correct clearance is obtained. Note the use of the correct tool

Normal. Grey-brown deposits, lightly coated core nose. Gap increasing by around 0.001 in (0.025 mm) per 1000 miles (1600 km). Plugs ideally suited to engine, and engine in good condition

Carbon fouling. Dry, black, sooty deposits. Will cause weak spark and eventually misfire. Fault: over-rich fuel mixture. Check: carburettor mixture settings, float level and jet sizes; choke operation and cleanliness of air filter. Plugs can be re-used after cleaning

Oil fouling. Wet, oily deposits. Will cause weak spark and eventually misfire. Fault: worn bores/piston rings or valve guides; sometimes occurs (temporarily) during running-in period. Plugs can be re-used after thorough cleaning

Overheating. Electrodes have glazed appearance, core nose very white — few deposits. Fault: plug overheating. Check: plug value, ignition timing, fuel octane rating (too low) and fuel mixture (too weak). Discard plugs and cure fault immediately

Electrode damage. Electrodes burned away; core nose has burned, glazed appearance. Fault: pre-ignition. Check: as for 'Overheating' but may be more severe. Discard plugs and remedy fault before piston or valve damage occurs

Split core nose (may appear initially as a crack). Damage is self-evident, but cracks will only show after cleaning. Fault: pre-ignition or wrong gap-setting technique. Check: ignition timing, cooling system, fuel octane rating (too low) and fuel mixture (too weak). Discard plugs, rectify fault immediately

there are no means of holding the legs these must be bound together with wire to stop them springing apart during removal.

13   Finally withdraw the shaft from the distributor body.

9   Distributor – inspection and repair

1   Check the contact breaker points for wear, burning or pitting. Check the distributor cap for signs of tracking indicated by a thin black line between the segments. Renew the cap if any signs of tracking are found.

2   If the metal portion of the rotor arm is badly burned or loose, renew the arm. If only slightly burned clean the end with a fine file. Check that the contact spring has adequate pressure and the bearing surface is clean and in good condition.

3   Check that the carbon brush in the distributor cap is unbroken and stands proud of its holder.

4   Examine the centrifugal weights and pivots for wear and the advance springs for slackness. They can be checked by comparing with new parts. If they are slack they must be renewed.

5   Check the points assembly for fit on the breaker plate, and the cam follower for wear.

6   Examine the fit of the spindle in the distributor body. If there is excessive side movement it will be necessary either to fit a new bush or obtain a new body.

10   Distributor (Bosch) – reassembly

1   Place the distributor cap retaining spring clip and retainers on the outside of the distributor body and secure the retainers with the two screws.

2   Position the contact breaker point assembly in the breaker plate in such a manner that the entire lower surface of the assembly contacts the plate. Refit the contact breaker points assembly securing screw but do not fully tighten yet.

3   Hook the diaphragm assembly pull rod into contact with the pivot pin.

4   Secure the diaphragm to the distributor body with the two screws. Also refit the condenser to the terrninal side of the diaphragm bracket securing screw. The condenser must firmly contact its lower stop on the housing.

5   Apply a little grease or petroleum jelly to the cam and also to the heel of the breaker lever.

6   Reset the contact breaker points, as described in Section 2, and then refit the rotor arm and distributor cap.

11   Distributor (Motorcraft) – reassembly

1   Reassembly is a straightforward reversal of the dismantling process but there are several points which must be noted.

2   Check that the drive gear is not 180° out of position, as the pin bores may be slightly misaligned. Secure it with a new pin.

3   Coat the upper shaft with a lithium based grease, ensuring that the undercut is filled.

4   When fitting the cam spindle assembly, first refit the thrust washer, then refer to the sketch in Section 8, paragraph 8. Check that the assembly moves freely without binding.

5   Position the spring clip legs opposite the rotor arm slot.

6   Before assembling the breaker plates make sure that the nylon bearing studs are correctly located in their holes in the upper breaker plate, and the small earth spring is fitted on the pivot post.

7   When all is assembled reset the contact breaker points, as escribed in Section 2.

12   Distributor – installation

1   If a new shaft or gear has not been fitted (ie; the original parts are still being used), it will not be necessary to re-time the ignition.

2   Align the rotor arm with the mark on the distributor body (Section 6, paragraph 5). Insert the distributor into its location with the vacuum advance assembly to the rear.

3   Note that the rotor arm rotates as the gears mesh. The rotor arm must settle in exactly the same direction that it was in before the

distributor was removed. To do this lift out the assembly far enough to rotate the shaft one tooth at a time, lowering it home to check the direction. With the assembly fully home fit the distributor clamp plate, bolt and plain washer.

4   With the distributor assembly fitted reconnect the low tension lead from the side of the distributor to the CB or negative (–) terminal on the coil. Reconnect the HT lead to the centre of the distributor cap and refit the rubber union of the vacuum pipe which runs from the induction manifold to the side of the vacuum advance unit.

5   If the engine has been disturbed, refer to Section 14.

13   Spark plugs and HT leads

1   The correct functioning of the spark plugs is vital for the correct running and efficiency of the engine.

2   At intervals of 6000 miles (10 000 km), the plugs should be removed, examined, cleaned and if worn excessively, renewed. The condition of the spark plugs will also tell much about the overall condition of the engine.

3   If the insulator nose of the spark plug is clean and white, with no deposits, this is indicative of a weak mixture, or too hot a plug (a hot plug transfers heat away from the electrode slowly – a cold plug transfers it away quickly).

4   The plugs fitted as standard are as listed in the Specifications at the beginning of this Chapter. If the tip and insulator noses are covered with hard black-looking deposits, then this is indicative that the mixture is too rich. Should the plug be black and oily, then it is likely that the engine is fairly worn, as well as the mixture being too rich.

5   If the insulator nose is covered with light tan to greyish brown deposits, then the mixture is correct and it is likely that the engine is in good condition.

6   If there are any traces of long brown tapering stains on the outside of the white portion of the plug, then the plug will have to be renewed, as this shows that there is a faulty joint between the plug body and the insulator, and compression is being allowed to leak away.

7   Plugs should be cleaned by a sand blasting machine which will free them from carbon more thoroughly than cleaning by hand. The machine will also test the condition of the plugs under compression. Any plug that fails to spark at the recommended pressure should be renewed.

8   The spark plug gap is of considerable importance, as, if it is too large or too small, the size of the spark and its efficiency will be seriously impaired. The spark plug gap should be set to the figure given in the Specifications at the beginning of this Chapter.

9   To set it, measure the gap with a feeler gauge, and then bend open, or close, the outer plug electrode until the correct gap is achieved. The centre electrode should never be bent as this may crack the insulation and cause plug failure if nothing worse.

10   When replacing the plugs, remember to use new plug washers, and refit the leads from the distributor in the correct firing order, which is given in the Specifications.

11   The plug leads require no routine attention other than being kept

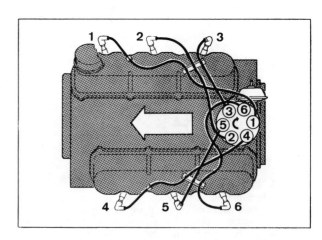

Fig. 4.12 Arrangement of HT leads to spark plugs (Sec 13)

clean and wiped over regularly.

12 At intervals of 6000 miles (10 000 km) or 6 months, pull the leads off the plugs and distributor one at a time and make sure no water has found its way onto the connections. Remove any corrosion from the brass ends, wipe the collars on top of the distributor, and refit the leads.

14 Ignition timing

1 When a new gear or shaft has been fitted or the engine has been rotated, or if a new assembly is being fitted, it will be necessary to retime the ignition.

2 Look up the initial advance (static) in the Specifications at the beginning of this Chapter.

3 Turn the engine until No. 1 piston is coming up to TDC on the compression stroke. This can be checked by removing No. 1 spark plug and feeling the pressure being developed in the cylinder. If this check is not made it is all too easy to set the timing 180° out. The engine can most easily be turned by placing a suitable sized socket and a ratchet on the crankshaft pulley bolt. Alternatively, it may be turned by engaging top gear and edging the car along (except automatic).

4 Continue turning the engine until the notch on the crankshaft pulley is in line with the appropriate mark on the timing scale bolted to the timing cover.

5 Now with the vacuum advance unit pointing to the left-hand side of the engine and the rotor arm in the same position as was noted before removal insert the distributor into its location. Note that the rotor arm rotates as the gears mesh. Lift out the distributor far enough to rotate the shaft one tooth at a time, lowering it home to check the direction of the rotor arm. When it points in the desired direction with the assembly fully home fit the distributor clamp plate, bolt and plain washer. Do not fully tighten yet.

6 Gently turn the distributor body until the contact breaker points are just opening when the rotor is pointing at the contact in the distributor cap which is connected to No. 1 spark plug. A convenient way is to put a mark on the outside of the distributor body in line with the segment in the cover, so that it shows when the cover is removed.

7 If this position cannot be reached check that the drive gear has meshed on the correct tooth by lifting out the distributor once more. If necessary, rotate the driveshaft gear one tooth and try again.

8 Tighten the distributor body clamp enough to hold the distributor but do not overtighten.

9 Set in this way, the timing should be approximately correct but a more accurate method is by using a stroboscopic timing light.

10 Clean the timing scale on the timing cover and mark the specified timing degree line, and also the notch on the crankshaft pulley, with quick drying white paint or chalk.

11 Disconnect and plug the vacuum pipe. Run the engine to normal operating temperature and check that the idling speed is correct.

12 Connect a timing light between No. 1 spark plug and the No. 1 spark plug lead.

13 Start the engine and point the timing light at the crankshaft pulley. The white painted marks will appear stationary and if the timing is correct they will be in alignment.

14 If they are not directly opposite each other, loosen the mounting plate clamp bolt and turn the distributor one way or the other until the marks line up. Tighten the clamp bolt and recheck the timing.

15 If the engine speed is now increased the white mark on the pulley will move away from the pointer indicating that the centrifugal advance is operating. If the vacuum pipe is unplugged and reconnected to the vacuum unit the operation of the vacuum unit can be checked by revving up the engine and watching the timing marks. Note: *To check the amount of ignition advance, the timing light must include an advance meter.*

16 Remove the timing light and reconnect the HT lead to the spark plug.

17 Since the ignition timing setting enables the firing point to be correctly related to the grade of fuel used, the fullest advantage of a change of grade from that recommended for the engine will only be attained by re-adjustment of the ignition setting.

15 Ignition system – fault finding

By far the majority of breakdown and running troubles are caused by faults in the ignition system either in the low tension or high tension circuits.

There are two main symptoms indicating ignition faults. Either the engine will not start or fire, or the engine is difficult to start and misfires. If it is a regular misfire, ie; the engine is running on only four or five cylinders, the fault is almost sure to be in the secondary or high tension circuit. If the misfiring is intermittent, the fault could be in either the high or low tension circuits. If the car stops suddenly, or will not start at all, it is likely that the fault is in the low tension circuit. Loss of power and overheating, apart from faulty carburation settings, are normally due to faults in the distributor or to incorrect ignition timing.

16 Fault diagnosis – engine fails to start

1 If the engine fails to start and the car was running normally when it was last used, first check that there is fuel in the petrol tank. If the engine turns over normally on the starter motor and the battery is evidently well charged, then the fault may be in either the high or low tension circuits. First check the HT circuit. If the battery is known to be fully charged, the ignition light comes on and the starter motor fails to turn the engine **check the tightness of the leads on the battery terminals** and also the secureness of the earth lead to its connection to the body. It is quite common for the leads to have worked loose, even if they look and feel secure. If one of the battery terminal posts gets very hot when trying to work the starter motor this is a sure indication of a faulty connection to that terminal.

2 One of the commonest reasons for bad starting is wet or damp spark plug leads and distributor. Remove the distributor cap. If condensation is visible internally dry the cap with a rag and also wipe over the leads. Refit the cap.

3 If the engine still fails to start, check that the current is reaching the plugs, by disconnecting each plug lead in turn at the spark plug end, and holding the end of the cable about $\frac{3}{16}$ inch (5mm) away from the cylinder block. Spin the engine on the starter motor.

4 Sparking between the end of the cable and the block should be fairly strong with a strong regular blue spark. (Hold the lead with rubber to avoid electric shocks). If current is reaching the plugs then remove them and clean and regap them to 0.025 inch (0.60 mm). The engine should now start.

5 If there is no spark at the plug leads take off the HT lead from the centre of the distributor cap and hold it to the block as before. Spin the engine on the starter once more. A rapid succession of blue sparks between the end of the lead and the block indicate that the coil is in order and that the distributor cap is cracked, the rotor arm faulty, or the carbon brush in the top of the distributor cap is not making good contact with the spring on the rotor arm. Possibly, the points are in bad condition. Renew them as described in this Chapter, Sections 2 and 3.

6 If there are no sparks from the end of the lead from the coil check the connections at the coil end of the lead. If it is in order start checking the low tension circuit.

7 Use a 12v voltmeter or a 12v bulb and two lengths of wire. With the ignition switched on and the points open, test between the low tension wire to the coil (it is marked SW or +) and earth. No reading indicates a break in the supply from the ignition switch. Check the connections at the switch to see if any are loose. Refit them and the engine should run. A reading shows a faulty coil or condenser, or broken lead between the coil and the distributor.

8 Take the condenser wire off the points assembly and with the points open test between the moving point and earth. If there is now a reading then the fault is in the condenser. Fit a new one as described in this Chapter, Section 4, and the fault is cleared.

9 With no reading from the moving point to earth, take a reading between earth and the CB or negative (–) terminal of the coil. A reading here shows a broken wire which will need to be renewed between the coil and distributor. No reading confirms that the coil has failed and must be renewed, after which the engine will run once more. Remember to refit the condenser wire to the points assembly. For these tests it is sufficient to separate the points with a piece of dry paper while testing with the points open.

17 Fault diagnosis – engine misfires

1 If the engine misfires regularly run it at a fast idling speed. Pull off each of the plug caps in turn and listen to the note of the engine. Hold

the plug cap in a dry cloth or with a rubber glove as additional protection against a shock from the HT supply.

2   No difference in engine running will be noticed when the lead from the defective circuit is removed. Removing the lead from one of the good cylinders will accentuate the misfire.

3   Remove the plug lead from the end of the defective plug and hold it about $\frac{3}{16}$ inch (5mm) away from the block. Re-start the engine. If the sparking is fairly strong and regular the fault must lie in the spark plug.

4   The plug may be loose, the insulation may be cracked, or the points may have burnt away giving too wide a gap for the spark to jump. Worse still, one of the points may have broken off.

5   If there is no spark at the end of the plug lead, or if it is weak and intermittent, check the ignition lead from the distributor to the plug. If the insulation is cracked or perished, renew the lead. Check the connections at the distributor cap.

6   If there is still no spark, examine the distributor cap carefully for tracking. This can be recognised by a very thin black line running between two or more electrodes, or between an electrode and some other part of the distributor. These lines are paths which now conduct electricity across the cap thus letting it run to earth. The only answer is a new distributor cap.

7   Apart from the ignition timing being incorrect, other causes of misfiring have already been dealt with under the section dealing with the failure of the engine to start. To recap – these are that:

a)   The coil may be faulty giving an intermittent misfire
b)   There may be a damaged wire or loose connection in the low tension circuit
c)   The condenser may be short circuiting
d)   There may be a mechanical fault in the distributor (broken driving spindle or contact breaker spring)

8   If the ignition timing is too far retarded, it should be noted that the engine will tend to overheat, and there will be quite a noticeable drop in power. If the engine is overheating and the power is down, and the ignition timing is correct, then the carburettor should be checked, as it is likely that this is where the fault lies.

Chapter 5 Clutch

For modifications, and information applicable to later models, see Supplement at end of manual

Contents

Specifications

Type . . . . Single dry plate, diaphragm spring, cable operated

Lining diameter
Inside diameter . . . . 6.12 in (155.5 mm)
Outside diameter . . . . 9.53 in (242 mm)
Lining thickness . . . . 0.15 in (3.8 mm)

Number of torsion springs 6

Pedal free travel . . . . 0.9 to 1.2 in (23 to 31 mm)

Total pedal stroke . . . . 6.69 in (170 mm)

Torque wrench setting	lbf ft	kgf m
Pressure plate to flywheel bolts	14	2

1 General description

All models covered by this manual are fitted with a single diaphragm spring clutch. The unit comprises a steel cover which is dowelled and bolted to the rear face of the flywheel and contains the pressure plate, diaphragm spring and fulcrum rings.

The clutch disc is free to slide along the splined first motion shaft and is held in position between the flywheel and the pressure plate by the pressure of the pressure plate spring. Friction lining material is rivetted to the clutch disc and it has a spring cushioned hub to absorb transmission shocks and to help ensure a smooth take off.

The circular diaphragm spring is mounted on shoulder pins and held in place in the cover by two fulcrum rings. The spring is also held to the pressure plate by three spring steel clips which are rivetted in position.

The clutch is actuated by a cable controlled by the clutch pedal. The clutch release mechanism consists of a release fork and bearing

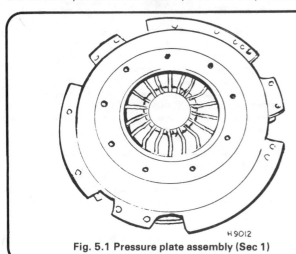
Fig. 5.1 Pressure plate assembly (Sec 1)

Fig. 5.2 Clutch disc assembly (Sec 1)

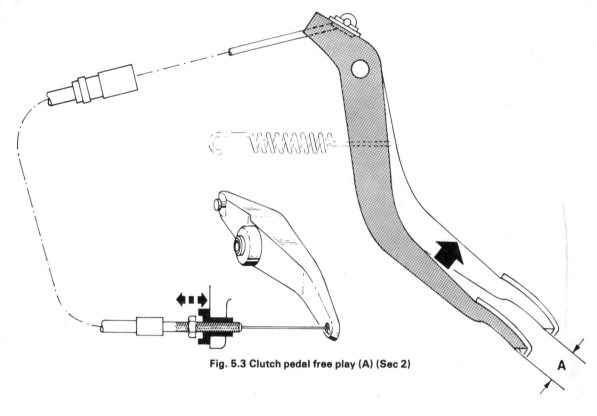

Fig. 5.3 Clutch pedal free play (A) (Sec 2)

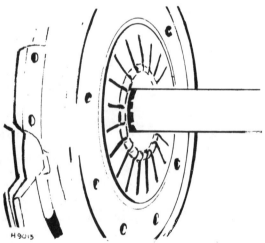

Fig. 5.4 Centralising the clutch disc (Sec 5)

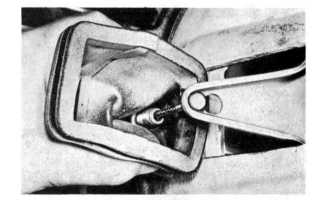

Fig. 5.5 Removing the clutch cable gaiter from the bellhousing (Sec 6)

which are in permanent contact with the release fingers on the pressure plate assembly. There should therefore never be any free play at the release fork. Wear of the friction material in the clutch is adjusted out by means of a cable adjuster at the lower end of the cable where it passes through the bellhousing.

Depressing the clutch pedal actuates the clutch release arm by means of the cable. The release arm pushes the release bearing forwards to bear against the release fingers so moving the centre of the diaphragm spring inwards. The spring is sandwiched between two annular rings which act as fulcrum points. As the centre of the spring is pushed in, the outside of the spring is pushed out, so moving the pressure plate backwards and disengaging the pressure plate from the clutch disc.

When the clutch pedal is released the diaphragm spring forces the pressure plate into contact with the friction linings on the clutch disc

and at the same time pushes the clutch disc a fraction of an inch forwards on its splines so engaging the clutch disc with the flywheel. The clutch disc is now firmly sandwiched between the pressure plate and the flywheel so the drive is taken up.

2 Clutch pedal free travel – adjustment

1   Adjust the clutch cable every 6000 miles (10 000 km) to compensate for wear of the clutch disc linings.
2   The clutch should be adjusted so that the free travel is as given in the Specifications (Fig. 5.3).
3   To obtain the correct adjustment pull the outer cable forward from the hexagon recess in the clutch housing and turn the adjusting nut until the specified pedal free travel is obtained, then allow the adjust-

ing nut to seat in the hexagon recess. Recheck the pedal free travel.

3 Clutch assembly – removal

1   This job may be carried out with the engine either in or out of the car. The gearbox must be detached from the rear of the engine as described in Chapter 6.
2   With a file or scriber mark the relative position of the clutch cover and flywheel which will ensure identical positioning when refitting. This is not necessary if a new clutch is to be fitted.
3   Undo and remove, in a diagonal and progressive manner, the six bolts and spring washers that secure the clutch cover to the flywheel. This will prevent distortion of the cover and also the cover suddenly flying off due to binding of the dowels.
4   With all the bolts removed lift the clutch assembly from the locating dowels. Note which way round the friction plate is fitted and lift it from the clutch cover.

4 Clutch – dismantling and inspection

1   It is not practical to dismantle the pressure plate assembly and the term 'dismantling' is usually used for simply fitting a new clutch friction plate.
2   If a new clutch disc is being fitted it is a false economy not to renew the release bearing at the same time. This will preclude having to renew it at a later date when wear on the clutch linings is still very small.
3   If the pressure plate assembly requires renewal an exchange unit must be purchased. This will have been accurately set up and balanced to very fine limits.

4   Examine the clutch disc friction linings for wear and loose rivets and the disc for rim distortion, cracks, broken hub springs, and worn splines. The surface of the friction linings may be highly glazed, but as long as the clutch material pattern can be clearly seen this is satisfactory. Compare the amount of lining wear with a new clutch disc at the stores in your local garage. If worn, the friction plate must be renewed.
5   It is always best to renew the clutch driven plate as an assembly to preclude further trouble, but, if it is wished to merely renew the linings, the rivets should be drilled out and not knocked out with a punch. The manufacturers do not advise that only the linings be renewed and personal experience dictates that it is far more satisfactory to renew the driven plate complete rather than try to economise by only fitting new friction linings.
6   Check the machined faces of the flywheel and the pressure plate. If either is grooved it should be machined until smooth, or renewed.
7   If the pressure plate is cracked or split it is essential that an exchange unit is fitted, also if the pressure of the diaphragm spring is suspect.
8   Check the release bearing for smoothness of operation. There should be no harshness or slackness in it. It should spin reasonably freely bearing in mind it has been pre-packed with grease. **Note:** *When the clutch disc is removed, a certain amount of asbestos dust is likely to be present. This* **should not** *be inhaled: the best method of cleaning is to use a vacuum cleaner.*

5 Clutch assembly – refitting

1   It is important that no oil or grease gets on the clutch plate friction linings, or the pressure plate and flywheel faces. It is advisable to refit the clutch with clean hands and to wipe down the pressure plate and

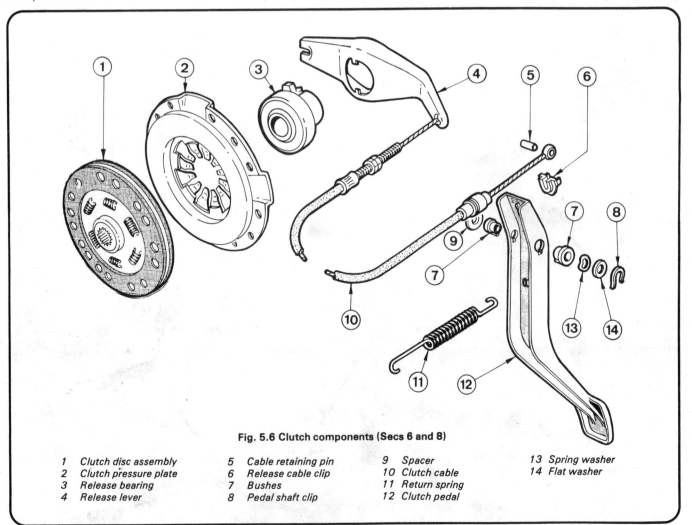

Fig. 5.6 Clutch components (Secs 6 and 8)

1 Clutch disc assembly	5 Cable retaining pin	9 Spacer	13 Spring washer
2 Clutch pressure plate	6 Release cable clip	10 Clutch cable	14 Flat washer
3 Release bearing	7 Bushes	11 Return spring	
4 Release lever	8 Pedal shaft clip	12 Clutch pedal	

Fig. 5.7 Cable retaining pin (Sec 6)

Fig. 5.8 Clutch release arm and bearing (Sec 7)

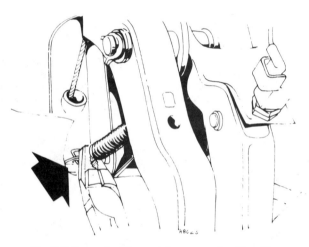

Fig. 5.9 Removing the pedal return spring (Sec 8)

Fig. 5.10 Pedal shaft retaining clip (Sec 8)

flywheel faces with a clean rag before assembly begins.

2   Place the clutch plate against the flywheel, ensuring that it is the correct way round. The projecting torsion spring plate should be furthest from the flywheel.

3   Refit the clutch cover assembly loosely on the dowels. Refit the six bolts and spring washers and tighten them finger-tight so that the clutch plate is gripped but can still be moved.

4   The clutch disc must now be centralised so that when the engine and gearbox are mated, the gearbox first motion shaft splines will pass through the splines in the centre of the driven plate.

5   Centralisation can be carried out quite easily by inserting a round bar or long screwdriver through the hole in the centre of the clutch, so that the end of the bar rests in the small hole in the end of the crankshaft containing the spigot bush. Ideally an old Ford first motion shaft should be used (Fig. 5.4).

6   Using the first motion shaft spigot bush as a fulcrum, moving the bar sideways or up and down will move the clutch disc in whichever direction is necessary to achieve centralisation.

7   Centralisation is easily judged by removing the bar and viewing the driven plate hub in relation to the hole in the centre of the clutch cover plate diaphragm spring. When the hub appears exactly in the centre of the hole all is correct. Alternatively the first motion shaft will fit the bush and centre of the clutch hub exactly, obviating the need for visual alignment.

8   Tighten the clutch bolts firmly in a diagonal sequence to ensure that the cover plate is pulled down evenly and without distortion of the flange. Finally tighten the bolts to the specified torque, see Specifications at the beginning of this Chapter.

6 Clutch cable – removal and refitting

1   Open the bonnet, and for safety reasons disconnect the battery.

2   Chock the rear wheels, jack up the front of the car and support it on firmly based axle-stands.

3   Slacken the clutch cable at the clutch adjusting nut, refer to Section 2. Ease off the release lever rubber gaiter from the side of the clutch housing (Fig. 5.5).

4   It will now be possible to lift the cable ball end from the slotted end of the release lever. Whilst this is being done take great care not to accidentally disengage the release lever from the bearing hub (Fig. 5.6).

5   Lever the cable eye end and pin from the cable retention bush in the pedal with a small screwdriver (see Fig. 5.7).

6   Withdraw the pin from the eye and withdraw the cable assembly from the abutment tube in the dash panel.

7   Refitting is a straightforward reversal of the removal sequence. Well lubricate the pivot pin. Refer to Section 2, and adjust the clutch pedal free travel.

7 Clutch release bearing – removal and refitting

1   With the gearbox and engine separated to provide access to the clutch, attention can be given to the release bearing located in the bellhousing, over the input shaft (Fig. 5.8).

2   The release bearing is a relatively inexpensive but important com-

ponent and unless it is nearly new it is a mistake not to renew it during an overhaul of the clutch.

3 The release bearing and arm can be withdrawn from the clutch housing.

4 To free the bearing from the release arm, simply rotate the bearing through 90° and remove. Note which way round the bearing is fitted (Fig. 5.6).

5 Refitting is a straightforward reversal of removal.

8 Clutch pedal – removal and refitting

1 Release the clutch cable from the pedal, refer to Section 6.

2 Disconnect the clutch pedal return spring (Fig. 5.9).

3 Remove the pedal shaft circlip (Fig. 5.10) flat washer and spring washer. Pull the pedal sideways off the shaft. Press out the clutch pedal spacers by hand (Fig. 5.6).

4 Refitting is a straightforward reversal of removal.

9 Fault diagnosis

There are four main faults to which the clutch and release mechanism are prone. They may occur by themselves or in conjunction with any of the other faults. They are clutch squeal, slip, spin and judder.

Clutch squeal

1 If on taking up the drive or when changing gear, the clutch squeals, this is a good indication of a badly worn clutch release bearing.

2 As well as regular wear due to normal use, wear of the clutch release bearing is much accentuated if the clutch is ridden, or held down for long periods in gear, with the engine running. To minimise wear of this component the car should always be taken out of gear at traffic lights and for similar holdups.

Clutch slip

3 Clutch slip is a c—— —— h occurs when the clutc— ——riction plate is badly wor— ——eel or pressure plate face—

4 ——e of the faults listed abov— ——e pressure plate, or insuff— —— solid drive.

5 If ——ey will be burnt off under —— process, gradually

darken the linings. Excessive oil on the clutch will burn off leaving a carbon deposit which can cause quite bad slip, or fierceness, spin and judder.

6 If clutch slip is suspected, and confirmation of this condition is required, there are several tests which can be made.

7 With the engine in second or third gear and pulling lightly up a moderate incline sudden depression of the accelerator pedal may cause the engine to increase its speed without any increase in road speed. Easing off on the accelerator will then give a definite drop in engine speed without the car slowing.

8 In extreme cases of clutch slip the engine will race under normal acceleration conditions.

9 If slip is due to oil or grease on the linings a temporary cure can sometimes be effected by squirting carbon tetrachloride into the clutch. The permanent cure is, of course, to renew the clutch driven plate and trace and rectify the oil leak.

Clutch spin

10 Clutch spin is a condition which occurs when the release arm travel is excessive, there is an obstruction in the clutch either on the primary gear splines or in the operating lever itself, or the oil may have partially burnt off the clutch linings and have left a resinous deposit which is causing the clutch disc to stick to the pressure plate or flywheel.

11 The reason for clutch spin is that due to any, or a combination of, the faults just listed, the clutch pressure plate is not completely freeing from the centre plate even with the clutch pedal fully depressed.

12 If clutch spin is suspected, the condition can be confirmed by extreme difficulty in engaging first gear from rest, difficulty in changing gear, and very sudden take up of the clutch drive at the fully depressed end of the clutch pedal travel as the clutch is released.

13 Check that the clutch cable is correctly adjusted and, if in order, the fault lies internally in the clutch. It will then be necessary to remove the clutch for examination, and to check the gearbox input shaft.

Clutch judder

14 Clutch judder is a self evident condition which occurs when the gearbox or engine mountings are loose or too flexible, when there is oil on the faces of the clutch friction plate, or when the clutch pressure plate has been incorrectly adjusted during assembly.

15 The reason for clutch judder is that due to one of the faults just listed, the clutch pressure plate is not freeing smoothly from the friction disc, and is snatching.

16 Clutch judder normally occurs when the clutch pedal is released in first gear or reverse gear, and the whole car shudders as it moves backwards or forwards.

1476583 Pin.

1528604 Clip

Chapter 6
Manual gearbox and automatic transmission

For modifications, and information applicable to later models, see Supplement at end of manual

Contents

Specifications

Manual gearbox

Type .... Four forward (all synchromesh) and one reverse. Floor mounted gear lever

Gear ratios
First .... 3.65 : 1
Second .... 1.97 : 1
Third .... 1.37 : 1
Fourth .... 1.00 : 1
Reverse .... 3.66 : 1

Lubricant capacity .... 3.0 pints (1.7 litre)

Countershaft
Countergear cluster endfloat .... 0.006 to 0.018 in (0.15 to 0.45 mm)
Thrust washer thickness .... 0.061 to 0.063 in (1.55 to 1.60 mm)
Diameter of countershaft .... 0.6817 to 0.6822 in (17.316 to 17.329 mm)

Automatic transmission

Type .... Ford C3

Torque converter
Type .... Trilock (hydraulic)
Converter ratio .... 2.15 : 1

Transmission ratios
First gear .... 2.47 : 1
Second gear .... 1.47 : 1
Third gear .... 1.00 : 1
Reverse gear .... 2.11 : 1

Fluid capacity (approx) .... 11.4 pints (6.5 litres), with converter and oil cooler

Torque wrench settings | lbf ft | kgf m |

Manual gearbox
Top cover-to-gearbox bolts .... 6.6 to 8.0 .... 0.9 to 1.1

Extension housing securing bolts	33 to 36	4.5 to 4.9
Drive gear bearing retainer bolts	6.6 to 8.0	0.9 to 1.1
Clutch housing-to-gearbox case	43 to 51	5.8 to 6.9
Clutch housing to engine	33 to 40	4.5 to 5.5
Gearbox to rear mounting	33 to 40	4.5 to 5.5
Gearbox support crossmember to body	13 to 16	1.8 to 2.2

Automatic transmission

Torque converter housing-to-engine	22 to 27	3.0 to 3.7
Torque converter drain plug	20 to 29	2.7 to 4.0
Drive plate-to-converter	27 to 30	3.6 to 4.1
Oil sump bolts	12 to 17	1.6 to 2.4
Fluid line to connector	7 to 10	0.9 to 1.4
Connector to transmission	10 to 15	1.4 to 2.0
Oil cooler line to connector	12 to 15	1.6 to 2.0
Downshift cable bracket	12 to 17	1.6 to 2.4
Downshift lever nut:		
Outer	7 to 11	1.0 to 1.5
Inner	30 to 40	4.1 to 5.4
Inhibitor switch	12 to 15	1.6 to 2.0

1 Manual gearbox – general description

The manual gearbox used on models covered by this manual is equipped with four four forward and one reverse gear. All forward gears are engaged through blocker ring synchromesh units to obtain smooth silent gear changes.

The bellhousing and gearbox case are of cast iron, and are bolted together.

The cast aluminium extension housing incorporates the remote control gearchange mechanism, which consists of a single selector rod.

The selector forks are free to slide on the selector rod which also serves as the gearchange shaft. At the gearbox end of this rod lies the selector arm, which, depending on the position of the gear lever, places the appropriate selector fork in the position necessary for the synchroniser sleeve to engage with the dog teeth on the gear selected.

It is impossible to select two gears at once because of an interlock guard plate which pivots on the right-hand side of the gearbox casing. The selector forks, when not in use, are positively held by the guard plate in their disengaged positions.

All forward gears on the mainshaft and input shaft are in constant mesh with their corresponding gears on the countershaft gear cluster and are helically cut to achieve quiet running.

The countershaft reverse gear has straight-cut spur teeth that drives the toothed 1st/2nd gear selector sleeve on the mainshaft through an interposed sliding idler gear.

The gearbox is of simple design using a minimum number of components. Where close tolerances and limits are required, manufacturing tolerances are compensated for and excessive endfloat or backlash eliminated by the fitting of selective circlips. When overhauling the gearbox always use new circlips, never re-use ones that have already been used.

2 Gearbox (manual) – removal and refitting

The gearbox can be removed by separating it from the rear of the engine at the bellhousing, then lowering and removing it from under the car.

1 If a hoist or an inspection pit is not available jack up the car and support it on axle-stands or solid blocks of wood. Make sure it is raised high enough to provide a good working height under the car.
2 Disconnect the battery earth terminal.
3 Working inside the car, push the front seats rearwards as far as possible. Remove the gearchange lever knob, then ease the gaiter from the body tunnel and slide the gaiter off the lever (photo).
4 Pull up the inner gaiter, then using a screwdriver bend back the locking tabs on the lock ring and unscrew the lock ring and gearchange lever retainer (photos).
5 Lift the gearchange lever upwards and out from the gearbox extension housing (photo).
6 Mark the mating flanges of the propeller shaft and final drive, so that they may be reconnected in their original positions, then undo and

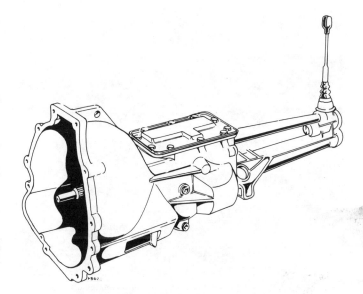

Fig. 6.1 Manual gearbox assembly (Sec 1)

2.3 Removing the gearchange lever knob

2.4a Pull off the inner gaiter

2.4b Removing the gearchange lever retainer

2.5 Lifting the gearchange lever out of the gearbox extension housing

2.6 Disconnect the propeller shaft from the final drive flange

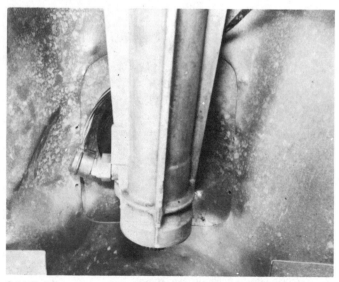
2.11 Pull the connector from the reversing light switch

2.13 Withdraw the speedometer cable

remove the four attaching bolts (photo).

7 Remove the two bolts securing the propeller shaft centre bearing assembly to the body then lower the propeller shaft at the rear and draw it rearwards to detach it from the gearbox (Fig. 6.2).

8 Secure a polythene bag over the end of the gearbox extension housing to prevent the oil draining out and also prevent the ingress of dirt.

9 Make a note of the wiring to the starter motor terminals and then disconnect the wiring.

10 Remove the two bolts securing the starter motor to the housing and lift away the starter motor.

11 Disconnect the wiring from the reversing light switch located on the side of the gearbox extension housing (photo).

12 Using a pair of circlip pliers remove the circlip retaining the speedometer drive cable end to the gearbox extension housing (Fig. 6.3).

13 Withdraw the speedometer cable from the side of the gearbox extension housing (photo).

14 Pull back the gaiter over the clutch operating arm and disconnect the clutch cable from the operating arm. Remove the clutch cable assembly from the locating hole in the clutch housing, refer to Chapter 5, Section 6.

15 Suitably support the weight of the gearbox with a jack or axle-stand. Insert a block of wood between the rear of the engine and the bulkhead. This will prevent the rear of the engine dropping when the gearbox extension housing mounting is removed.

16 Undo and remove the bolts securing the bellhousing to the rear of the engine.

17 Remove the bolt securing the rubber mounting to the gearbox extension housing (photo).

18 Remove the bolts securing the gearbox support crossmember to the body and lift away the crossmember (photo).

19 The assistance of a second person is now required to help in taking the weight of the gearbox as it is removed.

20 Separate the gearbox from the engine by pulling it rearwards from the guide bushes on the engine. Take care not to allow the weight of the gearbox to put any strain on the gearbox input shaft as it is easily bent. As the gearbox is moved rearwards it will be necessary to lower the rear end to give clearance from the underside of the body.

21 Refitting the gearbox is the reverse of the removal procedure but the following additional points should be noted:

a) Lightly grease the gearbox input shaft splines, but take care not to over-grease as the clutch disc could be contaminated
b) Ensure that the engine rear plate is correctly located on the bellhousing guide bushes (Fig. 6.4)
c) Tighten the bellhousing to engine securing bolts evenly to the specified torque
d) Adjust the clutch pedal free travel, refer to Chapter 5, Section 2
e) Fill the gearbox with the specified gear oil (photo)

Fig. 6.2 Removing the centre bearing retainer securing bolts (Sec 2)

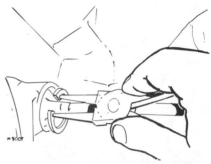

Fig. 6.3 Speedometer cable retaining circlip removal (Sec 2)

Fig. 6.4 Check that rear plate is correctly located (Sec 2)

2.17 Remove the rear mounting to gearbox housing securing bolts ...

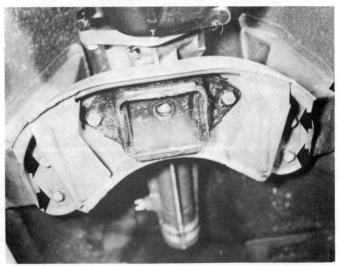

2.18 ... and then the support crossmember to body bolts (arrowed)

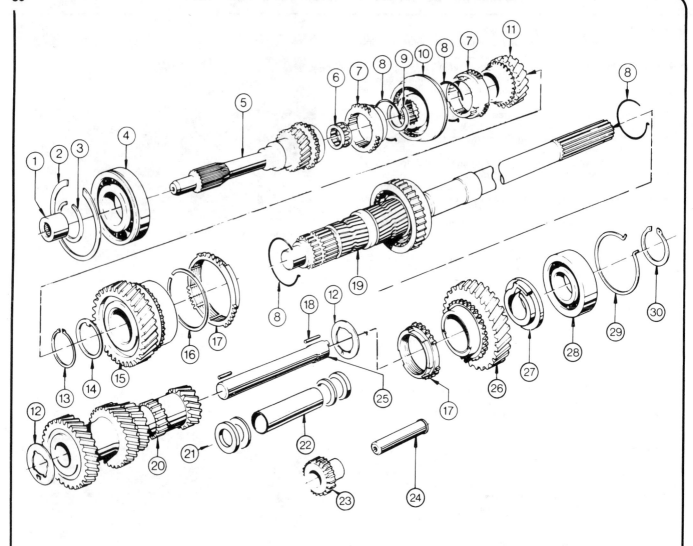

Fig. 6.5 Exploded view of gearbox internal components (Sec 3)

1	Bearing retainer bush	9	Circlip
2	Circlip	10	3/4 gear synchronising hub
3	Circlip	11	3rd gear
4	Ball bearing	12	Thrust washer
5	Input shaft	13	Circlip
6	Needle bearing	14	Thrust washer
7	3/4 gear synchroniser	15	2nd gear
	sleeve	16	Circlip
8	Synchroniser spring clip		

17	1/2 gear synchroniser sleeve	23	Reverse idler gear
18	Needle rollers (19 off)	24	Idler shaft
19	Mainshaft with 1/2 gear synchroniser hub	25	Countershaft
		26	1st gear
20	Countershaft gear cluster	27	Oil scoop ring
21	Spacer shims	28	Ball bearing
22	Spacer tube	29	Circlip
		30	Circlip

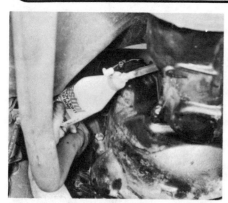

2.21 Don't forget to refill the gearbox with oil

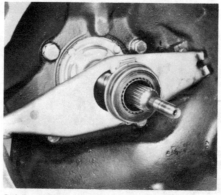

3.4 Removing the clutch release bearing

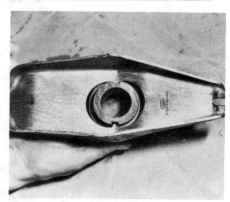

3.5 The release bearing location in the release lever

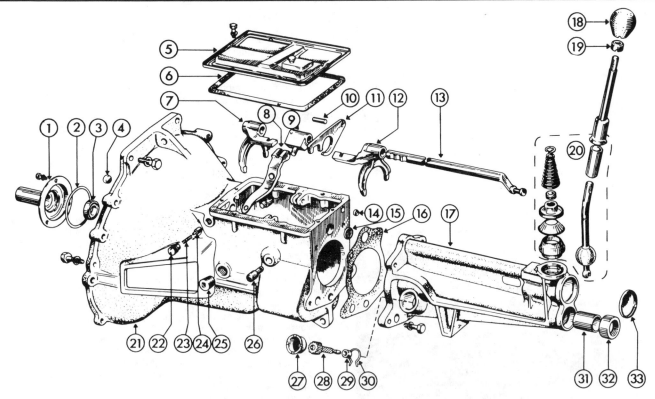

Fig. 6.6 Exploded view of gearbox casing and selector mechanism (Sec 3)

Note: *Some gearboxes have a detachable bellhousing*

1	Main drive gear bearing retainer	10	Spring pin
2	O-ring	11	Lock plate
3	Oil seal	12	1/2 gear selector fork
4	Blanking plug	13	Selector rail
5	Gearbox top cover	14	Blanking plug
6	Gasket	15	Oil seal
7	3/4 gear selector fork	16	Gasket
8	Reverse relay lever	17	Extension housing
9	Reverse selector boss		
18	Gearchange lever knob	26	Relay lever pin
19	Locknut	27	Speedometer drive cover
20	Gearchange lever	28	Speedometer drive gear
21	Gearbox casing	29	Oil seal
22	Side plug	30	Circlip
23	Spring	31	Bush, extension housing
24	Blocker bar, selector rail	32	Oil seal
25	Oil filler plug	33	Extension housing, rear cover

3 Gearbox (manual) – dismantling

1   Place the complete unit on a firm bench or table and ensure that you have the following tools available, in addition to the normal range of spanners etc.

    a)   *Good quality circlip pliers, 2 pairs – 1 expanding and 1 contracting*
    b)   *Soft-faced mallet, at least 2 lb (0.9 kg)*
    c)   *Drifts, steel and brass 0.375 inch (9.525 mm) diameter*
    d)   *Small containers for needle rollers*
    e)   *Engineer's vice mounted on firm bench*
    f)   *Selection of metal tubing*

Any attempt to dismantle the gearbox without the foregoing is not impossible, but will certainly be very difficult and inconvenient.
2   Read the whole of this Section before starting work.
3   The internal parts of the gearbox are shown in Fig. 6.5 and the casing and selector mechanism in Fig. 6.6.
4   Detach the release bearing from the release lever by turning the carrier through 90° and pulling forwards (photo).
5   The cut-outs in the release bearing carrier have to be lined up with the two protrusions in the release lever to enable removal of the bearing carrier (photo).
6   The B type gearbox occurs in two forms, one with a detachable bellhousing and one with an integral, cast bellhousing.

3.6 Removing the bellhousing to gearbox securing bolts

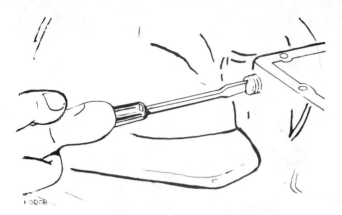

Fig. 6.7 Removing the blocker bar plug (Sec 3)

Fig. 6.8 Pull out the reverse gear idler shaft (Sec 3)

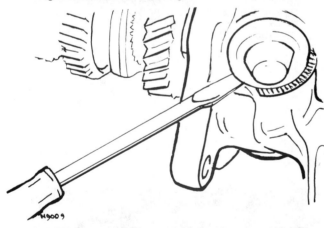

Fig. 6.9 Prise out the speedometer drive gear cover (Sec 3)

Fig. 6.10 Remove the mainshaft bearing circlip (Sec 3)

7   If possible remove the bellhousing. This will make it easier to work on the gearbox.

8   Using a suitable drift, working through the gear lever aperture, tap out the extension housing rear cover (photo).

9   Remove the eight top cover bolts, and remove the cover and gasket.

10 Turn the gearbox through 180° and allow the oil to drain.

11 Remove the slide plug (Fig. 6.7) and remove the spring and locking bar (photo).

12 Remove the blanking plug from the rear of the gearbox casing and drive out the lock plate spring pin using a suitable pin punch.

13 Remove the spring pin from the reverse selector boss (photo). Remove the selector rail rearwards (photo).

14 Lift out both selector forks, the lock plate and the selector boss (photo).

15 Unscrew and remove the bolts and spring washers that secure the extension housing to the main casing.

16 Rotate the extension housing until the cutaway is in such a position that the countershaft can be drawn from the main casing.

17 Using a suitable diameter soft metal drift tap the countershaft rearwards until it is possible to pull it from the rear face of the main case (photo).

18 Remove the countershaft from the main case (photo).

19 Allow the countershaft gear train to drop to the bottom of the main case.

20 Remove the gearbox extension housing and mainshaft assembly from the gearbox (photo).

21 Remove the input shaft needle roller bearing.

22 Undo and remove the bolts and spring washers that secure the bearing retainer to the front face of the main case.

23 Lift away the bearing retainer from over the input shaft. Recover the O-ring (photo).

24 Remove the input shaft assembly from the front of the gearbox and lift out the needle roller bearing.

25 Lift the countershaft gear train from inside the main case. Note which way round it is fitted (photo). Recover the two countershaft thrust washers.

26 Insert a suitable bolt into the reverse gear idler shaft with a nut, washer and suitable socket. Tighten the nut and withdraw the idler shaft (Fig. 6.8).

27 Withdraw the circlip from the pin, and remove the reverse gear relay lever.

28 Prise out the speedometer drive gear cover from the extension housing, and withdraw the drive gear (Fig. 6.9).

29 Remove the mainshaft bearing circlip from the extension housing (Fig. 6.10). Drive the mainshaft assembly from the extension housing using a soft-faced mallet (photo).

4 Gearbox (manual) – inspection

1   Thoroughly clean the interior of the gearbox, and check for dropped needle rollers and spring pins.

2   Carefully clean and then examine all the component parts for general wear, distortion, slackness of fit, and damage to machined faces and threads.

3   Examine the gearwheels for excessive wear and chipping of the teeth. Renew them as necessary.

4   Examine the countershaft for signs of wear, where the needle rollers bear. If a small ridge can be felt at either end of the shaft it will be necessary to renew it. Renew the thrust washers at each end.

5   The four synchroniser rings are bound to be badly worn and it is false economy not to renew them. New rings will improve the smoothness and speed of the gearchange considerably.

6   The needle roller bearing and cage, located between the nose of the mainshaft and the annulus in the rear of the input shaft, is also liable to wear, and should be renewed as a matter of course.

7   Examine the condition of the two ball bearing assemblies, one on the input shaft and one on the mainshaft. Check them for noisy operation, looseness between the inner and outer races, and for general wear. Normally they should be renewed on a gearbox that is being rebuilt.

8   If either of the synchroniser units are worn it will be necessary to buy a complete assembly as the parts are not sold individually. Also check the blocker bars for wear.

9   Examine the ends of the selector forks where they rub against the

3.8 Removing the extension housing rear cover

3.11 Blocker bar and spring removal

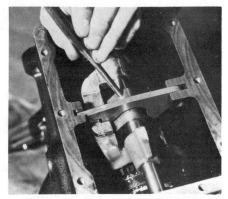

3.13a Removing the reverse selector boss spring pin

3.13b Removing the selector rail

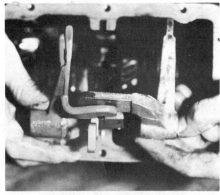

3.14 Removing the selector fork

3.17 Remove the countershaft using a drift

3.18 Lifting away the countershaft

3.20 Removing the extension housing and mainshaft assembly

3.23 Removing the bearing retainer and O-ring

3.25 Removing the countershaft gear train

3.29 Tap the mainshaft through the extension housing

4.11 Renew the seal in the main drive bearing retainer

5.1 Removing the input shaft bearing retaining circlip

5.5 Refitting the input shaft bearing

6.2 Removing the circlip from the end of the mainshaft

6.4 Removing the mainshaft rear bearing retainer circlip

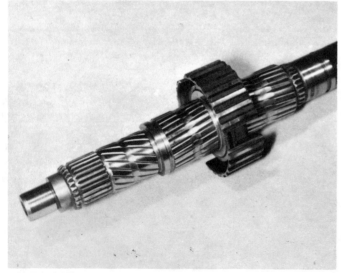

6.8 The 1st/2nd synchronizer hub cannot be removed from the mainshaft

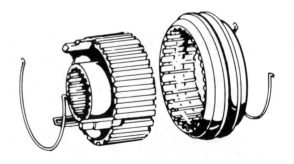

Fig. 6.11 Exploded view of synchroniser hub (Sec 6)

channels in the periphery of the synchroniser units. If possible compare the selector forks with new units to help determine the wear that has occurred. Renew them if worn.

10 If the bearing bush in the extension is badly worn it is best to take the extension to your local Ford garage to have the bearing pulled out and a new one fitted.

Note: *This is normally done with the mainshaft assembly still located in the extension housing.*

11 The oil seals in the extension housing and main drive gear bearing retainer should be renewed as a matter of course. Drive out the old seal with the aid of a drift or broad screwdriver. It will be found that the seal comes out quite easily (photo).

12 With a piece of wood or suitable sized tube to spread the load evenly, carefully tap a new seal into place ensuring that it enters the bore squarely.

5 Input shaft – dismantling and reassembly

1 The input shaft assembly may be dismantled by first removing the circlip using a pair of circlip pliers (photo).

2 Place the drive gear on the top of the vice with the outer track of the race resting on soft faces.

3 Using a soft-faced hammer drive the input shaft through the race inner track. The strain placed on the bearing does not matter, as the bearing would not be removed unless it was being renewed. Alternatively use a three-legged universal puller.

4 Lift away the race from the drive gear noting that the circlip groove on the outer track is offset towards the front.

5 To assemble the input shaft, place the race against soft metal (old shell bearing suitably straightened) on the top of the jaws of the vice and, using a drift located in the mainshaft spigot bearing hole in the rear of the input shaft, drift the shaft into the bearing. Make quite sure the bearing is the correct way round. Alternatively use a piece of long tube of suitable diameter (photo).

6 Refit the circlip that secures the bearing and also fit the circlip in the outer bearing race.

6 Mainshaft – dismantling and reassembly

1 With the mainshaft on the bench, remove the synchroniser sleeve from the front.

2 Using a pair of circlip pliers, expand the circlip that retains the third and top synchromesh hub on the mainshaft (photo).

3 Remove the third and top synchromesh assembly from the end of the mainshaft. Remove the synchroniser sleeve away from the third gear. Remove the third gear.

4 Using a pair of circlip pliers expand the circlip located at the rear of the mainshaft bearing, lift it from its groove and slide it down the mainshaft (photo).

5 Place the mainshaft on soft faces placed on the jaws of a vice so that the rear end is uppermost and the face of the first gear is on the vice.

6 Using a soft-faced mallet, drive the mainshaft through the gear and bearing assembly.

7 Lift away the speedometer gear, bearing, large circlip, oil scoop ring, 1st gear and synchroniser sleeve.

8 Remove the circlip, thrust washer, 2nd gear and the synchroniser sleeve. Note that the synchroniser hub cannot be removed from the mainshaft (photo).

9 Mark the synchromesh sleeve, hub and blocker bars for each synchromesh unit so that they may be refitted in their original positions.

10 Slide the synchromesh sleeve from the hub and lift away the blocker bars and springs (Fig. 6.11).

11 When new synchroniser assemblies are being fitted, they should be dismantled and thoroughly cleaned of all traces of preservative.

12 Lightly lubricate all parts with gearbox oil before reassembly.

13 The main reassembly procedure can now be commenced but first note that selective circlips will be needed at some stages during reassembly. It is therefore necessary to read through the procedure before reassembly commences so that the necessary circlips can be obtained.

14 Assemble the synchronisers by sliding the sleeve onto the hub with the mating marks aligned. Fit the blocker bars and springs, with the springs staggered, and the tagged ends of the springs in the same

6.15a Fitting the first gear ...

6.15b ... and then the oil scoop ring

Fig. 6.12 Alignment of synchroniser spring clips (Sec 6)

Fig. 6.13 Determine thickness of extension housing circlip (Sec 6)

Fig. 6.16 Fit the reverse idler gear in the casing (Sec 7)

Fig. 6.14 Location of speedometer drive gear (Sec 6)

Fig. 6.15 Locate the circlip in the extension housing groove (Sec 7)

blocker bar (Fig. 6.12).

15 Fit the first and second synchroniser sleeve and the first gear (photo). Slide on the oil scoop ring (photo).

16 It will now be necessary to select a new large circlip to eliminate endfloat of the mainshaft. To do this, first fit the original circlip in its groove in the gearbox extension and draw it outwards (ie; away from the rear of the extension). Now accurately measure the dimension from the base of the bearing housing to the outer edge of the circlip and record the figure. Also accurately measure the thickness of the

bearing outer track (Fig. 6.13) and subtract this figure from the depth already recorded. This will give the required circlip thickness.

17 Loosely fit the selected circlip, lubricate the bearing contact surfaces then press it onto the shaft. To press the bearing home, close the jaws of the vice until they are not quite touching the mainshaft, and with the bearing resting squarely against the side of the vice jaws draw the bearing on by tapping the end of the shaft with a soft-faced mallet (photo).

18 Refit the small circlip retaining the main bearing in place. This is also a selective circlip and must be fitted so that all endfloat between the bearing inner track and the circlip edge is eliminated (photo).

19 Fit the speedometer drive gear by driving it on with a suitable diameter tube until the dimension A in Fig. 6.14 is 1.44 in (49.25 mm).

20 Fit the blocker bars and the selector sleeve on the first and second synchroniser hub with the groove to the front (photos).

21 Slide the second gear synchroniser sleeve and second gear onto the mainshaft with the cone facing the rear. Fit the thrust washers and secure with a circlip (photos).

22 Slide on the third gear, with the dog teeth to the front, and fit the synchroniser sleeve onto the cone (photo).

23 Using a suitable diameter piece of tubing as a drift, drive the third/fourth gear synchroniser hub assembly with the longer hub to the front, onto the mainshaft. Fit the retaining circlip (photos).

7 Gearbox (manual) – reassembly

1 Heat the extension housing in hot water. Place the extension housing on its side and fit the mainshaft in the housing.

2 Position the extension housing on the edge of the bench so that the mainshaft end can protrude when fully home. Using a soft-faced hammer drive the mainshaft bearing into the extension housing bore (photo).

3 Using a pair of narrow pointed pliers and a small screwdriver fit the bearing retaining circlip. This is a tricky job and can take some time. Ensure that the circlip is correctly located in the groove in the housing (Fig. 6.15).

4 Smear the mating face of the extension housing and fit a new gasket.

5 Fit the reverse relay arm onto the relay arm pivot pin and secure with a circlip.

6 Fit the reverse idler gear into its location in the main casing with the selector groove facing rearward and engage it with the reverse relay arm. Insert the idler shaft and drive it home with a suitable drift and hammer (Fig. 6.16).

7 Fit the needle roller bearings in the countergear. There are 19 needle rollers at each end. The longer rollers are fitted at the rear end and the thick spacers at the outside ends (Fig. 6.17).

8 Slide the spacer tube into the countergear bore and smear some grease in both ends of the bore.

9 Insert one of the spacers, then fit the shorter needle rollers into the forward end of the bore. Fit the second spacer (photos).

10 Obtain a piece of bar or tube having approximately the same

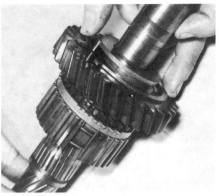

6.17 The large selected circlip is fitted loosely on the shaft at this stage

6.18 Fit the bearing retaining circlip

6.20a Fit the blocker bars and ...

6.20b ... the synchromesh sleeve into the hub

6.21a Fit the 2nd gear and thrust washer ...

6.21b ... and then the retaining circlip

6.22 Slide on the 3rd gear and synchroniser sleeve

6.23a Fit the 3rd/4th gear synchronizer hub assembly ...

6.23b ... and the retaining circlip

7.2 Mainshaft fitted in extension housing

7.9a Insert the thin spacer ...

7.9b ... then the needle rollers ...

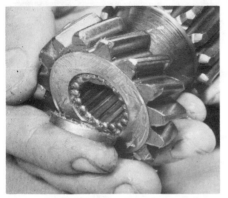
7.9c ... and the thick spacer

7.10 Slide dummy shaft into the countergear bore

7.14 Fit the thrust washers on the gearbox casing

7.15 Place the countershaft gear train in the main casing

7.16 Fit the needle roller bearing in the input shaft

7.18 Fitting a new O-ring

7.19 Slide the bearing retainer onto the input shaft

7.21 Fitting the mainshaft and extension housing

7.23 Insert the countershaft from the rear ...

7.24 ... and drive it in, pushing out the dummy shaft

7.25 Check that the countershaft is positioned correctly

7.26 Fit the extension housing retaining bolts

Fig. 6.17 Exploded view of countershaft gear cluster (Sec 7)

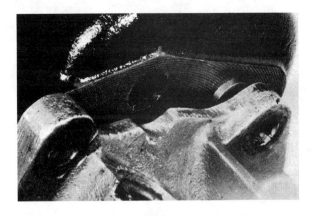

Fig. 6.18 Extension housing position when fitting countershaft (Sec 7)

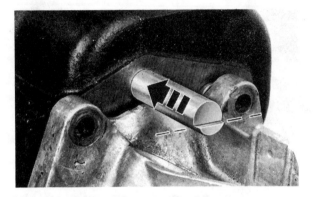

Fig. 6.19. Fitting the countershaft in the casing (Sec 7)

diameter as the countershaft and the same length as the countershaft gear train. Slide this halfway into the bore of the countershaft gear train so acting as a retainer for the needle rollers (photo).

11 Insert a spacer shim into the rear end of the countershaft gear train bore and fit the second set of needle rollers in the same manner as for the first set.

12 Fit the last spacer shim and push the previously obtained bar or tube through the second set of needle roller bearings.

13 Smear grease on each thrust washer face of the gearbox casing.

14 Fit the thrust washers to the casing (photo).

15 Carefully insert the countershaft gear train into the main casing making sure that the thrust washers are not dislodged (photo).

16 Oil the needle roller bearing that fits in the bore in the rear of the input shaft and insert the bearing in the bore (photo).

17 Support the main casing on the bench and insert the input shaft from the front.

18 Smear some grease in the groove on the front of the main casing and fit a new O-ring seal (photo).

19 Slide the bearing retainer over the input shaft and fit the four securing bolts, coated with sealing compound (photo).

20 Fit the top gear synchroniser sleeve over the cone on the rear of the input shaft.

21 Insert the mainshaft and extension housing assembly through the rear of the main casing (photo).

22 Turn the extension housing until the cutaway is positioned such that the countershaft can be inserted through the main casing rear face (Fig. 6.18).

23 Turn the input shaft and mainshaft so that the countershaft gear train can drop into engagement. Visually line up the countershaft bore hole in the main case with the centre of the countershaft gear train and slide the countershaft into position. The milled end of the countershaft is towards the rear of the main case (photo).

24 Turn the countershaft until it is positioned as shown in Fig. 6.19. Drive it in until the main part of the shaft is flush with the rear face (photo).

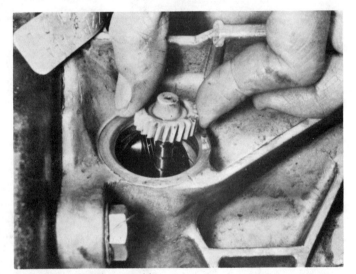

7.27a Fit the speedometer drive ...

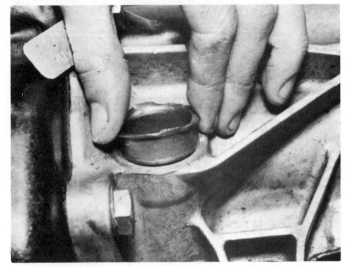

7.27b ... and the cover

7.27c Use a suitable socket to tap the cover into the casing

7.29a Insert both selector forks ...

7.29b ... and the reverse selector boss

7.30a Slide in the selector rail ...

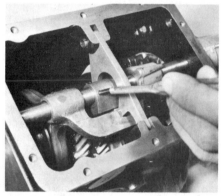

7.30b ... and fit the spring pin

7.31a Fit the blocker bar and spring ...

7.31b ... then the screw plug

7.32 Fit the top cover

7.33 Fitting the extension housing cover

7.34 Offer up the bellhousing to the main casing

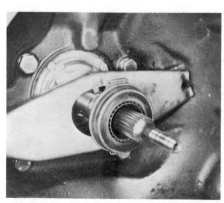

7.36 Fit the clutch release arm and bearing

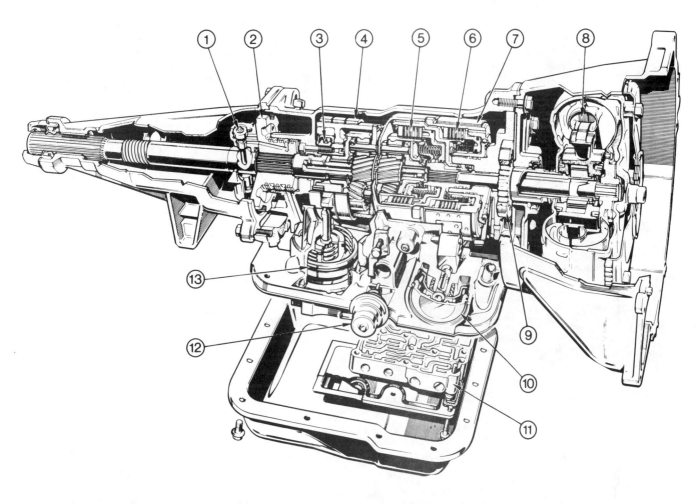

Fig. 6.20 Cut-away view of automatic transmission (Sec 8)

1	Governor assembly	5	Forward clutch
2	Governor hub	6	Reverse and top gear clutch
3	One-way clutch	7	Front brake band
4	Rear brake band		

8	Torque converter	11	Valve body
9	Hydraulic pump	12	Vacuum diaphragm
10	Front servo	13	Rear servo

25 Check that the idler shaft and countershaft protrusions line up with the slots in the extension housing and push the extension housing up to the rear face of the main casing (photo).

26 Coat the extension housing retaining bolts with sealing compound and fit the bolts (photo).

27 Fit the speedometer driven gear (photo) and its cover. Tap the cover into the casing (photos).

28 Fit the selector lock plate and secure with the spring pin. Fit a new blanking plug at the rear of the housing.

29 Insert both selector forks (photo) and the reverse selector boss (photo).

30 Slide the selector rail, from the rear through the bosses, and lock with the spring pin (photos).

31 Refit the blocker bar, spring and screw plug into the side of the housing (photos).

32 Fit the top cover and secure with the bolts (photo).

33 Fit the extension housing rear cover, coated with sealing compound. Secure with three blows from a pin punch, spread around the edge (photo).

34 Wipe the mating faces of the bellhousing and main casing and offer up the bellhousing (photo).

35 Secure the bellhousing with the bolts and spring washers.

36 Fit the clutch release arm to the clutch housing and then the release bearing to the release arm. Turn through 90° to lock (photo).

37 The gearbox is now ready for refitting. Do not forget to fill with the correct grade of oil.

8 Automatic transmission – general description

The automatic transmission takes the place of the clutch and gearbox, which are, of course, mounted behind the engine.

The unit has a large aluminium content which helps to reduce its overall weight and it is of compact dimensions. A transmission oil cooler is fitted as standard and ensure cooler operation of the transmission under trailer towing conditions. A vacuum connection to the inlet manifold provides smoother and more consistent downshifts under load than is the case with units not incorporating this facility.

The system comprises two main components:

a) A three element hydrokinetic torque converter coupling capable of torque multiplication at an infinitely variable ratio.

b) A torque/speed responsive and hydraulically operated epicyclic gearbox comprising planetary gearsets providing three forward ratios and one reverse ratio. Due to the complexity of the automatic transmission unit, if performance is not up to standard, or overhaul is necessary, it is imperative that this be left to the local main agents who will have the special equipment for fault diagnosis and rectification.

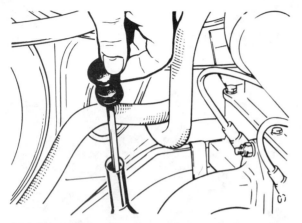

Fig. 6.21 Checking the automatic transmission fluid level (Sec 9)

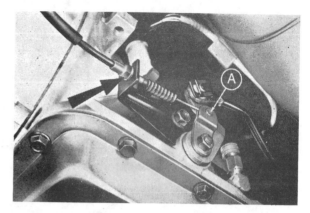

Fig. 6.22 Disconnect the kick-down cable (Sec 10)

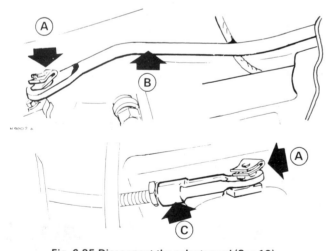

Fig. 6.23 Speedometer cable (A) and lock plate (Sec 10)

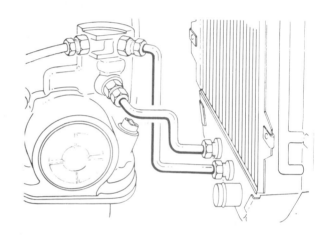

Fig. 6.24 Oil cooler pipes (Sec 10)

Fig. 6.25 Disconnect the selector rod (Sec 10)

A Spring clips   B Selector rod   C Adjuster

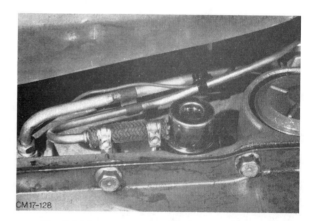

Fig. 6.26 Disconnect the vacuum pipe (Sec 10)

The content of the following sections is therefore confined to supplying general information and any service information and instruction that can be used by the owner.

9 Automatic transmission – fluid level checking

1   Every 6000 miles (10 000 km) bring the engine transmission to its normal operating temperature. Running the vehicle on the road for a minimum distance of 5 miles (8 km) will achieve this.
2   Select 'P' and allow the engine to idle for two or three minutes.
3   With the enginer still idling, withdraw the transmission dipstick.

Wipe it clean, re-insert it, withdraw it for the second time and read off the level (Fig. 6.21).
4   If necessary top-up with the specified oil, through the dipstick tube, to the MAX mark.
5   Always keep the exterior of the transmission unit clean and free from mud and oil and the air intake grilles must not be obstructed.

10 Automatic transmission – removal and refitting

Any suspected faults must be referred to the main agent before unit removal, as with this type of transmission the fault must be confir-

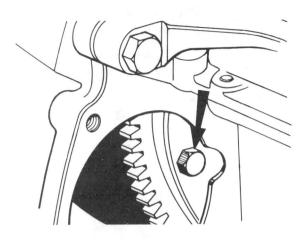

Fig. 6.27 Remove the converter to drive plate bolts (Sec 10)

Fig. 6.28 Remove the support crossmember (Sec 10)

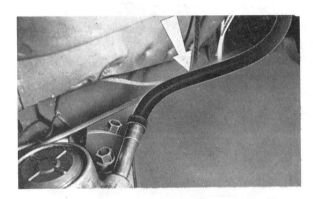

Fig. 6.29 Pull out the oil filler tube (Sec 10)

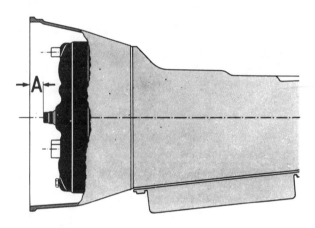

Fig. 6.30 Checking torque converter engagement (Sec 10)

med, using specialist equipment, before it has been removed from the car.
1   Open the engine compartment lid and place old blankets over the wings to prevent accidental scratching of the paintwork.
2   Undo and remove the battery earth connection nut and bolt from the battery terminal.
3   Remove the starter motor, refer to Chapter 10.
4   Position the vehicle on a ramp or over an inspection pit or, if these are not available, jack it up and support securely under the bodyframe. Make sure that there is sufficient clearance under the vehicle to permit withdrawal of the transmission.
5   Unscrew and remove the upper bolts which secure the torque converter housing to the engine. One of these bolts secures the dipstick tube support bracket.
6   Disconnect the 'kick-down' cable from the transmission downshift lever and bracket (Fig. 6.22).
7   Disconnect the plug from the reverse inhibitor switch.
8   Unscrew the lock plate bolt and remove the speedometer cable (Fig. 6.23).
9   Refer to Chapter 7, and remove the propeller shaft. To stop accidental dirt ingress, wrap some polythene around the end of the automatic transmission unit and secure with string or wire.
10 Undo and remove the two nuts that secure the exhaust downpipes to the manifolds on both sides. Ease the clamps from the studs, lower the downpipes and collect the sealing rings.
11 Remove the torque converter cover plate.
12 Disconnect the oil cooler pipes from the transmission (Fig. 6.24). Plug the pipe ends to prevent dirt ingress.
13 Remove the two selector rod spring clips and take out the selector rod (Fig. 6.25).
14 Disconnect the vacuum pipe from the vacuum diaphragm (Fig. 6.26).

15 The torque converter should next be disconnected from the crankshaft driving plate. Rotate the crankshaft until each bolt may be seen through the starter motor aperture. Undo each bolt and turn one at a time until all the bolts are free (Fig. 6.27).
16 Place an additional jack under the automatic transmission unit and remove the five bolts securing the transmission support crossmember to the transmission and the underside of the body (Fig. 6.28).
17 Slowly lower the transmission unit and engine jacks until there is sufficient clearance for the dipstick tube to be removed. Withdraw the dipstick and pull the oil filler tube (dipstick tube) sharply from the side of the transmission unit. Collect the O-ring. Plug the oil filler opening to prevent the ingress of dirt (Fig. 6.29).
18 Undo and remove the remaining bolts and spring washers that secure the converter housing to the engine.
19 Continue to lower the jacks until there is sufficient clearance between the top of the converter housing and underside of the floor for the transmission unit to be satisfactorily withdrawn.
20 Check that no cables or securing bolts have been left in position and tuck the speedometer cable out of the way.
21 The assistance of at least one other person is now required because of the weight of the complete unit.
22 Carefully pull the unit rearwards and, when possible, hold the converter in place in the housing as it will still be full of hydraulic fluid.
23 Finally withdraw the unit from under the car and place on wooden blocks so that the selector lever is not damaged or bent.
24 To separate the converter housing from the transmission case first lift off the converter from the transmission unit, taking suitable precautions to catch the fluid upon separation. Undo and remove the six bolts and spring washers that secure the converter housing to the transmission case. Lift away the converter housing.
25 Refitting is the reverse of removal but ensure that the torque converter drain plug is in line with the hole in the driveplate. To check that

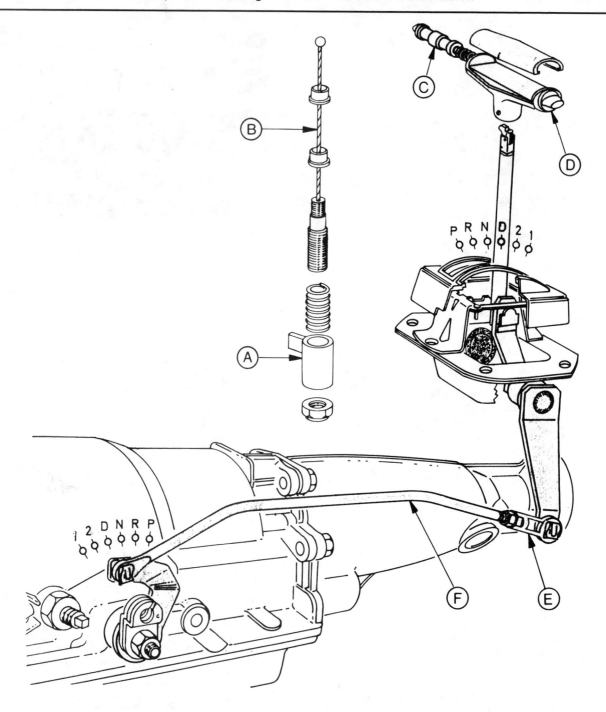

Fig. 6.31 Selector mechanism with both levers in position D (Sec 11 and 12)

A Selector inhibitor pawl
C Inhibitor push button
E Adjusting link

B Selector inhibitor cable
D Selector lever handle
F Selector rod

the torque converter is positively engaged, measure the distance A between the converter housing to engine mating face and the end of the stub shaft. This should be at least 0.4 in (10 mm) (Fig. 6.30).

26 Adjust the selector cable and inhibitor switch as described later in this Chapter.

27 Refill the transmission unit with the specified fluid before starting the engine and check the oil level as described in Section 9.

11 Automatic transmission selector mechanism – removal, overhaul and refitting

1   Prise off the selector lever escutcheon, and withdraw the illumination mounting from the selector lever.

2   Remove the spring clip and detach the selector rod from the

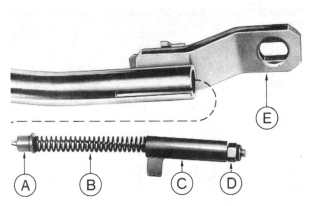

Fig. 6.32 Selector lever assembly (Sec 11)

A *Inhibitor cable bush*   B *Spring*
C *Pawl*   D *Locknut*
                    E *Selector lever*

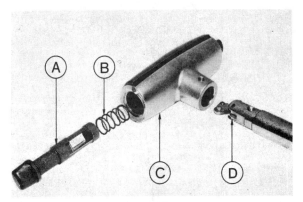

Fig. 6.33 Exploded view of selector lever handle (Sec 11)

A *Inhibitor push button*   B *Spring*
C *Selector handle*   D *Lever*

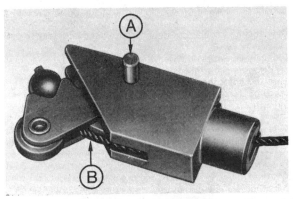

Fig. 6.34 Removing the inhibitor cable (Sec 11)

A *Straight pin*   B *Inhibitor cable*

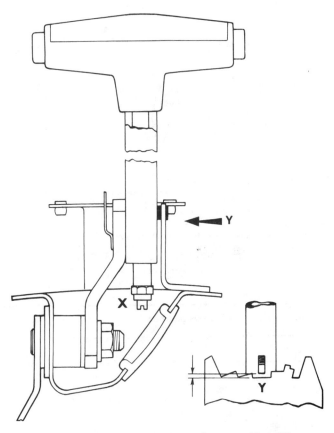

Fig. 6.35 Selector mechanism adjustment (Sec 12)

X *Locknut*   Y *0.004 to 0.008 in (0.1 to 0.2 mm)*

selector lever.
3   If required, remove the spring clip and detach the selector rod from the transmission selector lever.
4   Remove the four bolts retaining the selector lever housing to the transmission tunnel and remove the housing.
5   Remove the rubber plug from the side of the selector lever housing, unscrew the nut and press the lower lever out of the housing.
6   Unscrew the locknut on the inhibitor cable and withdraw the pawl, spring and guide bush (Fig. 6.33).
7   Remove the Allen screw from the T-handle and remove the handle. Remove the push button and spring (Fig. 6.33).
8   Using a pin punch, drive out the retaining pin and remove the inhibitor mechanism and inhibitor cable (Fig. 6.34).
9   Refitting is a reversal of the above procedure noting that the T-handle Allen screw is inserted from the front, so that the push button is nearest the driver (Fig. 6.34).
10 Adjust the mechanism, refer to Section 12.

12 Automatic transmission selector mechanism – adjustment

1   Prise off the selector lever escutcheon, and from underneath the car, remove the plug in the side of the selector housing.
2   Adjust the inhibitor cable locknut X to give a dimension at Y.
3   Refit the plug and escutcheon.
4   With the transmission shift lever and the manual selector lever in D, adjust the selector rod link until it can be reconnected without strain (Fig. 6.31).

13 Downshift cable – removal, refitting and adjustment

1   Remove the split pin and disconnect the cable from the carburettor linkage (Fig. 6.36).
2   Slacken the adjusting nut from the mounting bracket, pull back the outer sheath and unhook the cable from the slot.
3   Unhook the cable from the transmission lever and bracket (Fig. 6.22).
4   Refitting is a reversal of the above, but the inner nut at the upper

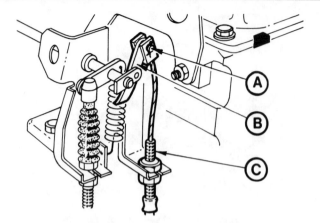

Fig. 6.36 Downshift cable removal (Sec 13)

A Retaining pin   B Connecting lever
          C Threaded sleeve

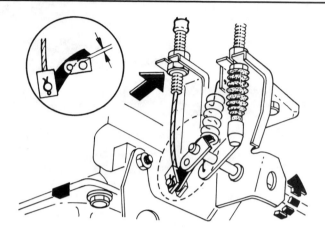

Fig. 6.37 Adjusting the downshift cable (Sec 13)

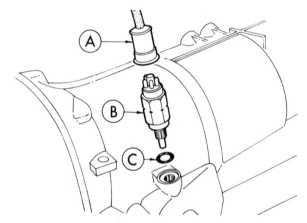

Fig. 6.38 Inhibitor switch renewal (Sec 14)

A Wiring connector   B Switch
          C O-ring seal

end should be screwed on completely, and the outer nut only a few turns.

5   Depress the accelerator pedal fully, and check that the throttle plate is fully open.

6   Using a screwdriver, lever the downshift cable lever upwards, pulling the inner cable fully upwards.

7   Turn the adjusting nut to lengthen or shorten the cable to give a clearance of 0.02 to 0.05 in (0.5 to 1.3 mm) between the downshift lever and the accelerator shaft (Fig. 6.37). Tighten the locknut.

14 Starter inhibitor/reverse lamp switch – removal and refitting

1   This switch is non-adjustable and any malfunction must be due to a wiring fault, a faulty switch or wear in the internal actuating cam.

2   When removing and installing the switch, always use a new O-ring seal and tighten to specified torque (Fig. 6.38).

15 Fault diagnosis – manual gearbox

Symptom	Reason/s
Weak or ineffective synchromesh	Synchronising cones worn, split or damaged Baulk ring synchromesh dogs worn, or damaged
Jumps out of gear	Broken gearchange fork rod spring Gearbox coupling dogs badly worn Selector fork rod groove badly worn
Excessive noise	Incorrect grade of oil in gearbox or oil level too low Bush or needle roller bearings worn or damaged Gear teeth excessively worn or damaged Countershaft thrust washers worn allowing excessive end play
Excessive difficulty in engaging gear	Clutch cable adjustment incorrect

16 Fault diagnosis – automatic transmission

Faults in these units are nearly always the result of low fluid level or incorrect adjustment of the selector linkage or downshift cable. Internal faults should be diagnosed by your main Ford dealer who has the necessary equipment to carry out the work.

Chapter 7 Propeller shaft

Contents

Specifications

Type (all two piece)
Manual gearbox .... Three universal joints or two universal joints and rubber coupling
Automatic transmission .... Two universal joints and one CV joint

Length
Manual gearbox .... 49.98 in (1269.5 mm)
Automatic transmission .... 51.12 in (1298.5 mm)

Number of splines 25

Yoke outside diameter .... 1.375 to 1.376 in (34.92 to 34.94 mm)

Grease specification .... Ford S–M1C–4515–6

*Note: *The length of driveshaft with constant velocity joint is measured from the rear axle flange to the centre of the front universal joint. Driveshafts with three universal joints or two universal joints and rubber coupling are measured from the centre of the rearmost universal joint to the centre of the front universal joint or rubber coupling.*

Torque wrench settings

	lbf ft	kgf m
Propeller shaft to drive pinion flange bolts	43 to 47	6.0 to 6.5
Centre bearing support bolts	13 to 17	1.8 to 2.3
Constant velocity joint bolts	30	4.1

1 General description

Drive is transmitted from the gearbox to the rear axle by means of a fairly balanced two-piece tubular propeller shaft.

Models with a manual gearbox have three universal joints or two universal joints and a rubber coupling at the front (Fig. 7.1). Automatic transmission models have two universal joints and a constant velocity joint. The constant velocity joint is located to the rear of the centre bearing.

All models are fitted with sealed universal joints. The propeller shaft assembly is a relatively simple component and reliable in service. It is not possible to obtain spare parts for the universal joints, therefore when these are worn a new assembly must be fitted.

2 Propeller shaft – removal and refitting

1 Jack up the rear of the car, or position the rear of the car over a pit or on a ramp.
2 If the rear of the car is jacked up, supplement the jack with support blocks so that danger is minimised should the jack collapse.
3 If the rear wheels are off the ground place the car in gear and apply the handbrake to ensure that the propeller shaft does not turn when an attempt is made to loosen the four nuts securing the propeller shaft to the rear axle.
4 The propeller shaft is carefully balanced to fine limits and it is important that it is refitted in exactly the same position it was in prior to removal. Scratch marks on the propeller shaft and rear axle flanges

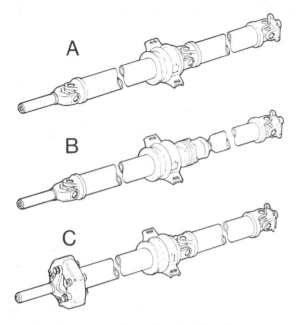

Fig. 7.1 The three types of propeller shaft (Sec 1)

A Propeller shaft with three universal joints
B Propeller shaft with two universal joints and constant velocity joint
C Propeller shaft with two universal joints and a rubber coupling

Fig. 7.2 Remove centre bearing securing bolts – note location of shims (Sec 2)

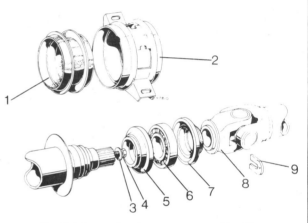

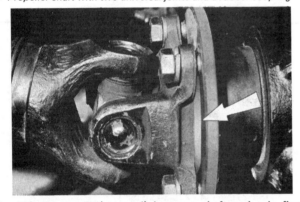

Fig. 7.3 Fit spacer (arrowed) between shaft and axle flanges (Sec 2)

Fig. 7.4 Centre bearing components (Sec 3)

1 Rubber bush   2 Bearing housing and retainer
3 Washer   4 Bolt
5 Dust cover   6 Ball race
7 Dust cover   8 Yoke
            9 U-shaped retainer

'A' shows flange which must be located at top of housing

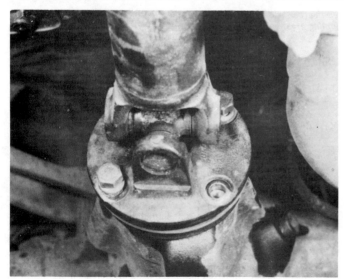

2.5 Disconnecting the propeller shaft from the rear axle

2.13 Position the centre bearing parallel to the shaft

to ensure accurate mating when the time comes for reassembly.

5   Unscrew and remove the four bolts and spring washers which hold the flange on the propeller shaft to the flange on the rear axle (photo).

6   Slightly push the shaft forward to separate the two flanges, then lower the end of the shaft.

7   To detach the centre bearing support, undo and remove the two bolts, spring and plain washers securing it to the underside of the body. Retain any mounting shims, noting their location (Fig. 7.2).

8   Lower the shaft and pull it rearwards to disengage the gearbox mainshaft splines.

9   Place a large can or tray under the rear of the gearbox extension to catch any oil which is likely to leak past the oil seal when the propeller shaft is removed.

10   Slide the front of the propeller shaft into the transmission, taking care not to damage the oil seal.

Manual gearbox models

11   Loosely fit the centre bearing, refitting the shims which were removed.

12   With the weight of the car on the wheels, fit a 0.16 in (4 mm) spacer between the propeller shaft and axle flange (Fig. 7.3). Tighten the bolts.

13   Position the centre bearing parallel to the shaft, and tighten the mounting bolts (photo).

14   Remove the spacer and fully tighten the bolts with the mating marks aligned.

Automatic transmission models

15   Loosely fit the centre bearing, refitting the shims which were removed.

16   Align the pinion flange mating marks and tighten the bolts.

17   With the rear of the car jacked up, so that the rear axle hangs down, pull the front of the shaft and the centre bearing forward.

18   When the CV joint is felt to bear against the rear of the centre bearing, tighten the centre bearing bolts, *ensuring that the bearing is square to the shaft.*

All models

19   Lower the car to the ground, and top-up the transmission with specified oil.

---

3   Propeller shaft centre bearing – removal and refitting

---

1   Refer to Section 2 and remove the complete propeller shaft assembly.

2   Using a blunt chisel carefully prise open the centre bearing support retaining bolt locking tab.

3   Slacken the bolt located in the end of the yoke and with a screwdriver ease out the U-shaped retainer through the side of the yoke. These parts are shown in Fig. 7.4.

4   Mark the propeller shaft and yoke for correct refitting. Disconnect the propeller shaft from the yoke and lift off the insulator rubber together with collar from the ball race.

5   Part the insulator rubber from the collar.

6   Refer to Fig. 7.5 and using a universal two-legged puller draw the bearing, together with the cap from the end of the propeller shaft.

7   To fit a new bearing and cap onto the end of the propeller shaft use a piece of suitable diameter tube and drive into position. Fill the space between the bearing and the caps with the specified grease.

8   With a pair of pliers bend the six metal tongues of the collar slightly outwards and carefully insert the insulator rubber. It is important that the flange of the insulator rubber, when fitted into the support, is uppermost see 'A' (Fig. 7.4).

9   Using a pair of 'parrot jaw' pliers or chisel bend the metal tongues rearwards over the rubber lip as shown in Fig. 7.6.

10   Next slide the support with the insulator rubber over the ball race.

11   Screw in the bolt together with the locking tab into the propeller shaft forward end bearing leaving just sufficient space for the U-shaped retainer to be inserted.

12   Assemble the two propeller shaft halves in their original positions as denoted by the two previously made marks or by the double tooth (Fig. 7.7).

13   Refit the U-shaped retainer with the boss towards the splines (Fig. 7.8).

14   Finally tighten the retainer securing bolt and bend over the lockwasher.

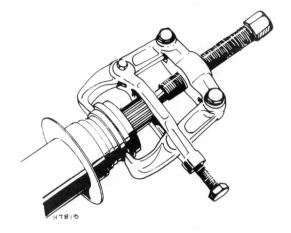

Fig. 7.5 Pulling off the bearing and caps (Sec 3)

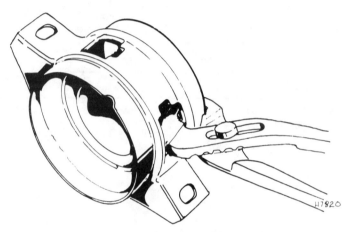

Fig. 7.6 Bending the six metal tabs over the rubber lip (Sec 3)

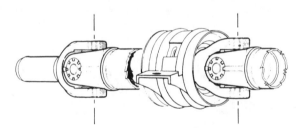

Fig. 7.7 Fitted position of the propeller shaft halves (Sec 3)

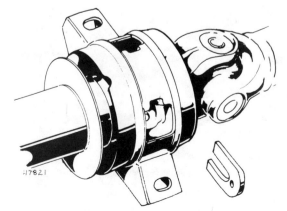

Fig. 7.8 Inserting U-retainer – note position of boss (Sec 3)

4 Constant velocity joint – renewal

1   Remove the propeller shaft, as previously described.
2   Place alignment marks on the constant velocity joint flange and the rear section of the propeller shaft so that the original balance can be maintained.
3   Remove the six bolts and circlip from the front face of the constant velocity joint.
4   Remove the joint from the splined shaft and then extract the cup spring through the opening of the rubber sleeve.
5   No further dismantling should be carried out, but the old joint should be discarded and a new one purchased.
6   Commence reassembly by inserting the cup spring through the rubber sleeve so that the spring rests against the outer circumference of the constant velocity joint.
7   Attach the joint to the flange with two bolts only, inserted finger-tight.
8   Offer up the propeller shaft (marks made before dismantling in alignment) and engage the splines. Now remove the two bolts, push the joint against the cup spring and fit the circlip.
9   Fill the constant velocity joint with 30 grams of specified grease, once again align the marks and connect the propeller shaft section.

Insert the bolts and tighten to the specified torque.

5 Universal joints – checking for wear

1   Wear in the needle roller bearings is characterised by vibration in the transmission, 'clonks' on taking up the drive, and in extreme cases of lack of lubrication, metallic squeaking and ultimately a grating and shrieking sound as the bearings break up.
2   It is easy to check if the needle roller bearings are worn, with the propeller shaft in position, by trying to turn the shaft with one hand, the other hand holding the rear axle flange when the rear universal joint is being checked, and the front half coupling when the front universal joint is being checked. Any movement between the propeller shaft and the front and the rear half couplings in indicative of considerable wear. If worn, a new assembly will have to be obtained. Check also by trying to lift the shaft and noticing any movement of the joints.
3   The centre bearing is a little more difficult to test for wear when mounted on the car. Undo and remove the two support securing bolts, spring and plain washers and allow the propeller shaft centre to hang down. Test the centre bearing for wear by holding the support and rocking it. If movement is evident the bearing is probably worn and should be renewed, as described in Section 3.

6 Fault diagnosis – propeller shaft

Symptom	Reason/s
Vibration when car running on road	Out of balance shaft
	Wear in splined sleeve
	Loose flange bolts
	Worn shaft joints

Chapter 8 Rear axle

Contents

Specifications

Type .... Hypoid, semi-floating

Axle ratio .... 3.44 : 1

Number of gear teeth

Crownwheel 31
Drive pinion 9

Backlash and preloads
Crownwheel and pinion backlash .... 0.004 to 0.008 in (0.10 to 0.20 mm)
Pinion bearing preload .... 0.001 to 0.003 in (0.03 to 0.07 mm)
Collapsible spacer length .... 0.453 to 0.461 in (11.5 to 11.7 mm)

Oil specification .... SQM-2C9002AA (SAE 90)

Torque wrench settings

	lbf ft	kgf m
Drive pinion self locking nut	Refer to text(Sec 4)	
Rear axle housing cover	22 to 19	3.0 to 4.0
Axleshaft to side flange retainer plate	19 to 23	2.7 to 3.2
Filler/level plug	25 to 30	3.5 to 4.2

1 General description

The rear axle is of the semi-floating type and is held in place by two lower swinging arms which are able to pivot on brackets welded to the chassis. Coil springs are located between the underside of the body and the swinging arms. Longitudinal and diagonal location of the rear axle is also controlled by two upper swinging arms which locate between the underside of the body and the outer ends of the final drive housing.

The differential unit is of the two pinion design and driven by a hypoid crownwheel and pinion. It is mounted in a cast iron differential housing into which the halfshaft and hub outer tubes are pressed.

The drive pinion is mounted in two taper roller bearings which are specially preloaded using a collapsible type spacer (Fig. 8.1).

The differential cage is also mounted on two taper roller bearings which are preloaded by spreading the differential carrier. The drive is taken through two differential side-gears to both axleshafts. The axleshafts are splined to the differential side-gears and run in ball races at their outer ends. These ball races have integral oil seals.

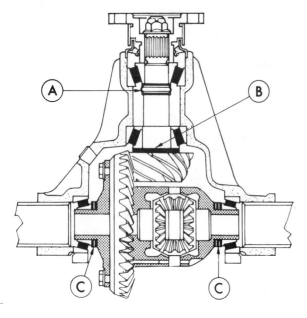

Fig. 8.1 Sectional view of the differential unit (Sec 1)

A   Collapsible spacer
B   Drive pinion shim
C   Differential bearing shim

Fig. 8.2 Removing the filler/level plug (Sec 2)

Fig. 8.4 Remove the brake flexible hose from the brake pipe (Sec 3)

Fig. 8.3 Disconnect the handbrake cable (Sec 3)

Fig. 8.5 Detach the shock absorber from the axle casing (Sec 3)

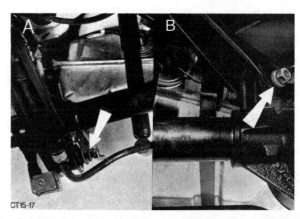

Fig. 8.6 Removing the lower (A) and upper (B) radius arms (Sec 3)

2   Oil level – checking

1   At the routine service intervals, the axle oil level should be checked and topped-up as required.
2   With the car standing on a *level* surface, remove the combined filler/level plug (Fig. 8.2).
3   The oil level should be up to the bottom edge of the hole. Add the specified type of oil as necessary and refit the plug.

3   Rear axle – removal and refitting

1   Remove the rear wheel trims and slacken the roadwheel nuts. Chock the front wheels, jack up the rear of the car and place on axle-stands located beneath the lower radius arms. Remove the two rear wheels.
2   Support the weight of the rear axle by placing the saddle of a jack (preferably trolley type) under the centre of the rear axle.
3   With a scriber or file mark a line across the propeller shaft and pinion driving flanges so that they may be refitted together in their original positions.
4   Refer to Chapter 7, Section 2, and remove the propeller shaft.
5   Release the handbrake. Undo and remove the two cheese head screws that secure the brake drums to the axleshaft. Using a soft-faced hammer carefully tap outwards on the circumference of each brake drum and lift away the brake drums.
6   Using a screwdriver placed between the brake shoe and relay lever, ease the handbrake cable relay lever inwards. Grip the handbrake cable end with a pair of pliers and release it from the relay lever. Pull the handbrake cable through each brake backplate (Fig. 8.3).
7   Wipe the top of the brake master cylinder reservoir and unscrew the cap. Place a piece of polythene sheeting over the reservoir neck and refit the cap. This is to stop hydraulic fluid syphoning out during subsequent operations.
8   Wipe the area around the brake flexible pipe to metal pipe union on the front of the rear axle and referring to Chapter 9, Section 3, detach the brake flexible hose from the metal pipe (Fig. 8.4).
9   With a trolley jack, slightly raise the axle and undo and remove the bolt, nut and plain washer that secures each shock absorber to the rear axle. Contract the shock absorbers (Fig. 8.5).
10   Undo and remove the bolt, nut and plain washer that secures each upper and each lower radius arm to the axle housing (Fig. 8.6).
11   Lower the rear axle and remove both coil springs, retaining the upper mounting rubber rings (Fig. 8.7).
12   The complete rear axle assembly may now be withdrawn.
13   Refit the rear axle in the reverse sequence to removal. Realign the marks on the propeller shaft and pinion flange.
14   Refer to Chapter 7, Section 3 to refit the centre bearing.
15   The radius arm mounting bolts must only be tightened to a torque wrench setting of 42–50 lbf ft (5·8–6·9 kgf m) when the roadwheels have been refitted and the car is standing on the ground.
16   It will be necessary to bleed the brake hydraulic system as described in Chapter 9, Section 2.
17   Check the amount of oil in the rear axle and top-up if necessary.

4   Drive pinion oil seal – renewal

Note: *Renewal of the drive pinion oil seal requires a great deal of care and the use of some special equipment. Without these, the collapsible spacer can be damaged which will require its renewal, and this operation is outside the scope of the do-it-yourself motorist because a special tool is required for removal of the pinion bearing. Whenever the pinion oil seal is renewed, it is essential that the self-locking pinion nut is also renewed.*

1   Jack up the rear of the vehicle and support it securely under the bodyframe.
2   Remove the rear roadwheels and brake drums.
3   Disconnect the propeller shaft from the rear axle drive pinion after marking them for correct alignment.
4   Using a spring balance and length of cord wound round the drive pinion flange, determine the torque required to turn the drive pinion and record it. Alternatively, a socket wrench fitted to the pinion nut and a suitable torque wrench may be used.
5   Mark the coupling in relation to the pinion springs to ensure that

they are refitted in the same position.
6   Hold the pinion coupling flange by placing two 2 inch long bolts through two opposite holes, bolting them up tight; undo the self-locking nut whilst holding a large screwdriver or tyre lever between the two bolts for leverage. Using a standard two- or three-leg puller, remove the coupling flange from the pinion shaft.
7   Using a hammer and a small chisel or screwdriver, remove the oil seal from the pinion housing. During this operation, great care must be taken to ensure that the pinion shaft is not scored in any way. Note that there will be some spillage of the axle oil as the seal is removed.
8   Carefully clean the contact area inside the pinion housing, then apply a film of general purpose grease to this surface and between the lips of the new oil seal. Do not remove the existing grease from the replacement seal.
9   Using a tube of suitable diameter, press in the new seal to its full depth in the pinion housing.
10   Refit the coupling in its correct relative position to the pinion shaft.
11   Using a new self-locking nut, prevent the flange from turning, then carefully and slowly tighten the nut until the same turning torque is achieved as recorded at paragraph 4. Continue tightening until an additional 2 to 3 lbf in (2 to 4 kgf cm) is achieved, to allow for the friction of the new oil seal. After this torque has been obtained, do not tighten the self-locking nut or the collapsible spacer will be damaged (see note at beginning of Section).
12   Remove the two bolts from the coupling flange then refit the propeller shaft taking note of the alignment marks made when removing.
13   Top up the rear axle with the correct grade of oil, then refit the brake drums and roadwheels.
14   Lower the car to the ground.

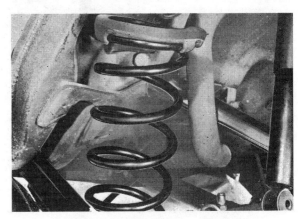

Fig. 8.7 Lift away the coil springs (Sec 3)

Fig. 8.8 Fitting a new collapsible spacer (Sec 3)

Fig. 8.9 Removing the bearing retainer plate (Sec 5)

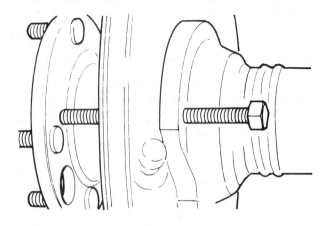

Fig. 8.10 Using long bolts to assist withdrawal of the axleshaft (Sec 5)

Fig. 8.11 Removing the bearing retaining ring (Sec 6)

Fig. 8.12 Renewing a wheel stub (Sec 7)

5 Axleshaft – removal and refitting

1   Chock the front wheels, remove the rear wheel trim and slacken the wheel nuts. Jack up the rear of the car and support on firmly based axlestands. Remove the roadwheel and release the handbrake.
2   Undo and remove the cheese head screw that secures the brake drum to the axleshaft. Using a soft-faced hammer, carefully tap outwards on the circumference of the brake drum and lift away the brake drum.
3   Using a socket wrench placed through the holes in the axleshaft flange, undo and remove the four bolts that secure the bearing retainer plate to the axle casing (Fig. 8.9).
4   Place a container under the end of the rear axle to catch any oil that may drain out once the axleshaft has been removed.
5   The axleshaft may now be withdrawn from the rear axle.
6   It is possible for the ball races to bind onto the axleshaft in which case screw in two long bolts through the rear end of the axle tube and thereby ease the axleshaft assembly out (Fig. 8.10).
7   Before refitting the axleshaft assembly, smear a little grease along the length of the axleshaft and also on the ball race to prevent corrosion due to moisture.
8   Insert the axleshaft into the rear axle tube, keep the shaft horizontal until its splines are felt to engage with those of the differential gears.
9   Secure the bearing retainer with the four bolts which should be tightened to the specified torque, see Specifications at the beginning of this Chapter.
10 Refit the brake drum and secure with the cheesehead screw.
11 Refit the roadwheel and lower the car to the ground.

6 Axleshaft bearing – renewal

1   Remove the axleshaft, as described in the preceding Section.
2   Secure the axleshaft in a vice fitted with jaw protectors and then carefully drill a hole in the bearing retaining collar. Do not drill right through the collar or the axleshaft will be damaged. Use a sharp cold chisel and cut the collar from the shaft (Fig. 8.11).
3   A press or suitable bearing extractor will be required to remove the bearing from the shaft. Do not damage the retainer plate during this operation.
4   Commence installation by fitting the retainer plate to the axleshaft, followed by the bearing (oil seal away from axleshaft flange) and a new bearing retaining collar.
5   Using a press or two-legged puller, apply pressure to the collar to draw all three components into their correct positions, tight against the axleshaft end-flange.
6   Apply a little grease to the bearing recess in the end of the axle tube and fit the axleshaft, as described in Section 5.

7 Roadwheel retaining stud – renewal

1   To renew a wheel retaining stud which has broken or has damaged threads, remove the roadwheel and brake drum then press the defective splined wheel stud nut of the axleshaft flange.
2   When fitting a new stud ensure that the splines are correctly aligned with those in the axleshaft flange then pull the new stud into the flange using a wheel nut and suitable washers (Fig. 8.12).
3   Refit the brake drum and roadwheel.

8 Rear axle – repair and overhaul

1   It is not recommended that servicing of the rear axle should go beyond the operations described in this Chapter.

2   Special tools and gauges are required to set up the differential, and dismantling and reassembly should be left to your Ford main dealer.

3   The latest trend is in fact for rear axle components not to be supplied individually but the complete factory-built unit only to be supplied as a spare.

4   Reference to the Fault Diagnosis chart will however assist the home mechanic in eliminating some sources of noise and wear before deciding that it is the rear axle which is undoubtedly due for major overhaul or reconditioning.

9 Fault diagnosis – rear axle

Symptom	Reason/s
Oil leakage	Faulty pinion oil seal Faulty axleshaft oil seals Defective cover gasket
Noise	Lack of oil Worn bearings General wear
'Clonk' on taking up drive and excessive backlash	Incorrectly tightened pinion nut Worn components Worn axleshaft splines Elongated roadwheel bolt holes Defective propeller shaft

Chapter 9 Braking system

For modifications, and information applicable to later models, see Supplement at end of manual

Contents

Specifications

System type	....	Dual line hydraulic, servo assisted on all four wheels
Front brake	....	Disc with twin piston caliper
Rear brake	....	Drum with leading and trailing shoes, self adjusting
Handbrake	....	Mechanical, or rear wheels only

Front brakes
Disc diameter		9.74 in (247.5 mm)
Swept brake area		194.49 in² (1254.8 cm²)
Maximum disc run-out		0.002 in (0.05 mm)
Caliper cylinder diameter		2.13 in (54.0 mm)
Minimum disc thickness		0.45 in (11.40 mm)
Minimum lining thickness		0.06 in (1.5 mm)

Rear brakes
Drum diameter		9.0 in (228.6 mm)
Shoe width		1.75 in (44.5 mm)
Wheel cylinder diameter		0.70 in (17.78 mm)

Vacuum servo unit
Boost ratio		2.2 : 1

Torque wrench settings
	lbf ft	kgf m
Caliper to stub axle	45 to 50	6.2 to 6.9
Brake disc to hub	30 to 34	4.1 to 4.7
Rear brake backplate to axle housing	15 to 18	2.0 to 2.5
Hydraulic pipe union	5 to 7	0.7 to 1.0
Bleed screw	5 to 7	0.7 to 1.0
Master cylinder to servo	17	2.3

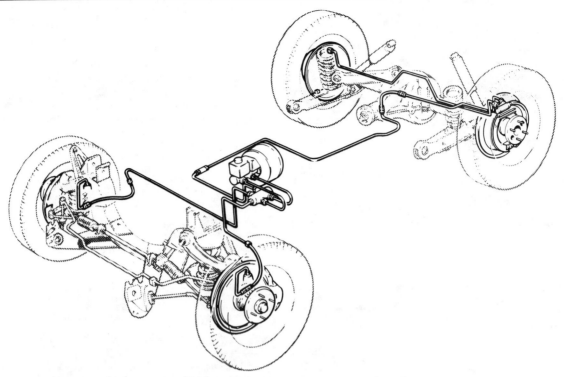

Fig. 9.1 Hydraulic braking system layout (Sec 1)

1 General description

Disc brakes are fitted to the front wheels and drum brakes to the rear. All are operated under servo assistance from the brake pedal, this being connected to the master cylinder and servo assembly, mounted on the bulkhead.

The hydraulic system is of the dual line principle whereby the front disc brake calipers have a separate hydraulic system to that of the rear drum brake wheel cylinders, so that, if failure of the hydraulic pipes to the front or rear brakes occurs, half the braking system is still operative (Fig. 9.1). Servo assistance in this condition is still available.

The front brake disc is secured to the hub flange and the caliper mounted on the steering knuckle and wheel stub, so that the disc is able to rotate in between the two halves of the calipers. Inside each half of the caliper is a hydraulic cylinder, this being interconnected by a drilling which allows hydraulic fluid pressure to be transmitted to both halves. A piston operates in each cylinder, and is in contact with the outer face of the brake pad. By depressing the brake pedal, hydraulic fluid pressure is increased by the servo unit and transmitted to the caliper by a system of metal and flexible hoses, whereupon the pistons are moved outwards so pushing the pads onto the face of the disc and slowing down the rotational speed of the disc.

The rear drum brakes have one cylinder operating two shoes. When the brake pedal is depressed, hydraulic fluid pressure, increased by the servo unit, is transmitted to the rear brake wheel cylinders by a system of metal and flexible pipes. The pressure moves the pistons outwards so pushing the shoe linings into contact with the inside circumference of the brake drum and slowing down the rotational speed of the drum.

The handbrake provides an independent means of rear brake application.

Also, attached to each of the brake units is an automatic adjuster which operates in conjunction with the footbrake.

Whenever it is necessary to obtain spare parts for the braking system great care must be taken to ensure that the correct parts are obtained.

2 Bleeding the hydraulic system

1   Removal of all the air from the hydraulic system is essential to the

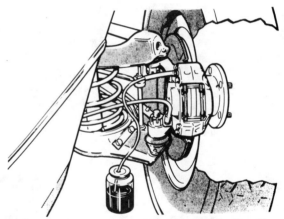

Fig. 9.2 Bleeding the front right-hand brake (Sec 2)

correct working of the braking system, and before undertaking this, examine the fluid reservoir cap to ensure that the vent hole is clear. Check the level of fluid in the reservoir, and top-up if required, ensuring that both halves are fitted.

2   Check all brake line unions and connections for possible seepage, and at the same time check the condition of the rubber hoses which may be perished.

3   If the condition of the caliper or wheel cylinders is in doubt, check for possible signs of fluid seepage.

4   If there is any possibility that incorrect fluid has been used in the system, drain all the fluid out and flush through with methylated spirits. Renew all piston seals and cups since they will be affected and could possibly fail under pressure.

5   Gather together a clean jam jar, a 12 inch (300 mm) length of tubing which fits tightly over the bleed screws and a tin of the correct brake fluid.

6   To bleed the system, clean the area around the bleed valves and start on the front right-hand bleed screw by first removing the rubber cup over the end of the bleed screw (Fig. 9.2).

3.1a Flexible brake hose to front brake caliper

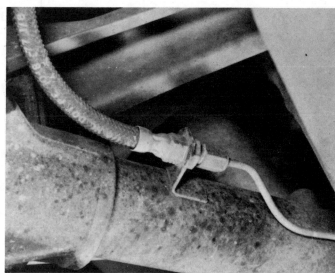

3.1b Flexible brake hose connection to rear axle

4.1 Front brake caliper and disc

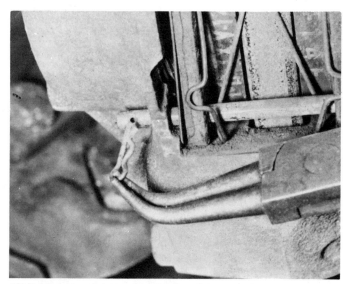

4.4 Remove the pad retaining pin spring clips ...

4.5 ... then the retaining pins and anti-rattle clips

4.9 The arrow on the shim must point upwards

7   Place the end of the tube in a clean jar which should contain sufficient fluid to keep the end of the tube underneath during the operation.

8   Open the bleed screw $\frac{1}{2}$ turn with a spanner and depress the brake pedal. After slowly releasing the pedal, pause for a moment to allow the fluid to recoup in the master cylinder and then depress it again. This will force air from the system. Continue until no more air bubbles can be seen coming from the tube. At intervals make certain that the reservoir is kept topped-up, otherwise air will enter at this point again.

9   Finally press the pedal down fully and hold it there whilst the bleed screw is tightened. To ensure correct seating it should be tightened to the specified torque.

10   Repeat this operation on the second front brake, and then the rear brakes, starting with the right-hand brake unit.

11   When completed, check the level of the fluid in the reservoir and then check the feel of the brake pedal, which should be firm and free from any 'spongy' action, which is normally associated with air in the system.

12   It will be noticed that during the bleeding operation the effort required to depress the pedal the full stroke will increase because of the loss of vacuum assistance as it is destroyed by repeated operation of the servo unit. Although the servo unit will be inoperative as far as assistance is concerned it does not affect the brake bleed operation.

3   Flexible hose – inspection, removal and refitting

1   Inspect the condition of the flexible hydraulic hoses leading to each of the front disc brake calipers and also the one at the front of the rear axle. If they are swollen, damaged or chafed, they must be renewed (photos).

2   Wipe the top of the brake master cylinder reservoir and unscrew the cap. Place a piece of polythene sheet over the top of the reservoir and refit the cap. This is to stop hydraulic fluid syphoning out during subsequent operations.

3   To remove a front flexible hose, wipe the union and brackets free of dust and undo the union nuts from the metal pipe ends.

4   Undo and remove the locknuts and plain washers securing each flexible hose end to the bracket and lift away the flexible hose.

5   To remove the rear flexible hose follow the instructions for the front flexible hose.

6   Refitting in both cases is the reverse sequence to removal. It will be necessary to bleed the brake hydraulic system as described in Section 2. If one hose has been removed it is only necessary to bleed either the front or rear brake hydraulic system.

4   Front brake pads – inspection, removal and refitting

1   Apply the handbrake, remove the front wheel nut caps, slacken the wheel nuts, jack-up the front of the car and place on firmly based axle-stands. Remove the front wheel (photo).

2   Inspect the amount of friction material left on the pads. The pads must be renewed when the thickness has been reduced to a minimum of 0.060 in (1.5 mm).

3   If the fluid level in the master cylinder reservoir is high, when the pistons are moved into their respective bores to accomodate new pads the level could rise sufficiently for the fluid to overflow. Place absorbent cloth around the reservoir or syphon a little fluid out so preventing paintwork damage caused by being in contact with the hydraulic fluid.

4   Using a pair of long nosed pliers extract the two small spring clips that hold the main retaining pins in place (photo).

5   Remove the main retaining pins and wire anti-rattle clips (photo).

6   The friction pads can now be removed from the caliper. If they prove difficult to remove by hand, a pair of long nosed pliers can be used. Lift away the shims.

7   Carefully clean the recesses in the caliper in which the friction pads and shims lie, and the exposed faces of each piston from all traces of dust or rust.

8   Using a piece of wood carefully retract the pistons (Fig. 9.3).

9   Fit new friction pads and shims, with the arrow on the shim pointing upwards (photo). Insert the pad retaining pins and anti-rattle clips and secure with the spring clips.

10   Refit the roadwheel and lower the car. Tighten the wheel nuts securely and refit the wheel nut caps.

11   To correctly seat the pistons pump the brake pedal several times

and finally top-up the hydraulic fluid level in the master cylinder reservoir as necessary.

5   Front brake caliper – removal and refitting

1   Apply the handbrake, remove the front wheel nut caps, slacken the wheel nuts, jack-up the front of the car and place on firmly based axle-stands. Remove the front wheel.

2   Wipe the top of the brake master cylinder reservoir and unscrew the cap. Place a piece of polythene sheet over the top of the reservoir and refit the cap. This is to stop hydraulic fluid syphoning out during subsequent operations.

3   Remove the friction pads, as described in Section 4.

4   If it is intended to fit new caliper pistons and/or the seals, depress the brake pedal to bring the pistons into contact with the disc and so assist subsequent removal of the pistons.

5   Wipe the area clean around the flexible hose bracket and detach the pipe as described in Section 3. Tape up the end of the pipe to stop the possibility of dirt ingress.

6   Using a screwdriver or chisel, bend back the tabs on the locking plate and undo the two caliper body mounting bolts. Lift away the caliper from its mounting flange on the steering knuckle and wheel stub.

7   To refit the caliper, position it over the disc and move it until the mounting bolt holes are in line with the two front holes in the steering knuckle and wheel stub mounting flange.

8   Fit the caliper and retaining bolts through the two holes in a new locking plate and insert the bolts through the caliper body. Tighten the bolts to the specified torque.

9   Using a screwdriver, pliers or chisel, bend up the locking plate tabs so as to lock the bolts.

10   Remove the tape from the end of the flexible hydraulic pipe and reconnect it to the union on the hose bracket. Be careful not to cross thread the union nut during the initial turns. The union nut should be tightened securely, if possible using a torque wrench, and special slotted end ring spanner attachment, set to the specified torque.

11   Push the pistons into their respective bores so as to accommodate the pads. Watch the level of hydraulic fluid in the master cylinder reservoir as it can overflow if too high whilst the pistons are being retracted. Place absorbent cloth around the reservoir or syphon a little fluid out so preventing paintwork damage caused by being in contact with the hydraulic fluid.

12   If the old pads are being re-used, refit them into their respective original positions. If new pads are being used it does not matter which side they are fitted. Refit the shims, and clips.

13   Insert the two pad and shim retaining pins and secure in position with the spring clips.

14   Bleed the hydraulic system as described in Section 2. Refit the roadwheel and lower the car.

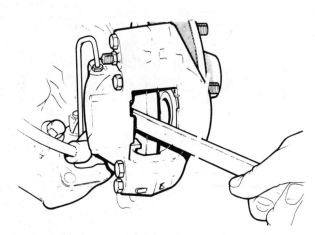

Fig. 9.3 Pushing the piston into the caliper hose (Sec 4)

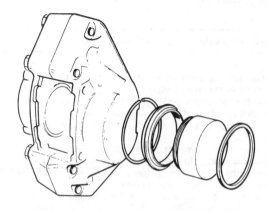

Fig. 9.4 Brake caliper body and one piston assembly (Sec 6)

Fig. 9.5 Pulling off the hub and disc assembly (Sec 7)

Fig. 9.6 Front hub assembly with disc removed (Sec 7)

Fig. 9.7 Refitting the disc to the hub (Sec 7)

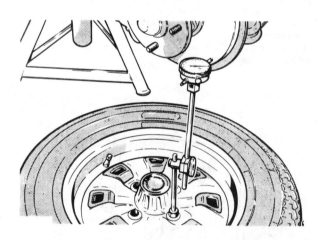

Fig. 9.8 Checking the disc runout using a dial gauge (Sec 7)

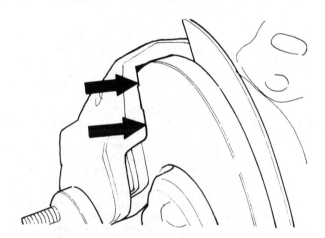

Fig. 9.9 Checking the disc runout using feeler gauges (Sec 7)

6 Front brake caliper – dismantling and reassembly

1   The pistons should be removed first. To do this, half withdraw one piston from its bore in the caliper body (Fig. 9.4).
2   Carefully remove the securing circlip and extract the sealing bellows from their location in the lower part of the piston skirt. Completely remove the piston.

3   If difficulty is experienced in withdrawing the piston use a jet of compressed air or a foot pump to move it out of its bore.
4   Remove the sealing bellows from their location in the annular ring which is machined in the cylinder bore.
5   Remove the piston sealing ring from the cylinder bore using a small screwdriver but do take care not to scratch the fine finish of the bore.
6   To remove the second piston repeat the operations in paragraphs

1 - 5 inclusive.

7   It is important that the two halves of the caliper are not separated under any circumstances. If hydraulic fluid leaks are evident, from the joint, the caliper must be renewed.

8   Thoroughly wash all parts in methylated spirits or clean hydraulic fluid. During reassembly new rubber seals must be fitted and these should be well lubricated with clean hydraulic fluid.

9   Inspect the pistons and bores for signs of wear, score marks or damage, and if evident, new parts should be obtained ready for fitting or a new caliper obtained.

10   To reassemble, fit one of the piston seals into the annular groove in the cylinder bore.

11   Fit the rubber bellows to the cylinder bore groove so that the lip is turned outwards.

12   Lubricate the seal and rubber bellows with clean hydraulic fluid. Push the piston, crown first, through the rubber sealing bellows and then into the cylinder bore. Take care as it is easy for the piston to damage the rubber bellows.

13   With the piston half inserted into the cylinder bore, fit the inner edge of the bellows into the annular groove that is in the piston skirt.

14   Push the piston down the bore as far as it will go. Secure the rubber bellows to the caliper with the circlip.

15   Repeat the operations in paragraphs 10 to 14 inclusive for the second piston.

16   The caliper is now ready for refitting. It is recommended that the hydraulic pipe end is temporarily plugged to stop any dirt ingress whilst being refitted, before the pipe connection is made.

7   Front brake disc and hub – removal and refitting

1   After jacking up the car and removing the front wheel, remove the caliper as described in Section 5.

2   By judicious tapping and levering remove the dust cap from the centre of the hub.

3   Remove the split pin from the nut retainer and lift away the adjusting nut retainer.

4   Unscrew the adjusting nut and lift away the thrust washer and outer tapered bearing.

5   Pull off the complete hub and disc assembly from the stub axle (Fig. 9.5).

6   From the back of the hub assembly carefully prise out the grease seal and lift away the inner tapered bearing (Fig. 9.6).

7   Carefully clean out the hub and wash the bearings with petrol making sure that no grease or oil is allowed to get onto the brake disc.

8   Should it be necessary to separate the disc from the hub for renewal or regrinding, first bend back the locking tabs and undo the four securing bolts. With a scriber mark the relative positions of the hub and disc to ensure refitting in their original positions and separate the disc from the hub.

9   Thoroughly clean the disc and inspect for signs of deep scoring or excessive corrosion. If these are evident, the disc may be reground to a minimum thickness of 0.45 in (11.40 mm). It is, however, desirable to fit a new disc if at all possible.

10   To reassemble make quite sure that the mating faces of the disc and hub are very clean and place the disc on the hub, lining up any previously made marks.

11   Fit the four securing bolts and two new tab washers and tighten the bolts in progressive and diagonal manner to the final torque wrench setting given in the Specifications. Bend up the locking tabs (Fig. 9.7).

12   Work some grease well into the bearing, fully pack the bearing cages and rollers. **Note:** *leave the hub and grease seal empty to allow for subsequent expansion of the grease.*

13   To reassemble the hub, first fit the inner bearing and then gently tap the grease seal back into the hub. A new seal must always be fitted as during removal it was probably damaged. The lip must face inwards to the hub.

14   Refit the hub and disc assembly on the stub axle and slide on the outer bearing and thrust washer.

15   Refit the adjusting nut and tighten it to a torque wrench setting of 27 lbf ft (3.7 kgf m) whilst rotating the hub and disc to ensure free movement and centralisation of the bearings. Slacken the nut back by 90° which will give the required endfloat of 0.001 – 0.005 in (0.03 – 0.13 mm). Fit the nut retainer and a new split pin but at this stage do not lock the split pin.

16   If a dial indicator gauge is available, it is advisable to check the disc for run out. The measurement should be taken as near to the edge of the worn yet smooth part of the disc as possible, and must not exceed 0.0035 in (0.09 mm). If the figure obtained is found to be excessive, check the mating surfaces of the disc and hub for dirt or damage and also check the bearings and cups for excessive wear or damage (Fig. 9.8).

17   If a dial indicator gauge is not available the runout can be checked by means of a feeler gauge placed between the casting of the caliper and the disc (Fig. 9.9). Establish a reasonably tight fit with the feeler gauge between the top of the casting and the disc and rotate the disc and hub. Any high or low spot will immediately become obvious by extra tightness or looseness of the fit of the feeler gauge. The amount of runout can be checked by adding or subtracting feeler gauges as necessary. It is only fair to point out that this method is not as accurate as when using a dial indicator gauge owing to the rough nature of the caliper casting.

18   Once the disc runout has been checked and found to be correct bend the ends of the split pin back and refit the dust cap.

19   Reconnect the brake hydraulic pipe and bleed the brakes as described in Section 2 of this Chapter.

8   Rear drum brake shoes – inspection, removal and refitting

After high mileages, it will be necessary to fit replacement shoes with new linings. Refitting new brake linings to shoes is not considered economic, or possible without the use of special equipment. However, if the services of a local garage or workshop having brake re-lining equipment are available then there is no reason why the original shoes should not be successfully relined. Ensure that the correct specification linings are fitted to the shoes.

1   Chock the front wheels, jack up the rear of the car and place on firmly based axle-stands. Remove the roadwheel.

2   Release the handbrake, remove the brake drum retaining screw, and using a soft-faced mallet on the outer circumference of the brake drum remove the brake drum (photo).

3   Should the situation exist whereby the shoes foul the drum making removal impossible, the shoes must be collapsed by detaching the handbrake cable from the body mounted brackets and then the plunger assembly removed from the backplate. Whenever the plunger is removed it must be discarded and a new one obtained.

4   The brake linings should be renewed when the lining material has worn down to 0.06 inch (1.52 mm) at its thinnest part.

5   Depress each shoe holding down spring and rotate the spring retaining washer through 90° to disengage it from the pin secured to the backplate. Lift away the washer and spring (Fig. 9.11).

6   Ease each shoe from its location slot in the fixed pivot and then detach the other end of each shoe from the wheel cylinder.

7   Note which way round and into which holes in the shoes the two

8.2 Removing the rear brake drum

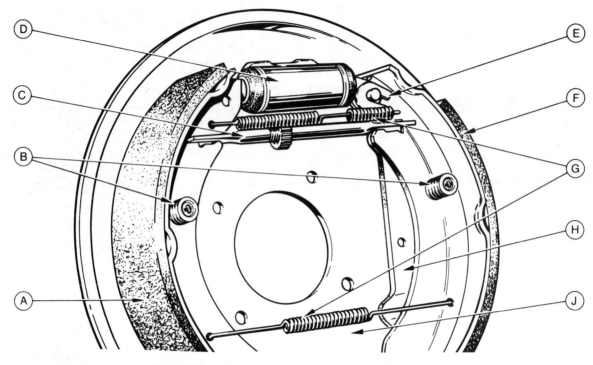

Fig. 9.10 Rear brake assembly with drum removed (Sec 8)

A Brake shoe
B Hold down spring
C Adjuster
D Wheel cylinder
E Handbrake lever retaining
   clip
F Brake shoe
G Return springs
H Handbrake lever
J Backplate

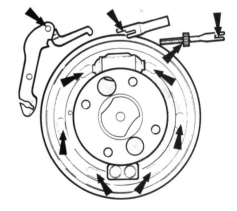

Fig. 9.12 Points to be smeared with brake grease (Sec 8)

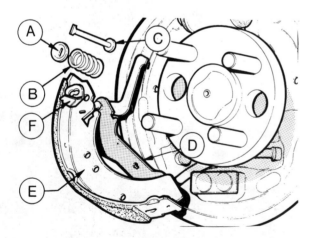

Fig. 9.11 Rear shoe assembly (Sec 8)

A Retaining washer
B Hold down spring
C Pin
D Relay lever
E Rear shoe
F Retaining bracket

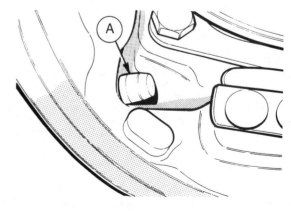

Fig. 9.13 Handbrake lever stop (Sec 8)

retracting springs fit and detach the retracting springs.

8   Lift away the front shoe followed by the self adjusting pushrod and ratchet assembly.

9   Completely remove the handbrake cable from the body mounted brackets and disconnect the cable from the relay lever.

10 Lift away the rear shoe together with the self adjusting mechanism.

11 If the shoes are to be left off for a while, place a warning on the steering wheel as accidental depression of the brake pedal will eject the pistons from the wheel cylinder.

12 To remove the relay lever assembly, release the shoe retaining bracket and lift away the relay lever assembly (Fig. 9.11).

13 Thoroughly clean all traces of dust from the shoes, backplates and brake drums using a stiff brush. It is recommended that compressed air is *not* used as it blows up dust which should *not* be inhaled. Brake dust can cause judder or squeal and, therefore, it is important to clean out as described.

14 Check that the pistons are free in the cylinder, that the rubber dust covers are undamaged and in position, and that there are no hydraulic fluid leaks.

15 Prior to reassembly smear a trace of brake grease on the shoe support pads, brake shoe pivots and on the ratchet wheel face and threads (Fig. 9.12).

16 Reassembly of the new shoes is a reversal of the removal and dismantling procedure, but note the following points:

    a)   Renew the handbrake lever stop, by withdrawing it from the carrier plate, if it is damaged or stiff to move (Fig. 9.13)

    b)   Check that the handbrake lever is positioned over its stop

    c)   The longer fork of the adjusting strut must be positioned against the rear brake shoe (Fig. 9.14)

    d)   Fit the upper retracting spring to the front shoe, then to the rear shoe retaining bracket (Fig. 9.15). Ensure that the tag on this bracket is located in the cut-out in the shoe (photo)

    e)   Expand the adjusting strut to remove all slack, and check that the pawl is correctly engaged in the ratchet wheel (Fig. 9.16)

17 Once the brake drum has been installed, apply the foot brake several times to adjust the shoes to their minimum drum clearance position.

9   Wheel cylinder (rear drum brake) – removal, inspection, overhaul and refitting

If hydraulic fluid is leaking from the brake wheel cylinder, it will be necessary to dismantle it and renew the seals. Should brake fluid be found running down the side of the wheel, or if it is noticed that a pool of liquid forms alongside one wheel or the level in the master cylinder drops it is also indicative of failed seals.

1   Refer to Section 8 and remove the brake drum and shoes. Clean down the rear of the backplate using a stiff brush. Place a quantity of

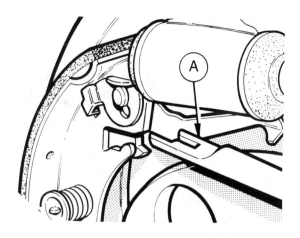

Fig. 9.14 Fitting the adjusting strut (Sec 8)

A Adjusting strut

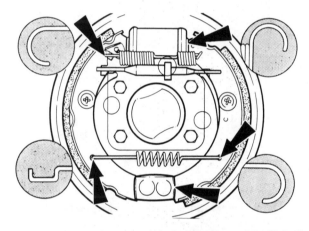

Fig. 9.15 Correct location of shoe retracting springs (Sec 8)

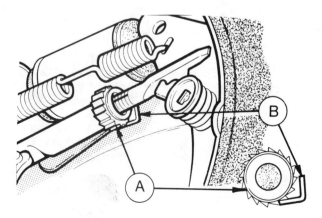

Fig. 9.16 Check that the pawl is correctly engaged (Sec 8)

A Ratchet wheel   *B Pawl*

8.16 Fitting the upper retracting spring

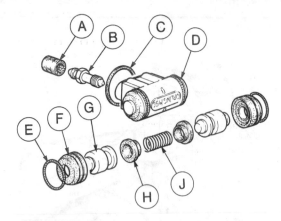

Fig. 9.17 Exploded view of wheel cylinder (Sec 9)

A Dust cap (where fitted)
B Bleed nipple (where fitted)
C Seal (where fitted)
D Wheel cylinder
E Retaining ring

F Dust cover
G Piston
H Piston seal
J Return spring

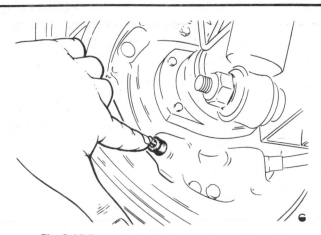

Fig. 9.18 Rear wheel adjustment plunger (Sec 11)

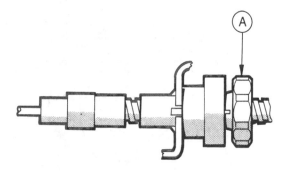

Fig. 9.19 Keyed sleeve engaged in bracket (Sec 11)

A Adjusting nut

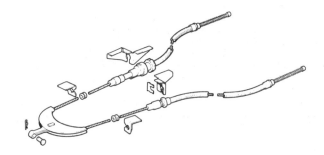

Fig. 9.20 Handbrake cable assembly (Sec 11)

11.5 Handbrake cable adjuster

13.2 The brake master cylinder is mounted on the servo unit

rag under the backplate to catch any hydraulic fluid that may issue from the open pipe or wheel cylinder.

2   Wipe the top of the brake master cylinder reservoir and unscrew the cap. Place a piece of polythene sheet over the top of the reservoir and refit the cap. This is to stop hydraulic fluid syphoning out.

3   Using an open ended spanner, carefully unscrew the hydraulic pipe connection union/s to the rear of the wheel cylinder. Note that on the left-hand wheel cylinder two pipes are attached to the wheel cylinder. Note the location of each pipe as these must not be interchanged. To prevent dirt ingress, tape over the pipe ends.

4   Undo and remove the two bolts and washers that secure the wheel cylinder to the brake backplate.

5   Withdraw the wheel cylinder from the front of the brake backplate. Remove the seal.

6   To dismantle the wheel cylinder first ease off each rubber dust cover retaining ring and lift away each rubber dust cover.

7   Carefully lift out each piston together with seal from the wheel cylinder bore. Recover the return springs.

8   Using the fingers only, remove the piston seal from each piston, noting which way round it is fitted (Fig. 9.17). Do not use a metal screwdriver as this could scratch the piston.

9   Inspect the inside of the cylinder for score marks caused by impurities in the hydraulic fluid. If any are found, the cylinder and pistons will require renewal. **Note:** *if the wheel cylinder requires renewal always ensure that the replacement is the same as the one removed.*

10   If the cylinder is sound, thoroughly clean it out with fresh hydraulic fluid.

11   The old rubber seals will probably be swollen and visibly worn. Smear the new rubber seals with hydraulic fluid and refit to the pistons making sure they are the correct way round with the flap of the seal adjacent to the piston rear shoulder (Fig. 9.17).

12   Wet the cylinder bore with clean hydraulic fluid and insert the return spring. Carefully insert the piston seal end first into the cylinder, making sure that the seals do not roll over as they are initially fitted into the bore.

13   Position the rubber boots on each end of the wheel cylinder and secure in position with the retaining rings.

14   Fit a new ring seal onto the rear of the wheel cylinder and position the cylinder in its slot in the backplate. Secure with the two bolts and washers.

15   Reconnect the brake pipe/s to the rear of the wheel cylinder, taking care not to cross thread the union nuts. On the left-hand wheel cylinder make sure the pipes are connected the correct way round as was noted during removal.

16   Refit the brake shoes and drum as described in Section 8.

17   Refer to Section 2 and bleed the brake hydraulic system.

10 Rear brake backplate – removal and refitting

1   To remove the backplate refer to Chapter 8, Section 5 and remove the axleshaft (halfshaft).

2   Detach the handbrake cable from the handbrake relay lever.

3   Wipe the top of the brake master cylinder reservoir and unscrew the cap. Place a piece of polythene sheet over the top of the reservoir and refit the cap. This is to stop hydraulic fluid syphoning out.

4   Using an open ended spanner, carefully unscrew the hydraulic pipe connection union/s to the rear of the wheel cylinder. Note that on the left-hand wheel cylinder two pipes are attached to the wheel cylinder. Note the location of each pipe as these must not be interchanged. To prevent dirt ingress tape over the pipe ends.

5   The brake backplate may now be lifted away.

6   Refitting is the reverse sequence to removal. It will be necessary to bleed the brake hydraulic system as described in Section 2.

11 Handbrake – adjustment

1   It is important to check that lack of adjustment is not caused by the cable becoming detached from the body mounted clips, that the equaliser bracket and pivot points are adequately lubricated and that the rear shoe linings have not worn excessively.

2   Chock the front wheels. Jack up the rear of the car and support on firmly based axle-stands located under the rear axle. Release the handbrake.

3   Check that there is no free movement at the rear wheel adjustment plungers (Fig. 9.18). If the plungers move, the footbrake should be operated several times until the ratchet is tightened.

4   At the adjusting bracket, on the right-hand side, separate the adjusting nut and sleeve using a screwdriver. Engage the keyed sleeve in the bracket (Fig. 9.19).

5   Now adjust the cable at the right-hand cable to body abutment bracket so as to give a plunger free movement of 0.04 to 0.06 in (1.0 to 1.5 mm) on each brake backplate (photo).

6   Equalise the movement of the plungers by gripping the handbrake at the equaliser bracket and adjusting the position of the cable.

7   Should adjustment of the cable not alter the plunger free movement, it is an indication that the cable is binding or the automatic brake adjuster is not operating correctly – usually due to seizure of the moving parts within the brake unit. It could also be that the adjustment plungers have seized in their locations in the backplate. Further investigation will therefore be necessary.

8   The adjusting nut and keyed sleeve will lock together automatically at the first application of the handbrake.

9   Remove the axle-stands and lower the car to the ground.

12 Handbrake cable – removal and refitting

1   Chock the front wheels, jack up the rear of the car and support on firmly based axle-stands located under the rear axle. Release the handbrake. Remove the two rear wheels.

2   From under the vehicle remove the spring clip and withdraw the clevis pin and wave washer from the handbrake lever yoke (Fig. 9.20).

3   Pull back and withdraw the cable from the two floor brackets. Using a pair of pliers withdraw the retaining U-shaped clip at the left-hand bracket. Remove the cable from the clips at the radius arms.

4   Remove the brake drums. If they are tight they may be removed using a soft-faced mallet on the outer drum circumference and tapping outwards.

5   Detach the brake cable from each brake unit relay lever and pull the cable through the rear of the backplate.

6   Detach the cable from the equaliser.

7   To refit the cable first feed the cable ends through the rear of the backplate and reconnect to the relay levers. Refit the brake drums.

8   Attach the cable to the underbody brackets and clips on the radius arms. Take care to make sure that the adjuster is correctly located in its bracket (Fig. 9.19).

9   Engage the cable within the groove of the equaliser and then connect the equaliser to the handbrake lever.

10   Refit the rear wheels and, referring to Section 11, adjust the handbrake cable.

11   Remove the axle-stands and lower the car to the ground.

13 Brake master cylinder – removal and refitting

1   Apply the handbrake and chock the front wheels. Drain the fluid from the master cylinder reservoir and master cylinder by attaching a plastic bleed tube to one of the brake bleed screws. Undo the screw one turn and then pump the fluid out into a clean glass container by means of the brake pedal. Hold the brake pedal against the floor at the end of each stroke and tighten the bleed screw. When the pedal has returned to its normal position loosen the bleed screw and repeat the process until the reservoir is empty.

2   Wipe the area around the three union nuts on the side of the master cylinder body and using an open ended spanner undo the three union nuts. Tape over the ends of the pipes to stop dirt ingress (photo).

3   Undo and remove the two nuts and spring washers that secure the master cylinder to the servo unit. Lift away the master cylinder taking care that no hydraulic fluid is allowed to drip onto the paintwork.

4   Refitting is the reverse sequence to removal. Always start the union nuts before finally tightening the master cylinder nuts. It will be necessary to bleed the hydraulic system: full details will be found in Section 2.

14 Brake master cylinder – dismantling, examination and reassembly

If a new master cylinder is to be fitted, it will be necessary to

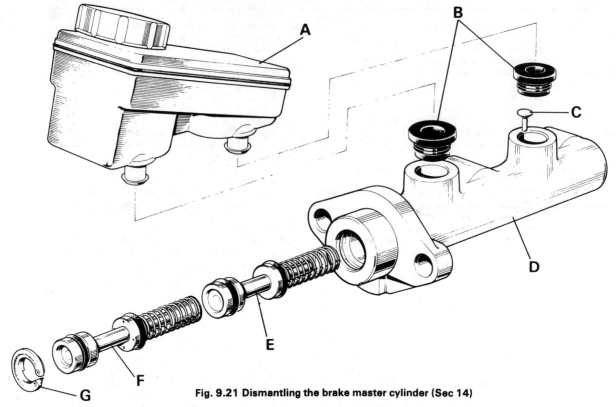

Fig. 9.21 Dismantling the brake master cylinder (Sec 14)

A Reservoir   B Reservoir seals   C Piston stop pin   D Master cylinder
E Secondary piston   F Primary piston   G Retaining circlip

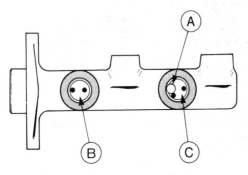

Fig. 9.22 Removing the stop pin (Sec 14)

A Stop pin   B Primary inlet
C Secondary inlet

Fig. 9.23 Remove the piston retaining circlip (Sec 14)

A Circlip   B Master cylinder

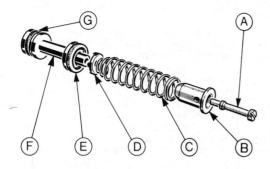

Fig. 9.24 Exploded view of primary piston assembly (Sec 14)

A Screw   B Sleeve
C Spring   D Retainer
E Seal   F Primary piston
G Seal

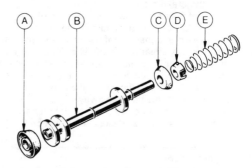

Fig. 9.25 Exploded view of secondary piston assembly (Sec 14)

A Seal   B Secondary Piston
C Seal   D Retainer
E Spring

lubricate the seals before fitting to the car as they have a protective coating when originally assembled. Remove the blanking plugs from the hydraulic pipe union seatings. Inject clean hydraulic fluid into the master cylinder and operate the primary piston several times so that the fluid spreads over all the internal working surfaces.

If the master cylinder is to be dismantled after removal proceed as follows:

1   Remove the reservoir by pulling upwards, and remove the rubber seals (Fig. 9.21).

2   Depress the operating rod to relieve the pressure on the piston stop pin, and remove the pin (Fig. 9.22). Using circlip pliers remove the retaining circlip (Fig. 9.23).

3   Using a compressed air jet, very carefully applied to the rear outlet connection, blow out all the master cylinder internal components. Alternatively, shake out the parts. Take care that adequate precautions are taken to ensure all parts are caught as they emerge.

4   To dismantle the primary piston, unscrew and remove the screw and sleeve. Remove the spring, retainer and seals (Fig. 9.24). Gently lever off the other seal, taking care not to scratch the piston.

5   To dismantle the secondary piston, remove the spring, retainer and seal (Fig. 9.25). Gently lever off the other seal, taking care not to damage the piston.

6   Examine the bore of the cylinder carefully for any signs of scores or ridges. If this is found to be smooth all over new seals can be fitted. If, however, there is any doubt about the condition of the bore, then a new cylinder must be fitted.

7   If examination of the seals shows them to be apparently oversize, or swollen, or very loose on the plungers, suspect oil contamination in the system. Oil will swell these rubber seals, and if one is found to be swollen, it is reasonable to assume that all seals in the braking system will need attention.

8   Thoroughly clean all parts in clean hydraulic fluid or methylated spirits. Ensure that the bypass ports are clear.

9   All components should be assembled wet by dipping in clean brake fluid.

10 Using the fingers only, fit the seals to the secondary piston, ensur-ing that they are the correct way round (Fig. 9.25). Fit the retainer and spring. Check that the master cylinder bore is clean, and smear with clean brake fluid.

11 Wet the secondary piston assembly with clean fluid, and insert into the master cylinder, spring first. Ease the lips of the seals into the cylinder bore taking care they do not roll over.

12 Fit the seals to the primary piston, ensuring that they are the correct way round (Fig. 9.24). Fit the retainer, spring, sleeve and screw.

13 Wet the primary piston assembly with clean fluid, and insert into the master cylinder, spring first. Ease the lips of the seals into the cylinder bore taking care they do not roll over.

14 Fit the circlip to retain the primary piston in the cylinder bore (Fig. 9.23).

15 Depress the operating rod and insert the piston stop pin (Fig. 9.22).

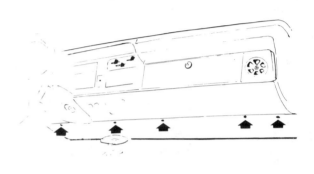

Fig. 9.26 Lower dash trim panel screw location (Sec 15)

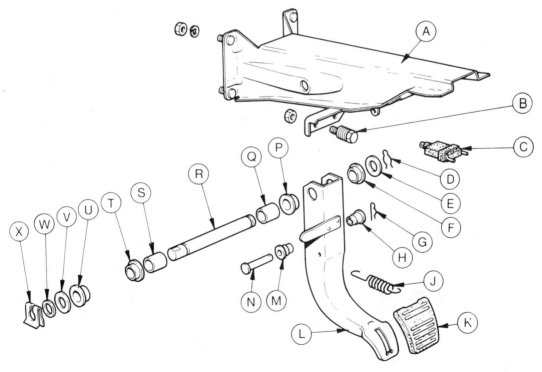

Fig. 9.27 Exploded view of brake pedal assembly (Sec 15)

A Pedal bracket	G Spring clip	N Clevis pin	T Bush
B Pedal stop	H Bush	P Bush	U Bush
C Stop light switch	J Pedal return spring	Q Spacer	V Flat washer
D Spring clip	K Pedal pad	R Shaft	W Wave washer
E Washer	L Brake pedal	S Spacer	X Spring clip
F Bush	M Bush		

16 Check the condition of the front and rear reservoir gaskets and if there is any doubt as to their condition they must be renewed.
17 Refit the hydraulic fluid reservoir.
18 The master cylinder is now ready for refitting to the servo unit. Bleed the complete hydraulic system and road test the car.

15 Brake pedal – removal and refitting

1 Open the bonnet and for safety reasons disconnect the battery.
2 Undo the five screws and remove the lower dash trim panel (Fig. 9.26).
3 Withdraw the spring clip from the brake servo pushrod to brake pedal clevis pin. Lift away the clevis pin and the bushes and allow the pushrod to drop (Fig. 9.27).
4 Detach the brake pedal return spring from the brake pedal bracket.
5 Remove the circlip and float washer and carefully push the shaft through the bracket and pedal.

6 Lift away the brake pedal. Remove the half bushes from each side of the brake pedal.
7 Inspect the bushes for signs of wear, and if evident, they must be renewed. Ensure that the key on each bush engages with the cut-out in the pedal.
8 Refitting the brake pedal is the reverse sequence to removal. Lubricate the bushes and shafts with a molybdenum disulphide grease.
9 Adjust the stop light switch if required, Section 19.

16 Handbrake lever – removal and refitting

1 Undo and remove the self-tapping screws that secure the handbrake lever rubber gaiter to the floor. Slide the gaiter up the handbrake lever (Fig. 9.28).
2 Lift away the carpeting from the handbrake area.
3 From under the vehicle remove the spring clip, clevis pin and wave washer securing the equaliser bracket to the handbrake lever (Fig. 9.29).

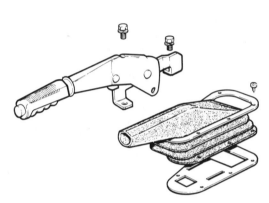

Fig. 9.28 Handbrake lever and gaiter assembly (Sec 16)

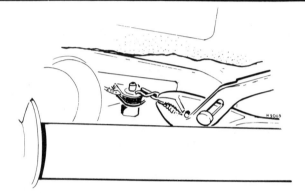

Fig. 9.29 Removing the spring clip from the handbrake clevis pin (Sec 16)

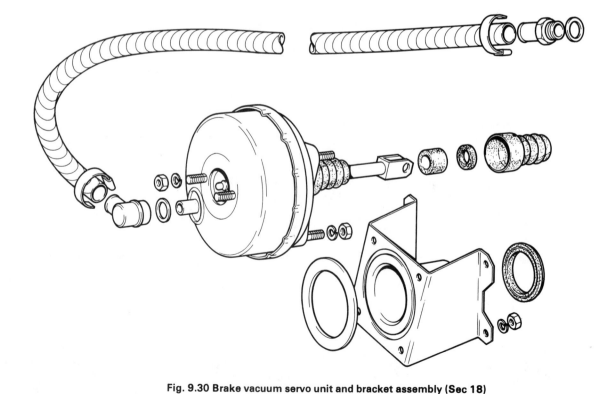

Fig. 9.30 Brake vacuum servo unit and bracket assembly (Sec 18)

4   Undo and remove the two bolts and spring washers that secure the handbrake lever to the floor. The handbrake lever assembly may be lifted away from its location on the floor.

5   Refitting is the reverse sequence to removal. Smear the clevis pin with a little grease. The handbrake lever seal must be installed with the paint spot uppermost.

17 Vacuum servo unit – description

A vacuum servo unit is fitted into the brake hydraulic circuit in series with the master cylinder, to provide assistance to the driver when the brake pedal is depressed. This reduces the effort required by the driver to operate the brakes under all braking conditions.

The unit operates by vacuum obtained from the induction manifold and comprises, basically, a booster diaphragm and check valve. The servo unit and hydraulic master cylinder are connected together so that the servo unit piston rod acts as the master cylinder pushrod. The driver's effort is transmitted through another pushrod to the servo unit piston and its built-in control system. The servo unit piston does not fit fit tightly into the cylinder, but has a strong diaphragm to keep its edges in constant contact with the cylinder wall, so assuring an air tight seal between the two parts. The forward chamber is held under vacuum conditions created in the inlet manifold of the engine and, during periods when the brake pedal is not in use, the controls open a passage to the rear chamber so placing it under vacuum conditions as well. When the brake pedal is depressed, the vacuum passage to the rear chamber is cut off and the chamber opened to atmospheric pressure. The consequent rush of air pushes the servo piston forward in the vacuum chamber and operates the main pushrod to the master cylinder.

The controls are designed so that assistance is given under all conditions and, when the brakes are not required, vacuum in the rear chamber is established when the brake pedal is released. All air from the atmosphere entering the rear chamber is passed through a small air filter.

Under normal operating conditions the vacuum servo unit is very reliable and does not require overhaul except at very high mileages. In this case it is far better to obtain a service exchange unit, rather than repair the original unit.

18 Vacuum servo unit – removal and refitting

1   Slacken the clip securing the vacuum hose to the servo unit and carefully draw the hose from its union.

2   Refer to Section 13 and remove the master cylinder.

3   Using a pair of pliers remove the spring clip in the end of the brake pedal to pushrod clevis pin. Lift away the clevis pin and bushes.

4   Undo and remove the nuts and spring washers that secure the servo unit mounting bracket to the bulkhead. Lift away the servo unit and bracket (Fig. 9.30).

5   Undo and remove the four nuts and spring washers that secure the bracket to the servo unit.

6   Refitting the servo unit is the reverse sequence to removal. It will be necessary to bleed the brake hydraulic system as described in Section 2.

19 Stop light switch – removal and refitting

1   Open the bonnet and for safety reasons, disconnect the battery.

2   Disconnect the wiring from the switch, remove the locking nut and detach the switch.

3   Refitting the switch is the reverse of the removal sequence. Adjust the switch position so that when the brake pedal is at the rest position the switch is depressed half its total length, then tighten the lock nut and reconnect the wiring.

4   Depress the brake pedal and check the operation of the switch.

20 Fault diagnosis – braking system

Symptom	Reason/s
Pedal travels almost to floor before brakes operate	Brake fluid level too low
	Caliper leaking
	Master cylinder leaking (bubbles in master cylinder fluid)
	Brake flexible hose leaking
	Brake line fractured
	Brake system unions loose
	Pad or shoe linings over 75% worn
Brake pedal feels springy	New linings not yet bedded in
	Brake discs or drums badly worn or cracked
	Master cylinder and/or vacuum servo unit securing nuts loose
Brake pedal feels spongy and soggy	Caliper or wheel cylinder leaking
	Master cylinder leaking (bubbles in master cylinder reservoir)
	Brake pipe line or flexible hose leaking
	Unions in brake system loose
Excessive effort required to brake car	Pad or shoe linings badly worn
	New pads or shoes recently fitted – not yet bedded-in
	Harder linings fitted than standard causing increase in pedal pressure
	Linings and brake drums contaminated with oil, grease or hydraulic fluid
	Vacuum servo unit not working
Brakes uneven and pulling to one side	Linings and discs or drums contaminated with oil, grease or hydraulic fluid
	Tyre pressures unequal
	Radial ply tyres fitted at one side of the car only
	Brake caliper loose
	Brake pads or shoes fitted incorrectly
	Different type of linings fitted at each wheel
	Anchorages for front suspension or rear suspension loose
	Brake discs or drums badly worn, cracked or distorted

Chapter 10 Electrical system

For modifications, and information applicable to later models, see Supplement at end of manual

Contents

Specifications

Battery

Type	Lead acid, 12 volt, negative earth
Capacity:	
Manual transmission	55 amp hour
Automatic transmission	66 amp hour
Specific gravity (charged)	1.27 to 1.29 at a temperature of 25°C (77°F) (Refer to Section 3)

Starter motor

Inertia	Lucas M35J
Pre-engaged:	
Standard	Lucas M35J
Heavy duty	Lucas 5M90
Number of brushes	4
Brush material	Carbon
Minimum brush length	0.32 in (8 mm)
Brush spring pressure	28 oz (800 gm)
Minimum commutator thickness	0.08 in (2.05 mm)
Armature endfloat*	0.01 in (0.25 mm)
Type of drive*	Solenoid
Direction of rotation	Clockwise
Maximum current draw	365 amps

Voltage   12
Not applicable to inertia motor

Alternator
Output:
Bosch G1 – 28A and Lucas 15ACR	28 amps
Bosch K1 – 35A and Lucas 17ACR	35 amps
Bosch K1 – 45A and Lucas 18ACR	45 amps
Femsa	32 amps

Maximum continuous speed . . . .   15 000 rev/min
Speed ratio to engine . . . .   1 : 1.9
Minimum brush length:
    Bosch and Lucas . . . .   0.2 in (5 mm)
    Femsa . . . .   0.3 in (7 mm)
Regulating voltage (4000 rev/min):
    Bosch and Femsa . . . .   13.7 to 14.5 volts
    Lucas . . . .   14.2 to 14.6 volts

Bulbs

Type	Wattage	Fitting
Headlamps (halogen)	55/60	Clip
Driving lamps (halogen)	55	Clip
Sidelights	4	Bayonet
Direction indicators	21	Bayonet
Rear lights	5	Bayonet
Stop lights	21	Bayonet
Number plate lamps	4	Bayonet
Reverse lamps	21	Bayonet
Instrument warning lamps/switches	1.3	Glass socket
Instrument illumination	2.6	Glass socket
Automatic selector illumination	1.4	Bayonet
Cigarette lighter illumination	1.4	Bayonet
Interior light(s)	5	Bayonet

1 General description

The electrical system is of the 12 volt negative earth type and the major components comprise a 12 volt battery of which the negative terminal is earthed, an alternator which is driven from the crankshaft pulley, and a starter motor.

The battery supplies a steady amount of current for the ignition, lighting and other electrical circuits and provides a reserve of electricity when the current consumed by the electrical equipment exceeds that being produced by the alternator.

The alternator has its own regulator which ensures a high output if the battery is in a low state of charge or the demand from the electrical equipment is high, and a low output if the battery is fully charged and there is little demand for the electrical equipment.

When fitting electrical accessories to cars with a negative earth system it is important, if they contain silicone diodes or transistors, that they are connected correctly, otherwise serious damage may result to the components concerned. Items such as radios, tape players, electronic ignition systems, electronic tachometer, automatic dipping etc, should all be checked for correct polarity.

It is important that the battery is disconnected before removing the alternator output lead as this is live at all times. Also if body repairs are to be carried out using electric arc welding equipment – the alternator must be disconnected otherwise serious damage can be caused to the more delicate instruments. Whenever the battery has to be disconnected it must always be reconnected with the negative terminal earthed. Do **not** disconnect the battery with the engine running. If 'jumper cables' are used to start the car, they *must* be connected correctly – positive to positive and negative to negative.

2 Battery – removal and refitting

1 The battery is on a carrier fitted to the left-hand wing valance of the engine compartment. It should be removed once every three months for cleaning and testing. Disconnect the negative and then the positive leads from the battery terminals by undoing and removing the

2.1 Battery cable connections

2.2 Battery securing clamp plate and bolt

plated nuts and bolts (photo). Note that two cables are attached to the positive terminal.

2   Unscrew and remove the bolt, and plain washer that secures the battery clamp plate to the carrier (photo). Lift away the clamp plate. Carefully lift the battery from its carrier and hold it vertically to ensure that none of the electrolyte is spilled.

3   Replacement is a direct reversal of this procedure. **Note:** *Refit the positive lead before the negative lead and smear the terminals with petroleum jelly to prevent corrosion. Never use an ordinary grease.*

3   Battery – maintenance and inspection

1   Normal weekly battery maintenance consists of checking the electrolyte level of each cell to ensure that the separators are covered by $\frac{1}{4}$ inch (6 mm) of electrolyte. If the level has fallen, top-up the battery using distilled water only. Do not overfill. If a battery is over-filled or any electrolyte spilled, immediately wipe away the excess as electrolyte attacks and corrodes any metal it comes into contact with very rapidly.

2   If the battery has the Auto-fill device as fitted on original produc-tion of the car, a special topping-up sequence is required. The white balls in the Auto-fill battery are part of the automatic topping-up device which ensures correct electrolyte level. The vent chamber should remain in position at all times except when topping-up or taking specific gravity readings. If the electrolyte level in any of the cells is below the bottom of the filling tube top-up as follows:

a) *Lift off the vent chamber cover*
b) *With the battery level, pour distilled water into the trough until all the filling tubes and trough are full*
c) *Immediately replace the cover to allow the water in the trough and tubes to flow into the cells. Each cell will automatically receive the correct amount of water*

3   As well as keeping the terminals clean and covered with petroleum jelly, the top of the battery, and especially the top of the cells, should be kept clean and dry. This helps prevent corrosion and ensures that the battery does not become partially discharged by leakage through dampness and dirt.

4   Once every three months remove the battery and inspect the battery securing bolts, the battery clamp plate, tray and battery leads for corrosion (white fluffy deposits on the metal which are brittle to touch). If any corrosion is found, clean off the deposit with ammonia and paint over the clean metal with an anti-rust/anti-acid paint.

5   At the same time inspect the battery case for cracks. If a crack is found, clean and plug it with one of the proprietary compounds marketed for this purpose. If leakage through the crack has been excessive, then it will be necessary to refill the appropriate cell with fresh electrolyte as detailed later. Cracks are frequently caused to the top of the battery by pouring in distilled water in the middle of winter *after* instead of *before* a run. This gives the water no chance to mix with the electrolyte and so the former freezes and splits the battery case.

6   If topping-up the battery becomes excessive and the case has been inspected for cracks that could cause leakage, but none are found, the battery is being overcharged.

7   With the battery on the bench at the three monthly interval check, measure the specific gravity with a hydrometer to determine the state of charge and condition of the electrolyte. There should be very little variation between the different cells and, if a variation in excess of 0·025 is present it will be due to either:

a) *Loss of electrolyte from the battery at some time caused by spillage or a leak, resulting in a drop in the specific gravity of the electrolyte when the deficiency was replaced with distilled water instead of fresh electrolyte*
b) *An internal short circuit caused by buckling of the plates or similar fault pointing to the likelihood of total battery failure in the near future*

8   The specific gravity of the electrolyte for fully charged conditions, at the electrolyte temperature indicated, is listed in Table A. The specific gravity of a fully discharged battery at different temperatures of the electrolyte is given in Table B.

Table A – Specific gravity – battery fully charged
1·268 at 100°F or 38°C electrolyte temperature
1·272 at 90°F or 32°C electrolyte temperature
1·276 at 80°F or 27°C electrolyte temperature
1·280 at 70°F or 21°C electrolyte temperature
1·284 at 60°F or 16°C electrolyte temperature
1·288 at 50°F or 10°C electrolyte temperature
1·292 at 40°F or 4°C electrolyte temperature
1·296 at 30°F or −1·5°C electrolyte temperature

Table B – Specific gravity – battery fully discharged
1·098 at 100°F or 38°C electrolyte temperature
1·102 at 90°F or 32°C electrolyte temperature
1·106 at 80°F or 27°C electrolyte temperature
1·110 at 70°F or 21°C electrolyte temperature
1·114 at 60°F or 16°C electrolyte temperature
1·118 at 50°F or 10°C electrolyte temperature
1·122 at 40°F or 4°C electrolyte temperature
1·126 at 30°F or −1·5°C electrolyte temperature

4   Battery – electrolyte replenishment

1   If the battery is in a fully charged state and one of the cells maintains a specific gravity reading which is 0·025 or more lower than the others, then it is likely that electrolyte has been lost from the cell at some time.

2   Top-up the cell with a solution of 1 part sulphuric acid to 2·5 parts of water. If the cell is already fully topped-up draw some electrolyte out of it with a pipette.

5   Battery – charging

1   In winter time when heavy demand is placed upon the battery, such as when starting from cold, and much electrical equipment is continually in use, it is a good idea to occasionally have the battery fully charged from an external source at the rate of 3·5 to 4 amps.

2   Continue to charge the battery at this rate, until no further rise in specific gravity is noted over a four hour period.

3   Alternatively, a trickle-charger charging at the rate of 1·5 amps can be safely used overnight.

4   Specially rapid 'boost' charges, which are claimed to restore the power of the battery in 1 to 2 hours, are not recommended as they can cause serious damage to the battery plates through overheating.

5   While charging the battery note that the temperature of the electrolyte should not exceed 100°F (37·8°C).

6   Alternator – general description

The main advantage of an alternator lies in its ability to provide a high charge at low revolutions. Driving slowly in heavy traffic, with a dynamo, invariably means no charge is reaching the battery. In similar conditions even with the wiper, heater, lights and perhaps radio switched on, the alternator will ensure a charge reaches the battery.

The three makes of alternator generate alternating current (ac) which is changed to a direct current (dc) by an internal diode system. They all have a regulator which limits the output to 14 volts maximum at all times. The regulator is mounted internally for Bosch and Lucas, and mounted on the inner wing for Femsa alternators. A warning lamp illuminates if the alternator fails to operate.

The alternator assembly basically consists of a fixed coil winding (stator) in an aluminium housing, which incorporates the mounting lugs. Inside this stator, rotates a shaft wound coil (rotor)). The shaft is supported at each end by ball-race bearings, which are lubricated for life.

Slip rings are used to conduct current to and from the rotor field coils via two carbon brushes which bear against them. By keeping the mean diameter of the slip rings to a minimum, relative speed between brushes and rings, and hence wear, are also minimal.

The rotor is belt-driven from the engine through a pulley keyed to the rotor shaft. A pressed steel fan adjacent to the pulley draws cooling air through the machine. This fan forms an integral part of the alternator specification. It has been designed to provide adequate air flow with a minimum of noise, and to withstand the high stresses associated with the maximum speed. Rotation is clockwise viewed on

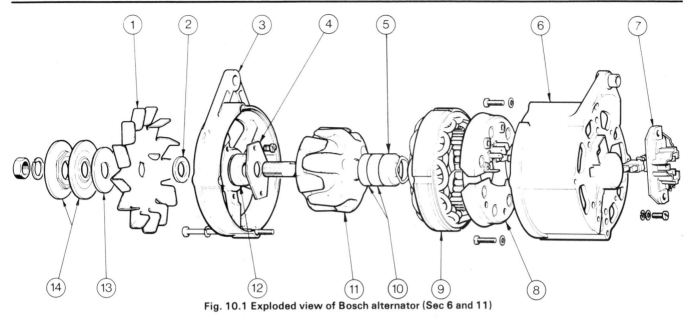

Fig. 10.1 Exploded view of Bosch alternator (Sec 6 and 11)

1	Fan	5	Slip ring end bearing	9	Stator	12	Drive end bearing
2	Spacer	6	Slip ring end housing	10	Slip rings	13	Spacer
3	Drive end housing	7	Brush box and regulator	11	Rotor	14	Pulley
4	Thrust plate	8	Rectifier (diode) pack				

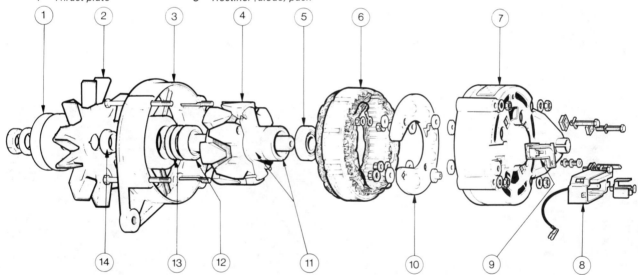

Fig. 10.2 Exploded view of Femsa alternator (Sec 6 and 12)

1	Pulley	5	Slip ring end bearing	9	Brush box	12	Drive end bearing
2	Fan	6	Stator	10	Rectifier (diode) box	13	Thrust washer
3	Drive end housing	7	Slip ring end housing	11	Slip rings	14	Spacer
4	Rotor	8	Terminal block				

the drive end.

The brush gear is housed in a moulding, screwed to the outside of the slip ring and bracket. This moulding thus encloses the slip ring and brush gear assembly, and together with the shielded bearing, protects the assembly against the entry of dust and moisture.

The regulator is set during manufacture and requires no further attention.

Electrical connections to external circuits are brought out to Lucas connector blades, these being grouped to accept a moulded connector socket which ensures correct connection. Detail design differences are shown in Fig. 10.1, 10.2 and 10.3.

7 Alternator – routine maintenance

1   The equipment has been designed for the minimum amount of maintenance in service, the only items subject to wear being the brushes and bearings.

2   Brushes should be examined after about 75 000 miles (120 000 km) and renewed if necessary. The bearings are pre-packed with grease for life, and should not require further attention.

3   Check the fan belt every 3000 miles (5000 km) for correct adjustment which should be 0·5 inch (13 mm) total movement at the centre of the run between the alternator and water pump pulleys.

8 Alternator – special procedures

Whenever the electrical system of the car is being attended to, or external means of starting the engine are used, there are certain precautions that must be taken otherwise serious and expensive damage can result.

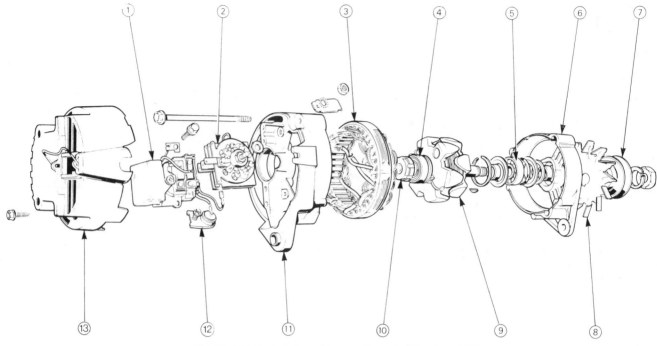

Fig. 10.3 Exploded view of Lucas alternator (Sec 6 and 13)

1 Regulator
2 Rectifier (diode) pack
3 Stator
4 Slip ring end bearing

5 Drive end bearing
6 Drive end housing
7 Pulley

8   Fan
9   Rotor
10 Slip ring

11 Slip ring end housing
12 Surge protection diode
13 End cover

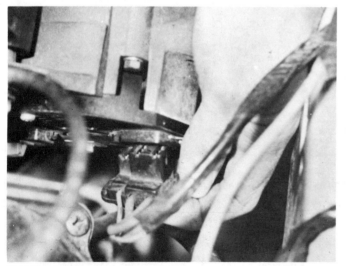

9.2 Disconnecting the multi-pin connector

9.4 Removing the alternator

1   Always make sure that the negative terminal of the battery is earthed. If the terminal connections are accidentally reversed or if the battery has been reverse charged, the alternator diodes will burn out.
2   The output terminal on the alternator marked 'BAT' or B+ must never be earthed but should always be connected directly to the positive terminal of the battery.
3   Whenever the alternator is to be removed, or when disconnecting the terminals of the alternator circuit, always disconnect the battery earth terminal first.
4   The alternator must never be operated without the battery to alter-

nator cable connected.
5   Should it be necessary to use a booster charger or booster battery to start the engine, always double check that the negative cable is connected to negative terminal and the positive cable to positive terminal.

9 Alternator – removal and refitting

1   Disconnect the battery leads.
2   Release the spring clip and disconnect the multi-pin connector

from the rear of the alternator (photo).

3   Loosen the alternator mounting bolts and push the alternator inwards towards the engine and remove the fan-belt from the pulley.

4   Remove the alternator mounting bolts and lift the alternator out of the engine compartment (photo).

5   Take care not to knock or drop the alternator as this can cause irrepairable damage.

6   Refitting the alternator is the reverse of the removal procedure. Adjust the tension of the fan-belt so that it has 0·5 in (13 mm) deflection at the centre of the run between the alternator and water pump pulley.

10 Alternator – fault finding and repair

Owing to the specialist knowledge and equipment required to test or service an alternator it is recommended that if the performance is suspect, the car be taken to an automobile electrician who will have the facilities for such work. Because of this recommendation, information is limited to the inspection and renewal of the brushes. Should the alternator not charge or the system be suspect, the following points may be checked before seeking further assistance:

1   Check the fan-belt tension, as described in Section 7.

2   Check the battery, as described in Section 3.

3   Check all electrical cable connections for cleanliness and security.

11 Alternator brushes (Bosch) – inspection, removal and refitting

1   Undo and remove the two screws, spring washers and plain washers that secure the brush box to the rear of the brush end housing (See Fig. 10.1). Lift away the brush box.

2   Check that the carbon brushes are able to slide smoothly in their guides without any sign of binding.

3   Measure the length of the brushes and if they have worn down to 0·2 inch (5 mm) or less, they must be renewed.

4   Hold the brush wire with a pair of engineer's pliers and unsolder it from the brush box. Lift away the two brushes.

5   Insert the new brushes (Fig. 10.4), and check to make sure that they are free to move in their guides. If they bind, lightly polish with a very fine file.

6   Solder the brush wire ends to the brush box, taking care that solder is allowed to pass to the stranded wire.

7   Whenever new brushes are fitted, new springs should be fitted.

8   Refitting the brush box is the reverse sequence to removal.

12 Alternator brushes (Femsa) – inspection, removal and refitting

1   Disconnect the wire from the brush box at the rear of the alternator, remove the retaining screw and withdraw the brush box (Fig. 10.2).

2   Measure the length of the brushes and if they have worn down to 0·3 in (7 mm) or less, they must be renewed.

3   Insert the new brushes (Fig. 10.5) and check to make sure that they are free to move in their guides. If they bind, lightly polish with a very fine file.

4   Refitting the brush box is the reverse sequence to removal.

13 Alternator brushes (Lucas) – inspection, removal and refitting

1   Refer to Fig. 10.3 and undo and remove the two screws that hold on the end cover. Lift away the end cover.

2   Remove the brush retaining screws (Fig. 10.6) and withdraw the brushes from the brush box.

3   Measure the length of the brushes and if they have worn down to 0·2 in (5 mm) or less, they must be renewed.

4   Insert the new brushes and check to make sure that they are free to move in their guides. If they bind, lightly polish with a very fine file.

5   Reassemble in the reverse order of dismantling. Make sure that leads which may have been connected to any of the screws are reconnected correctly.

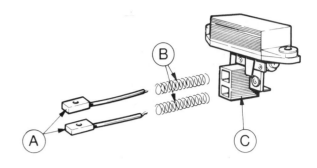

Fig. 10.4 Bosch brush box assembly (Sec 11)

A Brushes   C Brush box
B Springs

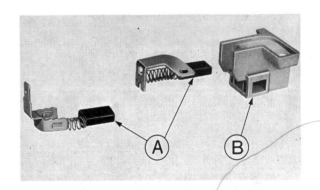

Fig. 10.5 Femsa brush box assembly (Sec 12)

A Brushes   B Brush box

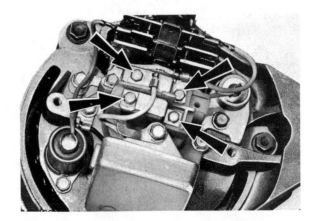

Fig. 10.6 Lucas brush securing screws (Sec 13)

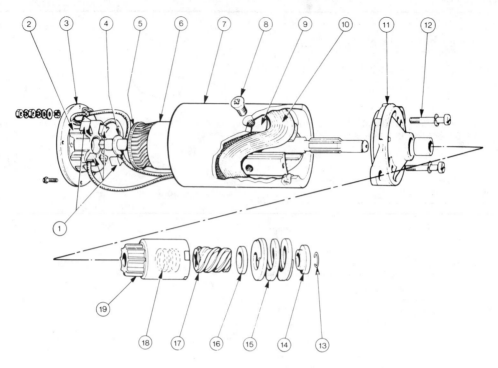

Fig. 10.7 Inertia starter motor (Sec 14 and 18)

1	Brushes	7	Main casing	11	Drive end plate	15	Cushion spring
2	Brushbox moulding	8	Pole piece retaining	12	Drive end plate retaining	16	Cushion washer
3	Commutator end plate		screw		screws	17	Screwed sleeve
4	Thrust washer	9	Pole piece	13	'C' clip	18	Anti-drift spring
5	Commutator	10	Field winding	14	Spring cup	19	Drive pinion
6	Armature						

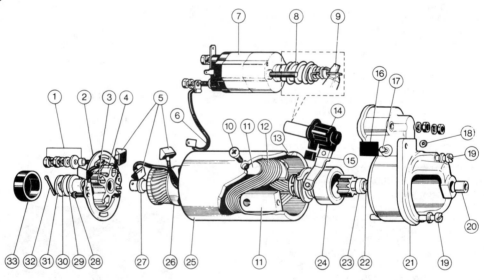

Fig. 10.8 Pre-engaged starter motor (Sec 14 and 17)

1	Terminal nuts and washers	9	Actuating lever	18	Retaining clip	26	Armature
2	Commutator end plate	10	Pole screw	19	Housing retaining screws (2)	27	Thrust washer
3	Brush housing	11	Pole shoe	20	Bearing bush	28	Commutator end plate retaining screws (2)
4	Brush springs	12	Field coils	21	Drive end housing	29	Bearing bush
5	Brushes	13	Field to earth connection	22	Jump ring	30	Thrust plate
6	Connector link, solenoid to starter	14	Rubber seal	23	Thrust collar	31	Shim washer
7	Solenoid unit	15	Rubber dust pad	24	Drive assembly	32	Cotter pin
8	Return spring	16	Rubber dust cover	25	Main casing	33	Dust cover
		17	Pivot pin				

14 Starter motor – general description

The starter motors fitted are of Lucas manufacture, and of either the inertial or pre-engaged type.

Both types are series wound, four pole, four brush motors. The bushgear is fully insulated, and comprises wedge shaped brushes actuated by coil springs onto the commutator face. The main case has two independently fixed end plates. The commutator end plate screws into the main body, while the drive end plate screws into the pole pieces. Access to the brushes is by removing the commutator end plate. The drive pinion fitted to the inertia motor runs on a screwed sleeve with an internal spline (Fig. 10.7). This sleeve, the pinion and the cushion spring are retained on the shaft by a 'C' clip. The pre-'engaged type of motor is fitted with a pre-engagement solenoid (Fig. 10.8).

Incorporated in the pinion assembly is a roller clutch which is able to transmit torque from the starter motor to the engine, but not in the reverse direction, thereby ensuring that the armature is not driven by the engine at any time.

The solenoid comprises a soft-iron plunger, starter switch contacts, main closing winding (series winding) and a hold on (short winding). When the starter ignition switch is operated both the coils are energised in parallel but the closing winding is shorted out by the starter switch contacts when they are closed.

The operating position of the engaging lever in the drive end bracket is pre-set and cannot be altered. This eliminates setting the pinion position to obtain the correct operation of the actuating solenoid. The lever pivots on a non-adjustable pivot pin, which is retained in the drive end bracket by a special type of retaining ring, which is a spring fit into a groove in the pin.

15 Starter motor – testing on engine

1   If the starter motor fails to operate, then check the condition of the battery by turning on the headlamps. If they flow brightly for several seconds and then gradually dim, the battery is in a discharged condition.

2   If the headlights continue to glow brightly and it is obvious that the battery is in good condition, then check the tightness of the battery wiring connections, in particular the earth lead from the battery terminal to its connection on the body frame. If the positive terminal on the battery becomes hot when an attempt is made to work the starter, this is a sure sign of a poor connection on the battery terminal. To rectify, remove the terminal, clean the mating faces thoroughly and reconnect. Check the connections on the rear of the starter solenoid. Check the wiring with a voltmeter or test lamp for breaks or shorts.

3   *On pre-engaged type starter motors,* test the continuity of the solenoid windings by connecting a test lamp circuit comprising a 12

volt battery and low wattage bulb between the STA terminal and the solenoid body. If the two windings are in order, the lamp will light. Next connect the test lamp (fitted with a high wattage bulb) between the solenoid main terminals. Energise the solenoid by applying a 12 volt supply between the unmarked 'Lucar' terminal and the solenoid body. The solenoid should be heard to operate and the test bulb light. This indicates full closure of the solenoid contacts.

4   *On inertia type starter motors,* check the solenoid by bridging the large solenoid terminals with a heavy cable. If the starter motor then operates, the solenoid is at fault.

5   If the battery is fully charged, the wiring in order, and the starter/ignition switch working and the starter motor still fails to operate, then it will have to be removed from the car for examination. Before this is done, ensure that the starter motor pinion has not jammed in mesh with the flywheel by engaging a gear *not automatic* and rocking the car to-and-fro. This should free the pinion if it is stuck in-mesh with the flywheel teeth.

16 Starter motor – removal and refitting

1   Disconnect the positive and negative terminals from the battery.

2   Make a note of the cable connections to the rear of the solenoid and detach the cable terminals from the solenoid. **Note:** *On inertia starter motors there is only one cable to remove from the motor.*

3   Undo and remove the starter motor, securing nuts, bolts and spring washers and lift away the starter motor.

4   Refitting is the reverse sequence of removal.

17 Starter motor (pre-engaged) – dismantling and reassembly

1   Clamp the starter motor in a vice with soft jaws, and remove the plastic cap from the commutator end plate.

2   Remove the retaining clip from the end of the armature shaft and discard the clip. Remove the thrust washer.

3   Disconnect and remove the connecting cable from the end of the solenoid. Remove the two securing nuts and washers and guide the solenoid away from the drive end housing. Unhook the solenoid armature from the actuating lever by moving it upwards and away from the lever (Fig. 10.8).

4   Remove the two drive end housing screws and guide the housing and armature assembly away from the body.

5   Remove the armature from the end housing, unhooking the actuating arm from the pinion assembly (Fig. 10.9). Remove the rubber block and sleeve from the housing.

6   Drive the pivot pin from the end housing, and remove the actuating lever. Discard the pivot pin clip, which will be distorted (Fig. 10.10).

7   If it is necessary to dismantle the starter pinion drive, place the

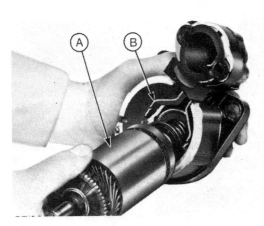

Fig. 10.9 Unhooking the pre-engaged actuating arm (Sec 17)

A Armature   B Arm

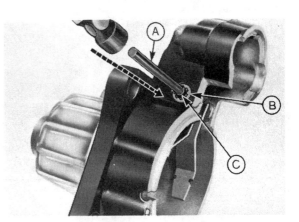

Fig. 10.10 Driving out the pivot pin (Sec 17)

A Drift   B Clip   C Pivot pin

armature between soft faces in a bench vice and using a universal puller draw the jump ring from the armature.

8 Tap down the circlip retaining cover and remove the washer, circlip and cover. The pinion assembly may now be removed.

9 Draw the actuating bush towards the pinion so as to expose the circlip and remove the circlip, bush, spring and large washer. It is very important that the one way clutch is not gripped in the vice at the point adjacent to the pinion whilst this is being carried out otherwise the clutch will be damaged.

10 The drive pinion and one way clutch are serviced as a complete assembly, so if one part is worn or damaged a new assembly must be obtained.

11 Remove the four commutator end plate screws and carefully tap the plate free from the body. Withdraw the plate slightly, remove the two field winding brushes and remove the plate.

12 To renew the field winding brushes, their flexible connectors must be cut leaving 0·25 in (7 mm) attached to the field coils. Discard the old brushes. Solder new brushes to the flexible connector studs. Check that the new brushes move freely in their holders.

13 The main terminal stud and its two brushes are available as a unit. To remove, take off the nut, washer and insulator and push the stud and second insulator through the end plate.

14 If cleaning the commutator with petrol fails to remove all the burnt areas and spots, then wrap a piece of glass paper round the commutator and rotate the armature.

15 If the commutator is very badly worn, remove the drive gear, (if still in place on the armature), and mount the armature in a lathe. With the lathe turning at high speed take a very fine cutout of the commutator and finish the surface by polishing with glass paper. *Do not undercut the mica insulators between the commutator segments. The minimum commutator thickness must never be less than 0·08 in (2 mm).*

16 With the starter motor dismantled, test the four field coils for an open circuit. Connect a 12 volt battery with a 12 volt bulb in one of the leads between the field terminal post and the tapping point of the field coils to which the brushes are connected. An open circuit is proved by the bulb not lighting.

17 If the bulb lights, it does not necessarily mean that the field coils are in order, as there is a possibility that one of the coils will be earthed to the starter yoke or pole shoes. To check this, remove the lead from the brush connector and place it against a clean portion of the starter yoke. If the bulb lights, then the field coils are earthing. Replacement of the field coils calls for the use of a wheel operated screwdriver, a soldering iron, caulking and riveting operations and is beyond the scope of the majority of owners. The starter yoke should be taken to a reputable electrical engineering works for new field coils to be fitted. Alternatively purchase an exchange starter motor.

18 If the armature is damaged this will be evident after visual inspection. Look for signs of burning, discolouration, and for conductors that have lifted away from the commutator.

19 With the starter motor stripped down, check the condition of the bushes. They should be renewed when they are sufficiently worn to allow visible side movement of the armature shaft.

20 The old bushes are simply driven out with a suitable drift and the new bushes inserted by the same method. As the bushes are of the phosphor bronze type it is essential that they are allowed to stand in engine oil for at least 24 hours before fitment. If time does not allow, place the bushes in oil at 100°C (212°F) for 2 hours.

21 Reassembly is the reverse sequence to dismantling, but the following points should be noted:

a) *When refitting the drive end housing, the peg on the housing should align with the notch in the casing (Fig. 10.11)*

b) *New retaining clips should be fitted to the actuating arm pivot pin and the armature shaft*

c) *When fitting the clip to the armature shaft end it should be pressed home firmly to eliminate any endfloat in the shaft*

18 Starter motor (inertia) – dismantling and reassembly

1 The procedure is basically similar to that for the pre-engaged starter motor, Section 17, with the following differences.

2 There is no retaining clip at the commutator end of the armature shaft.

3 The armature, drive end plate and pinion are removed as an assembly after removing the two retaining screws (Fig. 10.7).

4 Remove the drive pinion by compressing the large cushion spring and removing the C clip. (A small proprietary tool is available for this purpose). Remove the spring and drive pinion, then pull the drive end plate from the armature shaft.

19 Flasher circuit – fault tracing and rectification

1 The actual flasher unit consists of a small container positioned at the rear of the instrument panel.

2 If the flasher unit works twice as fast as usual when indicating either right or left turns, this is an indication that there is a broken filament, in the front or rear indicator bulb, on the side operating too quickly.

3 If the external flshers are working, but the internal flasher warning light has ceased to function, check the filament of the warning bulb and renew if necessary.

4 If a flasher bulb is sound but does not work, check all the flasher circuit connections with the aid of the wiring diagram.

5 With the ignition switched on, check that the current is reaching the flasher unit by connecting a voltmeter between the plug terminal and earth. If it is found that current is reaching the unit, connect the two flasher unit terminals together and operate the direction indicator switch. If one of the flasher warning lights comes on this proves that the flasher unit itself is at fault and must be renewed as it is not possible to dismantle and repair it.

20 Wiper mechanism – maintenance

1 Renew the screen wiper blades at intervals of 12 000 miles (20 000 km) or 12 months, or more frequently if found necessary.

2 The washer round the wheelbox spindle can be lubricated with several drops of glycerine every 6000 miles (10 000 km). The screen wiper linkage pivots may be lubricated with a little engine oil.

21 Wiper blades – removal and refitting

1 Lift the wiper arm away from the windscreen.

2 Press the spring clip to release the wiper-blade pivot and slide the wiper blade off the arm (photo).

3 Refitting is the reversal of the removal procedure.

22 Wiper arms – removal and refitting

1 Before removing a wiper arm, turn the wiper switch on and off to ensure that the arms are in their normal parked position.

2 Lift up the pivoted cap to expose the wiper-arm retaining nut (photo).

3 Remove the retaining nut and lift off the washer and wiper arm.

4 With the linkage in the parked position, fit the wiper arm on the pivot shaft. Fit the washer and retaining nut and press down the pivoted cap.

23 Wiper mechanism – fault diagnosis and rectification

1 Should the wipers fail, or work very slowly, then check the terminals on the motor for loose connections and make sure the insulation of all wiring has not been damaged, thus causing a short circuit. If this is in order, then check the current taken by the motor by connecting an ammeter in the circuit and turning on the wiper switch. Consumption should be between 2·3 and 3·1 amps.

2 If no current is passing through the motor, check that the switch is operating correctly.

3 If the wiper motor takes a very high current, check the wiper blades for freedom of movement. If this is satisfactory, check the gearbox cover and gear assembly for damage.

4 If the motor takes a very low current ensure that the battery is fully charged. Check the brush gear and ensure the brushes are bearing on the commutator. If not, check the brushes for freedom of movement and, if necessary, renew the tension springs. If the brushes are very worn, they should be replaced with new ones. Check the armature by substitution, if this part is suspect.

24 Wiper motor and linkage (front) – removal and refitting

1   For safety reasons disconnect the battery. Undo and remove the fixing screw and unclip the plastic wiper motor cover. Lift away the cover (photo).

2   Remove the five bolts and lift the wiper linkage cover plate clear. Note that one of these bolts secures the motor earth lead.

3   Undo and remove the bolts that secure the wiper assembly mounting bracket to the bulkhead, detach the multi-pin plug from the motor (photo).

4   Carefully lever off the wiper system linkage from the windscreen wiper motor. Undo and remove the three bolts and spring washers that secure the motor to the bracket assembly.

5   Undo and remove the bolts that secure the heater unit and draw the heater unit box to one side just sufficiently for the wiper motor and bracket assembly to be withdrawn.

6   Refer to Section 22 and remove the wiper arms and blades.

7   Carefully unscrew the spindle nuts and washers and, working within the engine compartment, lift away the wiper linkage (Fig. 10.12).

8   Refitting is the reverse sequence to removal. Lubricate all moving parts with engine oil, with the exception of the wiper spindles. Lubricate the wiper spindles with three drops of glycerine.

21.2 Removing the windscreen wiper blade

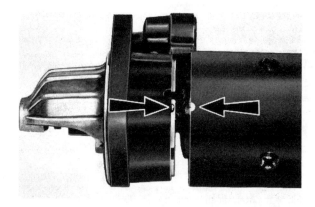

Fig. 10.11 Drive end housing to casing alignment (Sec 17)

22.2 Wiper arm retaining nut

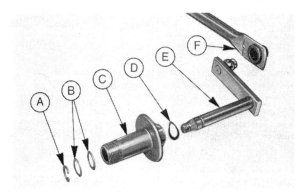

Fig. 10.12 Front wiper spindle components (Sec 24)

A Circlip   D Wave washer
B Shim and washer   E Pivot shaft
C Bush and housing   F Linkage

24.1 Removing the windscreen wiper motor cover

Fig. 10.13 Rear wiper motor bracket (Sec 25)

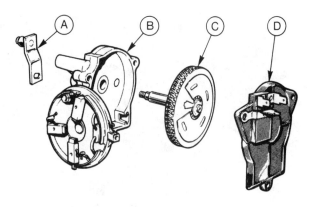

Fig. 10.14 Wiper motor assembly (Sec 26)

A *Operating arm*   B *Brushes*

C *Gear*   D *Cover plate*

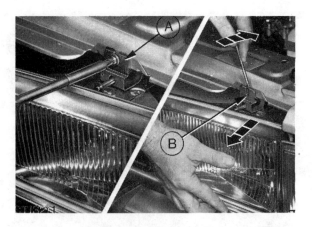

Fig. 10.15 Removing the headlight assembly (Sec 28)

A *Retaining screw*   B *Adjuster bracket*

25 Wiper motor and linkage (rear) – removal and refitting

1   For safety reasons disconnect the battery. Refer to Section 22, and remove the wiper arm and blade.
2   Lift off the spindle nut cover and remove the spindle nut, washer and seal.
3   Carefully remove the tailgate inner trim panel, and remove the three bolts securing the mounting bracket (Fig. 10.13).
    Remove the earth lead securing screw, disconnect the multi-plug and remove the motor and linkage assembly.
5   Prise the linkage from the motor link, remove the three bolts and detach the wiper motor.
6   Refitting is the reverse sequence of removal.

26 Wiper motor – dismantling, inspection and reassembly

1   Refer to Fig.14 ; undo and remove the two crosshead screws that secure the gearbox cover plate to the gearbox.
2   Undo and remove the nut that secures the operating arm to the gear shaft. Lift away the operating arm, wave washers and plain washers. Note the position of the arm relative to the 'park' cut-out segment of the gear contact plate.
3   Release the spring clips that secure the case and armature to the gearbox. Lift away the case and armature.
4   Wipe away all the grease from inside the gearbox and using a pair of circlip pliers remove the circlip that secures the gear to the shaft. Separate the gear from the shaft.
5   Undo and remove the screw that secures the brush mounting plate, detach the wiring loom plug and remove the brushes.
6   Clean all parts and then inspect the gears and brushes for wear or damage. Refit the spindle and check for wear in its bush in the gearbox body. Obtain new parts as necessary.
7   Reassembly is the reverse sequence to dismantling. Pack the gearbox with grease.

27 Horn – fault tracing and rectification

1   If the horn works badly or fails completely, first check the wiring leading to the horn for short circuits and loose connections. Also check that the horn is firmly secured and that there is nothing lying on the horn body (photo).
2   Using a test lamp check the wiring to the number 1 fuse on the fuse box located in the engine compartment. Check that the fuse has not blown.
3   If the fault is an internal one it will be necessary to obtain a new horn.
4   To remove the horn, disconnect the battery and remove the radiator grille.
5   Detach the lead at the rear of the horn and then undo and remove the retaining bolt, spring, horn bracket and star-washer.
6   Refitting the horn is the reverse sequence of removal.

28 Headlight assembly – removal and refitting

1   If the headlight bulb only is to be replaced, refer to Section 29.
2   Open the bonnet and for safety reasons, disconnect the battery.
3   Remove the single headlight retaining screw, unclip the adjuster bracket and lift the assembly forwards (Fig. 10.15), (photos).
4   Pull the multi-plug from the rear and remove the sidelight bulb by twisting and pulling clear (photo).
5   Remove the headlight bulb (Section 29) and unclip the headlight adjusters and the lower location guide.
6   Refitting is a reversal of this procedure, but ensure that the two adjuster guides are located with the respective body lugs.

29 Headlight bulb – removal and refitting

1   For safety reasons, disconnect the battery.
2   From inside the bonnet, pull off the multi-plug at the rear of the headlight. Pull off the rubber gaiter (photos).

24.3 Disconnect the wiper motor multi-pin plug

27.1 The horn is mounted behind the radiator grille

28.3a Remove the headlight retaining screw ...

28.3b ... and unclip the adjuster bracket

29.2a Pull off the multi-pin plug at the rear of the headlight ...

29.2b ... and remove the rubber gaiter

29.3a Twist the retaining ring anti-clockwise ...

29.3b ... then lift out the ring and bulb

31.2 Removing the sidelight bulb

3   Twist the bulb retaining ring anti-clockwise and lift out the ring and bulb (photos). **Note:** *The glass of the headlight bulb should **not** be touched with the fingers. If it is touched with the fingers it should be washed with methylated spirit.*
4   Refitting is a reversal of the above procedure.

30 Headlight and auxiliary light alignment

1   It is always advisable to have the lights aligned using special optical beam setting equipment but if this is not available the following procedure may be used.
2   Position the car on level ground, 10 ft (3 m) in front of a dark wall or board. The wall or board must be at right angles to the centre-line of the car.
3   Draw a vertical line on the board in line with the centre-line of the car.
4   Bounce the car on its suspension to ensure correct settlement and then measure the height between the ground and the centre of the lights.
5   Measure the distance between the centres of the lights to be adjusted, and mark the board as show in Figs. 10.16 and 10.17.
6   *Headlights* With the headlights on main beam, cover the other light(s) to prevent glare. By careful adjustment to the two adjusters at

the rear of the headlight assembly, set the horizontal position until point 'C' (Fig. 10.16) is at the cross on the aiming board. Adjust the vertical light position so that the top of the beam pattern just touches the dotted line (Fig. 10.16).
7   *Auxiliary lights* Turn the auxiliary lights on and cover the other lights to prevent glare. Slacken the lamp retaining nut and adjust until the centre of illumination lies at the area shown in Fig. 10.17.

31 Sidelight bulb – removal and refitting

1   The sidelight bulb is fitted within the headlamp assembly, and can be renewed from inside the engine compartment.
2   Disconnect the sidelight from the headlight assembly by twisting it anti-clockwise and pulling clear (Fig. 10.18). Remove the bayonet type bulb from the holder.
3   Refit the bulb, then push the holder into the headlight and twist clockwise to secure. Note that the lugs on the holder are not symmetrical, so that the holder can only be fitted in one position.

32 Front direction indicator light assembly and bulb – removal and refitting

1   From inside the engine compartment, disconnect the indicator wire and push it through the inner wing.
2   Working under the wheel arch, undo and remove the two retaining nuts and push the light assembly forwards away from its location in the front wing.
3   Refitting is the reverse sequence of removal.
4   If it is necessary to remove the bulb undo and remove the two crosshead screws that secure the lens to the light body. Lift away the lens (Fig. 10.19).
5   To detach the bulb press in and turn in an anti-clockwise direction to release the bayonet fixing and lift away the bulb. Refitting the bulb and lens is the reverse sequence of removal. Make sure that the lens gasket is correctly fitted to prevent dirt and water ingress (photo).

33 Rear direction indicator, stop and tail light bulbs – removal and refitting

1   *Saloon* Open the luggage compartment and pull off the protective cover from the rear of the lamp assembly (photo).
2   Press the retaining clip (Fig. 10.20) sideways and remove the bulb plate, then lift out the appropriate bulb. Refitting is the reverse sequence of removal (photo).
3   *Estate car:* Remove the two crosshead screws securing the lens to the rear of the vehicle, and renew the appropriate bulb (Fig. 10.21).

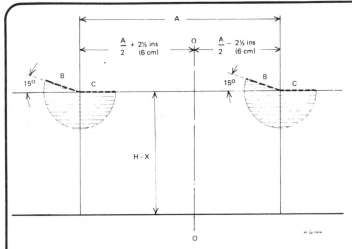

Fig. 10.16 Headlight alignment (Sec 30)

A   Distance between light centres
B   Dipped beam pattern
H   Height from ground to headlight centre
X   3.0 in (76 mm)
OO Vehicle centre line

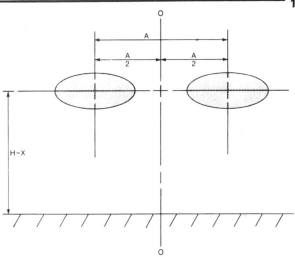

Fig. 10.17 Auxiliary lamp alignment (Sec 30)

A   Distance between lamp centres
H   Height from ground to lamp centre
X   2.0 in (50 mm)
OO Vehicle centre line

Fig. 10.18 Removing side light bulb (Sec 31)

A Holder   B Bulb
       C Location in headlight

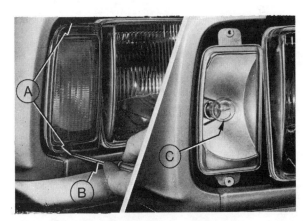

Fig. 10.19 Removing front direction indicator light bulb (Sec 32)

A Lens securing screws   B Screwdriver
           C Bulb

32.5 Refitting the front indicator light lens

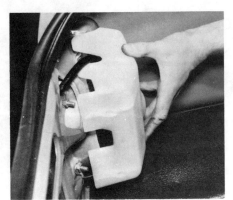

33.1 Removing the rear light cluster protective cover

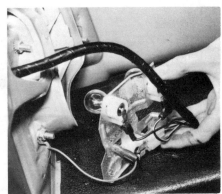

33.2 Rear light cluster bulb plate removed

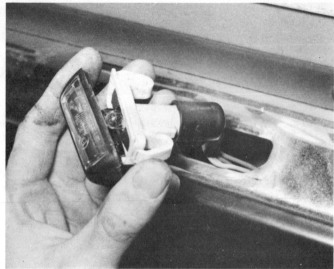

35.1 Removing the number plate light

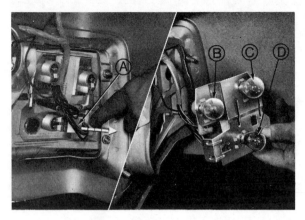

Fig. 10.20 Rear direction indicator, stop and tail light assembly (Sec 33)

A Securing tab
C Reverse light bulb
B Indicator bulb
D Stop/tail light bulb

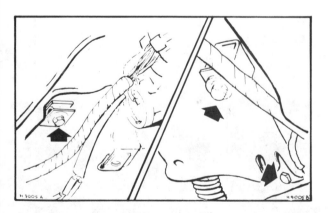

Fig. 10.21 Rear direction indicator, stop, tail and reverse light assembly – estate car (Sec 33)

A Indicator bulb
C Stop light bulb
B Tail light bulb
D Reverse light bulb

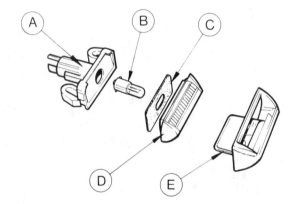

Fig. 10.22 Number plate light assembly (Sec 25)

A Body
C Gasket
B Bulb
D Lens
E Lens cover

Fig. 10.23 Steering column securing bolts (Sec 37)

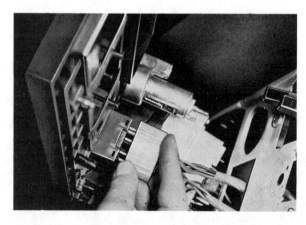

Fig. 10.24 Disconnecting multi-connectors at back of instruments (Sec 37)

34 Rear direction indicator, stop and tail light assembly – removal and refitting

1 *Saloon:* Refer to Section 33 to remove the lamp cover and lamp plate.
2 Remove the four retaining nuts and screws, and the earth wire, and lift the lamp assembly from the rear.
3 Refitting is the reverse sequence. Do not forget to reconnect the earth wire.
4 *Estate car:* With the rear seat's back folded forward, take out the two crosshead screws from the top edge of the rear trim panel, and unclip the panel.
5 Remove the two light assembly securing nuts and washers, and lift away the assembly.
6 Disconnect the wiring after carefully noting which wire goes to which light.
7 Refitting is a reversal of the above procedure.

35 Rear number plate light assembly and bulb – removal and refitting

1 From underneath the bumper, gently squeeze the two plastic clips inwards, and lift out the lamp (photo).
2 Pull off the two Lucar connectors.
3 Gently prise off the lens cover, which is retained by two lugs, lift away the lens and remove the bayonet bulb (Fig. 10.22).
4 Refitting the bulb, lens and assembly is the reverse sequence to removal. Take care to ensure that the lens sealing washer is correctly fitted to prevent dirt and water ingress.

36 Interior light – removal and refitting

1 Very carefully pull the interior light assembly from the location in the roof panel.
2 Disconnect the wires from the terminal connectors and lift away the light unit.
3 If the bulb requires renewal either lift the bulb from its clips (festoon type) or press and turn in an anti-clockwise direction (bayonet cap type).
4 Refitting the interior light is the reverse sequence of removal.

37 Instrument cluster and printed circuit – removal and refitting

1 Open the bonnet and disconnect the battery leads.
2 Unscrew the lower shroud from the steering column and remove it; then unclip the upper half.
3 Loosen the three steering column securing bolts (Fig. 10.23) so that the column can drop down approximately 0·25 in (6·35 mm) to give clearance for removal of the instrument panel.
4 Pull off the instrument panel light switch knob and the two radio control knobs.
5 Remove the six countersunk screws which retain the instrument cluster and its bezel.
6 Holding the bezel assembly square to the dashpanel, pull it forward far enough to allow disconnection of the two multi-connectors at the back of the instruments, also the leads from the cigar lighter, the hazard flasher switch and the heated rear window switch (Fig. 10.24).
7 Disconnect the speedometer cable from the speedometer by pressing on the grooved section of the sleeve (Fig. 10.25), and then remove the instrument cluster and bezel.
8 The instruments, warning light bulbs and their holders, and the printed circuit can now all be removed from the instrument assembly.
9 Refitting is a reversal of removal.

38 Instrument voltage regulator – removal and refitting

1 Remove the instrument panel, as described in the preceding Section.
2 Unscrew and remove the single screw which secures the voltage regulator to the printed circuit and withdraw it.
3 Refitting is a reversal of this procedure.

39 Instruments, warning lights and illumination lights – removal and refitting

1 Remove the instrument cluster (refer to Section 37).
2 The exact details concerning the number and type of securing nuts and/or screws will vary according to the instrument concerned, but this will be obvious from inspection.
3 Whenever the instrument cluster is dismantled, care must be taken not to crease or tear the printed circuit films, used to replace large clusters of wires.
4 When reassembling the instrument cluster, ensure that all printed circuit films and instrument housings are correctly located before tightening the fixing.
5 All light bulb holders should be twisted anti-clockwise for removal. The bayonet bulbs are also twisted anti-clockwise for removal.
6 Refitting the instrument cluster is the reverse sequence of removal.

40 Speedometer inner and outer cable – removal and refitting

1 *Manual gearbox:* Working under the car using a pair of circlip pliers, remove the circlip that secures the speedometer cable to the gearbox extension housing and withdraw the speedometer cable (Fig. 10.26).
2 *Automatic transmission:* Undo and remove the bolt, and spring washer that secures the forked plate to the extension housing. Lift away the forked plate and withdraw the speedometer cable.
3 Remove the clip that secures the speedometer outer cable to the bulkhead.

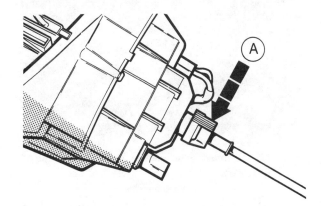

Fig. 10.25 Disconnecting the speedometer cable from the speedometer (Sec 37)

A Sleeve

Fig. 10.26 Disconnect the speedometer cable from the gearbox (Sec 40)

A Cable   *B Circlip*

42.2 Steering column switches with shroud removed

45.1 Fuse box with cover removed

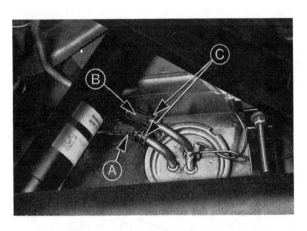

Fig. 10.27 Removing the fuel tank indicator unit (Sec 41)

A Return pipe   B Feed pipe
C Securing clips

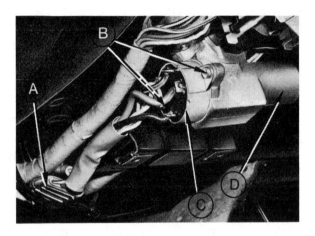

Fig. 10.28 Ignition switch and steering lock assembly (Sec 43)

A Multi-connector   B Securing screws
C Ignition switch   D Steering lock

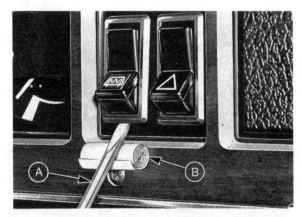

Fig. 10.29 Removing instrument panel switches (Sec 44)

A Screwdriver   B Protective pad

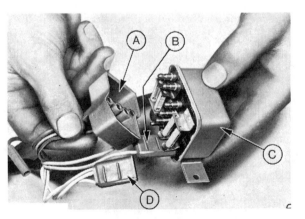

Fig. 10.30 Headlamp relay (Sec 46)

A Multi-connector cover   B Loom connector
C Relay   D Loom connector

4   Working under the facia depress the knurled pad on the speedometer cable ferrule and pull the cable from the speedometer head (Fig. 10.25).

5   Remove the grommet that seals the cable to the bulkhead. Withdraw the speedometer cable.

6   Refitting the speedometer cable is the reverse sequence of removal.

7   It is possible to remove the inner cable, whilst the outer cable is still attached to the car. Follow the instructions in paragraphs 1 and 4 and pull the inner cable from the outer cable.

41 Fuel tank indicator unit – removal and refitting

1   With the level of petrol in the tank lower than the bottom of the indicator unit, wipe the area around the unit free of dirt.

2   Detach the indicator unit cables, fuel feed and return pipes, and note their correct location (Fig. 10.27).

3   Using two crossed screwdrivers in the slots of the indicator unit body, or a soft metal drift carefully unlock the indicator unit. Lift away the indicator unit and sealing ring.

4   Refitting the indicator unit is the reverse sequence of removal. Always fit a new seal in the recess in the tank to ensure no leaks develop.

42 Steering column switches – removal and refitting

1   Open the bonnet and for safety reasons, disconnect the battery.

2   Unscrew the lower shroud from the steering column and remove it. Then unclip the upper half (photo).

3   Detach the multi-pin plugs from the underside of the switch.

4   Undo and remove the two screws and shakeproof washers located on the lever side of the switch and detach the switch assembly from the steering column.

5   Refitting the switch is the reverse sequence of removal.

43 Ignition switch and lock – removal and refitting

Ignition switch

1   The ignition switch can be removed by unscrewing the lower dash trim panel in the steering column area, and lowering the panel.

2   The switch is then removed by unscrewing the two screws, and disconnecting the multi-plug (Fig. 10.28).

Steering lock

3   To remove the steering lock refer to Chapter 11, Section 24 for the removal of the steering column.

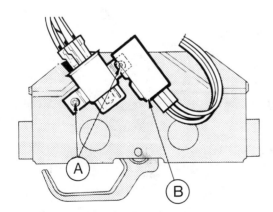

Fig. 10.31 Removing heated rear window relay (Sec 46)

A Heated rear window relay securing screws   *B Indicator relay*

4   Secure the steering column in a vice fitted with jaw protectors and drill out the two shear-bolts which retain the two halves of the steering column lock to the column.

5   Commence reassembly by fitting the new lock to the steering column so that the lock tongue engages in the cut-out in the column. Tighten the bolts slightly more than finger-tight and check the operation of the lock by inserting the ignition key. Move the lock assembly fractionally if necessary to ensure smooth and positive engagement when the key is turned.

6   Fully tighten the bolts until the heads shear.

7   Refit the steering column, refer to Chapter 11, Section 24.

44 Instrument panel switches – removal and refitting

1   The switches are removed from the instrument panel by inserting a screwdriver at their lower edge and then levering them from their locations. **Note:** *Use a pad of suitable material to prevent damage to the instrument panel* (Fig. 10.29).

2   Withdraw the switch far enough to permit the multi-plug to be disconnected.

3   To refit the switch, connect the multi-plug and push the switch firmly into its location.

45 Fuses

1   A fuse block is mounted on the right-hand inner wing panel, under a protective cover (photo).

2   The fuses, and their respective circuits are as follows:

Fuse	Size	Function
1	16 amp	Cigarette lighter, clock, interior light(s), hazard flashers, horn, glove compartment light
2	8 amp	LH side and tail light
3	8 amp	RH side and tail light, number plate light(s), instrument panel lights
4	8 amp	Main beam headlights
5	8 amp	Dipped beam headlights
6	8 amp	Wiper motor, washer motor, reversing lights, electric washer pump
7	8 amp	Direction indicators, stop lights, instrument cluster, heater motor

3   Four headlamp fuses are located within the relay, next to the windscreen washer reservoir.

Fuse	Size	Function
1	16 amp	LH dipped headlight
2	16 amp	RH dipped headlight
3	16 amp	RH main beam headlight and LH auxiliary light
4	16 amp	LH main beam headlight and RH auxiliary light

4   Two further fuses are located beneath the facia. These are a 16 amp fuse for the heated rear window, located within the relay (Section 46), and a 2 amp (slow blow) fuse in the radio supply lead.

5   Before any fuse that has blown is renewed, it is important to find the cause of the trouble and for it to be rectified, because a fuse acts as a safety device and protects the electrical system against expensive damage should a fault occur.

46 Relays – renewal

1   There are five relays incorporated in the electrical system: headlamp, heated rear window, indicator and hazard flasher, inhibitor switch (automatic transmission) and windscreen wipers.

Headlamp relay

2   This is located within the engine compartment on the side apron panel next to the windscreen washer reservoir.

3   Unplug the washer motor and lift out the reservoir. Unscrew the two crosshead securing screws and lift out the relay.

4   Pull the multi-plug and two double connectors from their terminals, carefully noting the correct connections (Fig. 10.30).

Heated rear window relay

5   This relay is located on the support bracket for the bonnet release

lever which is located under the instrument panel (Fig. 10.31).

6   Access to the relay can be facilitated if the instrument panel's lower insulation panel is first removed and the flasher unit extracted from its securing clip.

Indicator and hazard flasher relay

7   This relay is located on the support bracket for the bonnet release lever which is located under the instrument panel (Fig. 10.31).

8   Access to the relay can be facilitated if the instrument panel's lower insulation panel is first removed. The relay can then be pulled from its securing clip.

Inhibitor switch relay

9   This relay is located on the right-hand inner wing panel, and is retained by two crosshead screws.

Windscreen wiper relay

10   This relay is located on the ashtray guide bracket, and is retained by a clip (Fig. 10.32).

11   To remove the relay, first remove the instrument cluster and panel assembly, refer to Section 37.

---

47 Radios and tape players – installation

A radio or tape player is an expensive item to buy, and will only give its best performance if fitted properly. It is useless to expect concert hall performance from a unit that is suspended from the dash-panel by string with its speaker resting on the back seat or parcel shelf! If you do not wish to do the installation yourself there are many in-car entertainment specialists who can do the fitting for you.

Make sure the unit purchased is of the same polarity as the vehicle. Ensure that units with adjustable polarity are correctly set before commencing installation.

It is difficult to give specific information with regard to fitting, as final positioning of the radio/tape player, speakers and aerial is entirely a matter of personal preference. However, the following paragraphs give guidelines to follow, which are relevant to all installations.

Radios

Most radios are a standardised size of 7 inches wide, by 2 inches deep – this ensures that they will fit into the radio aperture provided in most cars. If your car does not have such an aperture, then the radio must be fitted in a suitable position either in, or beneath, the dash-panel. Alternatively, a special console can be purchased which will fit between the dashpanel and the floor, or on the transmission tunnel. These consoles can also be used for additional switches and instrumentation if required. Where no radio aperture is provided the following points should be borne in mind before deciding exactly where to fit the unit:

a) *The unit must be within easy reach of the driver wearing a seatbelt*

b) *The unit must not be mounted in close proximity to a tachometer, the ignition switch and its wiring, or the flasher unit and associated wiring*

c) *The unit must be mounted within reach of the aerial lead, and in such a place that the aerial lead will not have to be routed near the components detailed in the preceding paragraph 'b'*

d) *The unit should not be positioned in a place where it might cause injury to the car occupants in an accident; for instance, under the dashpanel above the driver's or passenger's legs*

e) *The unit must be fitted really securely*

Some radios will have mounting brackets provided, together with instructions: others will need to be fitted using drilled and slotted metal strips, bent to form mounting brackets – these strips are available from most accessory stores. The unit must be properly earthed, by fitting a separate earth lead between the casing of the radio and the vehicle frame.

Use the radio manufacturer's instructions when wiring the radio into the vehicle's electrical system. If no instructions are available, refer to the relevant wiring diagram to find the location of the radio 'feed' connection in the vehicle's wiring circuit. A 1 to 2 amp 'in-line' fuse must be fitted in the radio's 'feed' wire – a choke may also be necessary (see next Section).

The type of aerial used, and its fitted position, is a matter of personal preference. In general the taller the aerial, the better the reception. It is best to fit a fully retractable aerial – especially, if a mechanical car-wash is used or if you live in an area where cars tend to be vandalised. In this respect electric aerials which are raised and lowered automatically when switching the radio on or off, are convenient, but are more likely to give trouble than the manual type.

When choosing a site for the aerial the following points should be considered:

(a) *The aerial lead should be as short as possible; this means that the aerial should be mounted at the front of the vehicle*

(b) *The aerial must be mounted as far away from the distributor and HT leads as possible*

(c) *The part of the aerial which protrudes beneath the mounting point must not foul the roadwheels, or anything else*

(d) *If possible the aerial should be positioned so that the coaxial lead does not have to be routed through the engine compartment*

(e) *The plane of the panel on which the aerial is mounted should not be so steeply angled that the aerial cannot be mounted vertically (in relation to the 'end-on' aspect of the vehicle). Most aerials have a small amount of adjustment available*

Having decided on a mounting position, a relatively large hole will have to be made in the panel. The exact size of the hole will depend upon the specific aerial being fitted, although, generally, the hole required is of $\frac{3}{4}$ inch diameter. On metal bodied cars, a 'tank-cutter' of the relevant diameter is the best tool to be used for making the hole. This tool needs a small diameter pilot hole drilled through the panel, through which, the tool clamping bolt is inserted. On GRP bodied cars, a 'hole saw' is the best tool to use. Again, this tool will require the drilling of a small pilot hole. When the hole has been made the raw edges should be de-burred with a file and then painted, to prevent corrosion.

Fit the aerial according to the manufacturer's instructions. If the aerial is very tall, or if it protrudes beneath the mounting panel for a considerable distance it is a good idea to fit a stay between the aerial and the vehicle frame. This stay can be manufactured from the slotted and drilled metal strips previously mentioned. The stay should be securely screwed or bolted in place. For best reception it is advisable to fit an earth lead between the aerial body and the vehicle frame – this is essential on fibre glass bodied vehicles.

It will probably be necessary to drill one, or two holes through bodywork panels in order to feed the aerial lead into the interior of the car. Where this is the case ensure that the holes are fitted with rubber grommets to protect the cable, and to stop possible entry of water.

Positioning and fitting of the speaker depends mainly on its type. Generally, the speaker is designed to fit directly into the aperture already provided in the car (usually in the shelf behind the rear seats, or in the top of the dashpanel). Where this is the case, fitting the speaker is just a matter of removing the protective grille from the aperture and screwing or bolting the speaker in place. Take great care not to damage the speaker diaphragm whilst doing this. It is a good idea to fit a 'gasket' between the speaker frame and the mounting panel in order to prevent rattling – some speakers will already have such a gasket fitted.

If a 'pod' type speaker was supplied with the radio, the best acoustic results will normally be obtained by mounting it on the shelf behind the rear seat. The pod can be secured to the mounting panel with self-tapping screws.

When connecting a rear mounted speaker to the radio, the wires should be routed through the vehicle beneath the carpets or floor mats – preferably through the middle, or along the side of the floorpan, where they will not be trodden on by passengers. Make the relevant connections as directed by the radio manufacturer.

By now you will have several yards of additional wiring in the car; use PVC tape to secure this wiring out of harm's way. Do not leave electrical leads dangling. Ensure that all new electrical connections are properly made (wires twisted together will not do) and completely secure.

The radio should now be working, but before you pack away your tools it will be necessary to 'trim' the radio to the aerial. Follow the radio manufacturer's instructions regarding this adjustment.

Tape players

Fitting instructions for both cartridge and cassette stereo tape players are the same and in general the same rules apply as when fitting a radio. Tape players are not usually prone to electrical interference like radios – although it can occur – so positioning is not so critical. If possible the player should be mounted on an 'even-keel'. Also, it must be possible for a driver wearing a seatbelt to reach the unit in order to change, or turn over, tapes.

For best results from speakers, designed to be recessed into a panel, mount them so that the back of the speaker protrudes into an enclosed chamber within the vehicle (eg; door interiors or the boot cavity).

To fit recessed type speakers in the front doors first check that there is sufficient room to mount the speaker in each door without it fouling the latch or window winding mechanism. Hold the speaker against the skin of the door, and draw a line, around the periphery of the speaker. With the speaker removed draw a second 'cutting-line', within the first, to allow enough room for the entry of the speaker back, but at the same time providing a broad seat for the speaker flange. When you are sure that the 'cutting-line' is correct, drill a series of holes around its periphery. Pass a hacksaw blade through one of the holes and then cut through the metal between the holes until the centre section of the panel falls out.

De-burr the edges of the hole and then paint the raw metal to prevent corrosion. Cut a corresponding hole in the door trim panel ensuring that it will be completely covered by the speaker grille. Now drill a hole in the door edge and a corresponding hole in the door sur-round. These holes are to feed the speaker leads through – so fit grom-mets. Pass the speaker leads through the door trim, door skin and out through the holes in the side of the door and door surround. Refit the door trim panel and then secure the speaker to the door using self-tapping screws. **Note**: *If the speaker is fitted with a shield to prevent water dripping on it, ensure that this shield is at the top.*

'Pod' type speakers can be fastened to the shelf behind the rear seat, or anywhere else offering a corresponding mounting point on each side of the car. If the 'pod' speakers are mounted on each side of the shelf behind the rear seat, it is a good idea to drill several large diameter holes through to the trunk cavity, beneath each speaker – this will improve the sound reproduction. 'Pod' speakers sometimes offer a better reproduction quality if they face the rear window – which then acts as a reflector – so it is worthwhile experimenting before finally fixing the speakers.

48 Radios and tape players – suppression of interference (general)

To eliminate buzzes, and other unwanted noises, costs very little and is not as difficult as sometimes thought. With a modicum of common sense and patience whilst following the instructions in the following paragraphs, interference can be virtually eliminated.

The first cause for concern is the generator. The noise this makes over the radio is like an electric mixer and the noise speeds up when you rev-up the engine. The remedy for this is simple; connect a 1·0 mf to 3·0 mf capacitor between earth, probably the bolt that holds down the generator base, and the *large* terminal on the alternator. This is most important, because if you connect it to the small terminal you will probably damage the generator permanently (see Fig. 10.33).

A second common cause of electrical interference is the ignition system. Here a 1·0 mf capacitor must be connected between earth and the SW or + terminal on the coil (see Fig. 10.34). This may stop the tick-tick sound that comes over the speaker. Next comes the spark itself.

There are several ways of curing interference from the ignition HT system. One is the use of carbon-cored HT leads as original equip-ment. Where copper cable is substituted then you must use resistive spark plug caps (see Fig. 10.35) of about 10 000 ohm to 15 000 ohm resistance. If, due to lack of room, these cannot be used, an alternative is to use 'in-line' suppressors – if the interference is not too bad, you may get away with only one suppressor in the coil to distributor line. If the interference does continue (a 'clacking' noise) then modify all HT leads.

At this stage it is advisable to check that the radio is well earthed, also the aerial and to see that the aerial plug is pushed well into the set and that the radio is properly trimmed (see preceding Section). In addi-tion, check that the wire which supplies the power to the set is as short as possible. At this stage it is a good idea to check that the fuse is of the correct rating. For most sets this will be about 1 to 2 amps.

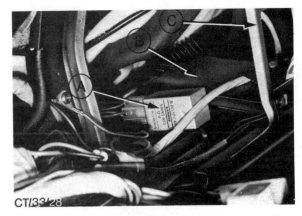

Fig. 10.32 Windscreen wiper relay removal (Sec 46)

A Wiper relay
B Bracket
C Dash panel

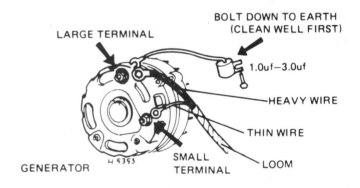

Fig. 10.33 The correct way to connect a capacitor to the generator (Sec 48)

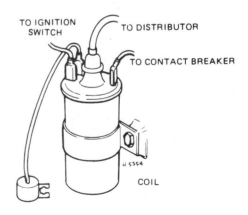

Fig. 10.34 The capacitor must be connected to the ignition switch side of the coil (Sec 48)

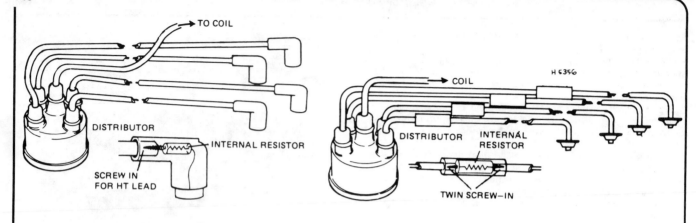

Resistive spark plug caps   'In-line' suppressors

Fig. 10.35 Ignition HT lead suppressors (Sec 48)

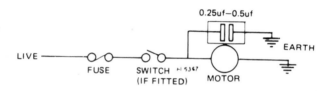

Fig. 10.36 Correct method of suppressing electric motors (Sec 48)

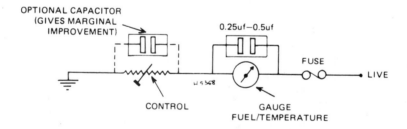

Fig. 10.37 Method of suppressing gauges and their control units (Sec 48)

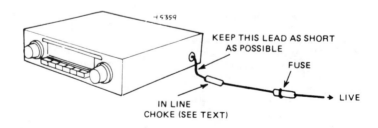

Fig. 10.38 An in-line choke should be fitted into the live supply lead as close to the unit as possible (Sec 48)

At this point the more usual causes of interference have been suppressed. If the problem still exists, a look at the cause of interference may help to pinpoint the component generating the stray electrical discharges.

The radio picks up electromagnetic waves in the air; now some are made by regular broadcasters, and some, which we do not want, are made by the car itself. The home made signals are produced by stray electrical discharges floating around in the car. Common producers of these signals are electrical motors, ie, the windscreen wipers, electric screen washers, electric window winders, heater fan or an electric aerial if fitted. Other sources of interference are flashing turn signals and instruments. The remedy for these cases is shown in Fig. 10.36 for an electric motor whose interference is not too bad and Fig. 10.37 for instrument suppression. Turn signals are not normally suppressed. In recent years, radio manufacturers have included in the line (live) of the radio, an 'in-line' choke in addition to the fuse. If your circuit lacks one of these, put one in as shown in Fig. 10.38.

All the foregoing components are available from radio stores or accessory stores. If you have an electric clock fitted this should be suppressed by connecting a 0·5 mf capacitor directly across it as shown for a motor in Fig. 10.36.

If after all this, you are still experiencing radio interference, first assess how bad it is, for the human ear can filter out unobtrusive unwanted noises quite easily. But if you are still adamant about eradicating the noise, then continue.

As a first step, a few 'experts' seem to favour a screen between the radio and the engine. This is OK as far as it goes – literally! – for the whole set is screened anyway and if interference can get past that then a small piece of aluminium is not going to stop it.

A more sensible way of screening is to discover if interference is coming down the wires. First, take the live lead; interference can get between the set and the choke (hence the reason for keeping the wires short). One remedy here is to screen the wire and this is done by buying screened wire and fitting that. The loudspeaker lead could be screened also to prevent 'pick-up' getting back to the radio, although this is unlikely.

Without doubt, the worst source of radio interference comes from the ignition HT leads, even if they have been suppressed. The ideal way of suppressing these is to slide screening tubes over the leads themselves. As this is impractical, we can place an aluminium shield over the majority of the lead area. In a vee- or twin-cam engine this is relatively easy, but for a straight engine, the results are not particularly good.

Now for the really difficult cases, here are a few tips to try out. When metal comes into contact with metal, an electrical disturbance is caused which is why good clean connections are essential. To remove interference due to overlapping or butting panels you must bridge the join with a wide braided earth strap (like that from the frame to the engine/transmission). The most common moving parts that could create noise and should be strapped are:

a) Silencer to frame
b) Exhaust pipe to engine block and frame
c) Air cleaner to frame
d) Front and rear bumpers to frame
e) Steering column to frame
f) Bonnet and boot lids to frame
g) Hood frame to bodyframe on soft tops

These faults are most pronounced when the engine is idling, or labouring under load. Although the moving parts are already connected with nuts, bolts, etc, these do tend to rust and corrode, thus creating a high resistance interference source.

If you have a 'ragged' sounding pulse when mobile, this could be wheel or tyre static. This can be cured by buying some anti-static powder and sprinkling it inside the tyres.

If the interference takes the form of a high pitched screeching noise that changes its note when the car is in motion and only comes now and then, this could be related to the aerial, especially if it is of the telescopic or whip type. This source can be cured quite simply by pushing a small rubber ball on top of the aerial as this breaks the electric field before it can form; but it would be much better to buy yourself a new aerial of a reputable brand. If, on the other hand, you are getting a loud rushing sound every time you brake, then this is brake static. This effect is most prominent on hot dry days and is cured only by fitting a special kit, which is quite expensive.

In conclusion, it is pointed out that it is relatively easy, and therefore, cheap, to eliminate 95 per cent of all noise, but to eliminate the final 5 per cent is time and money consuming. It is up to the individual to decide if it is worth it. Please remember also, that you cannot get a concert hall performance out of a cheap radio.

Finally, cassette players and eight track players are not usually affected by car noise but in a very bad case, the best remedies are the first three suggestions plus using a 3 to 5 amp choke in the 'live' line and in incurable cases screen the live and speaker wires.

Note: *If your car is fitted with electronic ignition, then it is not recommended that either the spark plug resistors or the ignition coil capacitor be fitted as these may damage the system. Most electronic ignition units have built-in suppression and should, therefore, not cause interference.*

49 Fault diagnosis – electrical system

Symptom	Reason/s
Starter motor fails to turn engine	Battery discharged
	Battery defective internally
	Battery terminal leads loose or earth lead not securely attached to body
	Loose or broken connections in starter motor circuit
	Starter motor switch or solenoid faulty
	Starter brushes badly worn, sticking, or brush wires loose
	Commutator dirty, worn or burnt
	Starter motor armature faulty
	Field coils earthed
Starter motor turns engine very slowly	Battery in discharged condition
	Starter brushes badly worn, sticking, or brush wires loose
	Loose wires in starter motor circuit
Starter motor operates without turning engine	Starter motor pinion sticking on the screwed sleeve
	Pinion or flywheel gear teeth broken or worn
Starter motor noisy or excessively rough engagement	Pinion or flywheel gear teeth broken or worn
	Starter motor retaining bolts loose
Battery will not hold charge for more than a few days	Battery defective internally
	Electrolyte level too low or electrolyte too weak due to leakage
	Plate separators no longer fully effective

Symptom	Reason/s
	Battery plates severely sulphated
	Fan/alternator belt slipping
	Battery terminal connections loose or corroded
	Alternator not charging properly
	Short in lighting circuit causing continual battery drain
Ignition light fails to go out, battery runs flat in a few days	Fan belt loose and slipping or broken
	Alternator faulty
Fuel gauge gives no reading	Fuel tank empty!
	Electric cable between tank sender unit and gauge earthed or loose
	Fuel gauge case not earthed
	Fuel gauge supply cable interrupted
	Fuel gauge unit broken
Fuel gauge registers full all the time	Electric cable between tank unit and gauge broken or disconnected
Horn operates all the time	Horn push either earthed or stuck down
	Horn cable to horn push earthed
Horn fails to operate	Blown fuse
	Cable or cable connection loose, broken or disconnected
	Horn has an internal fault
Horn emits intermittent or unsatisfactory noise	Cable connections loose
Lights do not come on	Blown fuse
	If engine not running, battery discharged
	Light bulb filament burnt out or bulbs broken
	Wire connections loose, disconnected or broken
	Light switch shorting or otherwise faulty
Lights come on but fade out	If engine not running battery discharged
Lights give very poor illumination	Lamp glasses dirty
	Reflector tarnished or dirty
	Lamps badly out of adjustment
	Incorrect bulb with too low wattage fitted
	Existing bulbs old and badly discoloured
	Electrical wiring too thin not allowing full current to pass
Lights work erratically – flashing on and off, especially over bumps	Battery terminals or earth connection loose
	Lights not earthing properly
	Contacts in light switch faulty
Wiper motor fails to work	Blown fuse
	Wire connections loose, disconnected or broken
	Brushes badly worn
	Armature worn or faulty
	Field coils faulty
Wiper motor works very slowly and takes excessive current	Commutator dirty, greasy or burnt
	Drive to wheelboxes bent or unlubricated
	Wheelbox spindle binding or damaged
	Armature bearings dry or unaligned
	Armature badly worn or faulty
Wiper motor works slowly and takes little current	Brushes badly worn
	Commutator dirty, greasy or burnt
	Armature badly worn or faulty
Wiper motor works but wiper blades remain static	Wheelbox gear and spindle damaged or worn
	Wiper motor gearbox parts badly worn

Key to wiring diagram on pages 144 and 145

Item No	Item
Item No	**Item**
Standard equipment	
1	Alternator (Bosch)
2	Distributor
3	Starter motor and solenoid switch
4	Ignition coil
5	Fuse link wire
6	Battery
7	Fuse box
8	Multi-plug (engine rear bulkhead – grey)
9	Multi-plug (engine rear bulkhead – black)
10	Steering lock/ignition switch
11	Instrument panel
	3 – charging current warning light
Optional extra equipment	
12	Relay – automatic transmission inhibitor switch
13	Selector inhibitor switch – automatic transmission

Wiring colour	Code	Wiring colour	Code
Blue	bl	Pink	rs
Brown	br	Red	rt
Yellow	ge	Black	sw
Grey	gr	Violet	vi
Green	gn	White	ws

Wire codes

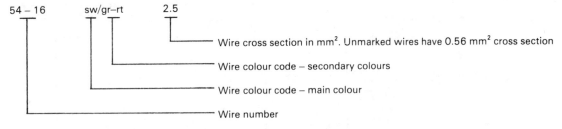

54 – 16   sw/gr–rt   2.5

Wire cross section in mm². Unmarked wires have 0.56 mm² cross section

Wire colour code – secondary colours

Wire colour code – main colour

Wire number

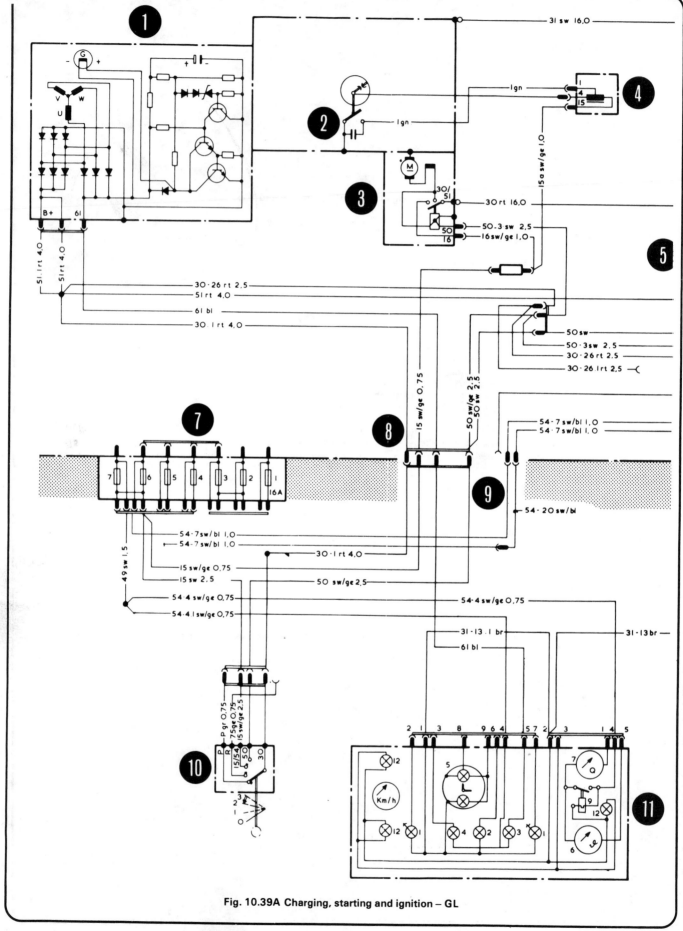

Fig. 10.39A Charging, starting and ignition – GL

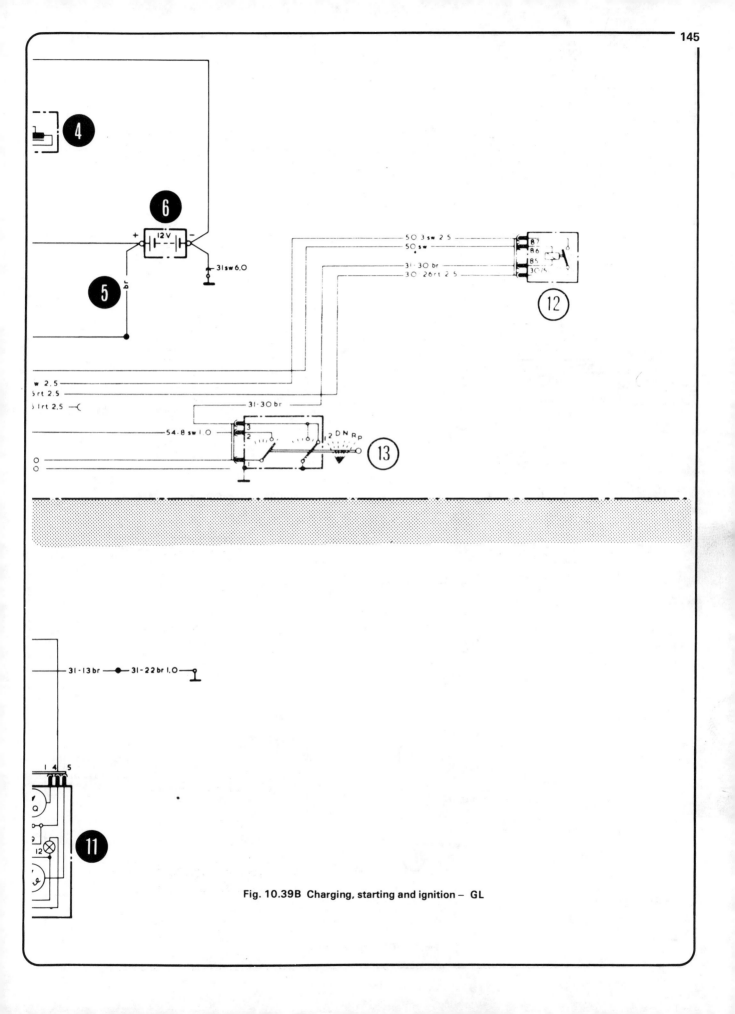

Fig. 10.39B Charging, starting and ignition – GL

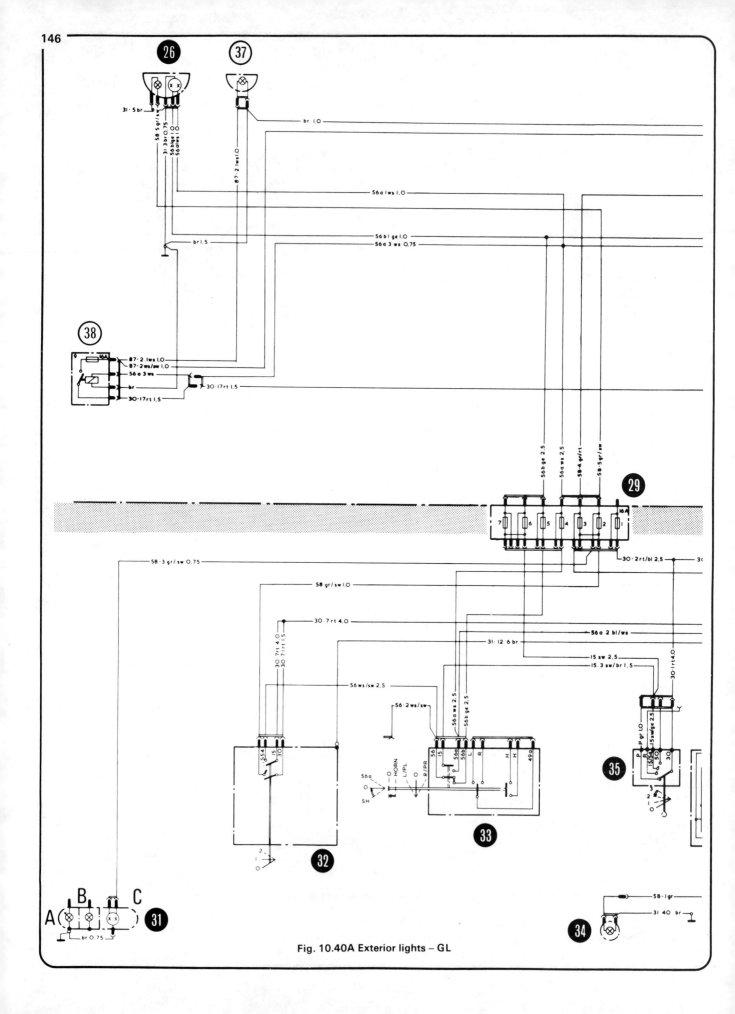

Fig. 10.40A Exterior lights – GL

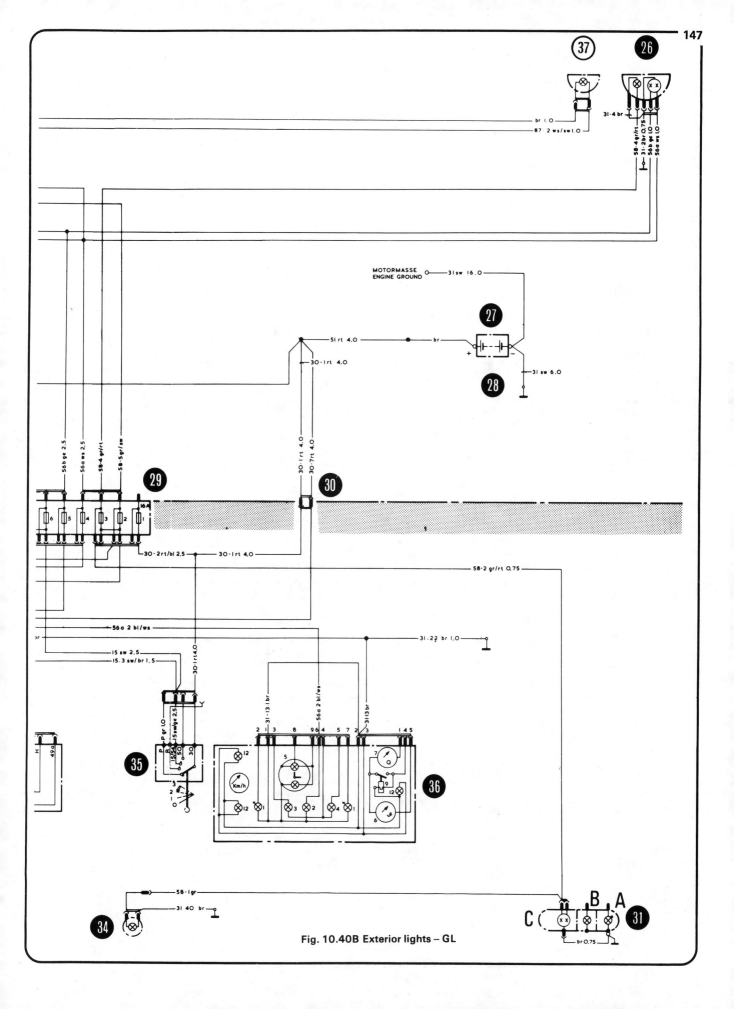

Fig. 10.40B Exterior lights – GL

Key to wiring diagram on pages 146 and 147

Item No	Item
Standard equipment	
26	Headlamp side lamp assembly
27	Battery
28	Fuse link wire
29	Fuse box
30	Multi-plug (engine rear bulkhead – grey)
31	Combined tail lamp assembly
	C – tail stop light
32	Lighting switch
33	Multi-function switch
34	Number plate lamps
35	Steering lock/ignition switch
36	Instrument cluster
	2 – main beam warning light
Optional extra equipment	
37	Auxiliary driving lamp
38	Auxiliary driving lamp relay

Wiring colour	Code	Wiring colour	Code
Blue	bl	Pink	rs
Brown	br	Red	rt
Yellow	ge	Black	sw
Grey	gr	Violet	vi
Green	gn	White	ws

Wire codes

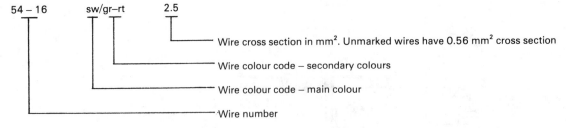

54 – 16   sw/gr–rt   2.5

Wire cross section in mm². Unmarked wires have 0.56 mm² cross section

Wire colour code – secondary colours

Wire colour code – main colour

Wire number

Key to wiring diagram on pages 150 and 151

Item No	Item
Standard equipment	
43	Fuse box
44	Fuse link wire
45	Multi-plug (engine rear bulkhead – black)
46	Battery
47	Courtesy light switches
48	Lamp – heater control illumination
49	Lighting switch
50	Interior light
51	Panel dimmer switch
52	Lamp cigar lighter illumination
53	Instrument cluster
	12 – illumination
54	Glove box lamp
55	Glove box lamp switch
Optional extra equipment	
56	Luggage compartment lamp switch
57	Luggage compartment lamp
58	Lamp – automatic transmission selector illumination

Wiring colour	Code	Wiring colour	Code
Blue	bl	Pink	rs
Brown	br	Red	rt
Yellow	ge	Black	sw
Grey	gr	Violet	vi
Green	gn	White	ws

Wire codes

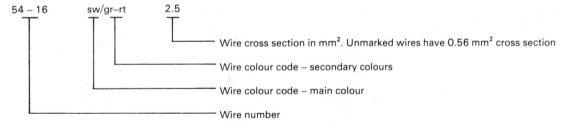

54 – 16   sw/gr–rt   2.5

Wire cross section in mm². Unmarked wires have 0.56 mm² cross section

Wire colour code – secondary colours

Wire colour code – main colour

Wire number

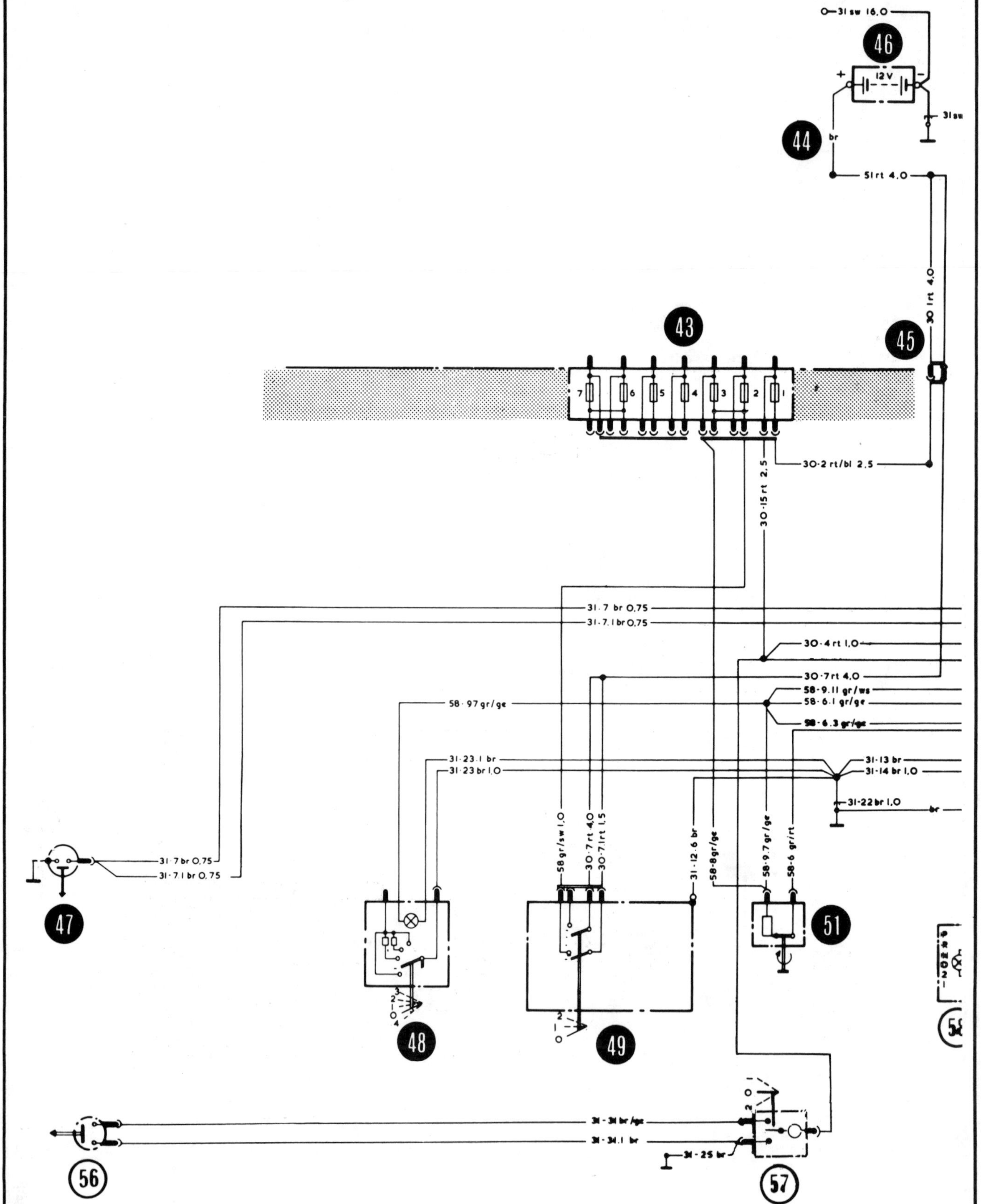

Fig. 10.41A Interior lights – GL

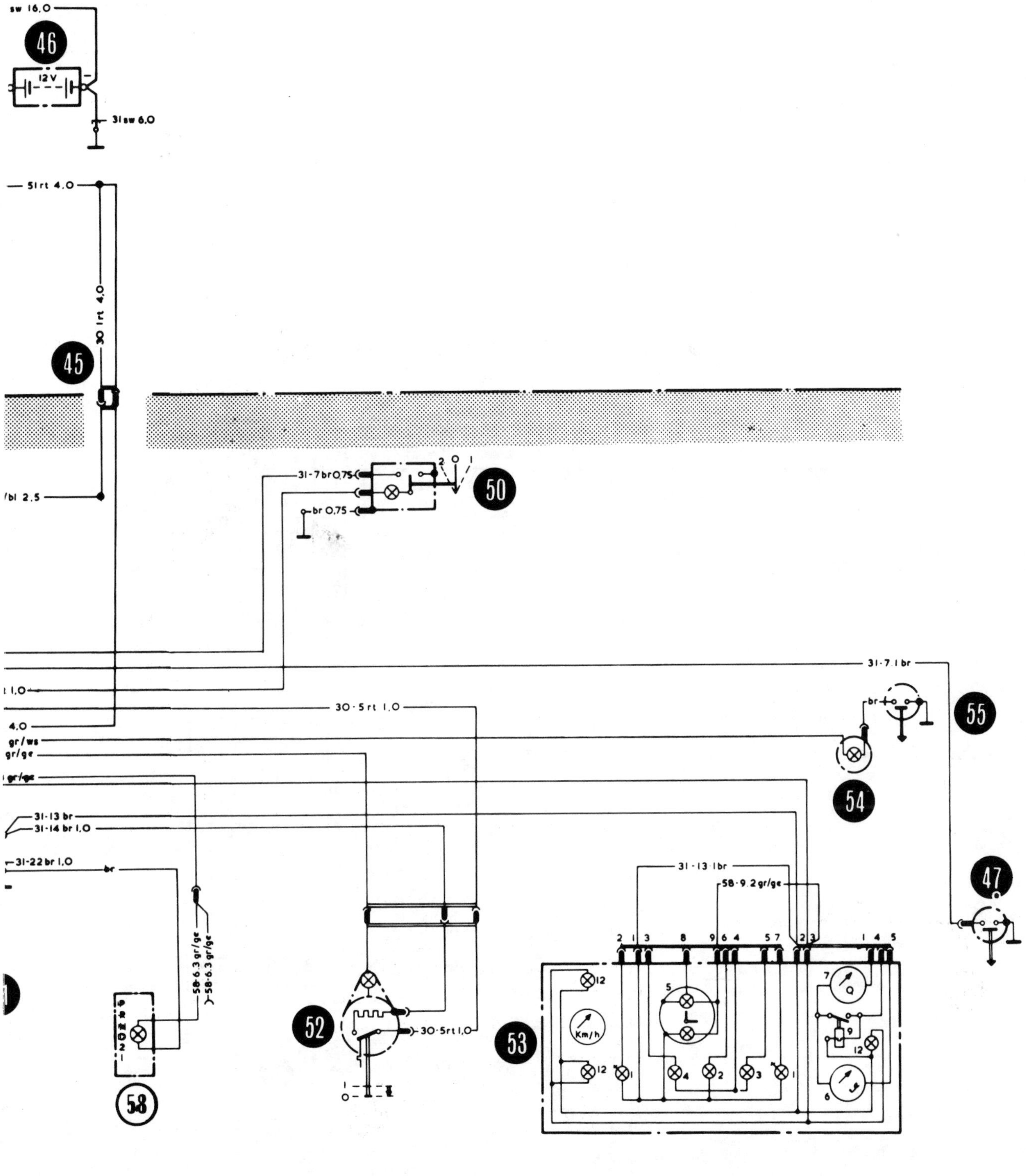

Fig. 10.41B Interior lights – GL

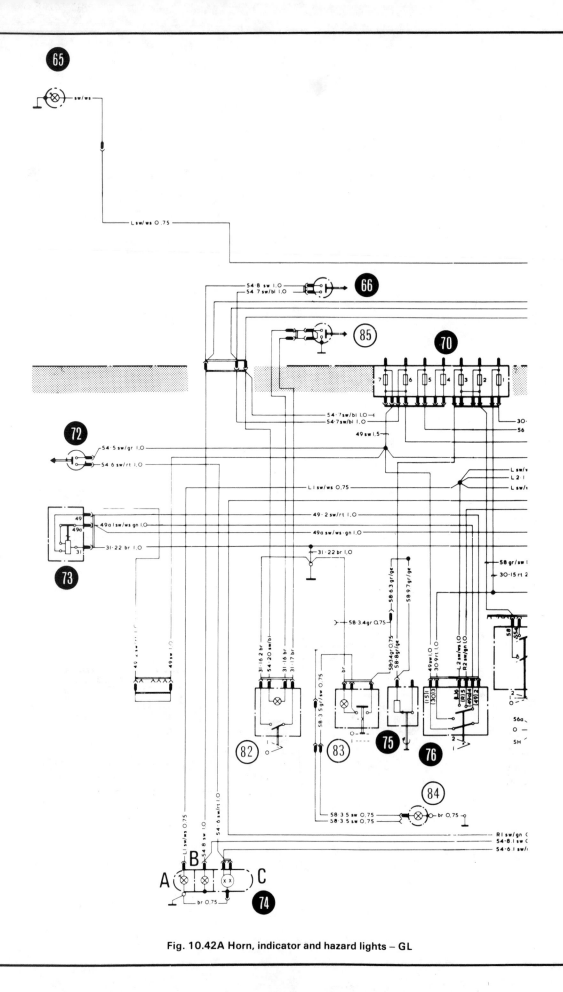

Fig. 10.42A Horn, indicator and hazard lights – GL

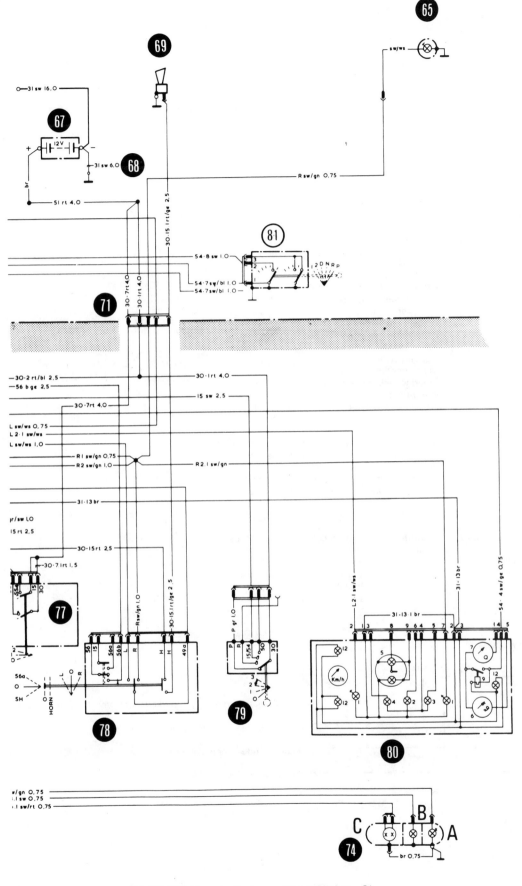

Fig. 10.42B Horn, indicator and hazard lights – GL

Key to wiring diagram on pages 152 and 153

Item No	Item
Standard equipment	
65	Front flasher lamp
66	Reversing lamp switch
67	Battery
68	Fuse link wire
69	Horn
70	Fuse box
71	Multi-plug (engine rear bulkhead – grey)
72	Stop switch
73	Flasher unit
74	Combined tail lamp assembly
	A – rear flasher lamps
	B – reversing lamps
	C – tail stop lamps
75	Panel dimmer switch
76	Hazard flasher switch
77	Lighting switch
78	Multi-function switch
79	Steering lock ignition switch
80	Instrument cluster
	1 – flasher indicator lamps

Item No	Item
Optional extra equipment	
81	Selector inhibitor switch – automatic transmission
82	Dual circuit brake warning system test switch
83	Rear fog lamp switch
84	Rear fog lamps
85	Dual circuit brake warning system switch

Wiring colour	Code	Wiring colour	Code
Blue	bl	Pink	rs
Brown	br	Red	rt
Yellow	ge	Black	sw
Grey	gr	Violet	vi
Green	gn	White	ws

Wire codes

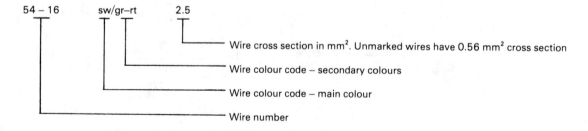

54 – 16   sw/gr–rt   2.5

Wire cross section in mm². Unmarked wires have 0.56 mm² cross section

Wire colour code – secondary colours

Wire colour code – main colour

Wire number

Key to wiring diagram on pages 156 and 157

Item

Standard equipment

90	Water temperature indicator sender unit
91	Oil pressure indicator sender unit
92	Fuse link wire
93	Battery
94	Windscreen washer pump
95	Windscreen wiper motor
96	Heater blower motor
97	Multi-plug (engine rear bulkhead – black)
98	Fuse box
99	Multi-plug (engine rear bulkhead – grey)
100	Relay–heated rear window
101	Heated rear window
102	Steering lock ignition switch
103	Instrument cluster
	4 – oil pressure warning lamp
	6 – water temperature indicator
	7 – fuel level indicator
104	Multi-function switch
105	Cigar lighter
106	Heated rear window switch
107	Windscreen wiper motor switch
108	Heater blower switch
109	Fuel indicator sender unit

Optional extra equipment

110	Headlamp washer pump
111	Headlamp washer pump fuse
112	Rear window wiper motor
113	Switch rear window washer pump
114	Switch rear window wiper motor
115	Radio
116	Radio fuse
117	Rear window washer pump
118	Windscreen wiper motor switch
119	Windscreen wiper intermittent relay
120	Timing relay – headlamp washer pump

Wiring colour	Code	Wiring colour	Code
Blue	bl	Pink	rs
Brown	br	Red	rt
Yellow	ge	Black	sw
Grey	gr	Violet	vi
Green	gn	White	ws

Wire codes

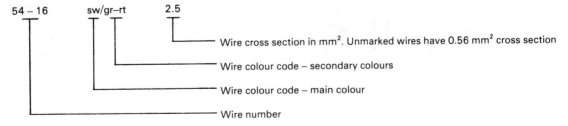

54 – 16   sw/gr–rt   2.5

Wire cross section in mm². Unmarked wires have 0.56 mm² cross section

Wire colour code – secondary colours

Wire colour code – main colour

Wire number

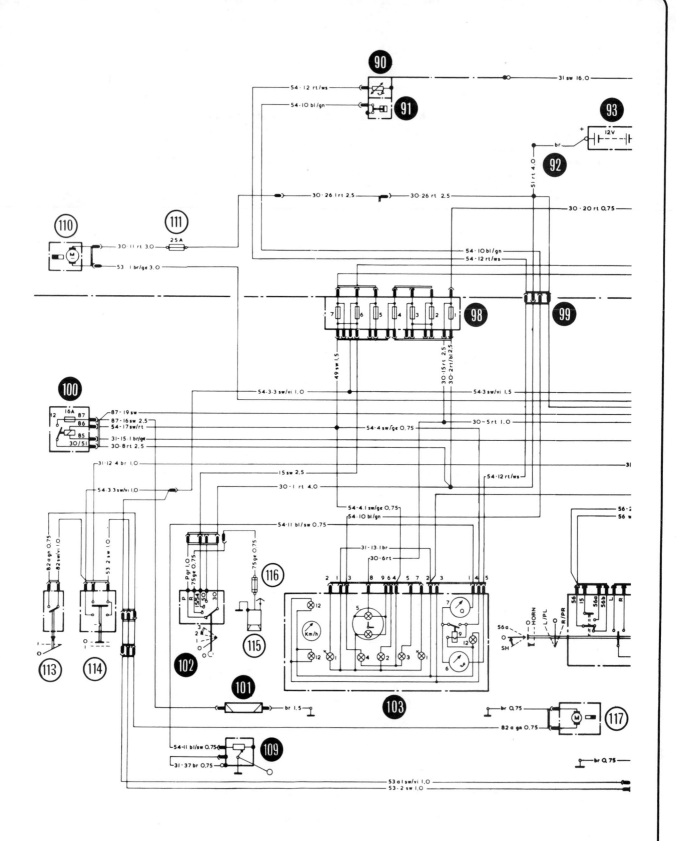

Fig. 10.43A Heater, wipers and auxiliary circuits – GL

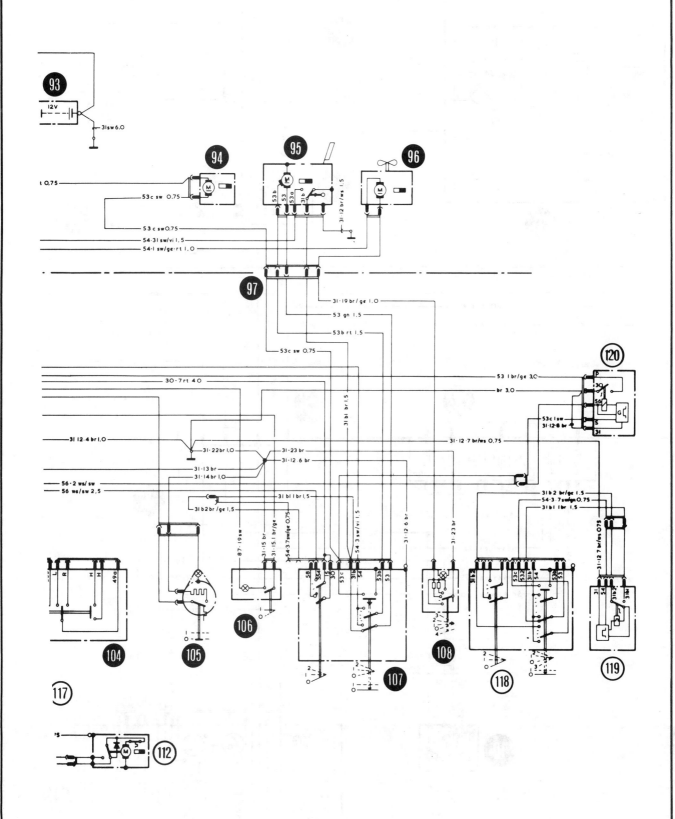

Fig. 10.43B Heater, wipers and auxiliary circuits – GL

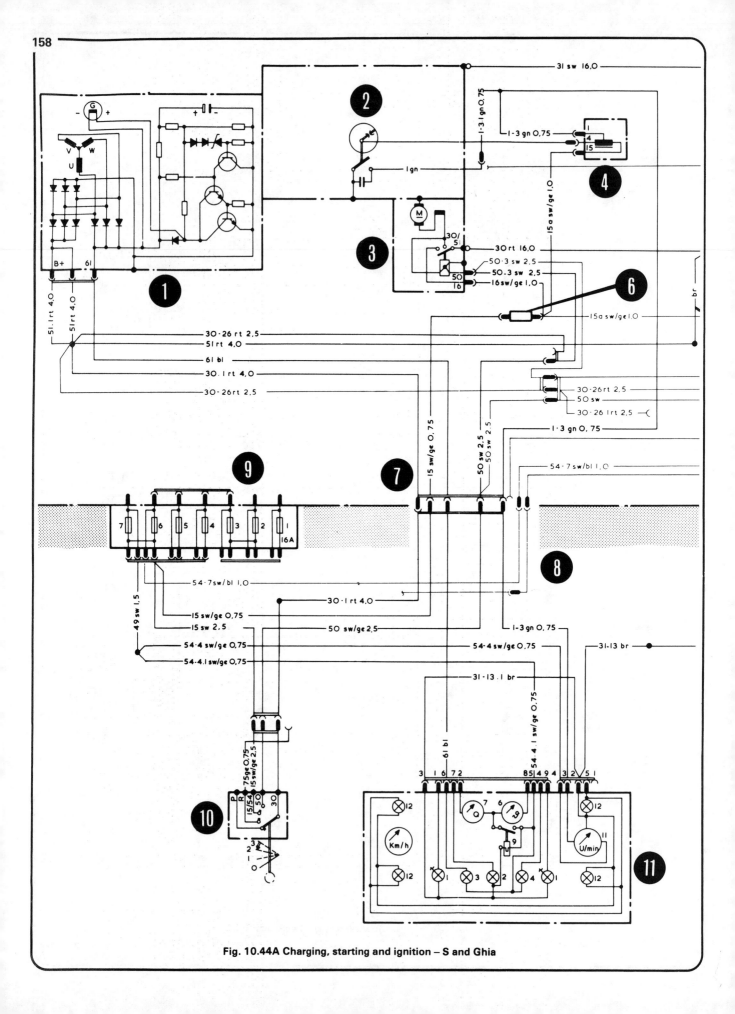

Fig. 10.44A Charging, starting and ignition – S and Ghia

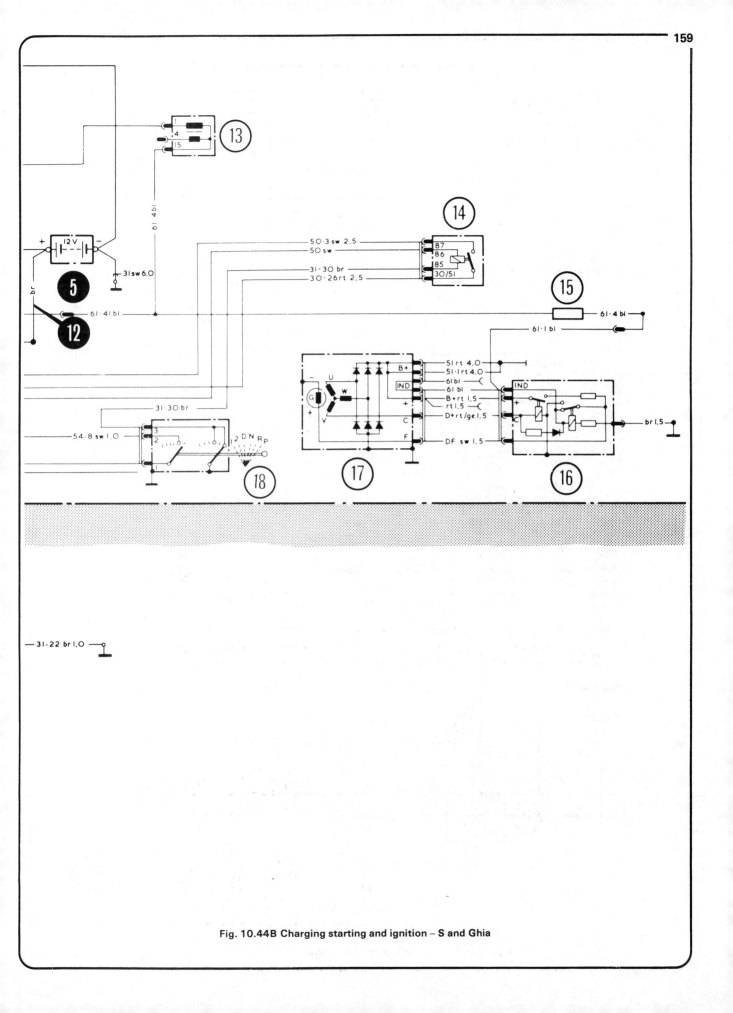

Fig. 10.44B Charging starting and ignition – S and Ghia

Key to wiring diagram on pages 158 and 159

Item No	Item
	Standard equipment
1	Alternator (Bosch)
2	Distributor
3	Starter motor and solenoid switch
4	Ignition coil
5	Battery
6	Ballast resistance
7	Multi-plug (engine rear bulkhead – grey)
8	Multi-plug (engine rear bulkhead) – black)
9	Fusebox
10	Steering lock ignition switch
11	Instrument panel
	3 – charging current warning lamp
12	Fuse link wire

	Optional extra equipment
13	Ignition coil
14	Relay–automatic transmission inhibitor switch
15	Resistance wire (Femsa)
16	Charging current regulator (Femsa)
17	Alternator (Femsa)
18	Selector inhibitor switch automatic transmission

Wiring colour	Code	Colour code	Code
Blue	bl	Pink	rs
Brown	br	Red	rt
Yellow	ge	Black	sw
Grey	gr	Violet	vi
Green	gn	White	ws

Wire codes

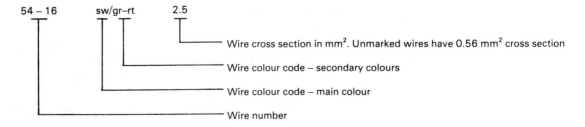

54 – 16   sw/gr–rt   2.5

Wire cross section in mm². Unmarked wires have 0.56 mm² cross section

Wire colour code – secondary colours

Wire colour code – main colour

Wire number

Key to wiring diagram on pages 162 and 163

Item No	Item
Standard equipment	
25	Auxiliary dimmer lamp relay
26	Headlamp side lamp assembly
27	Auxiliary driving lamp
28	Battery
29	Fuse box
30	Multi-plug (engine rear bulkhead – black)
31	Combined tail lamp assembly
	C – tail stop lamp
32	Lighting switch
33	Multi-function switch
34	Number plate lamp
35	Steering lock ignition switch
36	Instrument cluster
	2 – main beam warning lamp

Wiring colour	Code	Wiring colour	Code
Blue	bl	Pink	rs
Brown	br	Red	rt
Yellow	ge	Black	sw
Grey	gr	Violet	vi
Green	gn	White	ws

Wire codes

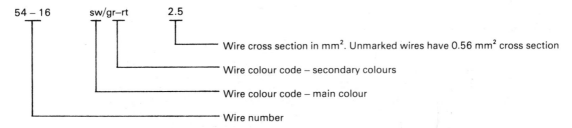

54 – 16   sw/gr–rt   2.5

Wire cross section in mm². Unmarked wires have 0.56 mm² cross section

Wire colour code – secondary colours

Wire colour code – main colour

Wire number

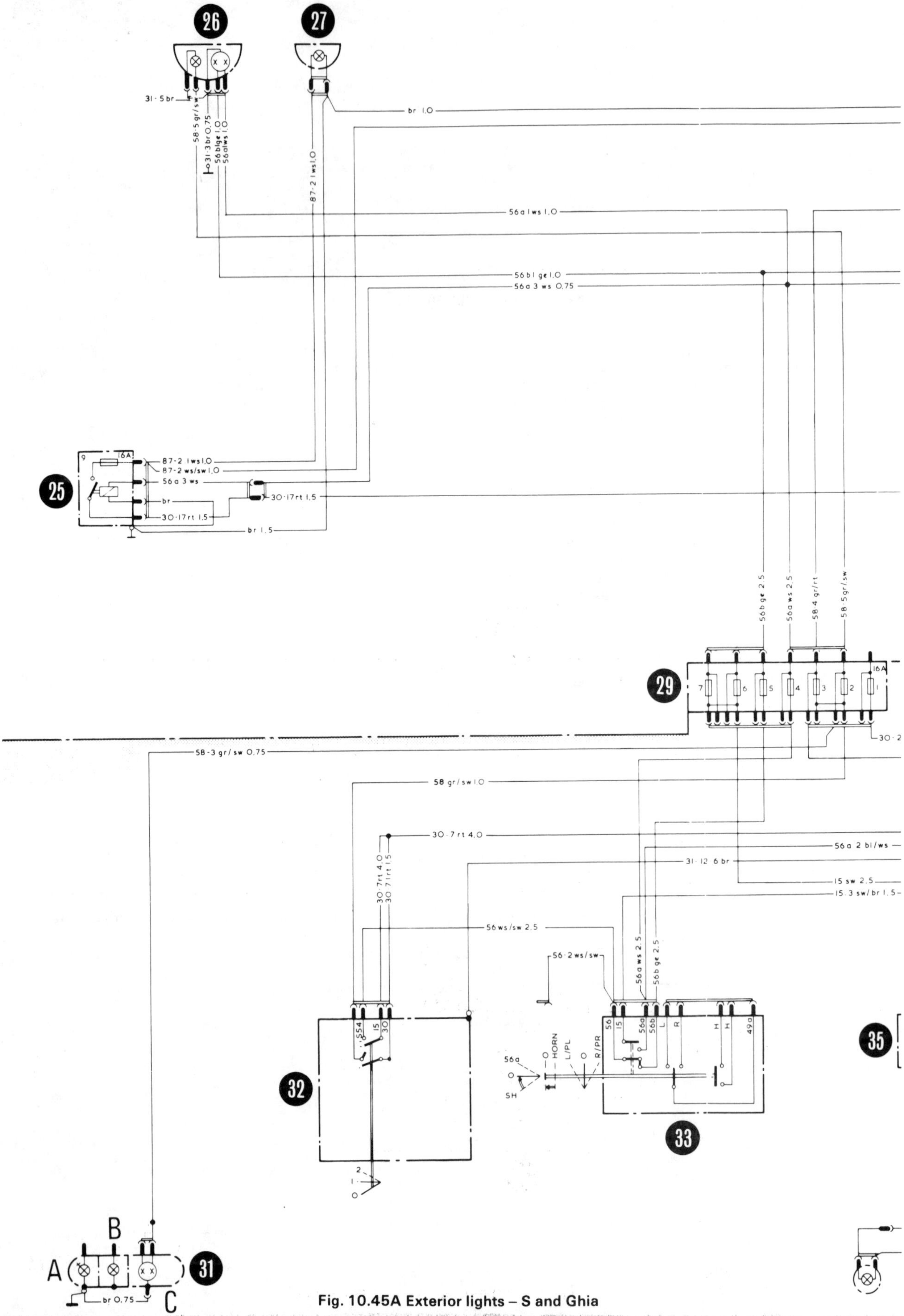

Fig. 10.45A Exterior lights – S and Ghia

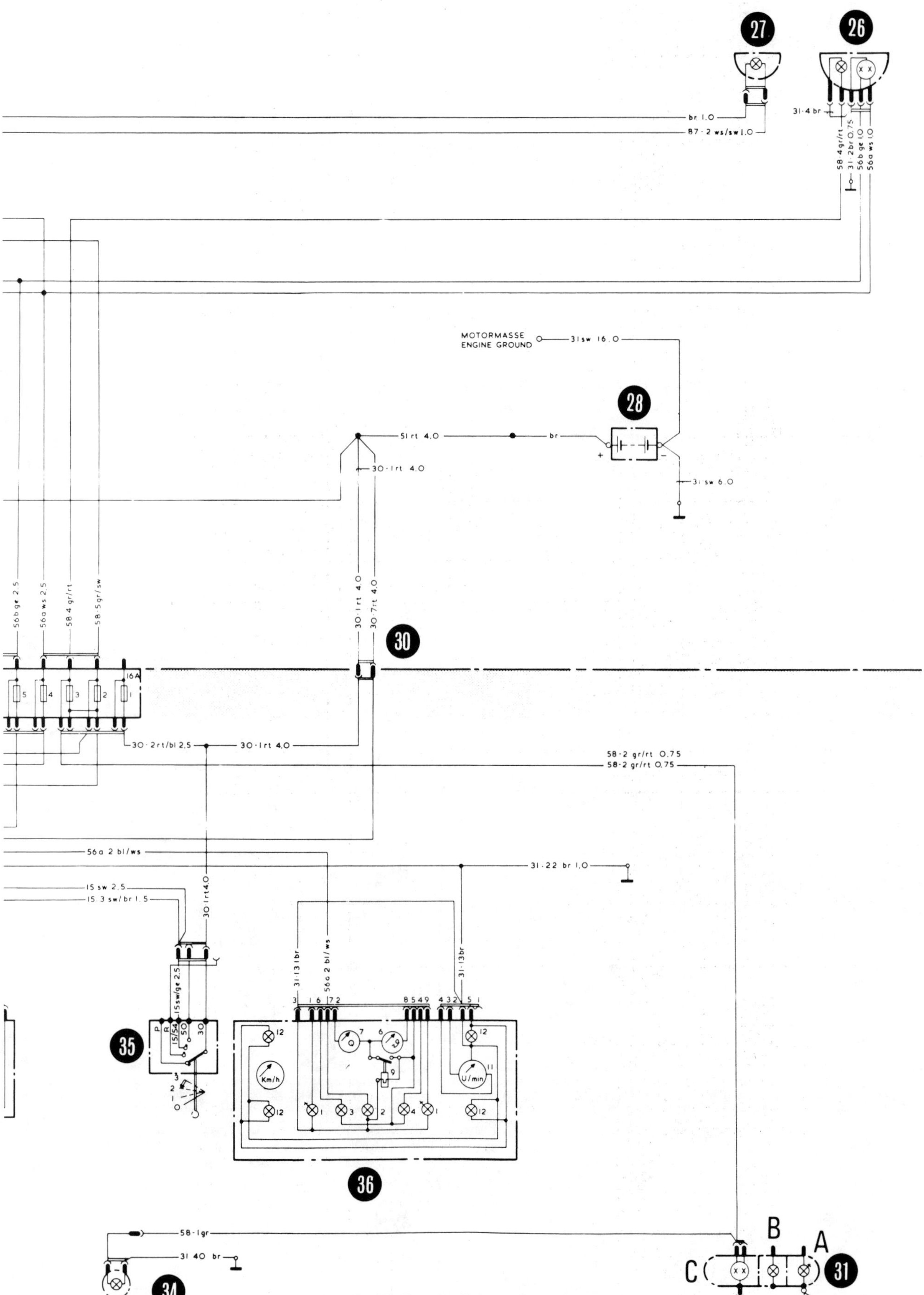

(27)

(26)

br 1.0
87·2 ws/sw 1.0

58·4 gr/rt
31·2 br 0.75
56b gr 1.0
56a ws 1.0

31·4 br

MOTORMASSE
ENGINE GROUND — 31 sw 16.0

(28)

51 rt 4.0 — br
30·1 rt 4.0

31 sw 6.0

56b gr 2.5
56a ws 2.5
58·4 gr/rt
58·5 gr/sw

16A

30·1 rt 4.0
30·7 rt 4.0

(30)

5 4 3 2 1

30·2 rt/bl 2.5 — 30·1 rt 4.0

58·2 gr/rt 0.75
58·2 gr/rt 0.75

56a 2 bl/ws

31·22 br 1.0

15 sw 2.5
15·3 sw/br 1.5
30·1 rt 4.0

31·13 br
56a 2 bl/ws
31·13 br

3 1 6 7 2
8 5 4 9
4 3 2 5 1

15 sw/gr 2.5

(35)

P R
15 50
30

(36)

12

7
6 9
12

Km/h
9
U/min 11

12
12
3 4 1
12

58·1 gr

31 40 br

(34)

C

B A

(31)

br 0.75

Fig. 10.45B Exterior lights – S and Ghia

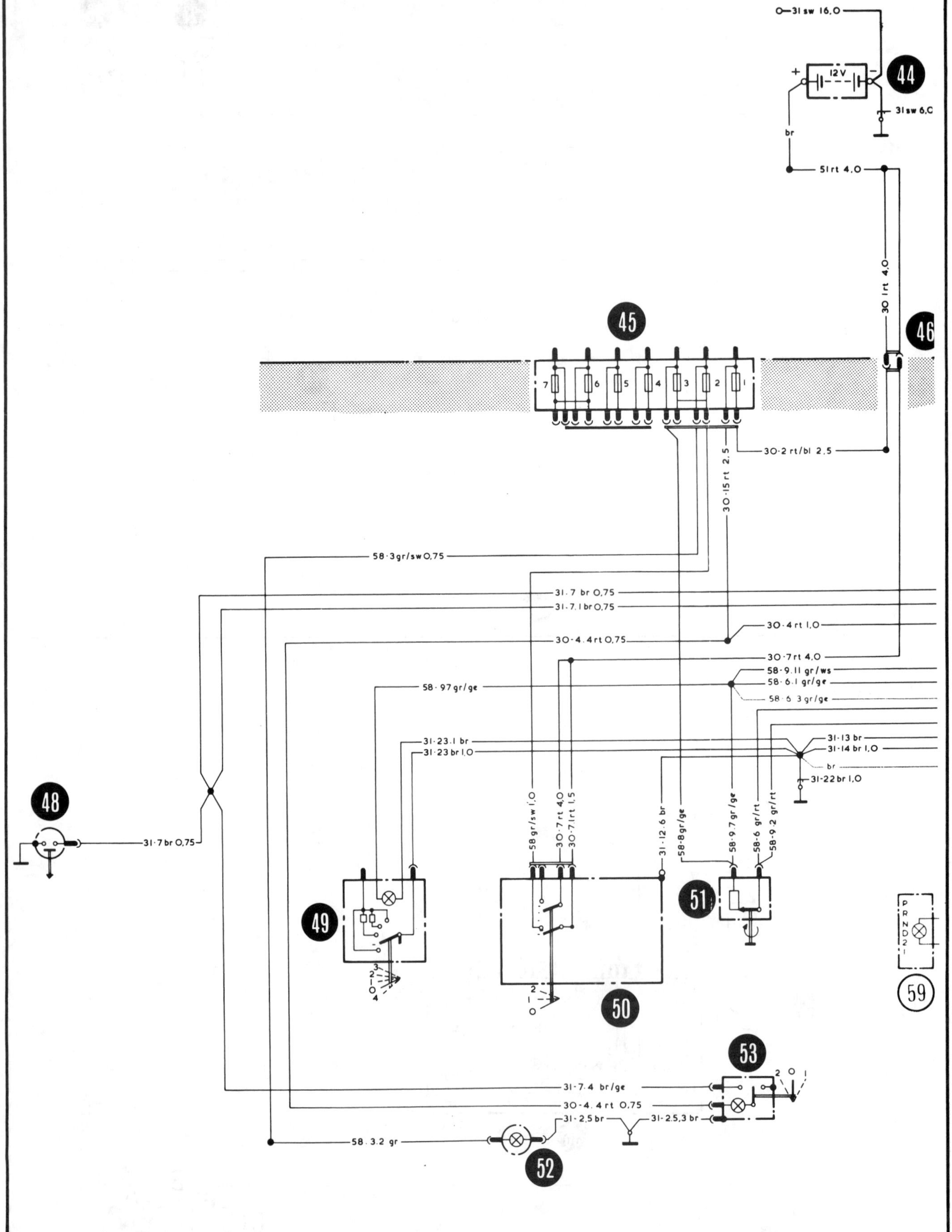

164

Fig. 10.46A Interior lights – S and Ghia

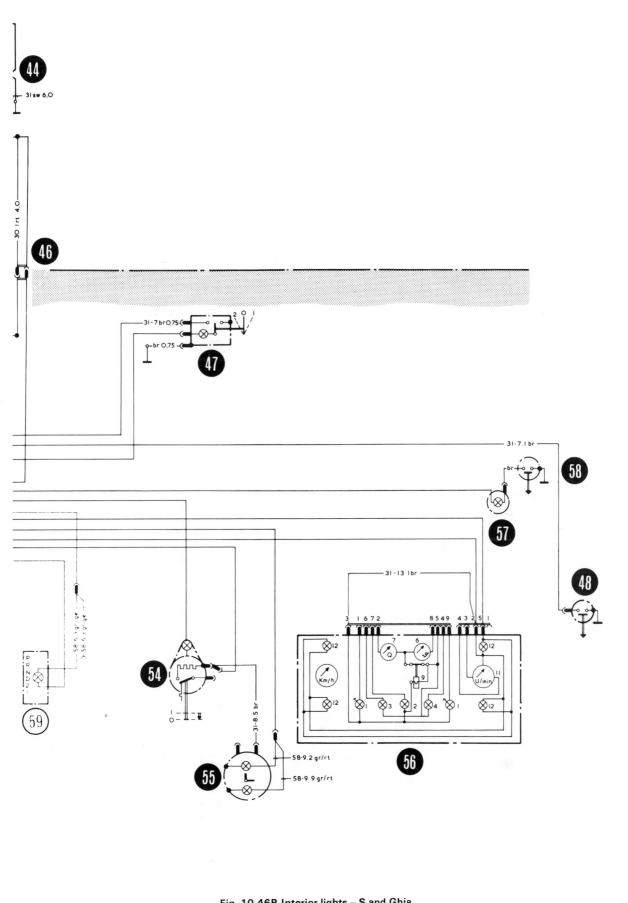

Fig. 10.46B Interior lights – S and Ghia

Key to wiring diagram on pages 164 and 165

Item No	Item
Standard equipment	
44	Battery
45	Fuse box
46	Multi-plug (engine rear bulkhead – grey)
47	Interior lamp
48	Courtesy lamp switches
49	Lamp–heater control illumination
50	Lighting switch
51	Panel dimmer switch
52	Luggage compartment lamp
53	Interior lamp
54	Lamp–cigar lighter illumination
55	Lamp–clock illumination
56	Instrument cluster
	12 – illumination
57	Glove box lamp
58	Glove box lamp switch

Optional extra equipment	
59	Lamp–automatic transmission selector illumination

Wiring colour	Code	Wiring colour	Code
Blue	bl	Pink	rs
Brown	br	Red	rt
Yellow	ge	Black	sw
Grey	gr	Violet	vi
Green	gn	White	ws

Wire codes

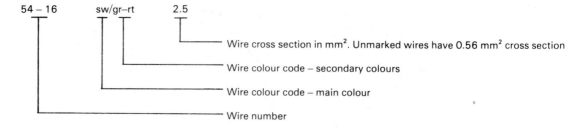

54 – 16   sw/gr–rt   2.5

Wire cross section in mm². Unmarked wires have 0.56 mm² cross section

Wire colour code – secondary colours

Wire colour code – main colour

Wire number

Key to wiring diagram on pages 168 and 169

Item No	Item
Standard equipment	
65	Front flasher lamps
66	Fuse link wire
67	Battery
68	Horn
69	Reversing lamp switch
70	Dual circuit brake warning system switch
71	Fuse box
72	Multi-plug (engine rear bulkhead – grey)
73	Stop lamp switch
74	Flasher unit
75	Dual circuit brake warning system test switch
76	Panel dimmer switch
77	Hazard flasher switch
78	Lighting switch
79	Multi-function switch
80	Steering lock/ignition switch
81	Instrument cluster
	1 – flasher indicator lamps
82	Combined tail lamp assembly
	A – rear flasher lamps
	B – reversing lamps
	C – tail stop lamps

Optional equipment	
83	Selector inhibitor switch automatic transmission
84	Rear fog lamp switch
85	Rear fog lamp
86	Hazard flasher switch link
	(System without switch warning lamp)

Wiring colour	Code	Colour code	Code
Blue	bl	Pink	rs
Brown	br	Red	rt
Yellow	ge	Black	sw
Grey	gr	Violet	vi
Green	gn	White	ws

Wire codes

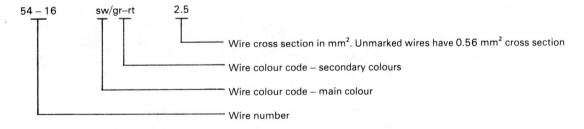

54 – 16   sw/gr–rt   2.5

— Wire cross section in mm². Unmarked wires have 0.56 mm² cross section
— Wire colour code – secondary colours
— Wire colour code – main colour
— Wire number

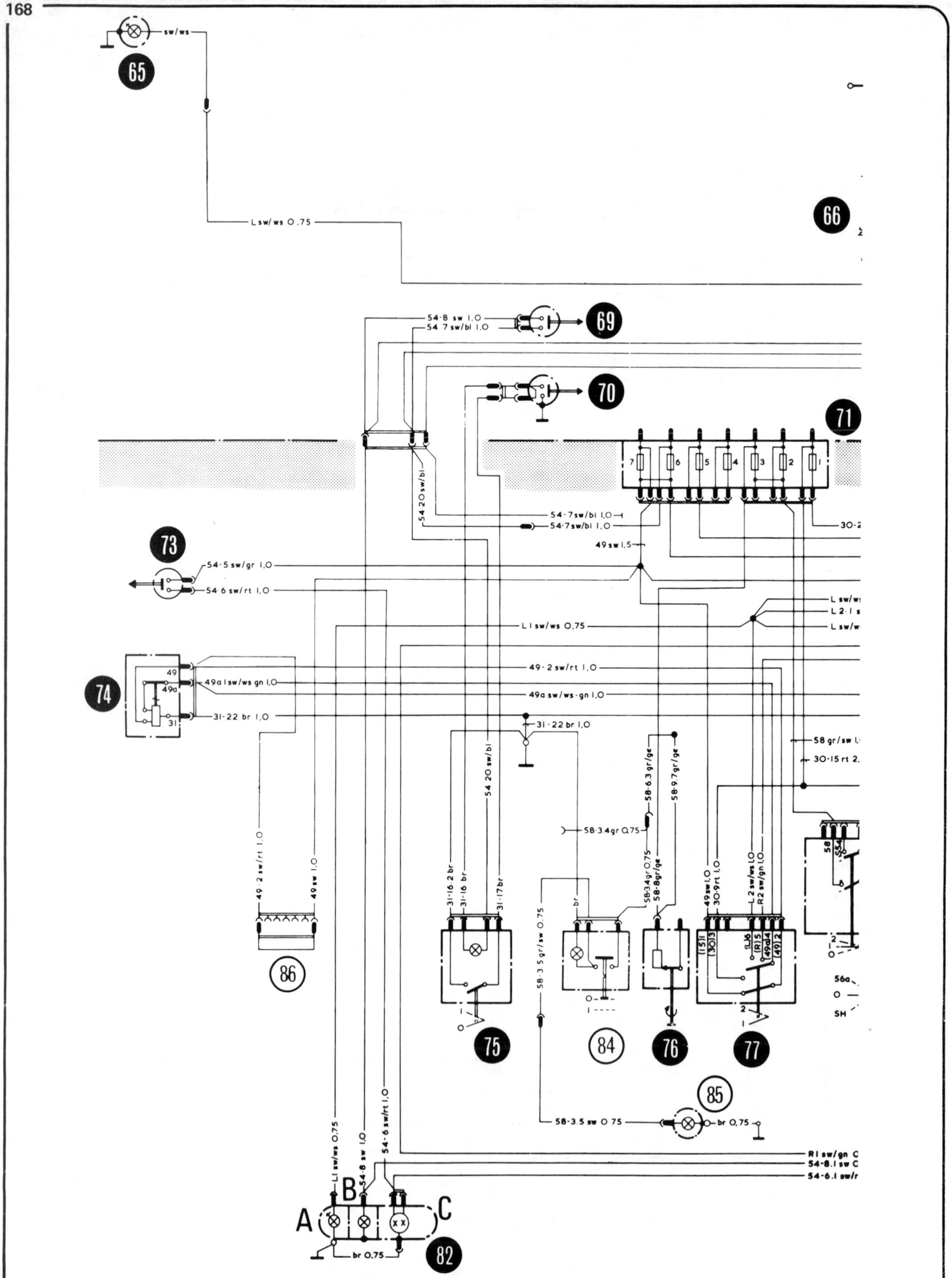

Fig. 10.47A Horn, indicator and hazard lights – S and Ghia

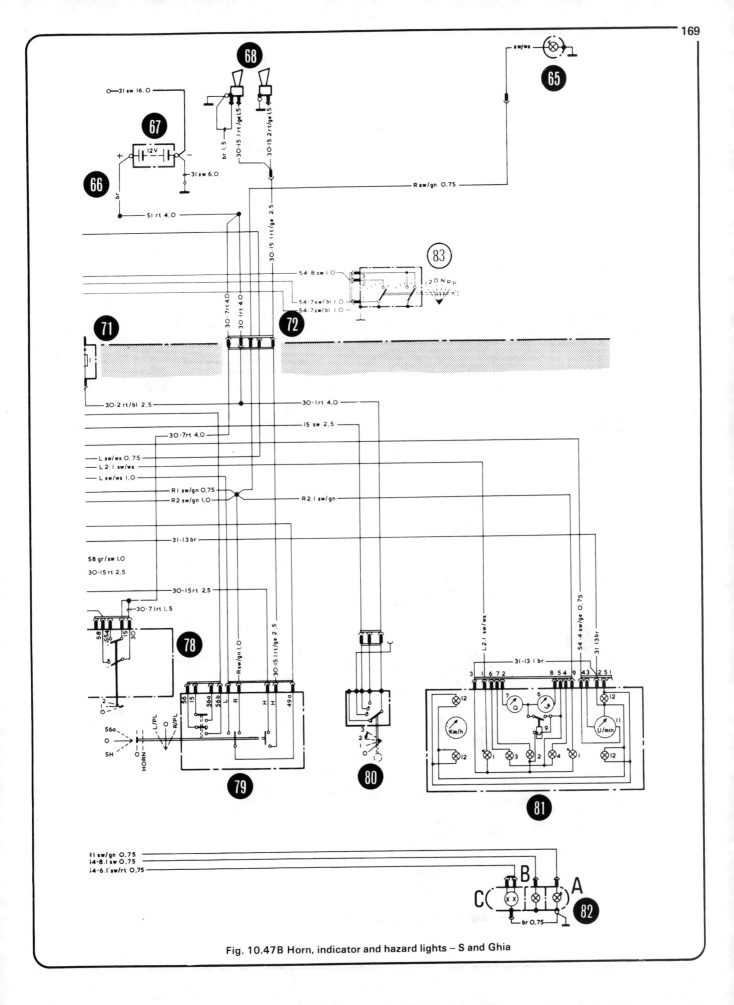

Fig. 10.47B Horn, indicator and hazard lights – S and Ghia

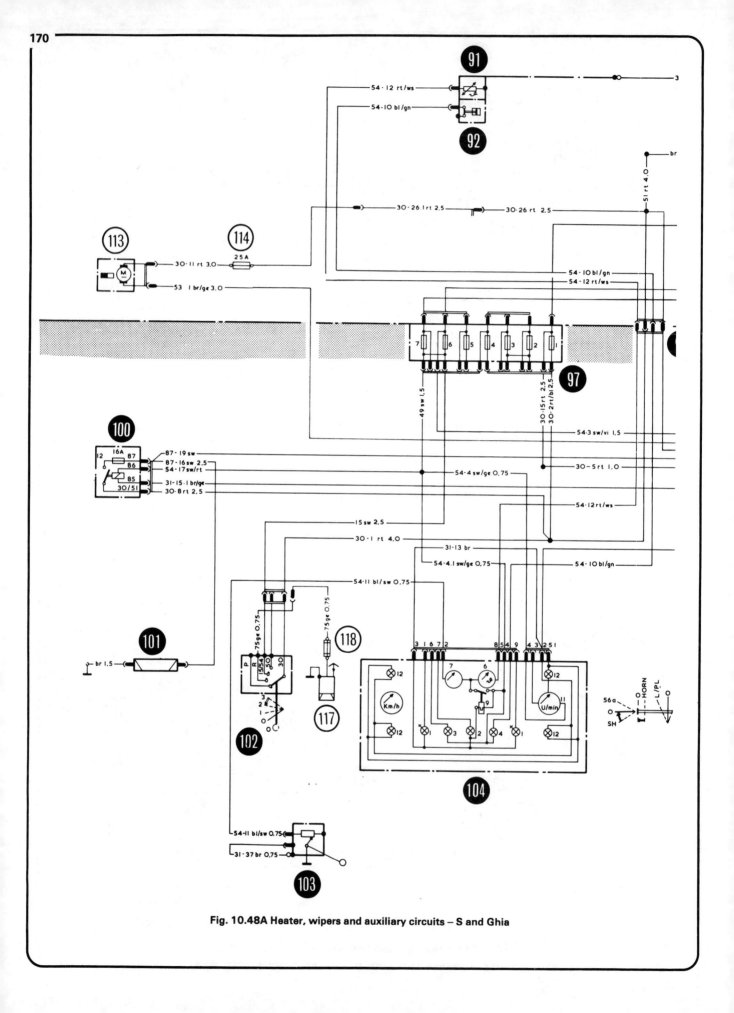

Fig. 10.48A Heater, wipers and auxiliary circuits – S and Ghia

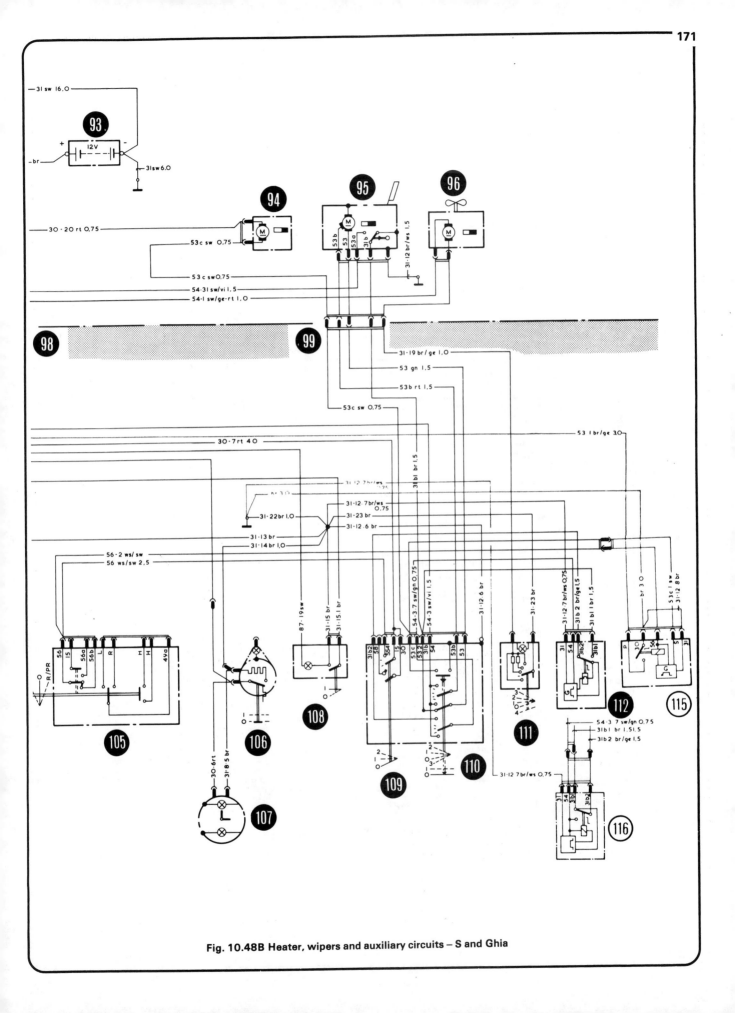

Fig. 10.48B Heater, wipers and auxiliary circuits – S and Ghia

Key to wiring diagram on pages 170 and 171

Item No	Item
Standard equipment	
91	Water temperature indicator sender unit
92	Oil pressure indicator sender unit
93	Battery
94	Windscreen washer pump
95	Windscreen wiper motor
96	Heater blower motor
97	Fuse box
98	Multi-plug (engine rear bulkhead – grey)
99	Multi-plug (engine rear bulkhead – black)
100	Relay heated rear window
101	Heated rear window
102	Steering lock ignition switch
103	Fuel indicator sender unit
104	Instrument cluster
	4 – oil pressure indicator
	5 – fuel level indicator
	6 – water temperature indicator
105	Multi-function switch
106	Cigar lighter
107	Clock
108	Heated rear window switch
109	Lighting switch
110	Windscreen wiper motor switch
111	Heater blower switch
112	Windscreen wiper intermittent relay

Item No	Item
Optional extra equipment	
113	Headlamp washer lamp
114	Headlamp washer pump fuse
115	Timing relay – headlamp washer pump
116	Windscreen wiper intermittent relay
117	Radio
118	Radio fuse

Wiring Colour	Code	Wiring colour	Code
Blue	bl	Pink	rs
Brown	br	Red	rt
Yellow	ge	Black	sw
Grey	gr	Violet	vi
Green	gr	White	ws

Wire codes

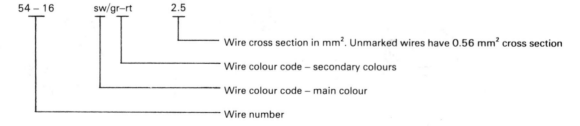

54 – 16   sw/gr–rt   2.5

Wire cross section in mm². Unmarked wires have 0.56 mm² cross section

Wire colour code – secondary colours

Wire colour code – main colour

Wire number

Chapter 11 Suspension and steering

For modifications, and information applicable to later models, see Supplement at end of manual

Contents

Specifications

Front suspension

Type	Independent, coil spring, long and short swinging arms. Double-acting hydraulic or gas-filled, telescopic shock absorbers
Spring identification	Colour-coded. For replacements use springs of same colour
Toe setting (toe-out)	0.04 in (1.0 mm) ± 0.04 in (1.0 mm)
Castor – standard	2° ± 1°
Castor – heavy duty	2° 32' ± 1°
Camber – standard	-0° 54' ± 0° 45'
Camber – heavy duty	-0° 51' ± 0° 45'
Maximum castor difference LH to RH	0° 45'
Maximum camber difference LH to RH	1° 00'

Rear suspension

Type	Radius arms, progressive coil springs, hydraulic or gas-filled double-acting telescopic shock absorbers, stabilizer bar
Springs identification	Colour-coded. For replacements use springs of same colour

Steering

Type	Rack-and-pinion, power assisted

Turns lock-to-lock 3.5
Turning circle
    Between kerbs . . . .   32.8 ft (10.0 m)
    Between walls . . . .   34.9 ft (10.64 m)
Steering ratio . . . .   17.73 : 1
Pinion bearing adjustment . . . .   Adjustable bearing
Rack slipper adjustment . . . .   Shims
Steering gear lubricant:
    Type . . . .   SAE 40 or SAE 20W oil
    Capacity . . . .   0.35 pint (0.2 litre)
Power assisted steering system . . . .   Automatic transmission fluid
                                                                                          (Ford specification SQ - M2C - 9007AA)

Power steering belt
Tension (cold)
    New . . . .   99 to 154 lbf (45 to 70 kgf)
    Used . . . .   77 to 99 lbf (35 to 45 kgf)

Roadwheels

Wheel size . . . . $4\frac{1}{2}$ J x 13 or $5\frac{1}{2}$ J x 13

Tyres

Tyre pressures – lbf in^2 (kgf m^2)

	Tyre size	Normally laden		Fully laden	
		Front	Rear	Front	Rear
Saloon	165 SR13	26 (1.8)	26 (1.8)	28 (2.0)	36 (2.5)
	185/70 SR13	23 (1.6)	23 (1.6)	28 (2.0)	36 (2.5)
Estate car	165 SR13	26 (1.8)	26 (1.8)	28 (2.0)	40 (2.8)
	185/70 SR13	23 (1.6)	24 (1.7)	28 (2.0)	40 (2.8)

Torque wrench settings

	lbf ft	kgf m
Front suspension		
Crossmember to body bolts	44 to 52	6.0 to 7.0
Stabiliser bar clamp bolts	13 to 18	1.7 to 2.4
Stabilizer bracket to body	13 to 18	1.7 to 2.4
Stub axle ball joints – first tightening	30 to 45	4.1 to 6.2
Stub axle ball joints – final tightening	43 to 66	5.8 to 9.2
Tie bar to lower arm	43 to 50	5.8 to 6.9
Tie bar insulator nuts	46 to 72	6.2 to 9.7
Upper arm pivot bolts	52 to 70	7.1 to 9.6
Lower arm to crossmember	52 to 59	7.1 to 8.2
Shock absorber mounts – top	28 to 35	3.9 to 4.8
Shock absorber mounts – bottom	6 to 9	0.8 to 1.2
Stabilizer bar to tie bar	7 to 9	1.0 to 1.3
Rear suspension		
Upper radius arm to body*	42 to 50	5.8 to 6.9
Upper radius arm to axle*	42 to 50	5.8 to 6.9
Lower radius arm to body*	42 to 50	5.8 to 6.9
Lower radius arm to axle*	42 to 50	5.8 to 6.9
Shock absorber mounts – top	30 to 35	3.9 to 4.8
Shock absorber mounts – bottom	42 to 50	5.8 to 6.9
Stabiliser bar to radius arm	30 to 35	4.0 to 5.0

These bolts must be tightened after the vehicle has been lowered to the ground

	lbf ft	kgf m
Steering		
Steering coupling clamp bolts	12 to 15	1.7 to 2.1
Steering coupling pinch bolt	12 to 15	1.7 to 2.1
Rack and housing locating peg	9 to 12	1.3 to 1.6
Pinion bearing cover plate	12 to 15	1.7 to 2.1
Control valve housing to pinion housing	12 to 15	1.7 to 2.1
Rack slipper cover plate	12 to 15	1.7 to 2.1
Feed hoses	19 to 23	2.7 to 3.2
Return hoses	12 to 15	1.7 to 2.1
Pulley hub securing bolts	15 to 20	2.0 to 2.7
Steering rack to crossmember bolts	32 to 37	4.1 to 5.1
Trackrod end locknuts	42 to 50	5.7 to 6.8
Trackrod end to steering arm	18 to 22	2.5 to 3.0
Trackrod end ballhousing	33 to 37	4.6 to 5.2
Steering column clamp nuts	13 to 17	1.7 to 2.4
Steering wheel to steering shaft	20 to 25	2.8 to 3.4
Wheel nuts		
Steel wheels	50 to 60	7 to 9
Aluminium wheels	90 to 105	12 to 14

1 General description

The independent front suspension (Fig. 11.1) comprises short and long swinging arms with coil springs and hydraulic or gas-filled (according to model) double-acting shock absorbers which operate on the lower swinging arms. The main suspension framework is located on the underbody side-members and acts as a mounting point for the wishbone type upper and single lower swinging arms. Attached to the upper frame are rubber bump stops to absorb excessive swinging arm movement. The suspension arms are mounted on rubber bushes and carry the stub axle balljoints at their outer ends.

Located on each axle stub are two taper roller bearings and these run in cups which are pressed into the wheel hubs. To keep the grease in the hub is a spring-loaded neoprene seal located in the inner end of the hub. The wheel studs are splined and pressed into the hub flange.

Bolted to the lower arm are rubber-mounted tie-bars which control the suspension castor angle. The tie-bars are connected to a stabilizer bar via a connecting link bushed at its connection points. It is mounted in split bushes which are clipped to brackets which are bolted to the body side-members.

The rear suspension (Fig. 11.2) comprises lower and upper radius arms and coil springs. The two lower radius arms are in position in the axial direction of the vehicle and the two upper radius arms are in a diagonal position so as to absorb any forces created during cornering. All four radius arms are mounted in insulated rubber blocks. Fitted between the rear axle casing and underside of the body are rubber mounted double-acting hydraulic or gas-filled telescopic shock absorbers. In addition, a stabilizer bar is fitted which passes along the lower radius arms and across the axle casing.

The coil springs are mounted on the lower radius arms and locate on a rubber ring between the spring and underside of the body.

The power-assisted steering consists of the steering gear, the power-assistance system and the steering column (Fig. 11.3).

The steering gear is of the rack-and-pinion type and is bolted onto the front crossmember. The pinion is connected to the steering column by a coupling assembly which has a universal joint and flexible coupling.

The upper end of the steering column is secured by a clamp with shear-off bolts. The steering shaft and column collapses on impact thus minimising injury in the event of an accident. This is achieved by convoluting the steering column tube and having shear-off inserts fitted in the column support brackets and in the steering shaft.

Turning the steering wheel causes the rack to move in a lateral direction and the track-rods attached to each end of the rack transmits this movement to the steering arms on the stub axle assemblies thereby moving the roadwheels.

Two adjustments are possible on the steering gear. Rack slipper

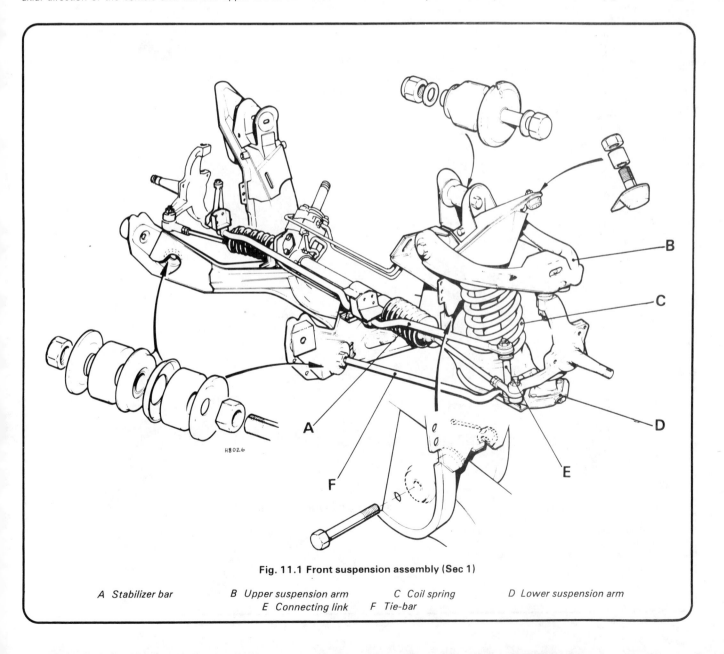

Fig. 11.1 Front suspension assembly (Sec 1)

A Stabilizer bar   B Upper suspension arm   C Coil spring   D Lower suspension arm

E Connecting link   F Tie-bar

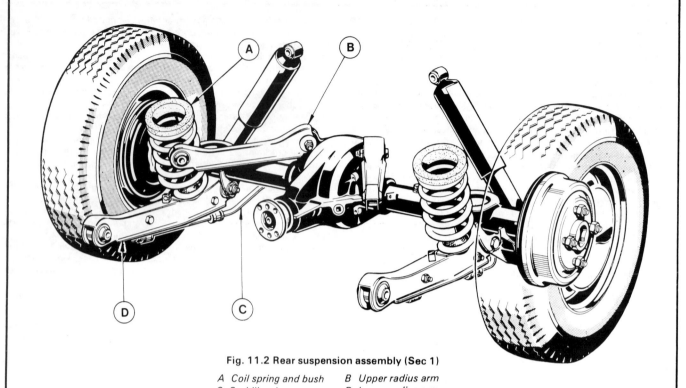

Fig. 11.2 Rear suspension assembly (Sec 1)

A Coil spring and bush   B Upper radius arm
C Stabilizer bar   D Lower radius arm

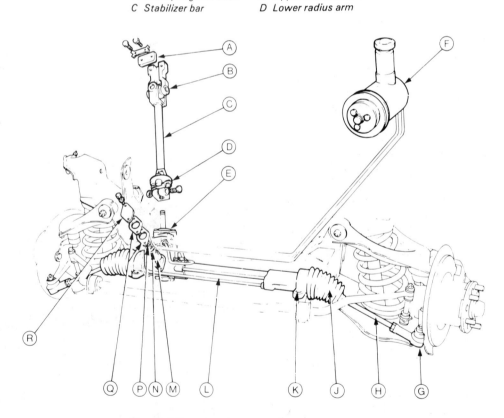

Fig. 11.3 Power assisted steering gear assembly (Sec 1)

A Clamp plate
B Universal joint
C Lower steering shaft
D Flexible coupling
E Control valve

F Power assistance pump and
   reservoir
G Track-rod balljoint
H Track-rod

J Rack gaiters
K Rack mounting
L Rack housing
M Slipper

N O-ring
P Slipper pre-load spring
Q Slipper bearing shim
R Slipper bearing cove

adjustment is carried out by varying the thickness of the shim pack, and pinion pre-load adjustment is by an adjustable roller bearing.

The two track-rods are adjustable in length to allow adjustment of the toe-out setting. Lock stops are built into the steering gear and are not adjustable.

Power-assistance is supplied by automatic transmission fluid. The fluid is pressurised by a roller-type pump and is fed to the control valve on the steering gear. The control valve passes the fluid to the appropriate side of the piston which is integral with the rack. The pump/reservoir is mounted on the left-hand side of the engine and is belt-driven from a pulley on the crankshaft. An idler pulley is fitted to provide for belt tension adjustment.

Should the power-assistance system fail for any reason normal manual steering is still available.

2 Front hub bearings – removal and refitting

1 Refer to Chapter 9, Section 5, paragraphs 1, 2, 3, 5 and 6 and remove the disc brake caliper.
2 By judicious tapping and levering remove the dust cap from the centre of the hub.
3 Remove the split pin from the nut retainer and lift away the adjusting nut retainer.
4 Unscrew the adjusting nut and lift away the thrust washer and outer tapered bearing (Fig. 11.4).
5 Pull off the complete hub and disc assembly from the stub axle.
6 From the back of the hub assembly carefully prise out the grease seal noting which way round it is fitted. Lift away the inner tapered bearing.
7 Carefully clean out the hub and wash the bearings with petrol making sure that no grease or oil is allowed to get into the brake disc.
8 Using a soft metal drift carefully remove the inner and outer bearing cups.
9 To fit new cups make sure they are the right way round and using metal tubes of suitable size carefully drift them into position.
10 Pack the cone and roller assembly with grease working the grease well into the cage and rollers. **Note:** *Leave the hub and grease seal empty to allow for subsequent expansion of the grease.*
11 To reassemble the hub first fit the inner bearing and then gently tap the grease seal back into the hub. A new seal must always be fitted as during removal it was probably damaged. The lip must face inwards to the hub.
12 Refit the hub and disc assembly to the stub axle and slide on the outer bearing and thrust washer.
13 Refit the adjusting nut, and tighten it to a torque wrench setting of 27 lbf ft (3.7 kgf m) whilst rotating the hub and disc to ensure free movement and centralisation of the bearings (Fig. 11.5). Slacken the nut back by 90° which will give the required endfloat. Fit the nut retainer and new split pin. Bend over the ears of the split pin.
14 Refit the dust cap to the centre of the hub.

15 Refit the caliper as described in Chapter 9, Section 5.

3 Front hub bearings – adjustment

1 To check the condition of the hub bearings, jack-up the front of the car and support on firmly based stands. Grasp the roadwheel at two opposite points to check for any rocking movement in the wheel hub. Watch carefully for any movement in the steering gear which can easily be mistaken for hub movement.
2 If a front wheel hub has excessive movement, this is adjusted by removing the hub cap and then tapping and levering the dust cap from the centre of the hub.
3 Remove the split pin from the nut retainer and lift away the adjusting nut retainer.
4 If a torque wrench is available tighten the centre adjusting nut to a torque wrench setting of 27 lbf ft (3.73 kgf m) as shown in Fig. 11.5 and then slacken the nut back 90° which will give the required endfloat. Replace the nut retainer and lock with a new split pin.
5 Assuming a torque wrench is not available however, tighten the centre adjusting nut until a slight drag is felt on rotating the wheel. Then loosen the nut very slowly until the wheel turns freely again and there is just a perceptible endfloat. Refit the nut retainer and lock with a new split pin.
6 Refit the dust cap to the centre of the hub.

4 Front hub – removal and refitting

1 Follow the instructions given in Section 2 of this Chapter up to and including paragraph 5.
2 Bend back the locking tab and undo the four bolts holding the hub to the brake disc.
3 If a new hub assembly is being fitted it is supplied complete with the new cups and bearings. The bearing cups will already be fitted in the hub. It is essential to check that the cups and bearings are of the same manufacture; this can be done by reading the name on the bearings and by looking at the initial letter stamped on the hub. 'T' stands for Timken and 'S' for Skefco.
4 Clean with scrupulous care the mating surfaces of the hub and check for blemishes or damage. Any dirt or blemishes will almost certainly give rise to the disc running out-of-true. Using new locking tabs bolt the disc and hub together and tighten the bolts to a torque wrench setting of 30 - 34 lbf ft (4.15 - 4.70 kgf m).
5 To grease and reassemble the hub assembly follow the instructions given in Section 2, paragraphs 10 onwards.

5 Front axle assembly – removal and refitting

1 Chock the rear wheels, jack-up the vehicle and support the body

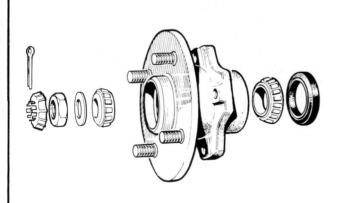

Fig. 11.4 Front hub assembly (Sec 2)

Fig. 11.5 Tightening the hub adjusting nut (Sec 2 and 3)

on firmly based axle-stands. Remove the front wheels.

2   Using a garage crane or overhead hoist support the weight of the engine.

3   Wipe the top of the brake master cylinder reservoir and unscrew the cap. Place a piece of polythene sheet over the top of the reservoir and refit the cap. This is to stop hydraulic fluid syphoning out during subsequent operations.

4   Disconnect the flexible brake hoses at the body support brackets and plug the hoses to prevent the entry of dirt.

5   Disconnect the feed and return pipes from the central valve on the steering gear and drain the fluid into a container. Plug the valve openings and the ends of the pipes to prevent dirt entering.

6   Remove the steering column to steering gear coupling as described in Section 26.

7   Undo and remove the engine mounting securing nuts at the underside of the mounting. There is one nut to each mounting.

8   Using a garage hydraulic jack or blocks support the weight of the front axle sub-assembly.

9   Remove the two stabilizer bars to body clamps. Unclip the two flexible fuel pipes.

10   Undo and remove the bolts which secure the front axle sub-assembly to the body sidemembers as shown in Fig. 11.6. Carefully lower the complete assembly and draw forwards from under the front of the vehicle.

11   Refitting the front axle sub-assembly is the reverse sequence to removal. It will be necessary to bleed the brake hydraulic system as described in Chapter 9, Section 2 and the power steering system as described in Section 28.

---

6   Front axle assembly – overhaul

After high mileage it may be considered necessary to overhaul the complete front axle assembly. It is far better to remove the complete unit as described in Section 5 and dismantle it rather than work on it still mounted on the car. Then proceed as follows:

1   Refer to Chapter 9, Section 5 and remove the caliper.

2   Prise off the hub dust cap and withdraw the split pin and nut retainer. Undo and remove the nut (Fig. 11.4).

3   Carefully pull the hub and disc assembly from the axle stub.

4   Undo and remove the ball stud securing nuts and then using a universal ball joint separator release the ball joint taper pins from the stub axle locations.

5   Next remove the trackrod-ends from their locations on the stub axles and remove the stub axle assembly.

6   Withdraw the long bolt that secures the upper arm to the axle frame and lift away the upper arm.

7   It is necessary to compress the spring. For this either make up a spring compressor tool comprising two parts as shown in Fig. 11.7 or borrow one from the local Ford garage. Do not attempt to use any makeshift tools as this can be very dangerous.

8   Using the spring compressors, contract the spring by at least 2 inches (51 mm).

9   Undo and remove the upper and lower shock absorber retaining nuts (lower fixing) and bolt (upper fixing). The shock absorber may now be lifted away through the coil spring and lower arm aperture.

10   Undo and remove the bolts that secure the tie bar to the lower arm. The lower arm should now be pulled down until there is sufficient clearances for the coil spring to be lifted away.

11   Bend back the lock tabs and unscrew and remove the four bolts that secure the steering rack to the front axle frame. Lift away the steering rack assembly.

12   Undo and remove the nut and bolt that secures the lower arm to the front axle frame. Lift away the lower arm.

13   Using a suitable diameter drift or long bolt, piece of metal tube, packing washers and nut, remove the lower arm bush.

14   The operations described in paragraphs 1 - 13 should now be repeated for the second front suspension assembly. It will be necessary to release the coil spring compressor.

15   Undo and remove the nuts that secure the tie bars to the axle frame. Lift away the connecting link, tie bar and stabilizer bar assembly.

16   Undo and remove the nuts and washers from each of the connecting links and part the stabilizer bar from the tie bars.

17   It is now beneficial to cut away the bushes in the tie bar and stabilizer which will make removal far easier.

18   Remove the nuts and washers securing each rubber bump stop. Remove the bump stops.

19   Dismantling is now complete. Wash all parts and wipe dry ready for inspection. Inspect all bushes for signs of wear and all parts for damage or excessive corrosion: if evident, new parts must be obtained. If one coil spring requires renewal the second one must also be renewed as it will have settled over a period of time.

20   During reassembly it is important that none of the rubber mounted bolts are fully tightened until the weight of the vehicle is taken on the front wheels.

21   Refit the rubber bump stops. If they are difficult to insert in their location smear with a little washing up liquid. Bolt the bump stops in position.

22   Fit new end bushes to the stabilizer and tie bar and then locate the connecting links in the stabilizer.

23   Next locate the connecting links in the tie bar and stabilizer bar bushes. Secure with their nut and washers.

24   Screw the nuts on the tie bar ends and follow with the washer together with the bush. Locate the tie bars in their respective positions on the frame and loosely refit the spacer, bush, washer and nut.

25   Using a bench vice and suitable diameter tube fit a new bush to the lower arm. The lower arm pivot bolt is fitted with a nylon nut and split pin. Tighten the nut to 55 lbf ft (7.6 kgf m).

26   Locate the lower arm in the frame and line up the holes with a screwdriver. Refit the pivot bolt and washers making sure that the bolt head is towards the front of the axle frame.

27   Refit the tie bar to the lower suspension arm and retain with the two nuts and bolts.

28   Place the coil spring between the frame and lower arm, with the feathered edge uppermost. Insert the shock absorber through the lower arm and spring and secure the shock absorber in position with the bolt (upper fixing) and nuts (lower fixing).

29   Unscrew the spring compressor and repeat the operations in paragraphs 22 to 28 for the second front suspension assembly.

30   Check the condition of the steering rack mounting rubbers and renew if necessary. Position the steering rack on the axle crossmember then fit and tighten the securing bolts to the specified torque.

31   Place the upper suspension arm on the axle frame, insert the pivot bolt through the arm and frame holes so that the head is towards the front of the axle frame. Secure with the washer and nut. Repeat this operation for the second upper suspension arm.

32   Connect the stub axle assembly to the suspension arm ball joints, locate the trackrod ends in the stub axle, and tighten all the nuts. The trackrod end to steering arm nuts should be tightened to the specified torque.

33   Refer to Section 4 and refit the hub and disc assemblies.

34   The complete front axle assembly may now be refitted to the car, as described in Section 5.

35   Check the wheel alignment and steering angles (Section 22).

---

7   Front axle mounting bushes – removal and refitting

1   Refer to Section 5, and remove the front axle assembly.

2   Using a piece of tube about 4 inches (101.6 mm) long and suitable diameter, a long bolt and nut and packing washers draw the bushes from the side member (Fig. 11.8).

3   Fit new bushes using the reverse procedure. The new bushes must be installed so that the arrows are in alignment with the indentation in the bodyframe. The flange position of the bushes must be: *front bush,* flange located *inside* sidemember; *rear bush,* flange located *outside* sidemember (Fig. 11.9).

4   Refit the front assembly, as described in Section 5.

---

8   Stub axle – removal and refitting

1   Refer to Section 2 and remove the front hub and disc assembly.

2   Undo and remove the three bolts and spring washers that secure the brake disc splash shield to the stub axle.

3   Extract the split pins and then undo and remove the castellated nuts that secure the three ball joint pins to the stub axle.

4   Using a universal ball joint separator, separate the ball joint pins from the stub axle. Lift away the stub axle.

5   Refitting the stub axle is the reverse sequence to removal. The trackrod end to steering arm retaining nut must be tightened to the

specified torque.

6 If a new stub axle has been fitted it is recommended that the steering geometry and front wheel toe-out be checked. Further information may be found in Section 22.

9 Upper suspension arm – removal and refitting

1 Chock the rear wheels, jack up the front of the car and place on firmly based axle stands. Remove the roadwheel.

2 Disconnect the flexible brake hoses at the body support brackets.

3 Remove the steering column to steering gear coupling as described in Section 26 (photo).

4 Using a crane or overhead hoist support the weight of the engine.

5 Undo and remove the engine mounting securing nuts at the underside of the mounting.

6 Using a garage hydraulic jack or blocks, support the weight of the front axle assembly.

7 Unclip the two flexible fuel pipes and the power steering hoses.

8 Undo and remove the rear bolts which secure the front axle assembly to the body sidemembers. Slacken but do not remove the front securing bolts.

9 Carefully lower the assembly, allowing it to pivot about the front securing bolts.

9.3 Steering column to steering gear coupling

Fig. 11.6 Location of front axle mounting bolts (Sec 5)

Fig. 11.7 Front coil spring with compressor tools fitted (Sec 6)

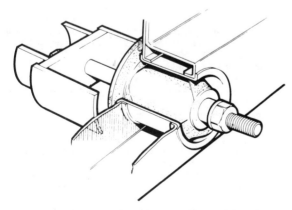

Fig. 11.8 Removing the mounting bush (Sec 7)

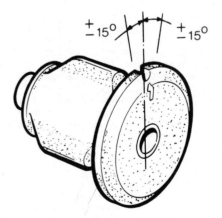

Fig. 11.9 Front axle mounting bush alignment mark (Sec 7)

14.4 Shock absorber lower mounting nuts

10 Undo and remove the upper arm to stub axle ball joint nut then using a ball joint separator release the joint. Undo the upper arm pivot bolt nut, withdraw the bolt and remove the upper arm.
11 Refitting is the reverse sequence of removal but the following points should be noted:

    a)   *Rubber mounted bolts and nuts should not be fully tightened until the weight of the vehicle is taken on the front wheels*
    b)   *The head of the upper arm pivot bolt should be towards the front*
    c)   *Check the steering geometry, Section 22*
    d)   *It will be necessary to bleed the braking system, Chapter 9, Section 2*

10 Lower suspension arm – removal and refitting

1 Chock the rear wheels, jack-up the front of the car and place on firmly based axle-stands. Remove the roadwheel.
2 Wipe the top of the brake master cylinder reservoir and unscrew the cap. Place a piece of polythene sheet over the top of the reservoir and replace the cap. Disconnect the flexible brake hoses at the body support brackets.
3 It is now necessary to compress the spring. For this either make up a spring compressor tool comprising two parts as shown in Fig. 11.8 or borrow one from the local Ford garage. Do not attempt to use any makeshift tools as this can be very dangerous.
4 Using the spring compressor, contract the spring by at least 2 inches (51 mm).
5 Undo and remove the upper and lower shock absorber retaining nuts (lower fixing) and bolt (upper fixing). The shock absorber may now be lifted away through the coil spring and lower arm aperture.
6 Withdraw the split pin, undo and remove the castellated nut that secures the lower wishbone ball joint pin to the stub axle. Using a universal ball joint separator separate the ball joint pin from the stub axle.
7 The lower suspension arm may now be parted and the coil spring removed.
8 Undo the tie-bar locknut and remove the two bolts and nuts that secure the tie-bar to the lower arm.
9 Undo and remove the bolt that secures the lower arm to the front axle frame. The suspension arm can now be lifted rearwards and downwards away from the front axle frame.
10 To fit a new bush first remove the old bush by using a piece of tube about 4 inches (101 mm) long and suitable diameter, a long bolt and nut and packing washer, draw the bush from the lower suspension arm. Fitting a new bush is the reverse sequence to removal.
11 Refitting the lower suspension arm is the reverse sequence to removal. The lower arm retaining bolts must be tightened once the car has been lowered to the ground.

12 If a new lower steering arm has been fitted it is recommended that the steering geometry and front wheel alignment be checked. Further information may be found in Section 22.

11 Stabilizer bar – removal and refitting

1 Undo and remove the bolt that secures each stabilizer bar mounting bush clip to the stabilizer bar mounting bracket.
2 Release the clips and then undo and remove the three bolts and spring washers that secure each mounting bracket to the body side-member.
3 Undo and remove the two nuts, dished washers and upper bushes and detach the connecting links from their locations in the stabilizer bar. The stabilizer bar may now be lifted away from the underside of the car.
4 Refitting the stabilizer bar is the reverse sequence to removal.

12 Stabilizer bar mounting bushes – removal and refitting

1 Undo and remove the bolt that secures each stabilizer bar mounting bush clip to the stabilizer bar mounting brackets.
2 Using a metal bar such as a tyre lever carefully ease the stabilizer bar downwards and push the split mounting bushes and washers clear of their locations.
3 Push the new bushes and washers onto the bar in their approximate positions and then align the bushes with the stabilizer bar mounting brackets and refit the retaining clips and bolts.

13 Stabilizer bar connecting link bush – removal and refitting

1 Refer to Section 11 and remove the stabilizer bar.
2 Using a sharp knife of hacksaw blade cut the cone ends off the connecting link bushes and discard the bushes.
3 Using a bench vice, a piece of tube of suitable diameter and a socket fit the new connecting link bushes.
4 Refit the stabilizer bar as described in Section 11.

14 Front shock absorber – removal and refitting

1 Chock the rear wheels, jack-up the front of the car and place on firmly based stands. Remove the roadwheel.
2 Locate a small jack under the lower suspension arm and partially compress the coil spring.
3 Undo and remove the shock absorber top mounting bolt.
4 Undo and remove the two nuts that secure the shock absorber lower mounting. The shock absorber may now be lifted away through the coil spring and lower arm aperture (photo).
5 Examine the shock absorber for signs of damage to the body, distorted piston rod, loose mounting or hydraulic fluid leakage which, if evident, means a new unit should be fitted.
6 To test for shock absorber efficiency, hold the unit in the vertical position and gradually extend and contract the unit between its maximum and minimum limit ten times. It should be apparent that there is equal resistance on both directions of movement. If this is not apparent a new unit should be fitted – always renew the shock absorbers in pairs.
7 Refitting the shock absorbers is the reverse sequence to removal.

15 Tie bar – removal and refitting

1 Chock the rear wheels, jack-up the front of the car and place on firmly based axle stands. Remove the roadwheel.
2 Undo and remove the bolts that secure the tie bar to the lower suspension arm.
3 Extract the split pin from the end of the bar. Undo and remove the forward of the two nuts that secure the tie bar to the chassis frame member.
4 Disconnect the stabilizer bar connecting link.
5 Remove the bush and spacer assembly from the threaded end of the tie bar. Lift away the tie-bar (Fig. 11.10).
6 If it is necessary to fit new bushes, use a sharp knife or hacksaw

blade and cut the cone ends from the tie bar bush. Discard the old bush.

7   Using a tube of suitable diameter, a socket and bench vice, fit a new tie bar end bush.

8   Refitting the tie-bar is the reverse sequence to removal. It is recommended that the steering geometry and front wheel alignment be checked. Further information will be found in Section 22.

16 Rear spring – removal and refitting

1   Chock the front wheels, jack-up the rear of the car and support the *body* on firmly based stands. Remove the rear wheels.

2   Using a suitable jack to relieve any tension on the through bolts, remove the stabilizer bar from the lower radius arm (Fig. 11.11).

3   Position the jack under the lower arm to remove the tension, and remove the front through bolt. Lower the jack and ease out the coil spring and rubber bush, noting its location (Fig. 11.12).

4   Refitting is the reverse of this procedure. The lower arm bolt should be fitted from the outside, and the stabilizer bar bolts from the inside. Do not tighten the nuts fully until the weight of the car is on its wheels (photo).

5   If one coil spring requires renewal the second one must also be renewed as it will have settled over a period of time. Make sure, by referring to a Ford dealer, that the correct type of spring is fitted.

17 Rear suspension upper radius arm – removal and refitting

1   Chock the front wheels, jack-up the rear of the car and support the body on firmly based axle-stands. Remove the rear wheels.

2   Disconnect the stabilizer bar from the radius arm and swing it to one side.

3   Jack-up the rear axle so that the shock absorber can be disconnected from the axle mounting.

4   Lower the jack and press the coil spring from its upper retainer. Now twist the spring from its lower retainer.

5   Again jack-up the rear axle and having relieved the radius arm bolts of any strain, remove the bolts and withdraw the radius arm.

6   Should it be necessary to fit new mounting insulator bushes the bushes may be removed using a piece of tube about 4 inches (101 mm) long and suitable diameter, a long bolt and nut and packing washers and drawing out the old bushes (Fig. 11.13).

7   Fitting new bushes is the reverse procedure as was used for removal.

8   The upper arm bolts should be fitted from the outside, the stabilizer bar bolts from the inside, and the shock absorber bolt from the front, with the spacer located as shown in Fig. 11.14. Do not tighten the nuts fully until the weight of the car is on its wheels.

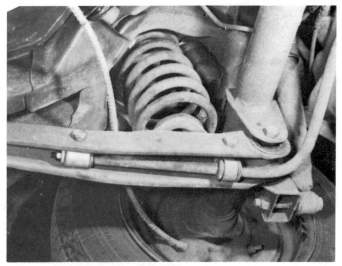

16.4 Stabilizer bar bolted to lower radius arm

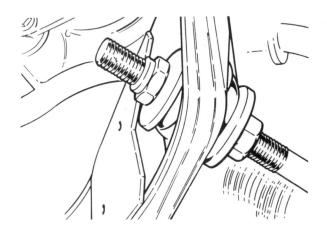

Fig. 11.10 Tie-bar end mounting (Sec 15)

Fig. 11.11 Rear stabilizer bar removal from lower radius arm (Sec 16)

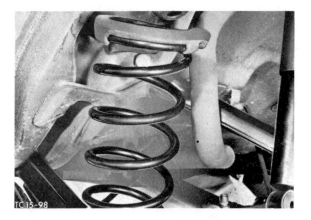

Fig. 11.12 Removing the rear suspension spring and bush (Sec 16)

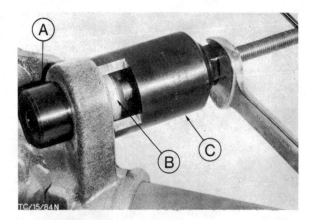

Fig. 11.13 Removing upper radius mounting bush (Sec 17)

A Nut and packing washers   B Bush
C Tube

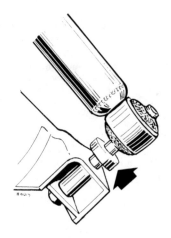

Fig. 11.14 Fitting spacer to rear shock absorber lower mounting bolt (Sec 18)

Fig. 11.15 Renewing shock absorber bushes (Sec 19)

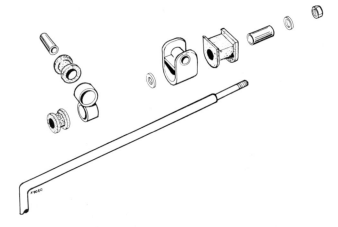

Fig. 11.16 Renewing stabilizer bar mounting bushes (Sec 20)

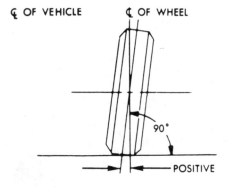

Fig. 11.17 Camber diagram (Sec 22)

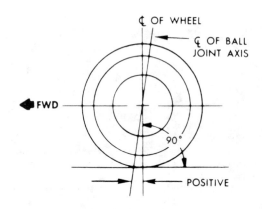

Fig. 11.18 Castor diagram (Sec 22)

18 Rear suspension lower radius arm – removal and refitting

1   Chock the front wheels, jack-up the rear of the car and support the body on firmly based axle-stands. Remove the rear wheels.
2   Disconnect the stabilizer bar from the radius arm and swing it to one side.
3   Jack-up the rear axle and disconnect the shock absorber lower mounting.
4   Lower the jack and press the coil spring from the upper retainer. Twist the spring from the lower retainer.
5   Remove the radius arm pivot bolts and withdraw the arm.
6   Should it be necessary to fit new mounting insulator bushes, the bushes may be removed using a piece of tube about 4 inches (101 mm) long and suitable diameter, a long bolt and nut and packing washers and drawing out the old bushes (Fig. 11.13).
7   Fitting new bushes is the reverse procedure as was used for removal. **Note** *the two bushes are of different diameters.*
8   Refitting the lower radius arm is the reverse sequence to removal. The upper spring rubber bush *must* be refitted correctly. The lower arm bolts should be fitted from the outside, the stabilizer bar bolts from the inside and the shock absorber bolt from the front, with the spacer located as in Fig. 11.14. Do not tighten the nuts fully until the weight of the car is on its wheels.

19 Rear shock absorber – removal and refitting

1   Chock the front wheels, jack-up the rear of the car and support the axle on firmly based stands. Remove the rear wheel.
2   Undo and remove the shock absorber upper and lower mounting nuts and bolt. Lift away the shock absorbers (photo).
3   Should it be necessary to fit new rubber bushes, use a suitable diameter drift and drive out the spacer sleeve and then the rubber bushes. Refitting new bushes is the reversal of the removal sequence (Fig. 11.15).
4   Examine the shock absorber for signs of damage to the body, distorted piston rod or hydraulic leakage which, if evident, means a new unit should be fitted.
5   To test for damper efficiency hold the unit in the vertical position and gradually extend and contract the unit between its maximum and minimum limits ten times. It should be apparent that there is equal resistance in both directions of movement. If this is not apparent a new unit should be fitted; always renew shock absorbers in pairs.
6   Refitting the shock absorber is the reverse sequence to removal (Fig. 11.14).

20 Rear stabilizer bar – removal and refitting

1   Remove the bolts which secure each end of the stabilizer bar to the radius arms (Fig. 11.11).
2   Unscrew the self-locking nuts and withdraw the front and rear mounting brackets together with the insulating bushes.
3   Bushes are renewed in a similar manner to those for the shock absorbers, by first removing the metal spacer. The use of a little brake fluid will facilitate installation of the rubber bush (Fig. 11.16).

21 Power assisted steering system – checking the fluid level

1   Remove the reservoir filler cap/dipstick. Wipe the dipstick with a non-fluffy cloth and refit the cap, then remove the cap and check the level of the fluid on the dipstick.
2   One side of the dipstick is marked *Full Cold* and the other side *Full Hot*. Top up, if necessary, with the specified power steering fluid to the appropriate mark on the dipstick.
3   Where topping-up is necessary, check all hoses and pipes in the system for leakage and rectify as required.

22 Front wheel – alignment and steering angles

1   Accurate front wheel alignment is essential to prevent excessive steering and tyre wear. Before considering the steering/suspension

19.2 Remove the shock absorber upper and lower mounting nuts and bolt

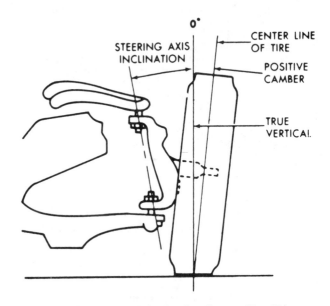

Fig. 11.19 Steering axis inclination diagram (Sec 22)

geometry, check that the tyres are correctly inflated, that the front wheels are not buckled, the hub bearings are not worn or incorrectly adjusted and that the steering linkage is in good order, without slackness or wear at the joints.
2   Wheel alignment consists of four factors:
Camber, which is the angle at which the front wheels are set from the vertical when viewed from the front of the car. Positive camber is the amount (in degrees) that the wheels are tilted outwards at the top from the vertical (Fig. 11.17).
Castor, is the angle between the steering axis and a vertical line when viewed from each side of the car. Positive castor is when the steering axis is inclined rearward (Fig. 11.18).
Steering axis inclination, is the angle, when viewed from the front of the car between the vertical and an imaginary line drawn between the upper and lower suspension control arm ball joints (Fig. 11.19).
Toe setting, is the amount by which the distance between the front inside edges of the roadwheels (measured at hub height) differs from the diametrically opposite distance measured between the rear inside edges of the front roadwheels (Fig. 11.20 shows toe-out).
3   Due to the need for special gauges it is not normally within the scope of the home mechanic to check and adjust any steering angle except toe. Where suitable equipment can be borrowed however, adjustment can be carried in the following way, setting the tolerances

to those given in Specifications.

4   Before carrying out any adjustment, place the vehicle on level ground, tyres correctly inflated and the front roadwheels set in the 'straight-ahead' position. Make sure that all suspension and steering components are securely attached and without wear in the moving parts.

The camber and steering axis inclination angles are set in production and they cannot be altered or adjusted. Any deviation from the angles specified must therefore be due to collision damage or gross wear in the components.

5   *To adjust the castor angle,* release the tie bar nuts and screw them in, or out, as necessary (Fig. 11.10).

6   *To adjust the toe,* (which must always be carried out after adjustment of the castor angle – where required), make or obtain a toe gauge. One can be made up from a length of tubing or bar, cranked to clear the sump, clutch or torque converter bellhousing and having a screw and locknut at one end.

7   Use the gauge to measure the distance between the two inner wheel rims at hub height and at the rear of the roadwheels.

8   Push or pull the vehicle to rotate the roadwheels through 180° (half a turn) and then measure the distance between the inner wheel rims at hub height and at the front of the roadwheels. This last measurement will differ from the first by the amount specified in the Specifications Section. This represents the correct toe-setting of the front wheels.

9   Where the toe-setting is found to be incorrect, loosen the locknuts on both the trackrod ends, also release the screws on the steering bellow clips (Fig. 11.21).

10 Turn each trackrod in opposite directions by not more than one quarter turn at a time and then recheck the toe-setting. When the adjustment is correct, tighten the locknuts without moving the trackrods and make sure that the trackrod ends are in their correct plane (centre position of arc of travel).

11 Tighten the steering bellows clips making sure that the bellows have not twisted during the adjustment operations.

12 It is important to always adjust each trackrod equally. Where new components have been fitted, adjust the length of each trackrod so that they are equal and the front roadwheels in approximately the 'straight-ahead' position, before commencing final setting with the gauge.

23 Steering wheel – removal and refitting

1   With the front wheels in the straight-ahead position note the position of the spokes of the steering wheel and mark the hub of the steering wheel and inner shaft to ensure correct positioning upon refitting.

2   Carefully prise out the steering wheel insert and using a socket or box spanner of the correct size slacken the steering wheel nut but leave it two or three turns on the thread (photo).

3   Remove the wheel by striking the rear of the rim adjacent to the spokes with the palms of the hands which should loosen the hub splines from the steering shaft spline. Fully remove the nut and lift off the steering wheel.

4   Refitting is the reverse procedure to removal. Correctly align the two marks previously made to ensure correct positioning of the spokes. Do not strike the steering wheel when refitting as it could cause the inner shaft to collapse. Refit the nut and tighten to the specified torque.

24 Steering column assembly – removal and refitting

1   Disconnect the battery and then working within the engine compartment, bend back the locktabs on the flexible coupling clamp plate. Slacken both bolts, extract one and swing the clamp plate to one side.

2   Refer to Section 23 and remove the steering wheel.

3   Unscrew and remove the steering column lower shroud and remove it, then unclip the upper shroud.

4   Unscrew and remove the dash lower insulation panel.

5   Remove the two bolts each from the wiper switch, light switch and multi-function switch. Note that one wiper switch bolt also has an earth wire.

6   Remove the section of air duct which passes over the steering column.

7   Remove the two screws which secure the wiring harness plug to

23.2 Steering wheel insert removed showing securing nut

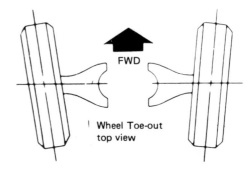

Fig. 11.20 Front wheel alignment (exaggerated toe-out shown) (Sec 22)

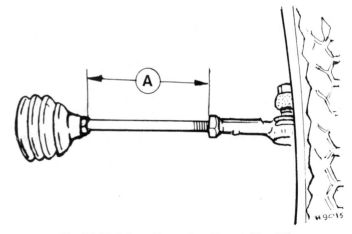

Fig. 11.21 Adjustable track rod length (Sec 22)

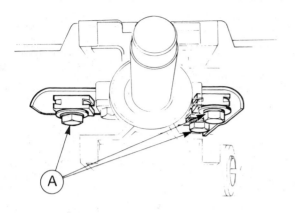

Fig. 11.22 Steering column removal (Sec 24)

A Mounting bolts

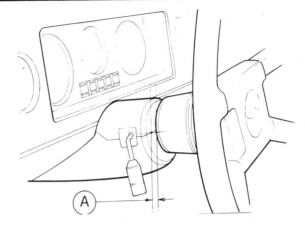

Fig. 11.23 Checking the steering column assembly location (Sec 24)

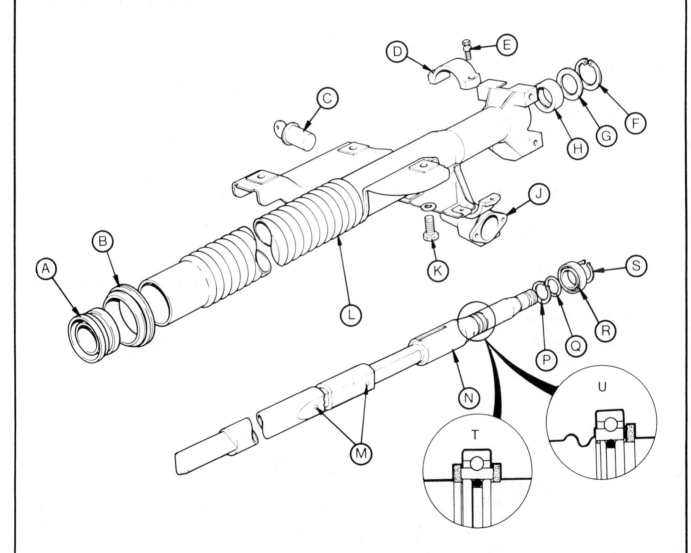

Fig. 11.24 Exploded view of steering column assembly (Sec 25)

A Lower bearing	G Washer	M Steering shaft shear-off inserts	S Circlip
B Seal	H Upper bearing	N Steering shaft assembly	T Upper bearing fixing using two circlips
C Lock barrel	J Steering lock	P Circlip	
D Steering lock clamp	K Steering column retaining bolts	Q O-ring	U Upper bearing fixing using one circlip (alternative design to insert T)
E Shear-off bolts	L Steering column outer tube	R Upper bearing	
F Circlip			

the bottom of the ignition switch.

8 Remove the upper and lower steering column bracket bolts (Fig. 11.22) lower the column and then withdraw it through the vehicle interior.

9 Refitting is the reverse of removal, but before tightening the column bracket bolts (Fig. 11.23) ensure that the dimension A in Fig. 11.24 is 2.87 – 3.03 in (73 – 77 mm).

25 Steering column shaft – removal and refitting

1 Refer to Section 24 and remove the steering column assembly.
2 Drill out the steering lock mounting bolt heads and remove the lock.
3 Lift away the lower bearing cover. Using a pointed chisel carefully prise open the staking and ease out the lower bearing.
4 With a pair of circlip pliers contract and withdraw the circlip and plain washer from the top end of the shaft.
5 Withdraw the steering shaft complete with the upper bearing from the column assembly (Fig. 11.24).
6 Using circlip pliers remove the upper bearing retaining circlip then remove the upper bearing. Remove the lower retaining circlip, where fitted.
7 Refitting is the reverse of removal. To fit the steering lock, position the clamp as shown in Fig. 11.25 ensuring that the lock tongue engages in the hole in the column tube. Tighten the new retaining

bolts until the heads break off.

26 Steering column flexible coupling and universal joint assembly – removal and refitting

1 Undo and remove the nut, clamp bolt and spring washer that secures the flexible coupling bottom half to the pinion shaft (photo).
2 Bend back the locktabs and undo and remove the two bolts securing the universal joint lock bar to the lower steering shaft. Lift away the tab washer and lock bar (Fig. 11.26).
3 The lower steering shaft may now be lifted away.
4 To refit place the lower steering shaft in the approximate fitted position and align the master splines on the shaft and pinion. Connect the shaft to the pinion.
5 Position the triangular clamp on the bottom of the steering column and secure with the clamp bar bolts and tab washer. Tighten the bolts fully and lock by bending up the tabs.
6 Refit the flexible coupling bottom half clamp bolt spring washer and nut. Tighten to the specified torque.

27 Steering gear assembly – removal and refitting

1 Set the steering wheel to the straight ahead position.
2 Jack-up the front of the car and place blocks under the wheels

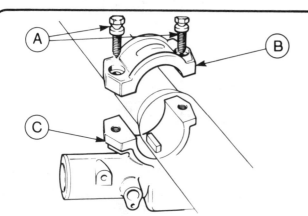

Fig. 11.25 Fitting the steering lock (Sec 25)

A Shear-off bolts   B Clamp
         C Steering lock

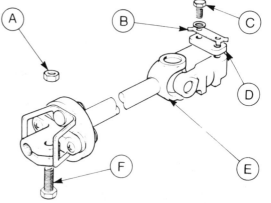

Fig. 11.26 Steering coupling assembly (Sec 26)

A Nut   B Lock tab
C Clamp bolt   D Clamp plate
E Universal joint F Clamp bolt

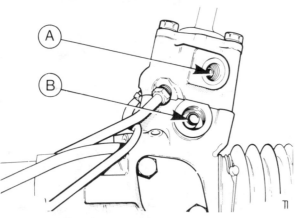

Fig. 11.27 Disconnect the feed and return pipes (Sec 27)

A Pressure feed pipe   B Return pipe

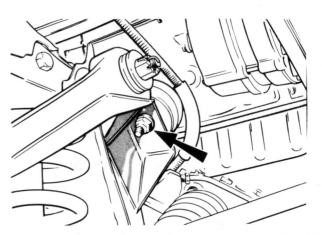

Fig. 11.28 Remove the right-hand engine mounting nut (Sec 27)

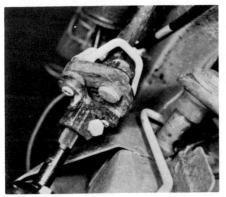
26.1 Steering column to pinion flexible coupling

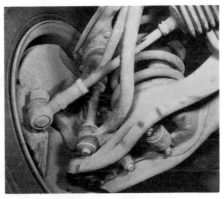
27.5 Trackrod to steering arm balljoint

27.6 The steering gear and rack assembly is secured to the crossmember by four bolts

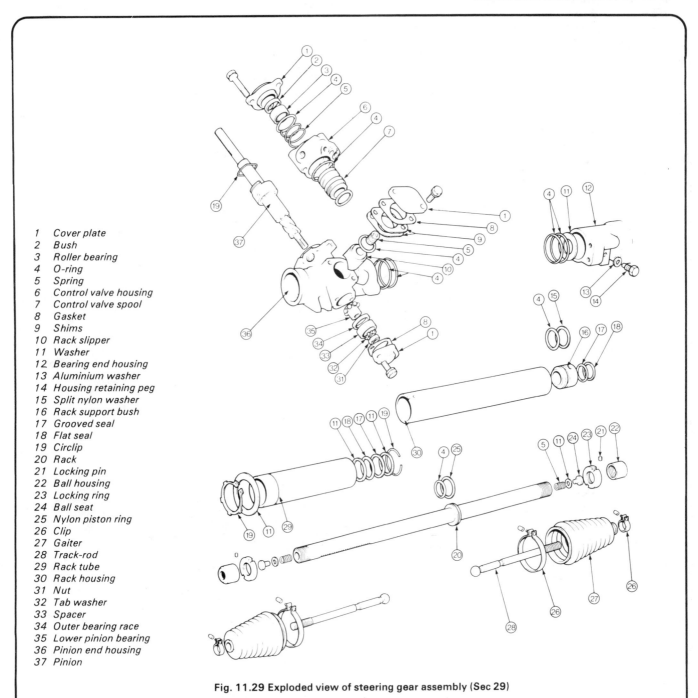

1   Cover plate
2   Bush
3   Roller bearing
4   O-ring
5   Spring
6   Control valve housing
7   Control valve spool
8   Gasket
9   Shims
10 Rack slipper
11 Washer
12 Bearing end housing
13 Aluminium washer
14 Housing retaining peg
15 Split nylon washer
16 Rack support bush
17 Grooved seal
18 Flat seal
19 Circlip
20 Rack
21 Locking pin
22 Ball housing
23 Locking ring
24 Ball seat
25 Nylon piston ring
26 Clip
27 Gaiter
28 Track-rod
29 Rack tube
30 Rack housing
31 Nut
32 Tab washer
33 Spacer
34 Outer bearing race
35 Lower pinion bearing
36 Pinion end housing
37 Pinion

Fig. 11.29 Exploded view of steering gear assembly (Sec 29)

then lower the car slightly so that the trackrods are in a near horizontal position. Remove the engine splash shield, if fitted.

3　Disconnect the fluid feed and return pipes from the control valve and drain the fluid into a container. Plug the ends of the pipes and the openings in the control valve to prevent the entry of dirt (Fig. 11.27).

4　Bend back the lock tabs on the coupling clamp plate, loosen the bolts and remove the clamp plate. Remove the bolt clamping the lower end of the coupling assembly to the pinion shaft, disengage the assembly from the pinion shaft and lift it out.

5　Withdraw the split pins and remove the castellated nuts from the ends of the trackrods where they are attached to the steering arms (photo). Using a universal balljoint separator, detach the trackrod ball pins from the steering arms.

6　Bend back the lock tabs, withdraw the split pins, then undo the nuts and remove the rack to cross-member securing bolts (photo).

7　Remove the fan shroud securing screws and lift the shroud out of the engine compartment.

8　Remove the right hand engine mounting securing nut (Fig. 11.28) and jack-up the engine approximately 5 in (125 mm). Move the rack to the left-hand side, and guide the right-hand trackrod over the top of the stabilizer bar then remove the steering gear assembly from the right-hand side.

9　Before refitting the steering gear assembly make sure the wheels are still in the straight-ahead position.

10　Check that the steering rack is in the centre of its travels. This can be done by ensuring that the distance between the ends of both trackrods and the rack housing on both sides are the same.

11　Slide the assembly in from the right-hand side of the car, and fit the steering coupling on the pinion shaft, with the master splines aligned, then loosely fit the clamp bolt and nut. Fit the steering gear assembly securing bolts using new locking tabs.

12　Fit the coupling clamp to the lower end of the steering shaft, fit new locking plate and refit the bolts loosely.

13　Tighten the steering gear to crossmember securing bolts to the specified torque and fit new split pins.

14　Reconnect the trackrod ends to the steering arms and tighten the castellated nuts to the specified torque. Fit new split pins.

15　Lower the engine and tighten the right-hand engine mounting nut to the specified torque.

16　Reconnect the power steering fluid feed and return pipes to the control valve.

17　Tighten the clamp bolts on the steering shaft flexible coupling and on the pinion shaft to the specified torque.

18　Refit the engine splash shield (if fitted) and the fan shroud.

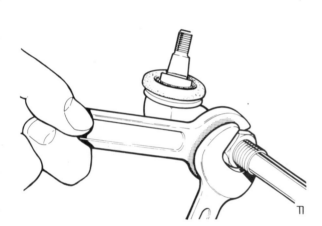

Fig. 11.30 Slackening the trackrod end locknut (Sec 29)

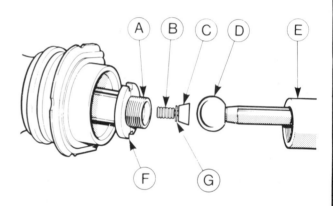

Fig. 11.31 Removing the trackrod from the steering rack (Sec 29)

A Steering rack　　　　B Spring
C Ball seat　　　　　　D Trackrod
E Housing　　　　　　 F Locknut
　　　　　G Washer

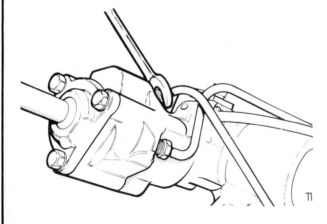

Fig. 11.32 Disconnecting the transfer pipes (Sec 29)

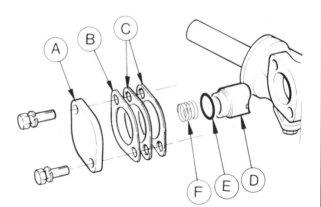

Fig. 11.33 Rack slipper and cover plate assembly (Sec 29)

A Cover　　　　　B Gasket
C Shims　　　　　D Slipper
E Sealing ring　　F Spring

19 Jack-up the car, remove the support blocks and lower the car to the ground.
20 Top-up the power steering fluid reservoir with the specified fluid and bleed the system as described in Section 28.
21 Check and adjust the toe-setting as described in Section 22.

28 Power assisted steering system – bleeding

1 Fill the reservoir to the maximum level, refer to Section 21, with the specified fluid, and jack-up the front of the car.
2 Wait for at least two minutes after filling the reservoir then start the engine and run it at approximately 1500 rpm.
3 Whilst an assistant slowly turns the steering wheel from lock-to-lock, top-up the reservoir until the level is stabilized and air bubbles can no longer be seen in the fluid. Fit the filler cap.
   Note: *When the car is raised from the ground with the front wheels clear and suspended, do not use any force or rapid movement when moving the wheels from lock-to-lock as this will cause fluid pressure to build up and burst or force off the rubber gaiters.*

29 Steering gear – dismantling and reassembly

1 Loosen the trackrod balljoint locknuts and unscrew the balljoints. To assist in obtaining an approximate setting for trackrod adjustment, mark the position of the balljoint on the trackrod or count the number of turns required to unscrew the balljoint (Fig. 11.30).
2 Slacken off the clips securing the rubber gaiters to each trackrod and rack housing end. Pull off the gaiters and collect the oil, which will drain out, in a container. **Note**: *Soft iron wire is used to secure the gaiters in production, instead of clips. At reassembly always use screw-type clips.*
3 Mount the steering gear assembly in a soft-jawed vice. Position the vice on an end casting, do not hold it by the tube as this is easily damaged.
4 Centre punch and drill out the pin securing each trackrod housing to lock nut with a 0.16 in (4 mm) drill. Great care must be taken not to drill too deeply or the rack will be damaged. Do not drill deeper than 0.35 in (9 mm).
5 Hold the locknut with a spanner, then grip the ball housing with a mole wrench and unscrew it from the threads on the rack.
6 Collect the spring and ball seat from the recess in the end of the rack and then unscrew the locknut from the threads on the rack. The spring and ball seat must be renewed during reassembly (Fig. 11.31).
7 Remove the two control valve body to rack housing transfer pipes (Fig. 11.32).
8 Undo and remove the two bolts securing the rack slipper cover plate, lift off the cover plate and remove the shim pack, sealing ring, spring and slipper (Fig. 11.33).
9 Undo the pinion lower bearing cover plate securing bolts and remove the cover plate and gasket. Bend back the lock tab and remove the lower bearing retaining nut. Protect the splines on the input shaft from damage when holding the shaft to remove the nut.
10 Remove the three securing bolts and lift off the control valve top cover, bearing and oil seal assembly. Take out the spool preload spring and withdraw the control valve body from the pinion shaft (Fig. 11.34).
11 Unscrew the pinion lower bearing (Fig. 11.35) then withdraw the pinion, spacer and outer race from the housing. Do not remove the middle bearing and oil seal unless the seal is suspected of being the cause of an oil leak or of being excessively worn. If either is suspect they both must be renewed.
12 Slide the spool off the pinion assembly after removing the retaining circlip (Fig. 11.36).
13 Remove the locating pegs from the end housings (Fig. 11.37), and using a rubber-faced hammer separate the end housings from the rack tube. This will also free the transfer pipe.
14 Pull the rack in the direction of the bearing end housing and disengage the rack from the inner tube. Pull the support bearing off the rack (Fig. 11.38).
15 Remove the inner tube from the rack tube.
16 Clean and examine all parts for signs of wear and damage. If the rack or pinion teeth are in any way damaged a new rack and pinion will have to be obtained. If either the pinion valve spool or valve housing is defective, both parts must be renewed. Renew all oil seals.
17 Commence reassembly by sliding the inner tube seals and

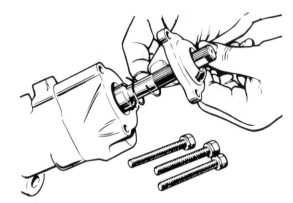

Fig. 11.34 Removing the spool pre-load spring (Sec 29)

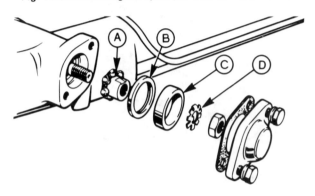

Fig. 11.35 Removing the pinion lower bearing (Sec 29)

A *Pinion lower bearing*   B *Bearing outer race*
C *Spacer*   D *Tab washer*

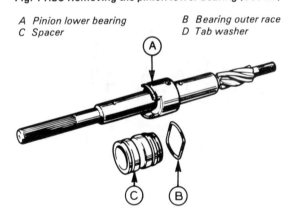

Fig. 11.36 Spool valve removal (Sec 29)

A *Pinion assembly*   B *Retaining circlip*
            C *Spool valve*

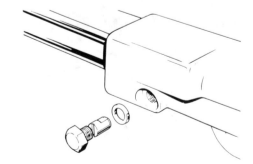

Fig. 11.37 Remove the end housing locating pegs (Sec 29)

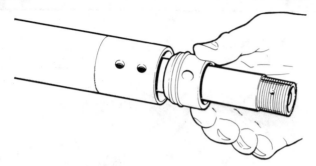

Fig. 11.38 Pull off the rack support bearing (Sec 29)

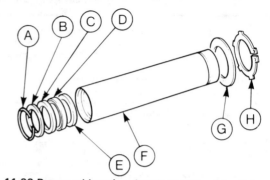

Fig. 11.39 Reassembly order of seals and clips (Sec 29)

A Circlip   E Washer
B Washer   F Inner tab
C Grooved seal   G Washer
D Flat seal   H Circlip

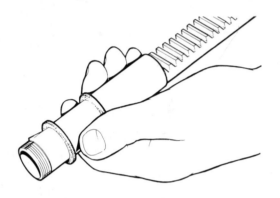

Fig. 11.40 Use a protective sleeve when fitting the seals (Sec 29)

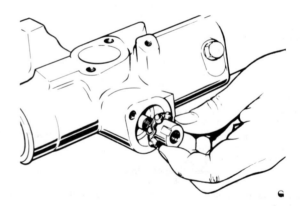

Fig. 11.41 Fit the seals and washers into the inner tube (Sec 29)

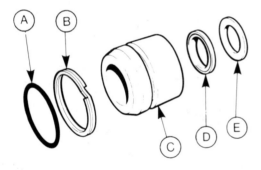

Fig. 11.42 Support bearing and seals (Sec 29)

A O-ring seal   D Grooved seal
B Nylon seal   E Flat seal
C Support bearing

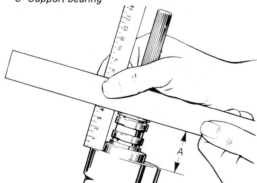

Fig. 11.44 Preliminary adjustment of pinion bearing (Sec 29)

Fig. 11.43 The lower bearing is screwed onto the pinion (Sec 29)

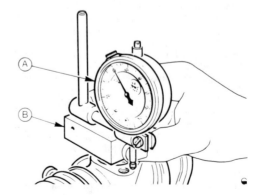

Fig. 11.45 Determining thickness of shim pack for rack slipper adjustment (Sec 29)

washers onto the rack from the toothed end in the following order: circlip, washer, grooved seal, flat seal and washer. A piece of thin foil or paper wrapped round the rack teeth will prevent possible damage to the seals as they are fitted (Fig. 11.39 and 11.40).

18 Lubricate the two O-ring seals with power steering fluid and insert them in the pinion end housing. Fit the circlip and washer to the inner tube and then push the inner tube into the end housing.

19 Slide the rack through the inner tube and pinion end housing, then fit the seals and washers that are on the rack, into the inner tube and secure with the circlip (Fig. 11.41).

20 Soak the piston O-ring and nylon piston ring in power steering fluid then fit the O-ring and piston ring in the piston groove.

21 Fit the rack tube over the rack with the end, with two round holes, towards the bearing support end. Take care to compress the piston ring carefully and push the rack tube firmly into the pinion end housing, checking that the locating peg holes are aligned, then fit the locating pegs. Use new aluminium washers.

22 Fit outer seals to the rack support bearing, slide the bearing over the rack then push it into the rack tube and align the locating peg holes.

23 Using a protective sleeve as described in paragraph 17, slide the inner seals over the rack, the grooved seal first, then fit the inner seals to the rack support bearing (Fig. 11.42).

24 Fit the large washer and two O-ring seals in the end housing and the transfer pipe seals in their locations, then locate the transfer pipe in the pinion end housing.

25 Fit the bearing end housing to the rack, rack tube and transfer pipe, ensure the locating peg holes are aligned and then fit the locating pegs.

26 Slide the spool onto the pinion assembly and fit the retaining circlip in the lower groove of the valve spool.

27 If the middle bearing was removed during dismantling fit a new bearing and oil seal. Fit the lower bearing inner race in the housing.

28 Position the rack in the centre of its travel (equal amount of rack protruding from each end housing) and slide the control valve and pinion assembly into the housing to engage with the rack.

29 Screw the lower bearing onto the pinion (Fig. 11.43) and make a preliminary adjustment of the control valve to locate the spool in an approximately neutral position. To do this pull the pinion to remove end float from the bearing and adjust dimension A in Fig. 11.44 to 1.61 – 1.65 in (41 – 42 mm) by screwing the lower bearing in or out as necessary. Fit a new lockwasher and nut, but do not bend the lock tab at this stage.

30 To adjust the pinion bearing cover plate, fit the outer bearing race, spacer and end cover to the pinion housing without shims. Tighten the bolts evenly to 9 – 12 lbf ft (1.2 – 1.6 kgf m), then using feeler gauges measure the gap between the cover plate and housing. Select shims to fit the measured gap. Remove the cover plate, fit the selected shims and then refit the cover plate and tighten the securing bolts to 12 – 15 lbf ft (1.7 – 2.1 kgf m). During this adjustment it may be necessary to re-adjust dimension A in Fig. 11.44.

31 Fit the control valve body, then pinion bearing preload spring (ensuring that the spring is not trapped in the roller bearing), the valve top cover assembly and the securing bolts. Tighten the bolts to the specified torque.

32 Fit the two transfer pipes connecting the control valve body to the rack housing.

33 For adjustment of the rack slipper a dial gauge and mounting block are required. Fit the dial gauge on the mounting block and with it positioned on a piece of glass, adjust the dial gauge to zero. Fit the slipper in the housing and hold the mounting block on the slipper with the probe of the dial gauge contacting the rack housing (Fig. 11.45). Move the rack from lock-to-lock by turning the pinion and note the maximum deflection of the dial gauge from zero. Make up a shim pack of thickness equal to the noted deflection plus 0.001 – 0.005 in (0.025 – 0.125 mm).

34 Fit the spring, O-ring seal, the selected shims, gasket cover plate and securing bolts (Fig. 11.33). Tighten the bolts to the specified torque.

35 Fit new springs and ball seats to the recess in the ends of the rack, and refit the locknuts onto the threads of the rack (Fig. 11.31).

36 Lubricate the balls, ball seats and ball housings with a small amount of the specified oil, then slide the ball housings over the trackrod and screw them onto the rack threads.

37 Hook a normal type of spring balance round the trackrod 0.25 in (6 mm) from the end and check the effort required to move it from the horizontal position.

38 By adjusting the tightness of the ball housing on the rack thread, the effort required to move the trackrod must be set at 5 lb (2.1 kg).

39 On the line where the locknut and ballhousing meet, drill a 0.16 in (4 mm) diameter hole, 0.35 in (9 mm) deep. Even if the existing holes align a new hole must be drilled.

40 Fit a new retaining pin into the hole and peen the end over to secure it (Fig. 11.46).

41 Refit the rubber gaiters and track rod ends ensuring that they are refitted in the same position from which they were removed. When fitting the gaiters fill the rack with 0.33 pints (0.2 litres) of the specified engine oil. Traverse the rack to distribute the oil. Do not over-fill. Tighten the gaiter securing clips.

42 After the steering gear assembly has been refitted to the car, the control valve adjustment must be finalised, and the toe-setting checked, as described in Sections 30 and 22.

30 Steering gear control valve – checking and adjusting

1 After overhaul the control valve must be finally checked and adjusted, if necessary, with the steering gear assembly fitted in the car. For this, a test gauge as shown in Fig. 11.47 will be required.

2 Connect the test gauge as shown in Fig. 11.47. Position the gauge

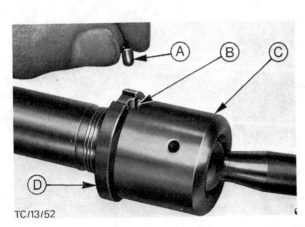

Fig. 11.46 Securing the trackrod ball joint assembly (Sec 29)

A Lock pin   B New hole
C Housing   D Lock ring

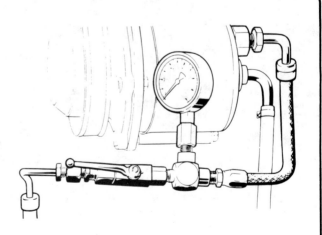

Fig. 11.47 Test gauge, control valve and fittings (Sec 30)

in front of the windscreen so that it can be seen from the driver's seat. Fill the reservoir with fluid and bleed the system as described in Section 28.

3   Start the engine and run it until the fluid reaches normal operating temperature, while rotating the steering wheel slowly to each lock in turn a maximum of five times. Do not hold on full lock for more than 30 seconds or damage to the pump may occur.

4   Remove the steering wheel insert and connect a torque gauge to the steering wheel nut with a socket and extension (Fig. 11.48).

5   With the engine running turn the steering wheel to each lock in turn and whilst on lock apply a torque of 34 lbf in (38 kgf cm) to the steering wheel nut and note the pressure registered on the gauge. Repeat two or three times on each lock. The pressure should be 160 lbf/in² (11.2 kgf/cm²) and the difference between right and left lock should not exceed 12 lbf/in² (0.85 kgf/cm²).

6   Adjustment is by means of the pinion lower bearing which is secured onto the pinion shaft. To adjust, proceed as follows:

   a) *Jack-up the car and support on axle-stands*
   b) *Disconnect the trackrod ends from the steering arms, see Section 27, paragraph 5*
   c) *Remove the rack to crossmember securing bolts and the right-hand engine mounting securing nut, then jack-up the engine approximately 5 in (125 mm), refer to Section 27*
   d) *Disconnect the steering coupling, see Section 26, and move the rack forward to gain access to the pinion lower cover plate. Remove the cover plate assembly. Collect the oil draining out in a container*
   e) *The bearing lockwasher has an internal offset tab, by inverting the washer, adjustments in 18 steps can be made. Each step alters the pressure difference by approximately 25 lbf/in² (1.7 kgf/cm²)*
   f) *Screwing the bearing onto the pinion shaft will increase the pressure on the left lock, screwing it out will increase the pressure on the right lock*
   g) *When the correct adjustment has been obtained bend one tab of the lockwasher into the cut-out in the pinion bearing and one tab over the nut*
   h) *Refitting the steering gear assembly in position is the reverse of the removal procedure*

7   Remove a rubber gaiter and top-up the steering gear with the same amount of specified oil as drained out when the lower cover plate was removed. Do not overfill.

8   Check the toe-setting as described in Section 22.

31 Steering rack rubber gaiters – removal and refitting

1   Jack-up the front of the car and place blocks under the wheels. Lower the car slightly so that the trackrods are in a near horizontal position.

2   Withdraw the split pin and undo the castellated nut holding the balljoint taper pin to the steering arm. Using a universal balljoint separator part the taper pin from the steering arm.

3   Undo the trackrod balljoint locknut and unscrew the balljoint. To assist in obtaining an approximate correct setting for trackrod adjustment mark the threads or count the number of turns required to undo the balljoint.

4   Slacken off the clips securing the rubber gaiter to the trackrod and rack housing end. Carefully pull off the gaiter. Have a quantity of rag handy to catch the oil which will escape when the gaiters are removed. **Note**: *on some steering gear assemblies soft iron wire is used instead of clips. Always secure the gaiter with clips.*

5   Fitting a new rubber gaiter is now the reverse sequence to removal. It will be necessary to refill the steering gear assembly with the specified oil. Insert the nozzle of an oil can into the rack housing and refill with the specified amount of oil.

6   Position the gaiter and tighten the clip quickly to prevent loss of oil and then move the steering wheel from lock-to-lock, very slowly, to distribute the oil in the housing.

7   It is recommended that the toe-setting be checked at the earliest opportunity, refer to Section 22.

32 Power steering pump drivebelt – removal and refitting

1   Slacken the two bolts securing the idler pulley bracket and slide the idler pulley towards the pump (Fig. 11.49).

2   Remove the drivebelt from the pump, idler and crankshaft pulleys.

3   Fit the drivebelt onto the pulleys and adjust the position of the idler pulley so that there is a deflection of 0.5 in (13 mm) at the midpoint of the longest run of the belt when moderate pressure is applied by hand.

4   Tighten the idler pulley bracket securing bolts.

33 Power steering pump assembly – removal and refitting

1   Remove the drivebelt, refer to Section 32 (photo).

32.3 Checking the steering pump drive belt tension

33.1 The power steering pump is mounted on the left-hand side of the engine at the front

2   Disconnect the fluid feed and return pipes from the pump and drain the fluid into a container. Plug the ends of the pipes and the openings in the pump.

3   To remove the pump from the mounting bracket requires a special wrench, but it is just as easy to undo the bracket to engine mounting bolts using a standard spanner and remove the pump and bracket as an assembly.

4   Refitting is the reverse of the removal procedure. Adjust the belt tension as described in Section 32. Top-up the reservoir with the specified power steering fluid and bleed the steering system as described in Section 28.

34 Power steering pump – dismantling and reassembly

Before dismantling the pump and reservoir assembly clean the exterior to prevent dirt from contaminating the internal components of the pump.

1   Undo the three securing bolts and remove the pulley.

2   Remove the outlet pipe adapter, copper washer and O-ring.

3   Free the reservoir by tapping it at opposite points, using a soft metal drift to avoid damaging the reservoir.

4   Remove the valve cap, spring and valve (Fig. 11.50) then take out the four Allen screws and prise off the end housing.

5   Prise the cover plate from the locating pins and carefully tip out the rollers from the carrier.

6   Ease the main body off the front housing, using two screwdrivers as levers, then remove the roller carrier circlip and lift off the carrier and drive pin (Fig. 11.51).

7   Pull the pump hub and shaft from the front housing and remove the locating pins.

8   Lever the oil seal out of the front housing.

9   Clean and examine all parts for signs of wear and damage. Renew as necessary. The front bush and housing, also the hub and shaft, are supplied as assemblies. Always fit a new seal at reassembly.

10 Fit the oil seal in the front housing with the inner lip facing to the rear.

11 Slide the pump shaft through the front housing.

12 Insert the locating pins in the front housing and fit the main body.

13 Fit the drive pin and roller carrier with the square indent towards the front. The leading edge of the carrier webs is longer than the trailing edge (Fig. 11.52).

14 Fit the carrier retaining circlip and then locate the twelve rollers in the carrier recesses.

15 Fit the cover plate with the circlip groove facing the carrier, then the end housing secured with the four Allen screws.

16 Refit the valve with the long spigot leading, (Fig. 11.50), and then the spring and cap.

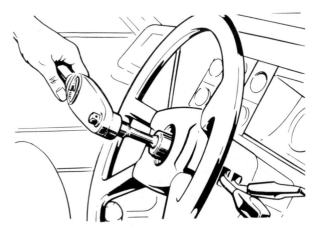

Fig. 11.48 Checking the turning torque (Sec 30)

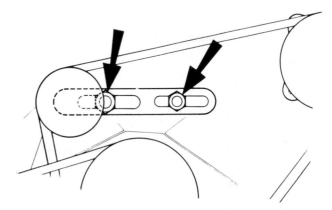

Fig. 11.49 Idler pulley bracket securing bolts (Sec 32)

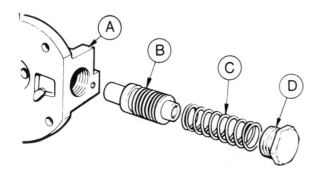

Fig. 11.50 Dismantling the pump valve (Sec 34)

A Housing   B Valve
C Spring   D Valve cap

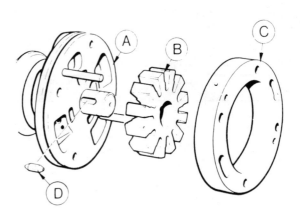

Fig. 11.51 Steering pump dismantled (Sec 34)

A Housing   B Roller carrier
C Body   D Drive pin

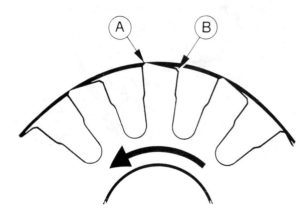

Fig. 11.52 Fitting the roller carrier (Sec 34)

A Leading edge   *B Trailing edge*

17 Fit a new O-ring in the front housing and, ensuring that the hole in the reservoir is aligned with the pressure adapter hole, tap the reservoir into its seating with a plastic hammer.
18 Fit new O-ring, copper washer and pressure adapter.
19 Fit the drivebelt pulley and securing bolts. Tighten the bolts to the specified torque.

35 Power steering fluid cooler – removal and refitting

1 Remove the five radiator grille securing screws and lift out the grille.
2 Loosen the power steering hoses securing clamps and pull the hoses off the cooler. Position the hoses with the ends pointing upwards to minimise fluid loss.
3 Remove the two bolts securing the cooler to the front panel and lift out the cooler (Fig. 11.53).
4 Refitting is the reverse of the removal procedure. Top-up the reservoir and bleed the steering system as described in Section 28.

36 Trackrod ends – removal and refitting

   Removal and refitting of the trackrod ends is described in Section 31.

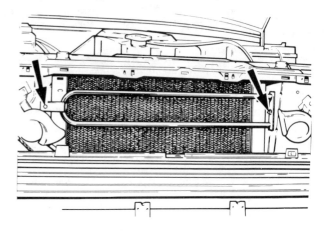

Fig. 11.53 Power steering fluid cooler securing bolts (Sec 35)

37 Wheels and tyres

1 The roadwheels are of the pressed steel or aluminium alloy type, and the tyres are of the radial ply type.
2 Check the tyre pressures weekly, including the spare.
3 The wheel nuts should be tightened to the appropriate torque as shown in the Specifications, and it is an advantage if a smear of grease is applied to the wheel stud threads.
4 Every 6000 miles (10 000 km) the roadwheels should be moved round the vehicle (this does not apply where the wheels have been balanced on the vehicle) in order to even out the tyre tread wear. With radial types it is recommended that the wheels are moved front-to-rear and rear-to-front, not from side-to-side of the car. To do this, remove each wheel in turn, clean it thoroughly (both sides) and remove any flints which may be embedded in the tyre tread. Check the tread wear pattern which will indicate any mechanical or adjustment faults in the suspension or steering components. Examine the wheel bolt holes for elongation or wear. If such conditions are found, renew the wheel.
5 Renewal of the tyres should be carried out when the thickness of the tread pattern is worn to a minimum of $\frac{1}{16}$ inch or the wear indicators (if incorporated) are visible.
6 Always adjust the front and rear tyre pressures after moving the wheels round as previously described.
7 All wheels are balanced initially, but have them done again halfway through the useful life of the tyres.

38 Fault diagnosis – suspension and steering

Symptom	Reason/s
Unbalanced steering	Tyre pressures uneven Dampers worn Spring gear ball joints worn Suspension geometry incorrect Fluid pipe damaged Control valve adjustment incorrect
Lack of power assistance	Pump belt needs adjustment Hoses or pipes restricted Fluid level low Hydraulic system may require bleeding of air Low fluid pressure perhaps caused by worn pump

Symptom	Reason/s
Poor self centring	Worn, damaged or badly adjusted suspension or steering
	Steering column badly misaligned
	Return fluid hose or pipe restricted
	Control valve spool sticking
	Stiff operation of rack caused by damaged rack piston or seals
Noisy operation of steering pump	Fluid level low
	Pump belt slack
	Flow control valve defective or worn pump components
Wheel wobble and vibration	Worn balljoints or swivels
	Wheel nuts loose
	Hub bearings loose or worn
	Steering ball joints worn
	Front spring weak or broken

Chapter 12 Bodywork and fittings

For modifications, and information applicable to later models, see Supplement at end of manual

Contents

Specifications

Overall length
Saloon	172.7 in (4384 mm)
Estate Car	176.7 in (4484 mm)

Overall width
	67 in (1700 mm)

Overall height
Saloon	53.7 in (1362 mm)
Estate Car	53.8 in (1366 mm)

Wheelbase
	101.6 in (2579 mm)

Track
Front	56 in (1422 mm)
Rear	56 in (1422 mm)

Nominal kerb weight
Saloon	2492 lb (1130 kg)
Estate	2591 lb (1175 kg)

Luggage capacity
Saloon	11.8 cu ft (0.33 cu m)
Estate Car	34 cu ft (0.96 cu m)
Estate Car with seat folded	64 cu ft (1.81 cu m)

1 General description

The combination body and underframe is of all-steel welded construction. This makes a very strong and torsionally rigid shell.

The Cortina 2.3 V6 is available in either Saloon or Estate versions with a seating capacity of five adults. The windscreen is slightly curved and is zone toughened for additional driver and passenger safety. In the event of windscreen shattering this zone breaks into much larger pieces than the rest of the screen thus giving the driver much better vision than would otherwise be possible.

The through-flow type of ventilation system is fitted. Air drawn in through a grille on the scuttle can either be heated or pass straight into the car. Used air passes out through a grille behind the rear side windows.

The Estate Cars have the same engine, technical and general specifications as the Saloon car except for the counterbalanced tailgate fitted with a lock.

Although the wheelbase for the Saloon and Estate car versions is the same, the overall length of the Estate Car is longer.

For additional occupant safety thick padding is used to surround the top of the dash panel.

2 Maintenance – bodywork and underframe

1 The condition of your car's bodywork is of considerable importance as it is upon this that the second-hand value of the car will mainly depend. It is much more difficult to repair neglected bodywork than to renew mechanical assemblies. The hidden portions of the body, such as the wheel arches, the underframe and the engine compartment are equally important, although obviously not requiring such frequent attention as the immediately visible paintwork.

2 Once a year or every 12 000 miles (20 000 km) it is a sound scheme to visit your local main agent and have the underside of the body steam-cleaned. All traces of dirt and oil will be removed and the underside can then be inspected carefully for rust, damaged hydraulic pipes, frayed electrical wiring and similar maladies.

3 At the same time, the engine compartment should be cleaned in a similar manner. If steam-cleaning facilities are not available then brush a water-soluble cleanser over the whole engine and engine compartment with a stiff paint brush, working it well in where there is an accumulation of oil and dirt. Do not paint the ignition system, and protect it with oily rags when the cleanser is washed off. As the cleanser is washed away it will take with it all traces of oil and dirt leaving the engine looking clean and bright.

4 The wheel arches should be given particular attention as undersealing can easily come away here and stones and dirt thrown up from the roadwheels can soon cause the paint to chip and flake, and so allow rust to set in. If rust is found, clean down to the bare metal with wet-and-dry paper, apply an anti-corrosive coating such as zinc primer or red lead, and renew the paintwork and undercoating.

5 The bodywork should be washed once a week or when dirty. Thoroughly wet the car to soften the dirt and then wash the car down with a soft sponge and plenty of clean water. If the surplus dirt is not washed off very gently, in time it will wear paint down as surely as wet-and-dry paper. It is best to use a hose if this is available. Give the car a final wash down and then dry with a soft chamois leather to prevent the formation of spots.

6 Spots of tar and grease thrown up from the road can be removed by a rag dampened with petrol.

7 Once every six months, or more frequently if wished, give the bodywork and chromium trim a thoroughly good wax polish. If a chromium cleaner is used to remove rust on any of the car's plated parts remember that the cleaner also removes part of the chromium, so use sparingly.

3 Maintenance – upholstery and carpets

1 Remove the carpets or mats and thoroughly vacuum-clean the interior of the car every three months or more frequently, if necessary.

2 Beat out the carpets and vacuum-clean them if they are very dirty. If the upholstery is soiled, apply an upholstery cleaner with a damp sponge and wipe off with a clean dry cloth.

4 Minor body damage – repair

The photo sequence on pages 198 and 199 illustrate the operations detailed in the following sub-sections.

Note: *For more detailed information about bodywork repair, the Haynes Publishing Group publish a book by Lindsay Porter called The Car Bodywork Repair Manual. This incorporates information on such aspects as rust treatment, painting and glass fibre repairs, as well as details on more ambitious repairs involving welding and panel beating.*

Repair of minor scratches in the car's bodywork

If the scratch is very superficial, and does not penetrate to the metal of the bodywork, repair is very simple. Lightly rub the area of the scratch with a paintwork renovator, or a very fine cutting paste, to remove loose paint from the scratch and to clear the surrounding bodywork of wax polish. Rinse the area with clean water.

Apply touch-up paint to the scratch using a thin paintbrush; continue to apply thin layers of paint until the surface of the paint in the scratch is level with the surrounding paintwork. Allow the new paint at least two weeks to harden: then blend it into the surrounding paintwork by rubbing the paintwork, in the scratch area, with a paintwork renovator or a very fine cutting paste. Finally, apply wax polish.

An alternative to painting over the scratch is to use a paint transfer. Use the same preparation for the affected area, then simply pick a patch of a suitable size to cover the scratch completely. Hold the patch against the scratch and burnish its backing paper; the paper will adhere to the paintwork, freeing itself from the backing paper at the same time. Polish the affected area to blend the patch into the surrounding paintwork.

Where the scratch has penetrated right through to the metal of the bodywork, causing the metal to rust, a different repair technique is required. Remove any loose rust from the bottom of the scratch with a penknife, then apply rust inhibiting paint to prevent the formation of rust in the future. Using a rubber or nylon applicator fill the scratch with bodystopper paste. If required, this paste can be mixed with cellulose thinners to provide a very thin paste which is ideal for filling narrow scratches. Before the stopper-paste in the scratch hardens, wrap a piece of smooth cotton rag around the top of a finger. Dip the finger in cellulose thinners and then quickly sweep it across the surface of the stopper-paste in the scratch; this will ensure that the surface of the stopper-paste is slightly hollowed. The scratch can now be painted over as described earlier in this Section.

Repair of dents in the car's bodywork

When deep denting of the car's bodywork has taken place, the first task is to pull the dent out, until the affected bodywork almost attains its original shape. There is little point in trying to restore the original shape completely, as the metal in the damaged area will have stretched on impact and cannot be reshaped fully to its original contour. It is better to bring the level of the dent up to a point which is about $\frac{1}{8}$ in (3 mm) below the level of the surrounding bodywork. In cases where the dent is very shallow anyway, it is not worth trying to pull it out at all.

If the underside of the dent is accessible, it can be hammered out gently from behind, using a mallet with a wooden or plastic head. Whilst doing this, hold a suitable block of wood firmly against the impact from the hammer blows and thus prevent a large area of the bodywork from being 'belled-out'.

Should the dent be in a section of the bodywork which has double skin or some other factor making it inaccessible from behind, a different technique is called for. Drill several small holes through the metal inside the area – particularly in the deeper section. Then screw long self-tapping screws into the holes just sufficiently for them to gain a good purchase in the metal. Now the dent can be pulled out by pulling on the protruding heads of the screws with a pair of pliers.

The next stage of the repair is the removal of the paint from the damaged area, and from an inch or so of the surrounding 'sound' bodywork. This is accomplished most easily by using a wire brush or abrasive pad on a power drill, although it can be done just as effectively by hand using sheets of abrasive paper. To complete the preparation for filling, score the surface of the bare metal with a screwdriver or the tang of a file, or alternatively, drill small holes in the affected area. This will provide a really good 'key' for the filler paste.

To complete the repair see the Section on filling and respraying.

This sequence of photographs deals with the repair of the dent and paintwork damage shown in this photo. The procedure will be similar for the repair of a hole. It should be noted that the procedures given here are simplified — more explicit instructions will be found in the text

In the case of a dent the first job — after removing surrounding trim — is to hammer out the dent where access is possible. This will minimise filling. Here, the large dent having been hammered out, the damaged area is being made slightly concave

Now all paint must be removed from the damaged area, by rubbing with coarse abrasive paper. Alternatively, a wire brush or abrasive pad can be used in a power drill. Where the repair area meets good paintwork, the edge of the paintwork should be 'feathered', using a finer grade of abrasive paper

In the case of a hole caused by rusting, all damaged sheet-metal should be cut away before proceeding to this stage. Here, the damaged area is being treated with rust remover and inhibitor before being filled

Mix the body filler according to its manufacturer's instructions. In the case of corrosion damage, it will be necessary to block off any large holes before filling — this can be done with aluminium or plastic mesh, or aluminium tape. Make sure the area is absolutely clean before ...

... applying the filler. Filler should be applied with a flexible applicator, as shown, for best results; the wooden spatula being used for confined areas. Apply thin layers of filler at 20-minute intervals, until the surface of the filler is slightly proud of the surrounding bodywork

Initial shaping can be done with a Surform plane or Dreadnought file. Then, using progressively finer grades of wet-and-dry paper, wrapped around a sanding block, and copious amounts of clean water, rub down the filler until really smooth and flat. Again, feather the edges of adjoining paintwork

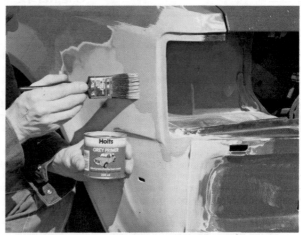

The whole repair area can now be sprayed or brush-painted with primer. If spraying, ensure adjoining areas are protected from over-spray. Note that at least one inch of the surrounding sound paintwork should be coated with primer. Primer has a 'thick' consistency, so will find small imperfections

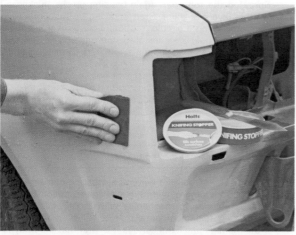

Again, using plenty of water, rub down the primer with a fine grade wet-and-dry paper (400 grade is probably best) until it is really smooth and well blended into the surrounding paintwork. Any remaining imperfections can now be filled by carefully applied knifing stopper paste

When the stopper has hardened, rub down the repair area again before applying the final coat of primer. Before rubbing down this last coat of primer, ensure the repair area is blemish-free — use more stopper if necessary. To ensure that the surface of the primer is really smooth use some finishing compound

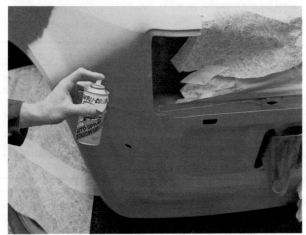

The top coat can now be applied. When working out of doors, pick a dry, warm and wind-free day. Ensure surrounding areas are protected from over-spray. Agitate the aerosol thoroughly, then spray the centre of the repair area, working outwards with a circular motion. Apply the paint as several thin coats

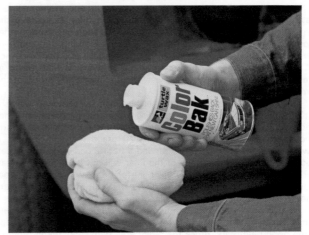

After a period of about two weeks, which the paint needs to harden fully, the surface of the repaired area can be 'cut' with a mild cutting compound prior to wax polishing. When carrying out bodywork repairs, remember that the quality of the finished job is proportional to the time and effort expended

Repair of rust holes or gashes in the car's bodywork

Remove all paint from the affected area and from an inch or so of the surrounding 'sound' bodywork, using an abrasive pad or a wire brush on a power drill. If these are not available a few sheets of abrasive paper will do the job just as effectively. With the paint removed you will be able to gauge the severity of the corrosion and therefore decide whether to renew the whole panel (if this is possible) or to repair the affected area. New body panels are not as expensive as most people think and it is often quicker and more satisfactory to fit a new panel than to attempt to repair large areas of corrosion.

Remove all fittings from the affected area except those which will act as a guide to the original shape of the damaged bodywork (eg headlamp shells etc). Then, using tin snips or a hacksaw blade, remove all loose metal and any other metal badly affected by corrosion. Hammer the edges of the hole inwards in order to create a slight depression for the filler paste.

Wire brush the affected area to remove the powdery rust from the surface of the remaining metal. Paint the affected area with rust inhibiting paint; if the back of the rusted area is accessible treat this also.

Before filling can take place it will be necessary to block the hole in some way. This can be achieved by the use of aluminium or plastic mesh, or aluminium tape.

Aluminium or plastic mesh is probably the best material to use for a large hole. Cut a piece to the approximate size and shape of the hole to be filled, then position it in the hole so that its edges are below the level of the surrounding bodywork. It can be retained in position by several blobs of filler paste around its periphery.

Aluminium tape should be used for small or very narrow holes. Pull a piece off the roll and trim it to the approximate size and shape required, then pull off the backing paper (if used) and stick the tape over the hole; it can be overlapped if the thickness of one piece is insufficient. Burnish down the edges of the tape with the handle of a screwdriver or similar, to ensure that the tape is securely attached to the metal underneath.

Bodywork repairs – filling and respraying

Before using this Section, see the Sections on dent, deep scratch, rust holes and gash repairs.

Many types of bodyfiller are available, but generally speaking those proprietary kits which contain a tin of filler paste and a tube of resin hardener are best for this type of repair. A wide, flexible plastic or nylon applicator will be found invaluable for imparting a smooth and well contoured finish to the surface of the filler.

Mix up a little filler on a clean piece of card or board – use the hardener sparingly (follow the maker's instructions on the pack) otherwise the filler will set very rapidly.

Using the applicator apply the filler paste to the prepared area: draw the applicator across the surface of the filler to achieve the correct contour and to level the filler surface. As soon as a contour that approximates the correct one is achieved, stop working the paste – if you carry on too long the paste will become sticky and begin to 'pick up' on the applicator. Continue to add thin layers of filler paste at twenty-minute intervals until the level of the filler is just proud of the surrounding bodywork.

Once the filler has hardened, excess can be removed using a Surform plane or Dreadnought file. From then on, progressively finer grades of abrasive paper should be used, starting with a 40 grade production paper and finishing with 400 grade wet-and-dry paper. Always wrap the abrasive paper around a flat rubber, cork, or wooden block – otherwise the surface of the filler will not be completely flat. During the smoothing of the filler surface the wet-and-dry paper should be periodically rinsed in water. This will ensure that a very smooth finish is imparted to the filler at the final stage.

At this stage the 'dent' should be surrounded by a ring of bare metal, which in turn should be encircled by the finely 'feathered' edge of the good paintwork. Rinse the repair area with clean water, until all of the dust produced by the rubbing-down operation has gone.

Spray the whole repair area with a light coat of primer – this will show up any imperfections in the surface of the filler. Repair these imperfections with fresh filler paste or bodystopper, and once more smooth the surface with abrasive paper. If bodystopper is used, it can be mixed with cellulose thinners to form a really thin paste which is ideal for filling small holes. Repeat this spray and repair procedure until you are satisfied that the surface of the filler, and the feathered edge of the paintwork are perfect. Clean the repair area with clean water and allow to dry fully.

The repair area is now ready for final spraying. Paint spraying must be carried out in a warm, dry, windless and dust free atmosphere. This condition can be created artificially if you have access to a large indoor working area, but if you are forced to work in the open, you will have to pick your day very carefully. If you are working indoors, dousing the floor in the work area with water will 'lay' the dust which would otherwise be in the atmosphere. If the repair area is confined to one body panel, mask off the surrounding panels; this will help to minimise the effects of a slight mis-match in paint colours. Bodywork fittings (eg chrome strips, door handles etc) will also need to be removed or masked off. Use genuine masking tape and several thicknesses of newspaper for the masking operations.

Before commencing to spray, agitate the aerosol can thoroughly, then spray a test area (an old tin, or similar) until the technique is mastered. Cover the repair area with a thick coat of primer; the thickness should be built up using several thin layers of paint rather than one thick one. Using 400 grade wet-and-dry paper, rub down the surface of the primer until it is really smooth. While doing this, the work area should be thoroughly doused with water, and the wet-and-dry paper periodically rinsed in water. Allow to dry before spraying on more paint.

Spray on the top coat, again building up the thickness by using several thin layers of paint. Start spraying in the centre of the repair area and then using a circular motion, work outwards until the whole repair area and about 2 inches of the surrounding original paintwork is covered. Remove all masking material 10 to 15 minutes after spraying on the final coat of paint.

Allow the new paint at least two weeks to harden, then, using a paintwork renovator or a very fine cutting paste, blend the edges of the paint into the existing paintwork. Finally, apply wax polish.

5   Major body damage – repair

1   Because the car is built without a separate chassis frame and the body is therefore integral with the underframe, major damage must be repaired by competent mechanics with the necessary welding and hydraulic straightening equipment.
2   If the damage has been serious it is vital that the body is checked for correct alignment as otherwise the handling of the car will suffer and many other faults such as excessive tyre wear and wear in the transmission and steering may occur.
3   There is a special body jig which most large body repair shops have, and to ensure that all is correct it is important that the jig be used for all major repair work.

6   Maintenance – PVC external roof covering

Under no circumstances try to clean any external PVC roof covering with detergents, caustic soaps or spirit cleaners. Plain soap and water is all that is required, with a soft brush to clean dirt that may be ingrained. Wash the covering as frequently as the rest of the car.

7   Maintenance – hinges and locks

Once every 6000 miles (10 000 km) or 6 months, the door, bonnet and boot or tailgate hinges and locks should be given a few drops of oil from an oil can. The door striker plates can be given a thin smear of grease to reduce wear and to ensure free movement.

8   Front bumper – removal and refitting

1   Open the bonnet and remove the radiator grille, as described in Section 30.
2   Undo and remove the bolt, washer and spacer assemblies that

secure the wrap round ends of the bumper bar. Then unscrew the two bolts that secure the underriders to the body (Fig. 12.1).

3   The front bumper assembly may now be lifted away taking care not to scratch the paintwork on the front wings.

4   If it is necessary to detach the underriders from the bumper bar, undo and remove the nut and washers that secure the bracket and underrider to the bumper bar.

5   Refitting the bumper bar and underriders is the reverse sequence to removal. Do not fully tighten the fixings until the bumper bar is perfectly straight and correctly located.

9   Rear bumper – removal and refitting

1   Press in the two plastic lugs securing the number plate lights, remove the lights and place to one side.

2   Open the luggage compartment lid and roll back the matting. Undo and remove the bolts and washers that secure the bumper bar brackets to the body (Fig. 12.2).

3   The rear bumper may now be lifted away taking care to not scratch the paintwork on the rear wings.

4   If it is necessary to detach the underriders and brackets undo and remove the bolts, spring and plain washers.

5   Refitting the bumper bar and underriders is the reverse sequence to removal. Do not fully tighten the fixings until the bumper bar is perfectly straight and correctly located.

10   Windscreen glass – removal and refitting

1   If you are unfortunate enough to have a windscreen shatter, or should you wish to renew your present windscreen, fitting a replacement is one of the jobs which the average owner is advised to leave to a professional. For the owner who wishes to attempt the job himself the following instructions are given.

2   Cover the bonnet with a blanket or cloth to prevent accidental damage and remove the windscreen wiper blades and arms as detailed in Chapter 10.

3   Put on a pair of lightweight shoes and get onto one of the front seats. An assistant should be ready to catch the glass as it is released from the body aperture.

4   Place a piece of soft cloth between the soles of your shoes and the windscreen glass and with both feet on one top corner of the windscreen push firmly.

5   When the weatherstrip has freed itself from the body aperture flange in that area repeat the process at frequent intervals along the top edge of the windscreen until from outside the car the glass and weatherstrip can be removed together.

6   If you are having to replace your windscreen due to a shattered screen, remove all traces of sealing compound from the weatherstrip and body flange.

7   Now is the time to remove all pieces of glass if the screen has shattered. Use a vacuum cleaner to extract as much as possible. Switch on the heater boost motor and adjust the screen controls to *screen defrost* but watch out for flying pieces of glass which might get blown out of the ducting.

8   Carefully inspect the rubber moulding for signs of splitting or deterioration.

9   To refit the glass first fit the weatherstrip onto the glass with the joint at the lower edge.

10 Insert a piece of thick cord into the channel of the weatherstrip with the two ends protruding by at least 12 in (300 mm) at the bottom centre of the screen.

11 Mix a concentrated soap and water solution and apply to the flange of the windscreen aperture.

12 Offer up the screen to the aperture, and with an assistant press the rubber surround hard against one end of the cord, moving round the windscreen and so drawing the lip over the windscreen flange of the body. Keep the draw-cord parallel to the windscreen. Using the palms of the hands, thump on the glass from the outside to assist the lip in passing over the flange and to seat the screen correctly onto the aperture.

13 To ensure a good watertight joint apply some Seelastik SR51 between the weatherstrip and the body and press the weatherstrip against the body to give a good seal.

14 Any excess Seelastik may be removed with a petrol-moistened cloth.

15 Lubricate the finisher strip groove with the soap and water solution and insert the strip.

16 Refit the wiper arms and blades.

11   Door rattles – tracing and rectification

1   The most common cause of door rattle is a misaligned, loose or worn striker plate; however other causes may be:

   a) Loose door or window winder handles
   b) Loose or misaligned door lock components
   c) Loose or worn remote control mechanism

2   It is quite possible for door rattles to be the result of a combination of the above faults so a careful examination should be made to determine their exact cause.

3   If striker plate wear or misalignment is the cause, the plate should be renewed or adjusted as necessary. The procedure is detailed in Section 13.

4   Should the window winder handle rattle, this can be easily rectified by inserting a rubber washer between the escutcheon and door trim panel.

5   If the rattle is found to be emanating from the door lock it will in all probability mean that the lock is worn and therefore should be

Fig. 12.1 Remove the front bumper retaining bolts (Sec 8)

Fig. 12.2 Remove the rear bumper retaining bolts (Sec 9)

13.2 The door striker is secured with four screws

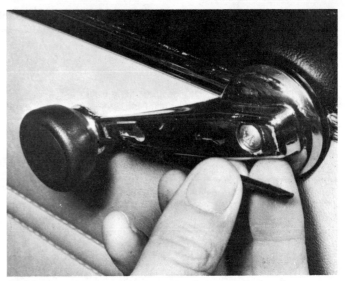

14.1 Remove the plastic trim from the window winder handle ...

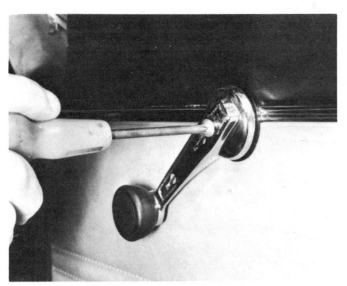

14.2 ... and then the handle retaining screws

14.3 Removing the armrest securing screws

14.4 Slide the door lock remote control housing bezel towards the door hinge

14.5 Removing the door trim panel

replaced with a new lock unit, as described in Section 15 or 16.
6   Lastly, if it is worn hinge pins causing rattles they should be renewed.

12   Front and rear door – removal and refitting

1   Using a pencil, accurately mark the outline of the hinge relative to the door. Remove the two bolts that secure each hinge to the pillar and lift away the complete door.
2   For storage it is best to stand the door on an old blanket and allow it to lean against a wall also suitably padded at the top to stop scratching.
3   Refitting the door is the reverse sequence to removal. If, after refitting, adjustment is necessary, it should be done at the hinges to give correct alignment, or the striker rest if the door either moves up or down on final closing.

13   Door striker plate – removal, refitting and adjustment

1   If it is wished to renew a worn striker plate, mark its position on the door pillar so a new plate can be fitted in the same position.
2   To remove the plates simply undo and remove the four crosshead screws which hold the plate in position. Lift away the plate (photo).
3   Refitting of the door striker is the reverse sequence to removal.
4   To adjust the striker plate, close the door to the first of the two locking positions. Check that the edges of the lock plate and the striker plate are parallel, and that the rear edge of the door stands 0.25 in (6.0 mm) proud of the body. Move the striker plate as necessary.
5   With the lock in the open position, check the clearance at A in Fig. 12.3. This can be checked by placing a ball of plasticine on the striker post and carefully closing the door. The dimension A should be set to 0.08 in (2.0 mm) by carefully moving the striker plate **vertically** as required.

14   Door trim – removal and refitting

1   Using a knife or thin bladed screwdriver, carefully prise the plastic trim from its recesses in the window winder handle. This will expose the handle retaining screw (photo).
2   Wind up the window and note the position of the handle. Undo and remove the crosshead retaining screw and lift away the handle (photo).
3   Undo and remove the two crosshead screws that secure the door pull. Lift away the door pull. Unscrew the interior lock knob (photo).
4   Using a screwdriver, carefully remove the door lock remote control housing bezel by sliding the bezel towards the hinge end of the door. Lift away the bezel (photo).
5   Insert a thin strip of metal with all the sharp edges removed, or a thick knife blade, between the door and the trim panel. This will release one or two of the trim panel retaining clips without damaging the trim. The panel can now be gently eased off by hand (photo).
6   Note that where a map pocket is fitted the trim panel is in two halves. Lack of care when releasing the trim clips could result in the fabric tearing.
7   Carefully remove the plastic weatherproof sheeting. Removal is now complete.
8   Refitting is generally a reversal of the removal procedure.
Note: *When replacing the panel ensure that each of the trim panel retaining clips is firmly located in its hole by sharply striking the panel in the approximate area of each clip with the palm of the hand. This will make sure the trim is seated fully.*

15   Door lock assembly (front) – removal and refitting

1   Refer to Section 14 and remove the door interior trim.
2   Remove the interior handle by sliding it forward to disengage it from the door. Remove the interior knob by unscrewing.
3   Working inside the door shell carefully prise the two exterior control rods from their locations in the lock assembly (Fig. 12.7).
4   Remove the three lock securing screws and push the lock assembly into the door shell. The assembly should be manoeuvred to disengage the interior lock rod, and the interior handle rod.

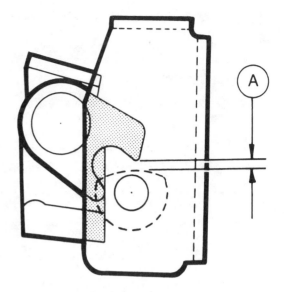

Fig. 12.3 Checking the door striker plate position (Sec 13)

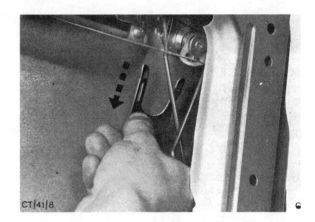

Fig. 12.4 Removing the exterior lock retaining clip (Sec 15)

Fig. 12.5 Driving out the pin securing the lock rod crank (Sec 16)

18.3 Removing the bonnet securing bolts

Fig. 12.6 Disengage the interior handle rod from the rear door
(Sec 16)

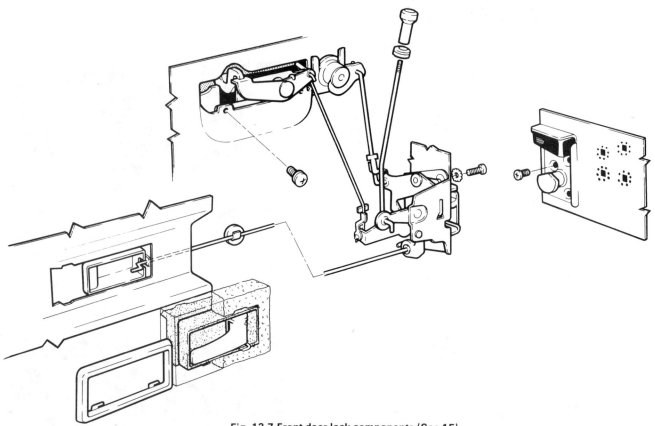

Fig. 12.7 Front door lock components (Sec 15)

5   To remove the exterior handle, remove the two crosshead screws from inside the door shell. To remove the exterior lock, pull down and remove the retaining clip (Fig. 12.4).
6   Refitting the door lock assembly is the reverse sequence to removal. Lubricate all moving parts with a little grease.

16 Door lock assembly (rear) – removal and refitting

1   Refer to Section 14 and remove the door interior trim.

2   Remove the interior lock rod crank from the door shell by drifting out the retaining pin with a suitable pin punch (Fig. 12.5).
3   Prise the exterior handle rod from its location in the lock assembly. Remove the interior door handle by sliding it forward to disengage it from the door.
4   Remove the three lock securing screws and push the lock assembly into the door shell. Turn the interior handle rod to disengage it from the lock (Fig. 12. 6). Remove the lock.
5   The exterior handle may be removed after unscrewing the two crosshead screws from inside the door shell.

Fig. 12.8 Removing the door window glass to the inside (Sec 17)

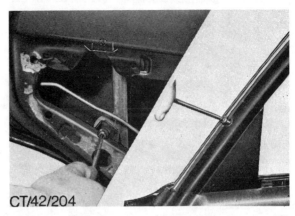

Fig. 12.9 Removing the window extension channel screws (Sec 17)

Fig. 12.10 Rear door window regulator retaining screws (Sec 17)

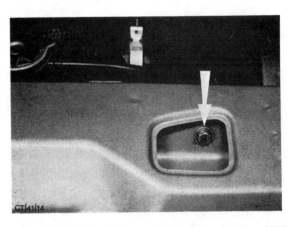

Fig. 12.11 Slacken the bonnet cable clamp bolt (Sec 20)

6   Refitting the door lock assembly is the reverse sequence. Lubricate all moving parts with a little grease.

17 Door glass and regulator – removal and refitting

1   Using a screwdriver carefully ease out the door inner and outer weatherstrips from their retaining clips on the door panel.
2   Undo and remove the two screws that secure the door glass to the window regulator. On rear doors, remove the two screws (Fig. 12.9) and remove the window frame extension channels. Tilt the glass and remove it upwards from the inside of the door (Fig.12.8).
3   Remove the three pairs of screws and the retaining clip on front doors, or remove the five screws on rear doors (Fig. 12.10), and lift away the regulator mechanism.
4   Should it be necessary to remove the glass run channel, start at the front lower frame end and carefully ease the glass run channel from its location in the door frame.
5   Refitting the door glass and regulator is the reverse sequence to removal. Lubricate all moving parts with a little grease. Before refitting the trim panel check the operation and alignment of the glass and regulator and adjust if necessary. When all is correct fully tighten all securing bolts.

18 Bonnet – removal and refitting

1   Open the bonnet and support it open using the bonnet stay. To act as a datum for refitting, mark the position of the hinges relative to the bonnet inner panel.
2   With the assistance of a second person hold the bonnet in the

open position and release the stay.
3   Undo and remove the two bolts, spring washers and plain washers that secure each hinge to the bonnet taking care not to scratch the top of the wings (photo).
4   Lean the bonnet up against a wall, suitably padded to prevent scratching the paint.
5   Refitting the bonnet is the reverse sequence to removal. Any adjustments necessary can be made either at the hinges or the bonnet catch.

19 Bonnet lock – adjustment

1   Should it be necessary to adjust the bonnet catch first slacken the locknut securing the shaft in position.
2   Using a wide-bladed screwdriver, screw the shaft in, or out, as necessary until the correct bonnet front height is obtained. Tighten the locknut.

20 Bonnet release cable – removal, refitting and adjustment

1   Unscrew the five screws securing the dash lower trim panel.
2   Detach the direction indicator flasher unit and the heated rear window relay from their mountings (see Chapter 10).
3   Through the holes in the side of the bonnet release lever bracket, insert a screwdriver and slacken the bracket securing screws.
4   Lift off the bracket and disengage the bonnet release cable.
5   Refer to Section 30 and remove the radiator grille.
6   Slacken the cable clamp bolt (Fig. 12.11) and unhook the cable from the lock spring.

22.2 Boot lid lock securing bolts

23.2 Boot lid lock striker plate securing bolts

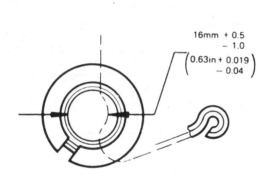

16mm + 0.5
      – 1.0

$\left(0.63\text{in} + 0.019 \atop -0.04 \right)$

Fig. 12.12 Setting dimension for the bonnet release spring (Sec 20)

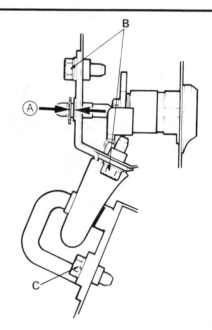

Fig. 12.13 Boot lid lock assembly (Sec 22 and 23)

A Spring clip clearance   B Lock retaining bolts
        C Striker plate retaining bolts

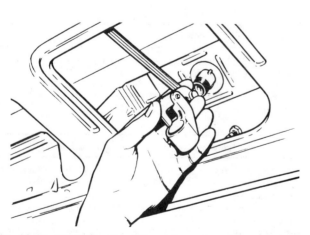

Fig. 12.14 Removing the linkage from the tailgate lock barrel (Sec 25)

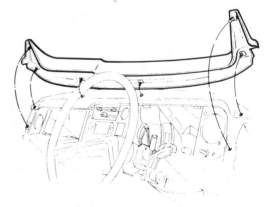

Fig. 12.15 Crash padding securing points (Sec 31)

7   Unclip the cable from its retaining clips around the engine compartment and pull through into the vehicle interior.

8   Installation is the reverse of removal ensuring that the bulkhead rubber grommet is correctly located.

9   The cable should be adjusted to give the dimension shown in Fig. 12.12 and the clamp bolt (Fig. 12.11) tightened.

21 Boot lid – removal and refitting

1   Open the boot lid to its fullest extent. To act as a datum for refitting, mark the position of the hinge relative to the lid inner panel.

2   With the assistance of a second person hold the boot in the open position and then undo and remove the two bolts, spring and plain washers that secure each hinge to the boot lid. Lift away the boot lid taking care not to scratch the top of the rear wings.

3   Lean the boot lid up against a wall, suitably padded to avoid scratching the paint.

4   Refitting the boot lid is the reverse sequence to removal. Any adjustment necessary can be made at the hinge.

22 Boot lid lock – removal and refitting

1   Open the boot lid and carefully withdraw the spring clip located at the end of the lock spindle.

2   Undo and remove the three bolts and spring washers that secure the lock to the boot lid (photo). Lift away the lock assembly.

3   Refitting the lock assembly is the reverse sequence to removal, noting that a small clearance is necessary at A in Fig. 12.13.

23 Boot lid lock striker plate – removal and refitting

1   Open the boot lid and with a pencil mark the outline of the striker plate relative to the inner panel to act as a datum for refitting.

2   Undo and remove the two bolts with spring and plain washers that secure the striker plate. Lift away the striker plate (photo).

3   Refitting the striker plate is the reverse sequence to removal. Line up the striker plate with the previously made marks and tighten the securing bolts.

24 Tailgate assembly – removal and refitting

1   Open the tailgate and with a pencil mark the outline of the hinges relative to the inner panel.

2   With the assistance of a second person hold the tailgate in position and then undo and remove the bolts, spring and plain washers that secure each hinge to the tailgate. Lift away the tailgate taking care not to scratch the side panels.

3   Refitting the tailgate is the reverse sequence to removal. Any adjustment may be made at the hinges.

25 Tailgate lock – removal and refitting

1   Use a wide bladed screwdriver or a thick knife blade between the tailgate and the trim panel. This will release one or two of the trim panel retaining clips without damaging the trim. The panel can now be gently eased out by hand.

2   Undo and remove the large hexagonal nut that retains the lock linkage to the handle, and remove the linkage (Fig. 12.14).

3   Remove the three screws securing the lock and handle assembly, and lift away from the tailgate.

4   To refit the lock assembly is the reverse sequence to removal.

26 Tailgate lock striker plate – removal and refitting

1   Open the tailgate and with a pencil mark the outline of the striker plate relative to the luggage compartment floor.

2   Undo and remove the bolts, spring and plain washers that secure the striker plate and lift away the striker plate.

3   Refitting the striker plate is the reverse sequence to removal. Line up the striker plate with the previously made mark and tighten the securing bolts.

27 Tailgate hinge and torsion bar – removal and refitting

1   Refer to Section 24 and remove the tailgate assembly.

2   With a pencil mark the outline of the hinge and torsion bar assembly to the body.

3   Undo and remove the four bolts, spring and plain washers that secure the hinge and torsion bar assembly to the body and lift away the assembly.

4   Refitting the tailgate hinge and torsion bar assembly is the reverse sequence to removal. Line up the hinge with the previously made mark and tighten the securing bolts.

28 Rear window glass – removal and refitting

Note: *Where a heated rear window is fitted, disconnect the electrical leads before commencing. Also, take great care that the electrical element is not damaged during handling.*

1   Undo and remove the self-tapping screws that secure the front edge of the rear seat cushion to the heel plate. Lift out the cushion taking care not to damage the upholstery or headlining.

2   Open the boot lid and undo and remove the screws that secure the top of the rear seat backrest to the body. Carefully life away the backrest.

3   Remove the retainers and bend back the lock tabs securing the rear parcel shelf. Lift away the parcel shelf.

4   Place a blanket over the boot lid so that it is not accidentally scratched and remove the rear window glass using the same procedure as for the front windscreen. Further information will be found in Section 10, paragraphs 3 to 6 inclusive.

5   Refitting the rear window glass is similar to the refitting of the front windscreen. Refer to Section 10, paragraphs 8 to 16 inclusive.

29 Tailgate window glass – removal and refitting

The procedure for removal and replacement of the tailgate window glass is similar to that for the windscreen glass. Refer to Section 10, paragraphs 3 to 6 and 8 to 16.

30 Radiator grille – removal and refitting

1   Open the bonnet and support in the open position. Undo and remove the crosshead screws that secure the radiator grille to the front body panels. Lift away the radiator grille. Refitting is the reverse sequence to removal but take care to locate the grille tabs in their respective slots in the front lower panel.

31 Instrument panel crash padding – removal and refitting

1   Refer to Chapter 10, Section 37 and remove the instrument cluster.

2   Remove the glove compartment lock striker, and the lid.

3   Remove the glove compartment securing screws, pull the assembly forward, disconnect the lamp leads and remove the assembly.

4   Remove the air vent surround and then remove the two exposed air vent securing screws and pull the vent from the facia so that the hose can be disconnected from it.

5   Access to the crash pad securing nuts can now be obtained through the apertures. Installation is a reversal of removal (Fig. 12.15).

32 Heater assembly – removal and refitting

1   Refer to Chapter 2 and drain the cooling system.

2   Locate the multi-pin plug connector for the heater unit blower motor and detach the plug from the socket, disconnect the

32.10 The heater assembly is mounted on the bulkhead

Fig. 12.16 Detach the heater motor plug and speedometer cable
(Sec 32)

Fig. 12.17 Disconnect the heater hoses (Sec 32)

A Feed hose   B Return hose

Fig. 12.18 Remove the four heater retaining screws (Sec 32)

Fig. 12.19 Remove the temperature control valve bracket (Sec 32
and 34)

speedometer drive cable from the clip on the heater assembly. (Fig. 12.16).

3   Remove the water drain pipe from the air inlet chamber.

4   Slacken the clips that secure the heater water pipes to the heater unit. Note which way round the pipes are fitted and carefully withdraw the two pipes (Fig. 12.17).

5   Undo and remove the self-tapping screws that secure the heater unit to the bulkhead. Their locations are shown in Fig. 12.18.

6   Remove the lower dash insulation panel, remove the bolt from the temperature control valve bracket (Fig. 12.19), and withdraw the control and bracket. Withdraw the heater from the bulkhead.

7   Note that there are three gaskets located between the heater housing flange and if these are damaged they must be renewed (Fig. 12.20 items B,M,N).

8   To refit the heater assembly, stick on three new gaskets to the heater joint face. If the original gaskets are to be retained apply some sealer to the free face of the gasket pack.

9   Move the flap located in the centre of the heater housing and the control lever inside the car to either the *cold* or *hot* position.

10   Fit the heater to the bulkhead and connect the quadrant of the control valve pivot. Secure the heater with self-tapping screws (photo).

11   Refit the water drain pipe and reconnect the multi-pin plug to the blower motor. Refit the speedometer cable.

12   Reconnect the two hoses to the heater unit and secure with the clips.

13   Refill the cooling system as described in Chapter 2.

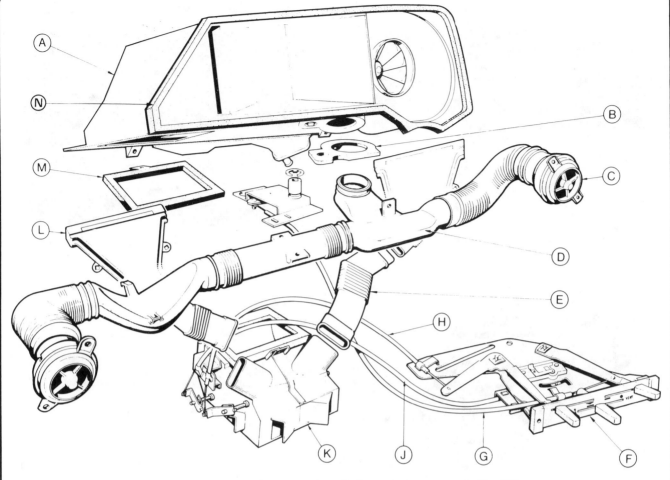

Fig. 12.20 Heating and ventilation system components (Sec 32)

A Heater assembly
B Ambient air duct/control
   valve shaft gasket
C Air vent
D Ambient air duct

E Demister
F Control panel
G Temperature control valve
   Bowden cable

H Air distribution valve
   Bowden cable
J Air inlet valve Bowden cable
K Air distribution valve

   assembly
L Demister vent
M Heating system air duct gasket
N Heater assembly gasket

Fig. 12.21 Removing the heater radiator lower panel bolts (Sec 33)

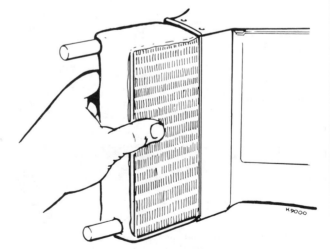

Fig. 12.22 Withdrawing the radiator and foam gasket (Sec 33)

Fig. 12.23 Removing the heater motor assembly (Sec 33)

Fig. 12.24 Disconnect the control cables from the air distribution valve (Sec 34)

Fig. 12.25 Location of heater motor resistance plate rivets (Sec 34)

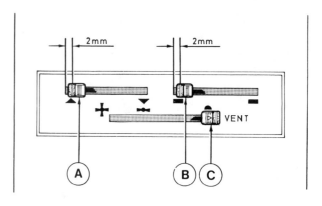

Fig. 12.26 Heater control cable adjustments (Sec 34)

A Air distribution lever   B Air temperature lever
C Boost fan switch

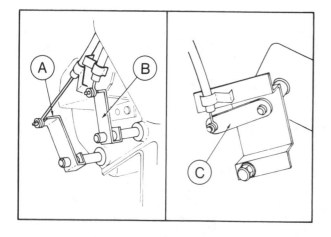

Fig. 12.27 Set heater flaps to end position and secure cable sheaths (Sec 34)

A Air inlet valve   B Air distribution valve
C Temperature control valve

33 Heater assembly – dismantling and reassembly

1   Refer to Section 3 and remove the heater assembly.
2   Undo and remove the two bolts that secure the heater radiator lower panel to the main casing. Lift away the lower panel (Fig. 12.21).
3   Carefully slide out the heater radiator together with its foam rubber packing (Fig. 12.22).
4   Undo and remove the three bolts that secure the blower motor baseplate and lift away the blower motor assembly (Fig. 12.23).
5   Inspect the heater radiator for signs of leaks which, if evident, may be repaired in a similar manner used for the engine cooling system radiator as described in Chapter 2. It is a good policy to reverse-flush the radiator to remove any sediment.
6   Reassembling the heater assembly is the reverse sequence to dismantling.
7   It is possible to remove the heater radiator and the blower motor whilst the heater assembly is still fitted in the car.

34 Heater controls – removal, refitting and adjustment

1   Refer to Chapter 10, Section 37 and remove the instrument panel.
2   Remove the lower dash insulation panel, and remove the Bowden cables from the temperature control valve and the air distribution valve assembly (Fig. 12.24).
3   Unscrew the three control panel securing screws, disconnect the

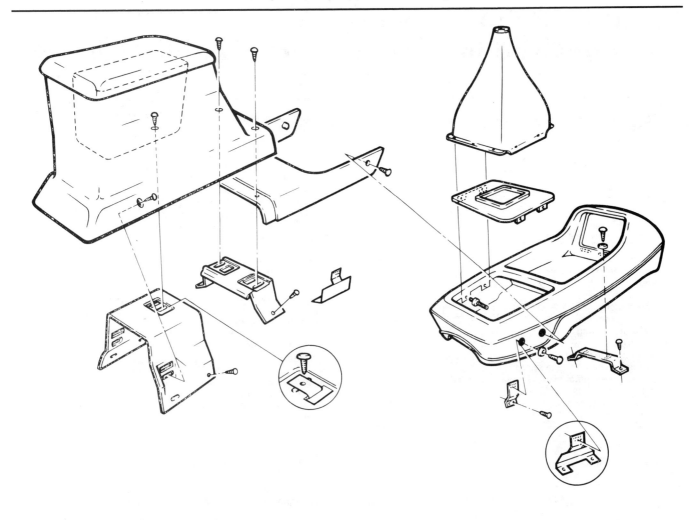

Fig. 12.28 Centre armrest and associated components (Sec 37)

electric cables at the rear and remove the control assembly complete with control cables.
4   If required, remove the cables from the controls, and the resistance plate by drilling out the rivets (Fig. 12.25).
5   Refitting is a reversal of the above procedure.
6   To adjust the control cables, set the upper heater control to a point approximately 0.1 in (2 mm) from their stops, and lock the booster switch in the *vent* position by pulling outwards (Fig. 12.26). Set the heater flaps in their end positions and clamp the cable sheaths with the spring clips (Fig. 12.27).

35 Trinket tray – removal and refitting

1   Remove the four screws (two each side) and lift off the tray. Refitting is a reversal of this procedure.

36 Centre console – removal and refitting

1   Refer to Section 37 and remove the centre armrest if fitted.

2   Prise out the lock (or the blanking plate) and disconnect the clock leads.
3   Unscrew and remove the two screws accessible through the clock aperture and the two located at the rear side of the console.
4   Unscrew the gearlever knob, or remove the T-handle from the selector lever, and lift up the centre console.
5   Refitting is a reversal of this procedure.

37 Centre armrest – removal and refitting

1   Position the front seats as required to remove one armrest retaining screw from each side (Fig. 12.28).
2   Open the armrest lid, and remove the screw from the bottom of the box.
3   Remove the two screws from the front of the armrest, and lift the armrest forward over the handbrake lever.
4   Refitting is a reversal of this procedure.

Chapter 13 Supplement:
Revisions and information on later models

Contents

2 Specifications

The following are additions to, or modifications of, the Specifications given at the beginning of Chapters 1 to 12

Engine
General

Compression ratio	9.0:1
Piston ring gap position:	
Top compression ring	150° to spreader gap
Centre compression ring	150° on other side of spreader gap
Top oil control ring	1 in (25 mm) from spreader gap
Centre oil control ring	Rear of piston
Bottom oil control ring	1 in (25 mm) on other side of spreader gap
Cylinder head:	
Cast mark	A9
Valve timing:	
Inlet opens	25° BTDC
Inlet closes	51° ABDC
Exhaust opens	67° BBDC
Exhaust closes	9° ATDC
Inlet valve:	
Head diameter	39.67 to 40.06 mm

Free spring length	53 mm	
Exhaust valve:		
Head diameter	33.83 to 34.21 mm	
Free spring length	53 mm	

Torque wrench settings

	lbf ft	kgf m
Cylinder head bolts:		
First stage	30 to 40	4.1 to 5.5
Second stage	40 to 50	5.5 to 6.9
Third stage (after 10 to 20 minutes wait)	70 to 85	9.7 to 11.7
After 15 minutes running at 1000 rpm	70 to 85	9.7 to 11.7
Inlet manifold:		
Stage 1	3 to 6	0.4 to 0.8
Stage 2	6 to 11	0.8 to 1.5
Stage 3	11 to 15	1.5 to 2.1
Stage 4	15 to 18	2.1 to 2.5
Stage 5 (After running engine for 15 minutes at 1500 rpm)	15 to 18	2.1 to 2.5
Exhaust manifold	18 to 22	2.5 to 3.0

Cooling system
General

Fan type (Aug '79 on)	Thermo-viscous clutch
Thermostat (Aug '79 on):	
Type	Wax
Opening temperature	192 to 200°F (89 to 93°C)
Fully open temperature	217 to 223°F (103 to 106°C)
Antifreeze type	Motorcraft Antifreeze Super-Plus

Torque wrench settings

	lbf ft	kgf m
Fan blades to viscous clutch	6 to 9	0.8 to 1.0

Fuel system
General

Carburettor:	
Part number:	
Manual transmission	80 TF 9510 AEA
Automatic transmission	80 TF 9510 AFA, AGA or AJA
Float level setting	0.57 in ± 0.02 (14.5 mm ± 0.5)
Throttle barrel diameter	35 mm
Venturi diameter	26/26 mm
Main jet	137, 5/137, 5
Idle jet	47, 5/47, 5

Torque wrench settings

	lbf ft	kgf m
Fuel pump retaining nuts	10 to 13	1.4 to 1.8

Ignition system
General

Distributor type	Breakerless
Dwell angle	Governed by electronic module (does not require checking)
Distributor shaft endfloat	0.6 to 1.05 mm
Coil:	
Type	High output breakerless ignition coil
Output	30 kV (minimum) on open circuit
Primary resistance	0.75 to 0.85 ohms
Secondary resistance	5000 to 6000 ohms
Spark plugs	Motorcraft Super AGR 22C
Distributor capacitor (conventional distributor)	0.24 to 0.32 µ F

Clutch
General

Adjustment method	Automatic, from August 1979
Lining external diameter	9.13 in (232.3 mm)

Suspension and steering
Front suspension (1980 on)

Toe setting:	
Checking value	0.16 in (4.0 mm) toe-in to 0.8 in (2.0 mm) toe-out
If outside checking limits adjust to	0.8 in (2.0 mm) toe-in to Zero (straight-ahead)
Castor:	
Saloon (standard)	1°40' nominal (0°55' to 2°55' tolerance range)
Saloon (heavy duty)	2°17' nominal (1°17' to 3°32' tolerance range)
Estate (standard)	1°57' nominal (1°12' to 3°12' tolerance range)

Estate (heavy duty)	2°17' nominal (1°17' to 3°32' tolerance range)
Estate (business)	1°21' nominal (0°21' to 2°36' tolerance range)

Camber:
Saloon (standard)	-0°53' (-0°08 to -1°38' tolerance range)
Saloon (heavy duty)	-0°51' (-0°06' to -1°36' tolerance range)
Estate (standard)	-0°53' (-0°08' to -1°38' tolerance range)
Estate (heavy duty)	-0°51' (-0°06' to -1°36' tolerance range)
Estate (business)	-0°54' (-0°09' to -1°39' tolerance range)

Torque wrench settings

	lbf ft	kgf m
Power steering pump mounting stud	25 to 40	3.5 to 5.4
Power steering pump union	25 to 40	3.5 to 5.4

1 Introduction

This additional Chapter details modifications to the models covered in Chapter 1 to 12, and also includes the repair and adjustment procedures of the new features introduced on the 1980 model Cortina.

3 Engine

1 The engine has been modified to improve performance and economy, the principal changes being that the compression ratio has been increased and there have been changes to the inlet manifold, cylinder heads, pistons and exhaust manifold. Details of the changes are as follows.

Inlet manifold

2 An improved and more even lubrication of the mixture has been achieved by modifying the inlet manifold (Fig. 13.1). A passage through the inlet manifold connects the exhaust manifolds of both banks of cylinders and gives preheating of the inlet gases.

Inlet manifold gasket

3 From August 1978 (Build Code UP), all 2.3 litre Cologne engines have the same type of inlet manifold gasket as used on the 2.8 litre Cologne V6 engine. This type of gasket is immersed in Ford sealing compound, Part Number A70SX-19554-BA prior to assembly.

4 The gasket should be installed in the following manner. Carefully clean all the mating surfaces of the cylinder block, inlet manifold and cylinder heads and then coat them with the above mentioned sealing compound.

5 Apply a thin film of sealing compound $\frac{1}{8}$ to $\frac{1}{2}$ in (3 to 12 mm) wide around all coolant and induction port apertures on both sides of the new inlet manifold gasket.

6 Position the inlet manifold and tighten the retaining bolts in the five stages given in the Specification and in the sequence shown in Fig. 1.16 of Chapter 1. A special tool 21-092 (Fig. 13.2) is available for use on the more inaccessible inlet manifold bolts and it is necessary to remove the throttle control bracket before tightening.

Exhaust manifolds

7 The exhaust manifolds have been strengthened and they have been modified to enlarge the passages (Fig. 13.3).

8 To minimise the risk of cracking the exhaust manifold, a revised tightening torque and installation procedure was introduced from February 1978 and applies to any vehicle fitted with a Cologne V6 engine.

9 Ensure that the manifold retaining studs protrude from the cylinder head by 1.14 ± 0.06 in (29.0 ± 1.5 mm) and that the mating surfaces are clean and free from burrs.

10 Install the manifold using only graphite grease for sealing between the manifold and cylinder head. Gaskets should NOT be used on new manifolds, but a gasket may be used if an old manifold is installed and cannot otherwise be sealed adequately.

11 Install the flat washers and nuts, and torque tighten to the value given in the Specifications. It is essential that this torque is applied correctly and is not exceeded because failure to do so will result in damage to the manifold.

Cylinder heads

12 In addition to the changes in inlet and exhaust porting already mentioned, the shape of the combustion chambers has been changed (Fig. 13.4), and new cylinder head gaskets have been introduced.

13 When installing a cylinder head and retightening the bolts, or when retightening the cylinder head bolts in service, the following points should be noted in order to achieve effective and long lasting sealing.

   (a) To overcome 'stiction', back each bolt off half a turn before tightening to the specified torque
   (b) Do not back off and re-torque more than one bolt at a time. Do not slacken all the bolts simultaneously, because this might destroy the gasket seal
   (c) Take care to tighten the bolts according to the correct sequence, which is shown in Fig. 1.15 of Chapter 1
   (d) Observe the revised torque wrench settings given in the Specifications Section of this Supplement

Valves and valve stem seals

14 In October 1978, all engines produced with standard sized valves had nylon instead of rubber valve stem seals. When overhauling any engine with standard sized valves, nylon stem seals should be used whether or not the ones removed are rubber.

15 There are two patterns of oversized valve which were in use from October 1978 until the 1980 modifications were introduced. Oversize valves can be identified by having the stem diameter stepped in the area of the grooves for the valve spring collet (Fig. 13.5); the old and new type differ as follows:

Nominal dimension X	Old design	New design
Inlet valve	0.66 in	0.48 in
	(16.8 mm)	(12.1 mm)
Exhaust valve	0.82 in	0.48 in
	(20.9 mm)	(12.1 mm)

16 When renewing valve stem seals on oversize valves, use nylon seals, except on oversized inlet valves of the old design.

17 When installing nylon seals, it is important that they are pushed onto the stem squarely and not at an angle, and they must be secure on the valve stem.

18 When using nylon seals on oversized valves of the old type, the seals must not be pressed past the step on the valve stem, because this will damage the seal. Take care when fitting the valve spring collets that the spring retainer does not push the valve seal down the valve stem more than $\frac{5}{8}$ in (16 mm).

19 Nylon valve stem seals have a colour code identification as follows:

Standard	–	White
0.2 mm oversize	–	red
0.4 mm oversize	–	blue

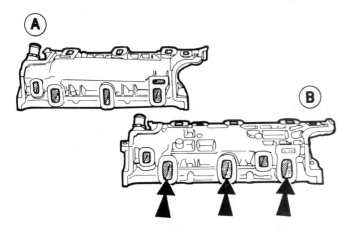

Fig. 13.1 Inlet manifold (Sec 3)

A   Old version   B   Modified version

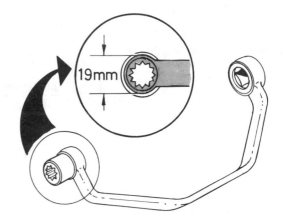

Fig. 13.2 Special tool for inlet manifold bolts (Sec 3)

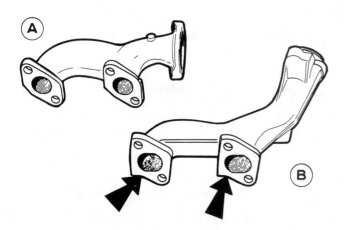

Fig. 13.3 Exhaust manifold (Sec 3)

A   Old version   B   Modified version

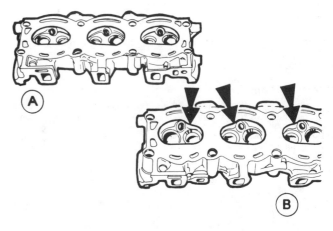

Fig. 13.4 Cylinder head combustion chambers (Sec 3)

A   Old version   B   Modified version

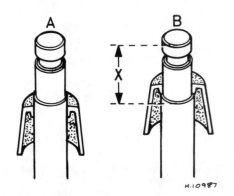

Fig. 13.5 Position of nylon seals on old design oversize valves (Sec 3)

A   Incorrect   See text for dimension 'X'
B   Correct

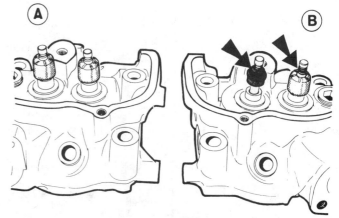

Fig. 13.6 1980 valve stem oil seals (Sec 3)

A   Old version   B   Modified version
Note the three grooves on the stem of the exhaust valve

0.6 mm oversize   –   green
0.8 mm oversize   –   black

It should be noted that some production engines are fitted with 0.2 mm and 0.4 mm oversize valves, but 0.6 and 0.8 mm oversize valves are for service use only.

20 With the introduction of the 1980 model modifications, was a new type of valve stem seal for inlet valves (Fig. 13.6). The exhaust valve has the same type of sealing cap as that used previously.

21 The diameters of the heads of the inlet and exhaust valves have been increased on 1980 model engines (see Specifications)., The stems of the exhaust valves now have three grooves in them (Fig. 13.6) and have to be assembled with valve spring cotters having corresponding grooves.

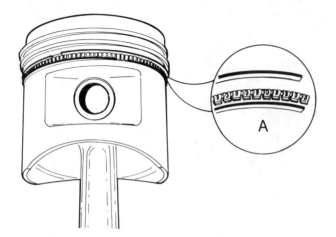

Fig. 13.7 Modified piston of higher compression engine (Sec 3)

A   Low friction oil scraper ring

Valve springs

22   The larger valves introduced as part of the 1980 model modifications, have uprated valve springs with a greater free length (see Specifications).

Pistons and rings

23   The 1980 model engine has an increased compression ratio (see Specifications), and this has been achieved by increasing piston height. To reduce friction, a new type of oil scraper ring has been introduced (Fig. 13.7).

Camshaft and camshaft gear

24   The 1980 model engine has a camshaft which has been advanced 2.5°, changing the valve opening and closing times (see Specifications). The camshaft is now mounted in bronze bearings and the drivegear is of nylon.

4   Cooling system

Antifreeze

1   The cooling systems of all 1981 models are filled with Motorcraft Antifreeze Super-Plus.

2   The new antifreeze was developed to meet the requirements of the CVH engine of the new Escort, and has significantly improved high temperature performance and corrosion resistance.

3   It is recommended that the new antifreeze is used for refilling all Ford engines and the following points should be noted.

4   The new antifreeze is coloured pink, to distinguish it from Motorcraft Antifreeze Plus, which is blue/green. The two products are fully compatible and Super-Plus can be used for topping up engines already filled with Motorcraft Antifreeze Plus. The resultant colour will be brownish, but the colour is unrelated to performance.

5   Although such action is discouraged, Motorcraft Antifreeze Super-Plus can also be used to top up systems which have been filled with other proprietary antifreeze compounds.

Thermo-viscous fan – description

6   To increase engine performance and provide better fuel economy, a thermo-viscous fan clutch (Fig. 13.8) is now fitted to all models from 1980 on. This type of fan has several advantages over the type used originally, the advantages being:

- (a)   The engine warms up faster
- (b)   Less power is required to drive the fan, so that fanbelt life is increased and the power saved results in increased performance and decreased fuel consumption
- (c)   The fan is quieter

7   The fan is multibladed and is manufactured from plastic. It is mounted on a viscous coupling whose operation is controlled thermostatically. On initial start-up, when the engine is cold, the fan rotates at idle speed, irrespective of engine speed. As the engine warms up, a bimetallic element in the fan hub actuates the control valve in the fan hub, progressively opening the inlet port to permit fluid

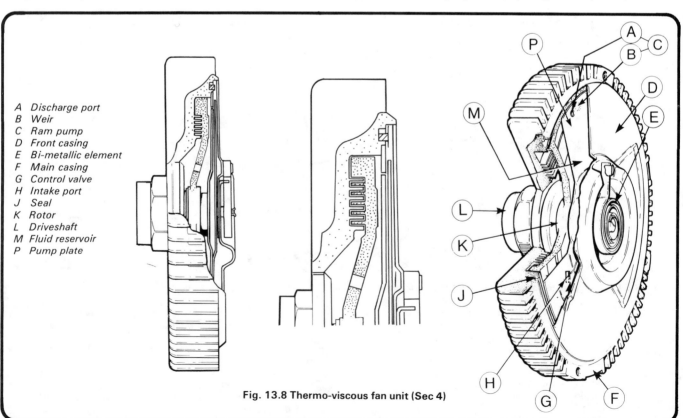

A   Discharge port
B   Weir
C   Ram pump
D   Front casing
E   Bi-metallic element
F   Main casing
G   Control valve
H   Intake port
J   Seal
K   Rotor
L   Driveshaft
M   Fluid reservoir
P   Pump plate

Fig. 13.8 Thermo-viscous fan unit (Sec 4)

to enter the rotor chamber. The fluid in the rotor chamber increases the coupling between the driveshaft and the rotor, increasing the rotor drive torque and thereby increasing fan speed.

8   The fluid is transferred into the fluid reservoir at the front by the rotation of the rotor and a ram pump. The fluid is kept in the reservoir until the engine starts to warm up and it is then transferred to the rotor chamber progressively as described previously.

9   The unit is not repairable and must be renewed if it becomes defective.

Thermo-viscous fan – removal and installation

10   To remove the thermo-viscous fan necessitates the use of a cranked spanner to unscrew it from the water pump hub. An open-ended 1.25 in AF (32 mm) spanner with a thickness not exceeding 0.196 in (5 mm) should be modified as shown in Fig. 13.9.

11   Hold the water pump pulley to prevent it from rotating. Engage the special spanner over the fan clutch unit and unscrew it. The nut has a left-hand thread, so the spanner must be turned clockwise when viewed from the front. If the nut is tight, the end of the spanner should be tapped with a hide-faced hammer.

12   After screwing the assembly off the water pump, separate the fan from the clutch assembly by removing the four bolts securing the fan to the clutch.

13   Installation is the reverse of removal, it being necessary to screw the clutch assembly anticlockwise onto the water pump shaft. When assembling the fan to the clutch, do not exceed the specified torque when tightening the fan retaining bolts. This is very important, because otherwise the aluminium clutch housing may be damaged.

Coolant expansion tank

14   A coolant expansion tank is now fitted (photo) and this assists the cooling system to retain the correct volume of coolant. The tank is connected to the radiator by a pipe which is attached to the radiator filler neck, and any coolant which is expelled when the radiator

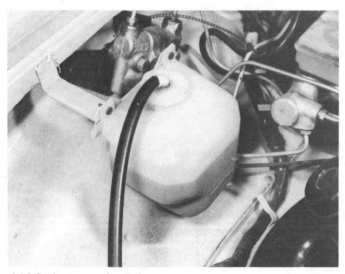

4.14 Coolant expansion tank

temperature rises flows into it. When the system cools, coolant is sucked from the expansion tank back into the radiator.

15   Only check the coolant level when the engine is cold, otherwise the flow of coolant between the radiator and the expansion tank may be interrupted and an incorrect level indication obtained.

16   Coolant level must be checked at the radiator filler neck and not at the expansion tank. If the radiator level is low, add coolant until the level is up to the base of the radiator filler neck.

17   The coolant level in the expansion tank should never exceed $\frac{1}{4}$ full. If the level exceeds this and if it tends to increase with time, it is likely that the system pressure is incorrect because of an incorrect, or defective, radiator pressure cap. Check the cap and renew it if necessary.

Coolant expansion tank – removal and installation

18   Allow the engine to cool and then remove the expansion tank cap.

19   Unscrew and remove the two retaining screws, and remove the tank by lifting its locating lug clear of the bottom mounting.

20   Drain the contents of the tank into a clean container, so that the coolant can be re-used.

21   With the overflow tank empty, install it as the reverse of removal.

22   Remove the radiator filler cap, pour the coolant drained from the overflow tank back into the radiator until the coolant level is to the base of the filler neck, and discard any excess.

Radiator bottom hose

23   On some V6 Cortina variants there is a danger of the bottom hose chafing on the flange of the front crossmember (photo).

24   There should be a minimum clearance of 0.8 in (20 mm) at this point and, if this does not exist, slacken the hose clamp at the radiator and twist the radiator end of the lower hose anticlockwise when viewed from the front of the vehicle. When the clearance is correct, tighten the hose clamp.

25   Stick a 2 in (50 mm) length of door weatherstrip to the edge of the

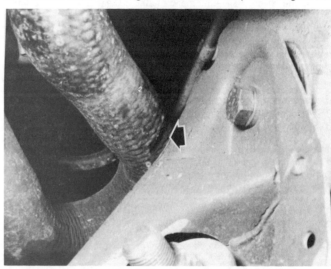

4.23 Chafing (arrowed) of bottom hose on front crossmember

crossmember beneath the forward end of the hose loop.

26   Start the engine to check for coolant leaks and to make certain that the hose no longer chafes.

Thermostat – testing

27   The operating range of the thermostat has been changed to increase the operating temperature of the engine (see Specifications).

28   To test the thermostat, remove it from the vehicle and suspend it in water in a suitable container, ensuring that the thermostat does not touch the container sides.

29   Gradually heat the water, checking its temperature frequently with an accurate thermometer. Note the temperature at which the thermostat starts to open, which should be between 192 and 200°F (89 to 93°C).

30   It is not possible to check the fully open temperature of the thermostat by this method because this is in the range 217 to 223°F (103 to 106°C) which is above the boiling point of water at normal atmospheric pressure.

31   It is not possible to repair the thermostat and if defective it must be renewed.

5   Fuel system

Oil leaks from fuel pump gasket

1   On vehicles built prior to January 1979 there is a tendency for oil to leak from the fuel pump-to-engine cylinder block joint. To overcome this, the original black coloured gasket should be replaced with the current gasket which is lighter in colour.

2   Remove the fuel pump (Chapter 3, Section 7), and carefully clean the mating surfaces of the cylinder block and fuel pump.

3   Install the pump onto the engine without any gasket and tighten the retaining nuts to a torque of 1.5 to 3.0 lbf ft (0.2 to 0.4 kgf m).
4   Try and insert a 0.004 in (0.10 mm) feeler gauge between the cylinder block and the pump. If the gauge can be inserted, the pump flange is distorted and a new pump must be installed.
5   If the pump is satisfactory, remove it from the engine and install it using a new gasket (Part No 79TM-9417-AA).
6   Tighten the nuts to a torque of 10 to 13 lbf ft (1.4 to 1.8 kgf m). Do not exceed this torque, because it will result in the fuel pump flange being distorted.

Electrically operated choke system

7   An electric choke system (photo) has been introduced to reduce emission levels and fuel consumption during the warm-up period. On coolant temperature controlled units as used previously, the choke does not start to open until the engine coolant is hot enough to operate the bi-metal coil and this time lag results in a mixture which is richer than necessary during warm up.
8   In the electric system, the bi-metal is heated by two electric heaters. One heater is powered directly by the alternator and starts to heat and open the choke as soon as the engine starts, but the power of the heater is insufficient to open the choke fully. The second heater is controlled by a thermo-switch in the coolant system so that the choke does not open fully until the engine has reached a specific temperature. A simplified wiring diagram is shown in Fig. 13.10.

Electrically operated choke – removal and installation

9   Disconnect the battery leads and remove the air cleaner (Chapter 3, Section 4).
10 Disconnect the wiring loom plug from the thermostat housing.
11 Note the choke alignment marks (photo) and, if they are not co-incident, make marks to ensure that the choke is reinstalled to the same position as before removal.
12 Remove the three screws and remove the choke thermostat and its clamping plate.
13 When installing, connect the bi-metal coil to the choke lever and position the assembly with the three retaining screws loose.
14 Turn the choke thermostat until the alignment marks are coincident and then tighten the clamping screws (photo).

Slow running and basic idle systems

15 The bypass idle (slow running) and basic idle systems have been changed, the most important change being that the adjusting screws which controlled the fuel mixture strength for the basic idling system have been eliminated.

Slow running adjustment

16 Slow running adjustment is the same as described in Chapter 3 Section 17, but the position of the adjuster screws has been changed and they are now protected by tamper-proof plugs (photos). The alternative positions of both adjuster screws are shown in Fig. 13.11.

Basic idle setting

17 There is no basic idle setting on 1980 carburettors. The tapered needle jets formerly used have been replaced by fixed jets and the speed screw controlling throttle plate position is set in production and its end is then sheared off to prevent any subsequent alteration (photo).

Fast idle adjustment

18 Because difficulty may be experienced in locating the phase point position of the choke mechanism, it is now recommended that the choke is set in the 'high cam' position. The information given in paragraphs 8 and 9 of Chapter 3, Section 22 should be disregarded and the following method used for water heated and electrically heated choke systems.
19 Remove the fixings of the air cleaner assembly, but do not disconnect the vacuum supply pipe. Position the air cleaner so that it is clear of the carburettor.
20 Start the engine and allow it to run until it achieves normal operating temperature, then stop the engine and connect a tachometer in accordance with its maker's instructions.
21 Hold the throttle partially open and, while doing so, close the throttle plates fully and then release the throttle; the throttle will then

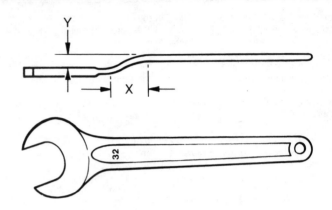

Fig. 13.9 Special spanner for removing thermo-viscous fan (Sec 5)

X = 1 in (25 mm)   Y = 0.5 in (12 mm)

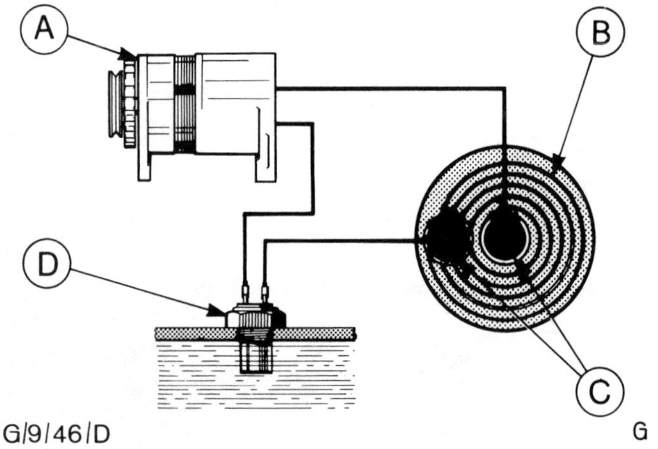

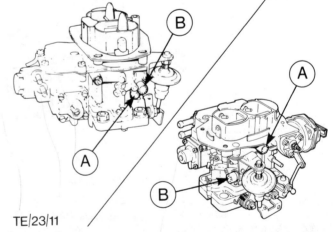

G/9/46/D   G

Fig. 13.10 Electric choke simplified wiring diagram (Sec 5)

A Alternator   C Heater elements
B Bi-metal coil   D Thermo-switch

TE/23/11

Fig. 13.11 Alternative positions of bypass (slow running) adjusters (Sec 5)

A Bypass mixture screw   B Bypass idle speed screw

hold the choke mechanism in the high cam/fast idle setting position.
22 Release the choke plates and, without touching the throttle pedal, start the engine. Record the indicated engine speed, which should be 2900 rpm. If any adjustment is necessary, follow the procedure of Chapter 3, Section 21.

5.7 Electrically heated choke

5.14 Choke alignment marks (arrowed)

5.16 Tamperproof plug (arrowed) covering adjuster screw

5.17 Sheared off throttle adjustment screw (arrowed)

6 Ignition system

Breakerless ignition system – general description

1   The breakerless ignition system has an electronic module to switch the primary circuit of the ignition coil. The module receives electrical pulses from the distributor, these pulses being produced by a coil in a magnetic field whose strength is varied cyclically by a toothed rotor connected to the distributor spindle (photo).

2   The distributor rotor and cap are of conventional design as are the coil and HT leads, except that the coil is designed to give an increased output voltage and does not operate in conjunction with a series resistor.

3   Ignition timing of an engine with breakerless ignition is essentially the same as for an engine with a conventional distributor, and the vacuum and centrifugal advance mechanisms are similar. In the breakerless system there is no provision for adjusting dwell angle. This is done by the electronic module, which continually varies the dwell angle to correspond to engine speed.

Breakerless ignition system – precautions

4   The high tension voltage generated by the coil of the breakerless ignition system is about 30 000 volts, some 25% higher than that of a normal coil so that any electric shock received from the breakerless ignition will be correspondingly more severe.

5   It is possible to receive a shock from the breakerless ignition system under circumstances which would not result in a shock from a conventional system and it is necessary to take care to avoid such shocks.

6   The instant that the ignition is switched off, or if the distributor is knocked while the ignition is switched ON, a single high tension pulse will be produced and directed to one of the spark plugs. If handling any spark plug or HT lead, take care that neither of the conditions mentioned can be produced.

Breakerless ignition system – component identification

7   The high output ignition coils have a red label on them to identify them. They also have a black protective cap over their ends and this cap must not be removed. The positive and negative LT terminals are clearly marked on this cap.

8   The principal method of identifying the distributor of a breakerless ignition system is that the distributor cap is brick red in colour. In addition, they have their LT leads emerging from the distributor and terminating in a plug, and they do not have a capacitor mounted on the outside of the distributor body.

Ignition coil – removal and installation

9   The ignition coil is mounted on the upper face of the rear bulkhead on the driver's side (photo). Pull the HT lead out of the centre of the

coil and after labelling the two LT wires so that they are reconnected correctly, disconnect them.

10 The coil may be removed complete with its clamp bracket by removing the two bolts, or the bracket clamping bolt may be slackened and the coil pulled out of the clamp bracket.

11 Installation is the reverse of removal. Take care to connect the two LT wires correctly (green to negative terminal, black/red to positive). If the coil was removed from its clamp, do not overtighten the clamp bolt after the coil has been reinstalled. Over-tightening can cause crushing of the ignition coil case and may do internal damage.

Electronic module – removal and installation

12 The electronic module is mounted adjacent to the ignition coil (photo).

13 The module is connected to the main loom by a special flat multi-pin connector which is protected by a rubber boot.

14 Pull back the rubber boot, release the clips at the sides of the plug and pull the plug off the module (photo).

15 Remove the two crosshead screws securing the module and remove the module.

16 Installation is the reverse of removal. The plug of the module is of the coded type and cannot be connected improperly. When reinstalling the rubber boot, make sure that its upper edge engages in the groove in the electronic module.

17 The electronic module has a very high reliability and in the event of any suspected ignition fault check the connections, but do not change the module until all other possible causes have been eliminated.

Distributor – removal and installation

18 The removal of the distributor is essentially the same as for the conventional distributor (see Chapter 4, paragraph 6). Distributor removal is facilitated by the use of a special cranked spanner (Fig. 13.12), because the distributor clamp bolt (photo) is not very accessible, but this tool is not essential. A short ring spanner, or a $\frac{3}{8}$ in square drive socket and a flexible handle are equally suitable.

19 Install the distributor as described in paragraphs 1 to 5 of Chapter 4, Section 14 and then initially adjust the timing as follows so that the engine can be started.

20 Turn the engine to 9°BTDC for No 1 cylinder and check that the rotor arm points to the slot cut in the distributor housing (Fig. 13.13).

21 Remove the rotor arm and turn the distributor until the teeth of the rotor are directly opposite the teeth of the stator. The angle Z between the rear face of the cylinder block and the distributor diaphragm axis should then be between 0° and 14° anticlockwise (Fig. 13.14).

22 Tighten the distributor clamp bolt.

Fig. 13.12 Special spanner for distributor clamp bolt (Sec 6)

Ignition timing

23 An engine with breakerless ignition cannot be timed statically in the same way as is used for conventional ignition. Having set the timing approximately as described in paragraphs 20 to 22 above, ignition timing must be set as follows.

24 Turn the engine manually to locate the timing notch on the crankshaft pulley and highlight the notch and the timing pointer with chalk, or white paint.

6.1 Distributor rotor and stator teeth

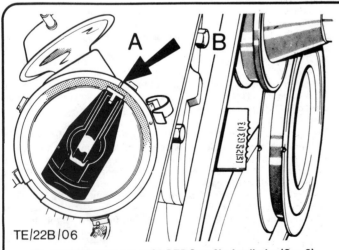

Fig. 13.13 Engine set at 9° BTDC on No 1 cylinder (Sec 6)

    A   Rotor arm pointing to slot in distributor housing
    B   Timing pointer at 9° BTDC

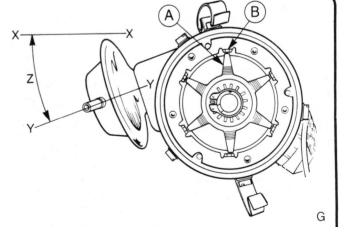

Fig. 13.14 Correct position of distributor (Sec 6)

A	Rotor teeth	YY	Vacuum unit axis
B	Stator teeth	Z	Angle between 0° and 14°
XX	Cylinder block rear face		

6.9 Ignition coil of breakerless system

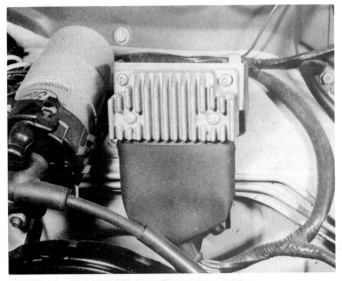
6.12 Electronic module of breakerless ignition system

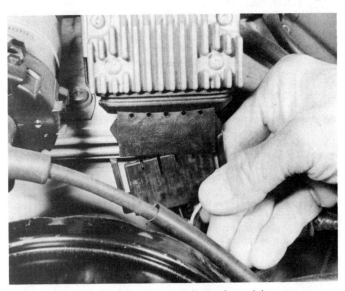
6.14 Disconnecting the plug from the electronic module

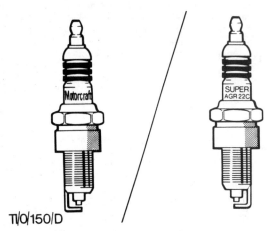

TI/0/150/D

Fig. 13.15 Identification of copper cored spark plugs (Sec 6)

25 Connect a timing light in accordance with its manufacturer's instructions, start the engine and allow it to run at idle speed.
26 Disconnect and plug the vacuum pipe to the distributor and then check the ignition timing.
27 If the timing requires adjustment, stop the engine, slacken the distributor clamp bolt and rotate the complete distributor assembly a few degrees. Tighten the clamp bolt and re-check the timing. To advance the timing, the distributor should be turned anticlockwise and vice versa.

Spark plugs

28 Because of misfiring during the warming up period on some engines, a new type of spark plug was introduced in October 1978. The new plugs had a copper core and were designated AGR 22C.
29 An improved version, designated Super AGR 22C was introduced in February 1980 and is fitted to all new engines from January 1980. The new plugs are identified by having three red rings towards the top of the insulator and the inscriptions 'Motorcraft' and 'Super AGR 22C' in red on opposite sides at the base of the insulator (Fig. 13.15). A non-resistor version of the plug is available and is designated Super AG 22C.
30 It is recommended that when replacement plugs are required Super AGR 22C, or Super AG 22C plugs are fitted, regardless of the type previously used.
31 On models with breakerless ignition it is not necessary to check the plugs at 6000 miles (10 000 km) intervals, but they should be renewed every 12 000 miles (20 000 km).

6.18 Distributor clamp bolt (arrowed)

32 On models with conventional ignition, it is still advisable to clean and check the gaps of the spark plugs at 6000 miles (10 000 km).

7   Clutch

Automatically adjusted clutch cable

1   All 1980 models fitted with manual transmission have an automatically adjusted clutch operating cable, the adjustment being made by a ratchet device fitted to the clutch pedal. The main components of this device are shown in Fig. 13.16.
2   When the clutch pedal is not being depressed, the pawl is not engaged in the clutch pedal quadrant and the cable is tensioned by the spring between the pedal and the quadrant. When the pedal is depressed, the pawl engages in the nearest available tooth in the quadrant, locking the quadrant to the pedal lever so that the lever pulls the clutch cable and operates the clutch.

Automatically adjusted clutch cable – removal and installation

3   Raise the front of the car and support it securely on axle stands, or substantial wood blocks. Alternatively use ramps, or position the car over an inspection pit. Ensure that the handbrake is fully applied.
4   Working beneath the car, pull the clutch release lever gaiter out of its hole in the bell housing. While holding the clutch release lever, pull on the clutch cable and release the ball end of the clutch cable from the key hole aperture in the end of the release lever. Remove the rubber damper from the end of the clutch release lever.
5   Working inside the car, push the driver's seat back as far as possible to give adequate room to work, then unscrew and remove the dash lower trim panel.
6   Pull the clutch cable and detach it from the quadrant, then withdraw the clutch cable through the recess between the pedal and the adjusting mechanism (Fig. 13.17).
7   Withdraw the clutch cable assembly from the engine compartment.
8   Installation is the reverse of removal. Ensure that the cable is free from kinks and sharp bends, and that all components are installed properly. On completion check that the action of the clutch is satisfactory.

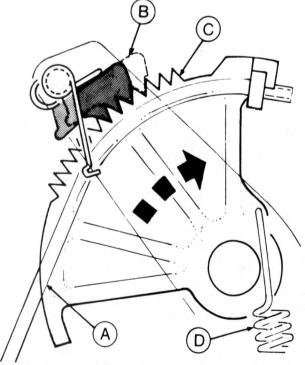

Fig. 13.16 Automatic clutch cable adjuster on Cortina 80 models (Sec 7)

A   Clutch cable   C   Quadrant
B   Pawl   D   Tension spring

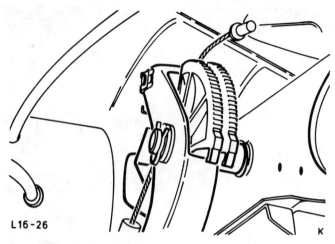

L16-26   K

Fig. 13.17 Detaching the clutch cable from the quadrant (Sec 7)

Clutch pedal/automatic adjustment mechanism – removal and installation

9   Referring to the preceding sub-section, disconnect the clutch cable from the clutch operating lever and from the clutch pedal lever quadrant, but do not remove the clutch cable assembly from the car.
10   Prise off the locking clip and remove the washer from the pedal pivot, then remove the clutch pedal and automatic adjuster mechanism sideways off the pedal pivot.
11   To dismantle the pedal assembly (Fig. 13.18), extract the pivot pin bushes and lift out the quadrant and tension spring, then remove the pawl pivot clip to allow the pivot, pawl and spring to be removed.
12   Renew any parts which show significant wear, paying particular attention to the tension and pawl springs, and the pedal pivot bushes.
13   Before assembling, lubricate the pedal pivot and bushes with graphite grease. Insert the pawl and spring into the pedal and secure the pawl pivot with its clip. Attach the tension spring to the quadrant and the pedal, insert the quadrant into the pedal and secure it in place by inserting the pivot bushes.
14   Lift the pawl and turn the quadrant so that the pawl teeth rest on the quadrant face (Fig. 13.19). Slide the pedal and quadrant assembly onto the pedal pivot and install the washer and spring clip to secure it.
15   Hook the clutch cable into the quadrant and then, from beneath the car, connect the cable to the clutch operating lever. Finally, install the rubber damper on the clutch operating lever and the rubber gaiter into the clutch housing.

Clutch squeal

16   To overcome the squeal which some vehicles produced when the clutch engaged on starting from rest, engines from October 1980 have a clutch pilot bearing in the end of the crankshaft which gives an increased clearance between the gearbox input shaft and the needle rollers of the bearing.
17   If clutch squeal is a problem on earlier vehicles, the new bearing (Part No 79ET-7120-AA) can be installed.

8   Manual gearbox and automatic transmission

Gear lever rattles

1   In unfavourable conditions, vibrations from the engine, clutch and driveshafts can combine to produce a rattling noise from the gear lever.
2   From August 1980 an improved gear lever assembly was installed. This can be identified by it not having any staking tabs on the inside of the metal cup (item D in Fig. 13.20).
3   On vehicles which do not have the improved gear lever assembly, the following steps should be taken to eliminate gear lever rattle.
4   Remove the gear lever (see Chapter 6, Section 2) and fit a new damping bush in place of the existing bush.
5   Coat the gear lever fork with grease, engage 3rd gear, and insert the gear lever and damping bush back into the transmission.

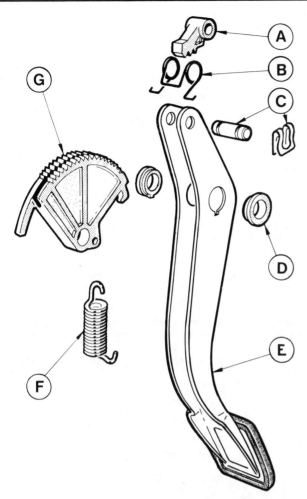

Fig. 13.18 Clutch pedal and automatic cable adjuster (Sec 7)

A Pawl
B Pawl spring
C Pawl pivot and clip
D Pedal pivot bushes
E Pedal
F Quadrant tension spring
G Quadrant

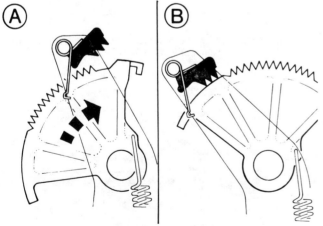

Fig. 13.19 Pawl and quadrant installation (Sec 7)

A Lift pawl and turn quadrant
B Rest pawl on smooth face of quadrant

6   If not already fitted, press a rubber strap (item A in Fig. 13.20) over the gear lever and secure it to the reversing light switch.
7   A double gaiter for fitting to the transmission tunnel is available if further damping is required and, if the problem still remains intractable, a new gear lever assembly may be installed.

Automatic transmission fluid

8   A new type of automatic transmission fluid has been introduced and is known as CJ fluid. This new fluid must never be mixed with the old type of fluid because it may result in the transmission assembly being damaged.
9   When topping up an automatic transmission ensure that only the new fluid (SQM-2C 9010-A) is used if the vehicle has a red dipstick/filler tube.
10 If the vehicle has a black (or bright finish) tube and a black dipstick, use only the old fluid (SQM-2C 9007-AA).

Revised fluid level and new dipstick

11 From May 1979, the fluid level in C3 automatic transmissions has been raised and a new dipstick has been introduced.
12 The new dipstick has a recess (Fig. 13.21) and the fluid level must lie between the recesses in the dipstick. The hole in the bottom of the dipstick is of no significance.
13 Check the fluid level when the vehicle is standing on level ground. With the engine idling, apply the handbrake and footbrake, move the selector lever three times through all positions, then select the P position and wait one to two minutes.
14 With the engine idling, raise the bonnet and extract the ATF dipstick. Take care to keep well clear of moving parts and avoid the risk of any items of loose clothing becoming trapped.
15 Wipe the dipstick with a clean, lint-free cloth, insert the dipstick fully and withdraw it again to check the fluid level, which should be between the recesses of the dipstick.
16 If the level is too low, stop the engine and add fluid SQM-2C 9007 AA through the filler tube until it reaches the upper limit of the recess in the dipstick.
17 If the fluid level is too high, fluid must be drained from the transmission to correct the level.
18 If the transmission fluid is dark brown in colour, it indicates that one of the clutches or brake bands inside the transmission is worn or slipping, and advice should be sought from a Ford agent.

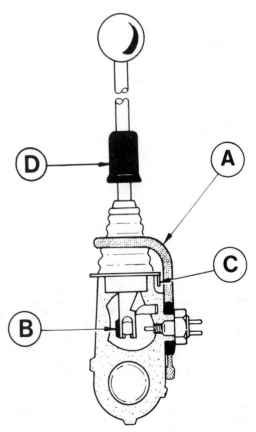

Fig. 13.20 Gear lever modification (Sec 8)

A Rubber strap
B Damping bush
C Lock plate
D Metal cup

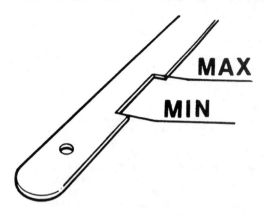

Fig. 13.21 New ATF dipstick (Sec 8)

9   Braking system

Brake fluid

1   The fluid used in the hydraulic braking system should be one of the two given in the Specifications. Although of different colours, the two fluids are fully miscible and either fluid may be used, even in a system containing the other.

2   A fluid which does not comply with the specification fully, may cause deterioration of the rubber, metal or synthetic components of the braking system and might result in unjustifiable risk.

Brake pad/shoe materials

3   Due to the different performance and braking characteristics of different types of vehicle, a friction material suitable for one vehicle may not be suitable for another vehicle of higher performance.

4   To ensure that only pads and shoes of the correct friction material are fitted, it is essential that only genuine Ford parts are used.

5   To ensure quieter operation of the front disc brakes, later models have a PVC coating applied either to the outer face of the brake pad backplate, or to the brake pad shims. When renewing pads it is important that PVC coated pads are not fitted to vehicles having PVC cooled shims. *Under no circumstances is it permissible to have a PVC coating on both the pad and the shim.*

Renewal of brake discs

6   It is essential that brake discs are matched pairs and, if only one disc is renewed, the replacement must be of the same Part Number as the remaining disc. This ensures that both discs are from the same casting source and that a disc with a fine-turned finish and a disc with a ground finish are not installed on the same vehicle.

7   The only exception to the above is that it is permissible to fit one each of brake discs Part Nos 71 BB-1125-BA and 71 BB-1125-CA because both come from the same casting source and both have a ground finish.

Brake master cylinder modifications

8   On master cylinders having three ports (Fig. 13.22) it is important that the brake pipes are connected to the correct ports as shown.

9   Later models have a brake fluid warning indicator incorporated in the master cylinder reservoir cap (Fig. 13.23); this is a float and switch assembly connected to a warning light on the facia.

10 The float is set to operate the switch and illuminate the lamp when the fluid is below a pre-set level, but is marginally above the minimum level.

11 If the light is illuminated, it indicates either that the brake pads/linings have worn sufficiently to allow the fluid to drop to compensate for the wear, or that there is a fluid leak in the braking system. Do not delay investigating and rectifying the reason for the warning light being illuminated.

Brake pressure control valve

12 When fitted, the brake pressure control valve (photo) is in the brake circuit between the master cylinder and the rear brakes. It has

the effect of allowing the line pressure to the rear brakes to rise at a lower rate than the line pressure to the front brakes once a deceleration cut-in point has been reached.

13 This reduces the possibility of the rear wheels locking and increases stability by reducing the tendency to skid.

14 The unit cannot be repaired and must not be dismantled.

Brake fluid replacement

Note: *A piston retracting tool will be required for this operation*

15 At the mileage or time interval specified in Routine Maintenance at the beginning of the manual the brake fluid should be completely changed to maintain maximum efficiency of the system.

16 Raise both the front and rear of the vehicle and support it securely on axle stands. The vehicle should be reasonably level when raised.

17 Disconnect the battery. Remove the front wheels.

18 Remove the cap from the master cylinder reservoir.

Note: *Any brake fluid spilt on the paintwork must be washed off the paintwork immediately using cold water.*

19 Fit a bleed tube to each front caliper bleed screw in order to simultaneously bleed both caliper units of old fluid.

20 Place the free end of each bleed tube in a clean transparent container.

21 Unscrew both bleed screws half a turn. Depress the brake pedal fully, then allow the brake pedal to return to its 'rest' position quickly. This will have expelled some fluid.

22 Allow three seconds pause for the master cylinder to recuperate.

23 Repeat depressing the brake pedal, pausing after each stroke, until all the fluid is expelled and only air is being pumped from each front circuit.

24 Remove the brake pads from one caliper (see Chapter 9, Section 4).

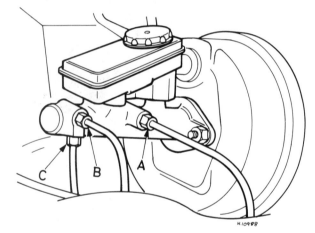

Fig. 13.22 Brake pipe connections to master cylinder with three ports (Sec 9)

A   To rear brake circuit   C   To LH front brake
B   To RH front brake

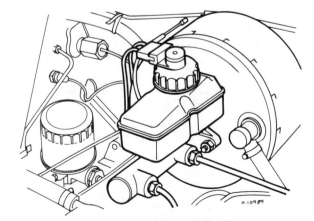

Fig. 13.23 Brake master cylinder with fluid level warning indicator (Sec 9)

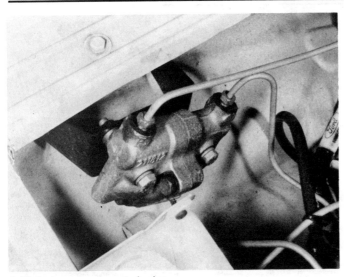

9.12 Brake pressure control valve

29 Unscrew the bleed screw of this second caliper.
30 Fill the fluid reservoir with brake fluid of the correct specification. Begin depressing the brake pedal, pausing between strokes as before, until fresh, air-free fluid can be seen coming through the bleed tube.
31 With the pedal held fully depressed, tighten the bleed screw. Top up the fluid reservoir with fresh fluid. On no account use old fluid for topping-up purposes.
32 Unscrew the piston retractor, but leave it installed in the caliper.
33 Depress the brake pedal slowly to move the pistons to their fully extended position. Hold the pedal down and unscrew the bleed screw. Now, using the piston retractor, drive the pistons into their housings and tighten the bleed screw.
34 Remove the piston retractor and refit the brake pads to this caliper.
35 Now, turning to the first caliper, install the piston retractor and move the pistons to their retracted position.
36 Repeat the operations described in paragraphs 28 to 34 for this caliper.
37 Bleed the rear brakes, as described in Chapter 9, Section 2.
38 Maintain the fluid level in the reservoir, topping-up as required. Check that the cap vent is clean and unblocked.
39 Refit the front wheels and lower the vehicle to the ground.
40 Reconnect the battery.

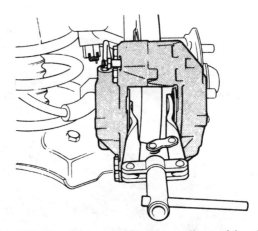

Fig. 13.25 Piston expander fitted to caliper with caliper pistons fully retracted (Sec 9)

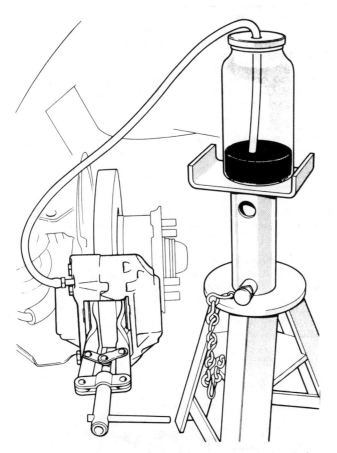

Fig. 13.24 Bleed jar positioned 300 mm (12 in) above the caliper bleed screw (Sec 9)

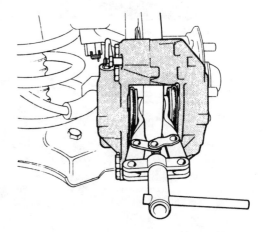

Fig. 13.26 Piston expander fitted to caliper with caliper pistons fully extended (Sec 9)

25 Using either a proprietary or substitute piston retracting tool, completely retract the caliper pistons.
26 Depress the brake pedal again until only air is being pumped into the jar. Tighten the bleed screw and refit the brake pads.
27 Repeat paragraphs 24, 25 and 26 for the second brake caliper, but leave the piston retractor in the caliper.
28 Reposition the container of old fluid at least 12 in (300 mm) above the caliper bleed screw. This will prevent air leaking past the bleed screw during subsequent operations. Ensure that the end of the bleed tube remains immersed in the fluid.

Handbrake cable – adjustment
41 During 1982, a new type of handbrake cable adjuster was fitted.
42 The knurled locknut is released simply by unscrewing it with the fingers. Adjustment is carried out by turning the adjuster sleeve.
43 After adjustment is achieved hold the sleeve and tighten the locknut onto it until two clicks are heard. This indicates that the locking rings have engaged. Over tightening may distort the cable.

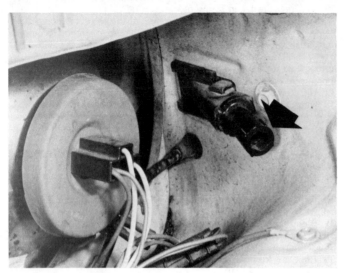

10.3 Indicator securing nut (arrowed)

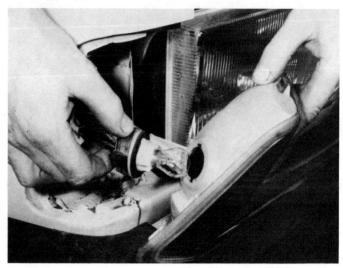

10.4 Removing the bulbholder of the front direction indicator

10.6 1980 style combination rear light

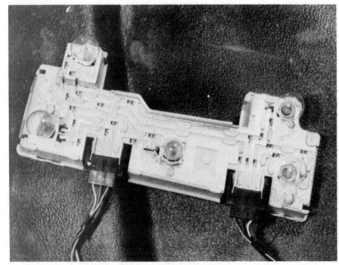

10.7 Bulb holder assembly of combination rear light

10 Electrical system

Front direction indicator lights – bulb renewal

1   On 1980 models the front indicator lights were changed and are now individual units separate from the headlights. They are immediately recognizable, being larger than the older type and being of wrap-round design so that they are visible from the side as well as the front. To renew a bulb, proceed as follows.

2   Raise and support the bonnet.

3   The light unit nut is accessible from inside the engine compartment, and is outboard of the rear of the headlamp. While supporting the front of the light unit, unscrew and remove the securing nut (photo).

4   Remove the light unit from the front of the vehicle and extract the bulb holder (photo), then remove the bulb from its bayonet fitting holder.

5   Refitting is the reverse of removal. Check that the rubber cover is fully fitted over the bulb holder. On completion, check that the indicator works satisfactorily.

Rear combination lights – bulb renewal

6   The 1980 Saloon models have a redesigned tail light unit on each side (photo), and each unit now incorporates a high intensity rear light for use in fog. Estate models retain the original type of rear light unit and have a high intensity rear light mounted separately. To remove a light unit and renew a bulb, proceed as follows.

7   Open the boot lid and remove the complete bulb holder unit by gripping it and pushing it sideways as shown in Fig. 13.27. When it is clear of the lamp body clips, remove it (photo).

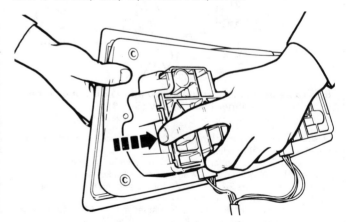

Fig. 13.27 Rear combination light bulb holder removal (Sec 10)

Press at point arrowed

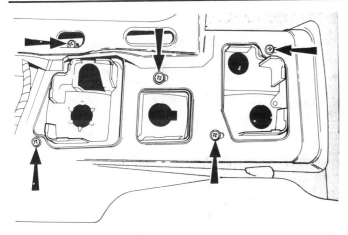

Fig. 13.28 Rear light assembly retaining screws (Sec 10)

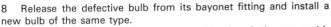

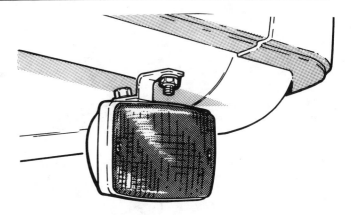

Fig. 13.29 Fog rear light (Estate models) (Sec 10)

8   Release the defective bulb from its bayonet fitting and install a new bulb of the same type.

9   To remove the lamp unit as an assembly, detach the two multi-plugs; then unscrew the five retaining screws (Fig. 13.28) and remove them with their washers, while holding the unit to prevent it from falling out. Remove the unit from outside the vehicle.

10 Refitting is the reverse of removal. Check that the multi-plugs are installed securely, and on completion check that all the lights in the unit operate satisfactorily.

Rear fog light (Estate models) – removal and installation

11 On 1980 models a fog light is installed under the rear bumper (Fig. 13.29).

12 To renew the bulb, remove the two screws securing the lens and remove the lens for access to the bayonet type bulb.

13 To remove the complete unit, disconnect the wiring to the light unit, unscrew the retaining nut (removing both the nut and the serrated washer) then detach the lamp unit.

14 Installation is the reverse of removal. On completion, check that the light is properly aligned and that it functions correctly.

Reversing light switch

15 The reversing light switch is located in the gear selector extension housing, in line with the gear lever (Fig. 13.20).

16 If renewal is necessary, engage neutral, disconnect the cables from the switch then unscrew the switch from the housing. Refitting is the reverse of removal; on completion check that reverse gear can be engaged properly and that the reversing lights function correctly.

Rear windscreen washer hoses (Estate models) – renewal

17 Open the tailgate and carefully prise free the trim panel which is attached to the tailgate by snap clips.

18 Similarly remove the trim panel from the rear load space, then disconnect the hose from the nozzle and attach a length of cord to it. Release the hose from the retaining clips in the tailgate and carefully pull it out, leaving the cord threaded in its place.

19 Remove the side panel access cover to the reservoir, detach the reservoir retaining strap and lift it clear.

20 Detach the hose from the washer unit pump and tie some cord to the end of the hose. Pull the hose out leaving the cord threaded through the body channel.

21 Use the cords to pull in the new hoses. Fit the hose ends securely to the nozzle and the pump, and top up the reservoir. Check the operation of the washer and wiper before refitting the trim panels.

Ignition switch lock barrel – removal and installation

22 Disconnect the battery leads.

23 Unscrew and unclip the upper and lower parts of the steering column shroud.

24 Turn the ignition key to position 1 (accessories) to align the key barrel retaining circlip with the keyway register in the housing. Use a scriber or fine punch, and depress the leaf spring through the hole (Fig. 13.28) while simultaneously pulling on the key to withdraw the

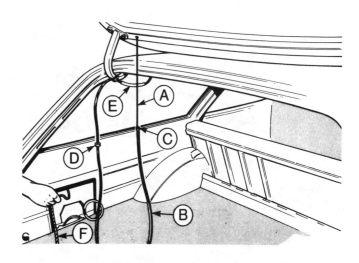

Fig. 13.30 Renewing the rear window washer hoses (Estate models) (Sec 10)

A Cord
B Hose
C Cord-to-hose joint
D Grommet
E Protective sleeve
F Cord

cylinder and lock barrel. Oscillate the key sideways slightly to ease removal.

25 With the key inserted fully into the barrel, remove the circlip and check that the circlip groove in the barrel is in good condition.

26 Withdraw the key about 0.2 in (5 mm), but no more than this. This will allow an additional ward to be flush with the barrel and the barrel can then be withdrawn from the cylinder. **CAUTION:** *Do not withdraw the key from the barrel while the barrel is out of the cylinder because this will allow the springs and wards to be detached from the barrel.*

27 When installing, withdraw the key by approximately 0.2 in (5 mm), so that all the wards are flush with the barrel, and insert the barrel into the cylinder. The barrel will only fit the cylinder in one position. With the barrel inserted, push the key in fully and check that it can be turned from position O to position III without difficulty. If undue force is necessary to turn the key, it is probable that the lock barrel components are not assembled correctly.

28 Turn the key to position I (accessory) and install the retaining circlip. The open jaws of the circlip must align with the keyway register on the cylinder (Fig. 13.33).

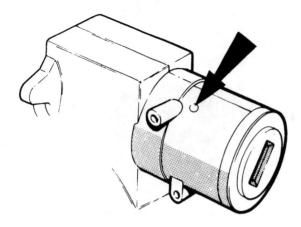

Fig. 13.31 Depress spring in cylinder through hole arrowed
(Sec 10)

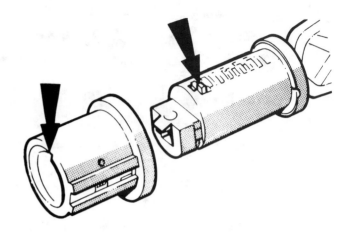

Fig. 13.32 Barrel and key cylinder. Align ward with slot (arrowed)
when assembling (Sec 10)

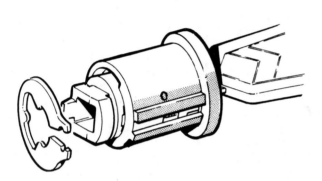

Fig. 13.33 Locate the retaining clip (Sec 10)

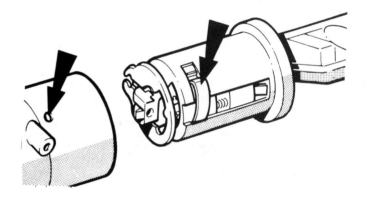

Fig. 13.34 Leaf spring must align with hole (arrows) on
reassembly (Sec 10)

29 Insert the cylinder assembly into the housing, ensuring that it is pushed fully in, and that the leaf spring locates in the undercut slot in the housing (Fig. 13.34). As in the removal operation, it may be necessary to rock the cylinder slightly to align it with the lock housing.
30 Before installing the steering column shroud and reconnecting the battery leads, check that the switch operates in all positions and that the key can be removed.

Windscreen wipers
31 From 1980 some models are fitted with either intermittent wipe action, or flick wipe action windscreen wipers.
32 The intermittent wipe action operates via a relay unit which is located on the underside of the instrument panel and gives to the wipers a single sweep about every five seconds.
33 Flick action is produced by the wiper switch arm which, when pressed against the action of a spring, will operate the wipers until the pressure on the switch is released. If the switch is released when the blades are not in their parked position, the full sweep cycle will be completed and the blades will stop in the parked position.
34 Removal and refitting procedures are identical with those of earlier types described in Chapter 10, but when ordering spares it is important to quote the vehicle model and year, to ensure that replacement parts are of the correct type.

Heated seats
35 On some models, heated front seats are available as an optional

extra. The seats are essentially the same, but a heater pad is inserted under the covering of both the seat and the backrest. Both pads are secured to the tie-rods of the seat padding by three hub rings at one end and by tapes at the other.
36 Power is supplied to each pad by a relay which is positioned near and controlled by a switch on the upper console.
37 The pads require no maintenance and are unaffected if the seats become wet.
38 Removal and installation of the pads is best left to a Ford dealer, or a car upholsterer because it requires the removal of the seat trim and the pads need to be tensioned correctly. Allowance must be made for seat stretch without straining the pads, but sagging must also be avoided because pads which are too loose may wrinkle and cause damage to the heater elements.

Revised temperature sender
39 On some engines the temperature indication on the gauge is rather low, even though the engine is at normal temperature and thermostat calibration is correct. A revised temperature sender Part No C 5 EH-10884-B is available which will give a higher indication at normal running temperature with negligible effect on the readings at the upper and lower ends of the scale.

Wire codes

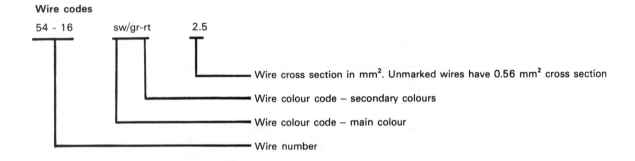

54 - 16   sw/gr-rt   2.5

Wire cross section in mm². Unmarked wires have 0.56 mm² cross section

Wire colour code – secondary colours

Wire colour code – main colour

Wire number

Wiring colour	Code	Wiring colour	Code
Blue	bl	Pink	rs
Brown	br	Red	rt
Yellow	ge	Black	sw
Grey	gr	Violet	vi
Green	gn	White	ws

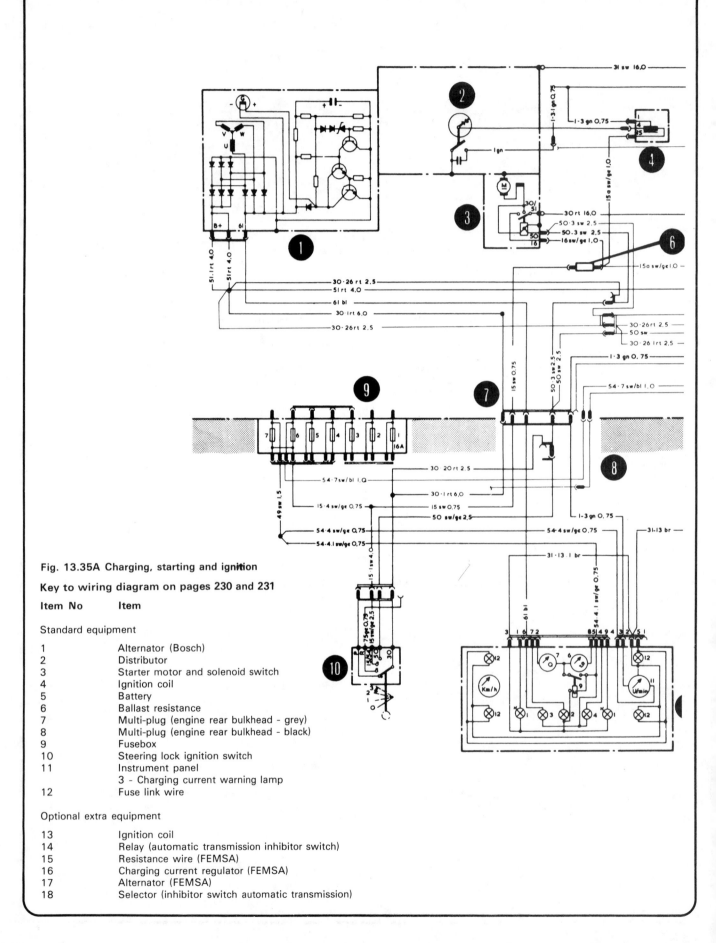

Fig. 13.35A Charging, starting and ignition

Key to wiring diagram on pages 230 and 231

Item No	Item
	Standard equipment
1	Alternator (Bosch)
2	Distributor
3	Starter motor and solenoid switch
4	Ignition coil
5	Battery
6	Ballast resistance
7	Multi-plug (engine rear bulkhead - grey)
8	Multi-plug (engine rear bulkhead - black)
9	Fusebox
10	Steering lock ignition switch
11	Instrument panel
	3 - Charging current warning lamp
12	Fuse link wire

Optional extra equipment

13	Ignition coil
14	Relay (automatic transmission inhibitor switch)
15	Resistance wire (FEMSA)
16	Charging current regulator (FEMSA)
17	Alternator (FEMSA)
18	Selector (inhibitor switch automatic transmission)

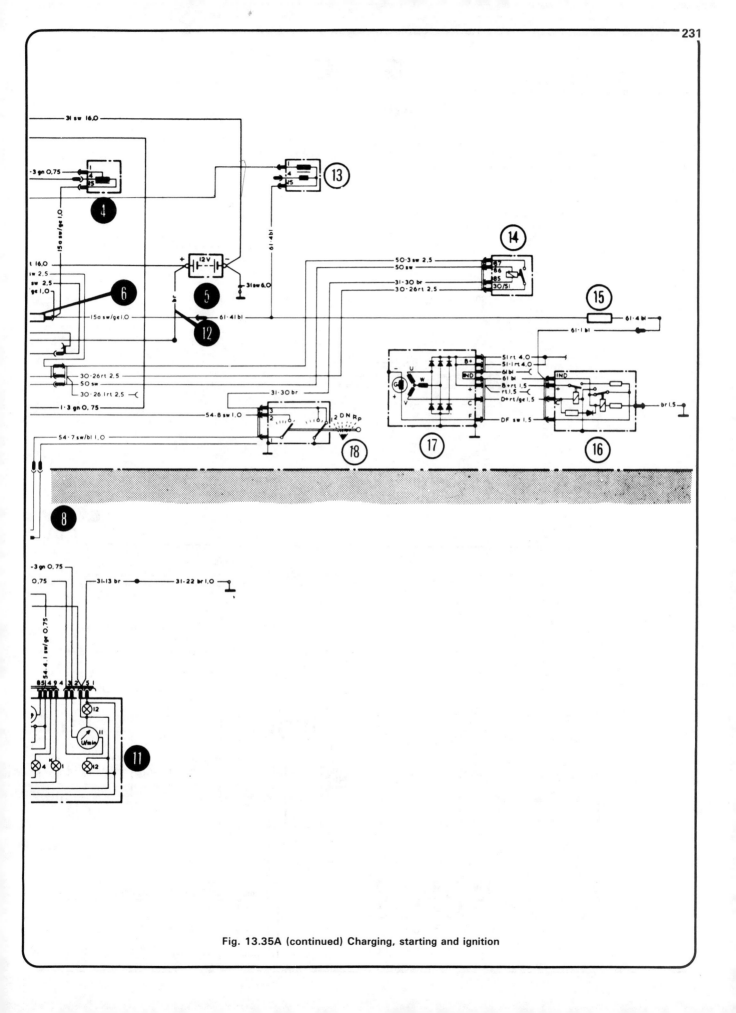

Fig. 13.35A (continued) Charging, starting and ignition

Fig. 13.35B Exterior lights
Key to wiring diagram on pages 232 and 233

Item No	Item

Standard equipment

25	Auxiliary dimmer lamp relay
26	Headlamp side lamp assembly
27	Auxiliary driving lamp
28	Battery
29	Fusebox
30	Multi-plug (engine rear bulkhead - black)
31	Combined tail lamp assembly
	B - Tail stop lamp
	C - Tail lamp
32	Light switch
33	Multi-function switch
34	Number plate lamp
35	Steering lock ignition switch
36	Instrument cluster
	2 - Main beam warning lamp

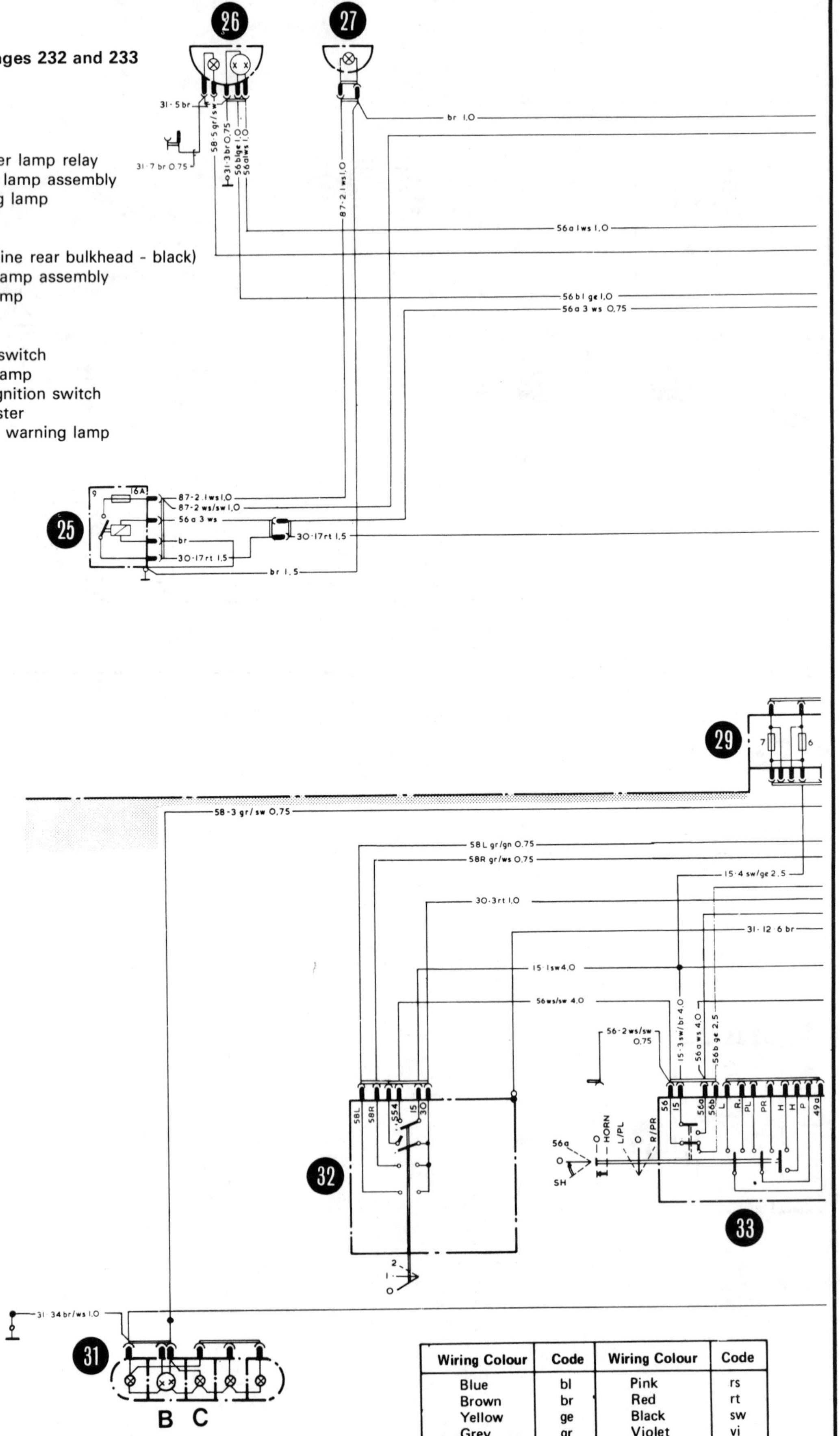

Wiring Colour	Code	Wiring Colour	Code
Blue	bl	Pink	rs
Brown	br	Red	rt
Yellow	ge	Black	sw
Grey	gr	Violet	vi
Green	gn	White	ws

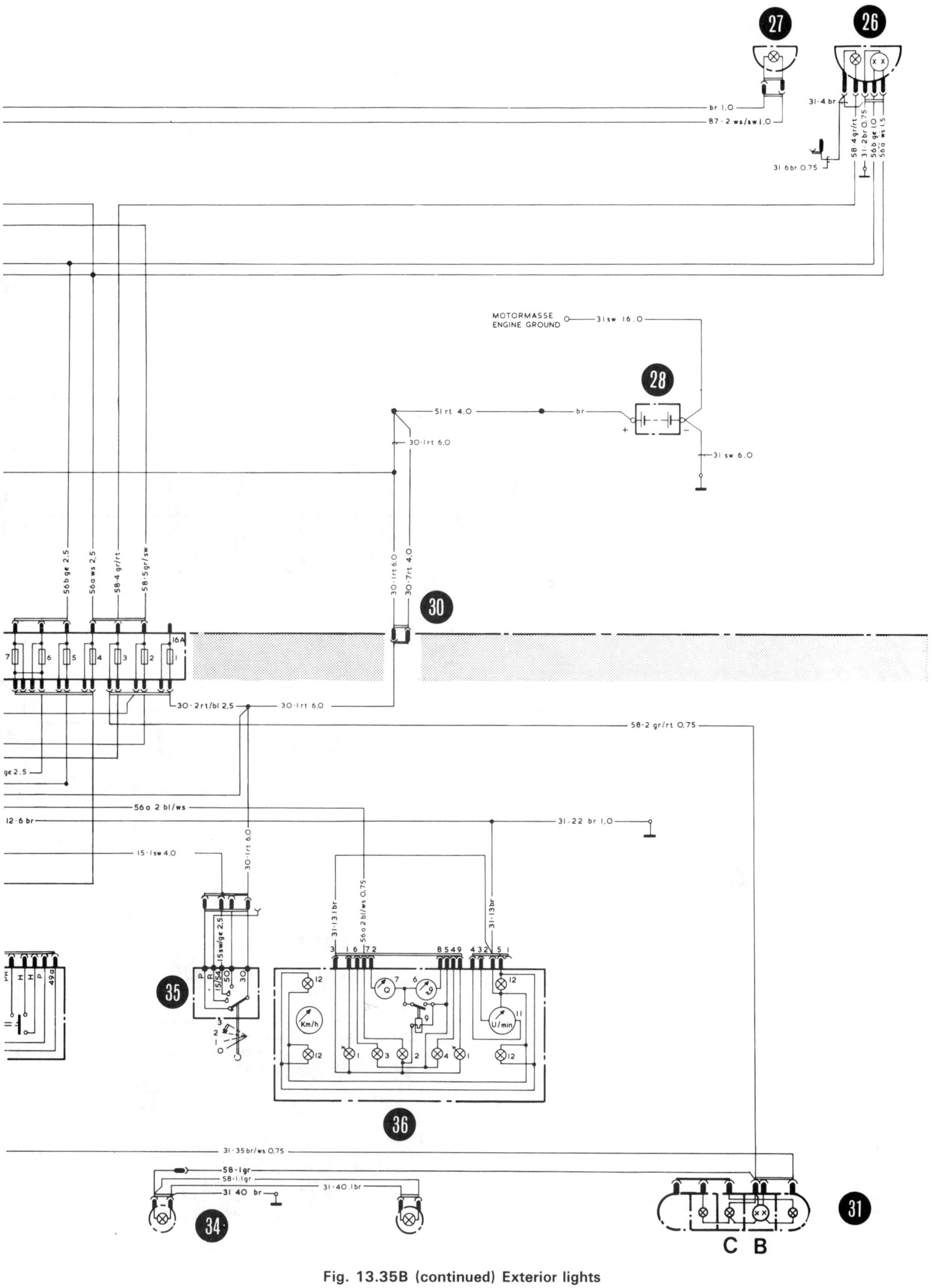

Fig. 13.35B (continued) Exterior lights

Fig. 13.35C Interior lights

Key to wiring diagram on pages 234 and 235

Item No	Item

Standard equipment

44	Battery
45	Fusebox
46	Multi-plug (engine rear bulkhead - grey)
47	Interior lamp
48	Courtesy lamp switches
49	Lamp (heater control illumination)
50	Light switch
51	Panel dimmer switch
52	Luggage compartment lamp
53	Interior lamp
54	Lamp (cigar lighter illumination)
55	Lamp (clock illumination)
56	Instrument cluster
	12 - Illumination
57	Glove box lamp
58	Glove box lamp switch

Optional extra equipment

59	Lamp (automatic transmission selector illumination)

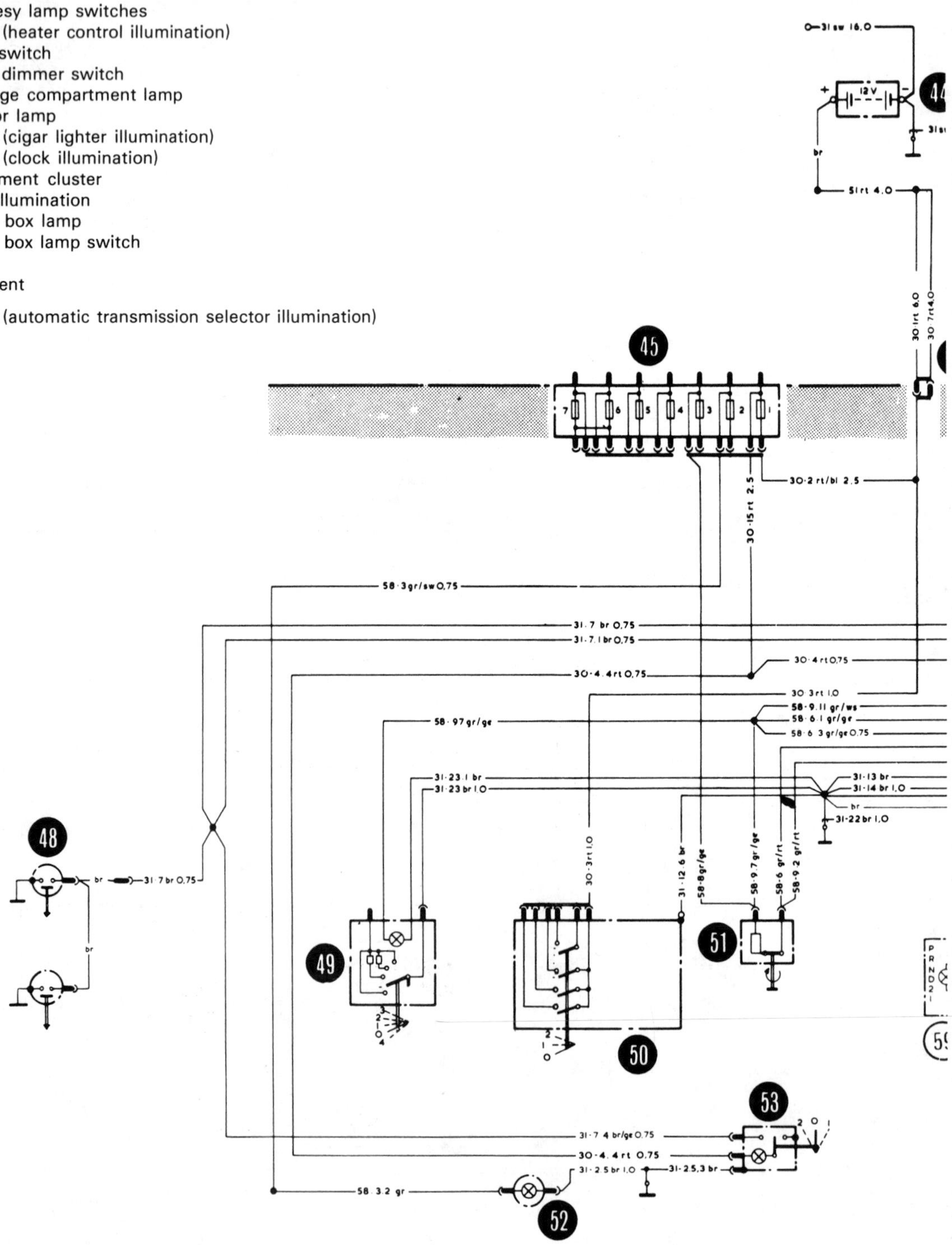

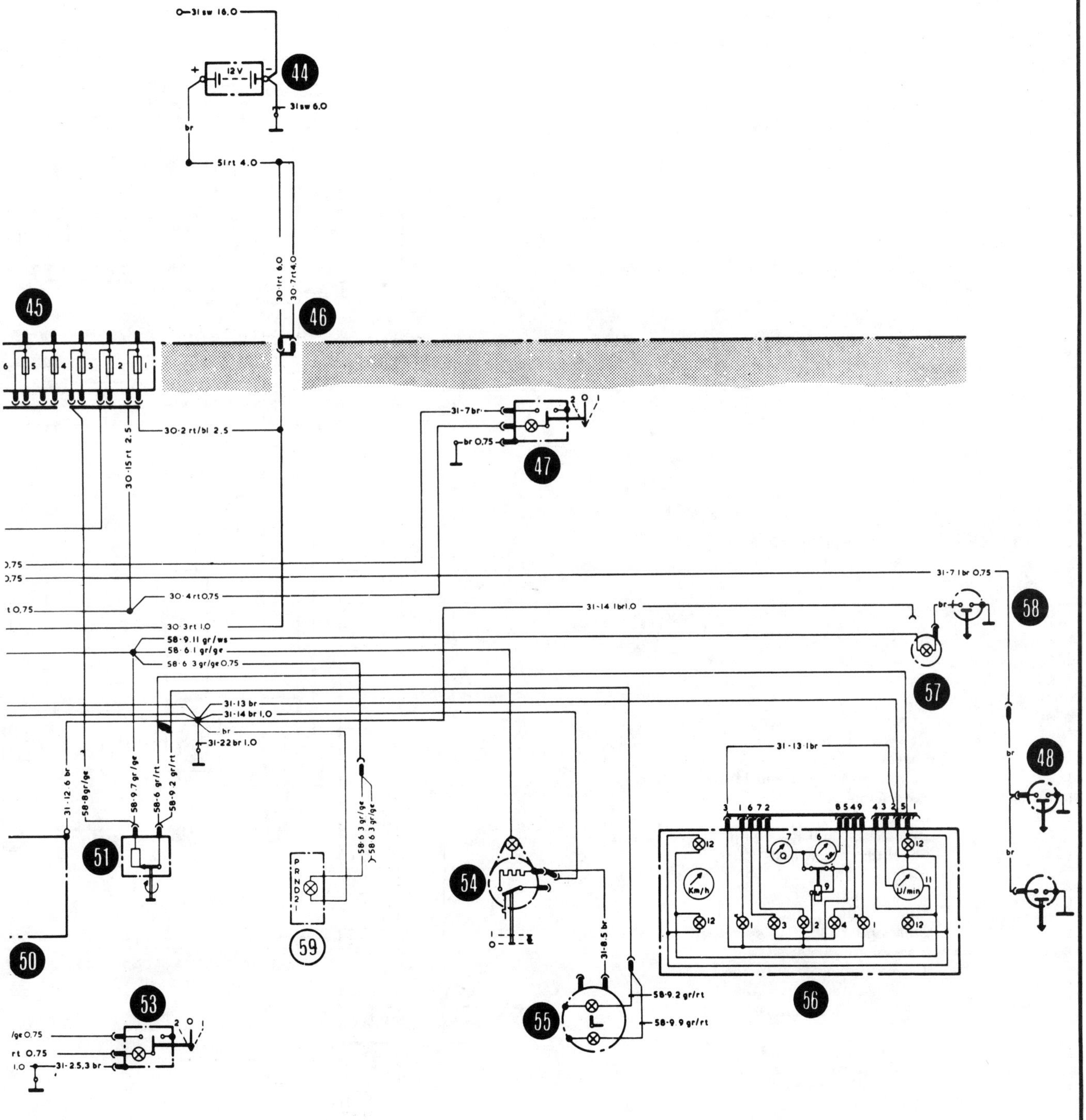

Fig. 13.35C (continued) Interior lights

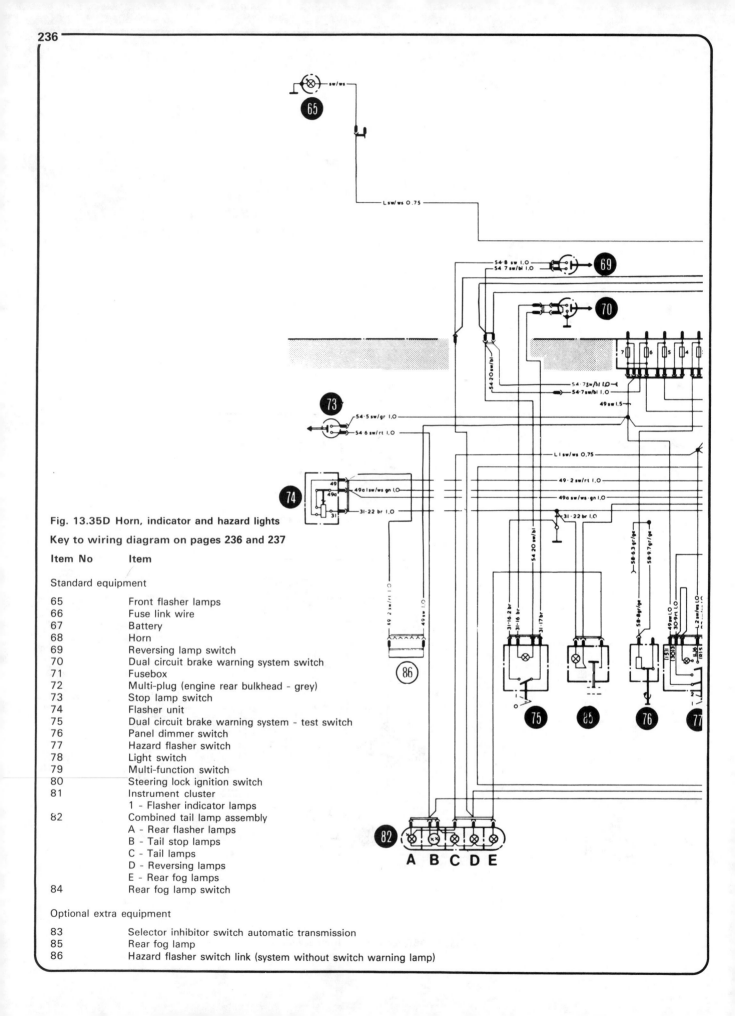

Fig. 13.35D Horn, indicator and hazard lights

Key to wiring diagram on pages 236 and 237

Item No	Item
	Standard equipment
65	Front flasher lamps
66	Fuse link wire
67	Battery
68	Horn
69	Reversing lamp switch
70	Dual circuit brake warning system switch
71	Fusebox
72	Multi-plug (engine rear bulkhead - grey)
73	Stop lamp switch
74	Flasher unit
75	Dual circuit brake warning system - test switch
76	Panel dimmer switch
77	Hazard flasher switch
78	Light switch
79	Multi-function switch
80	Steering lock ignition switch
81	Instrument cluster
	1 - Flasher indicator lamps
82	Combined tail lamp assembly
	A - Rear flasher lamps
	B - Tail stop lamps
	C - Tail lamps
	D - Reversing lamps
	E - Rear fog lamps
84	Rear fog lamp switch
	Optional extra equipment
83	Selector inhibitor switch automatic transmission
85	Rear fog lamp
86	Hazard flasher switch link (system without switch warning lamp)

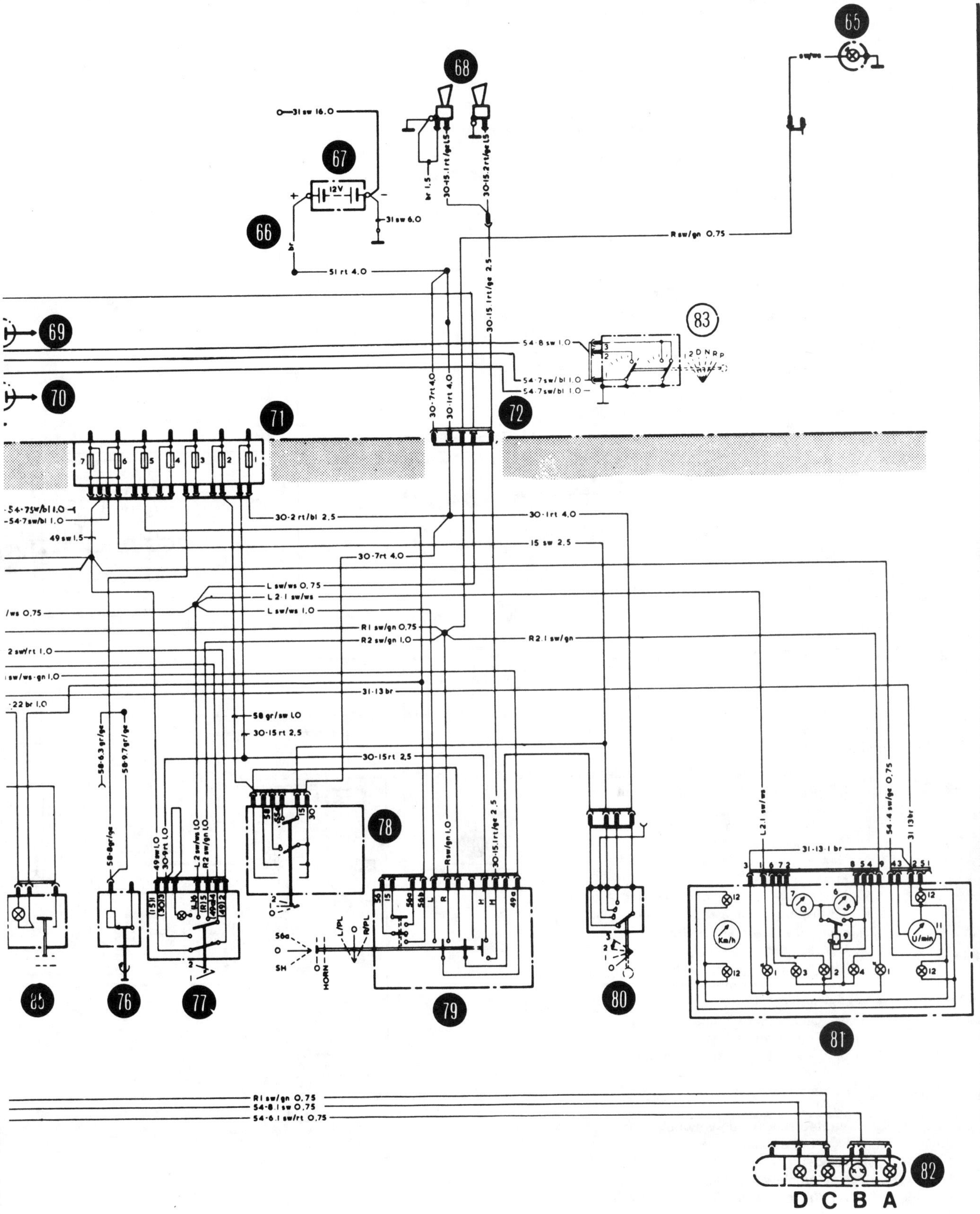

Fig. 13.35D (continued) Horn, indicator and hazard lights

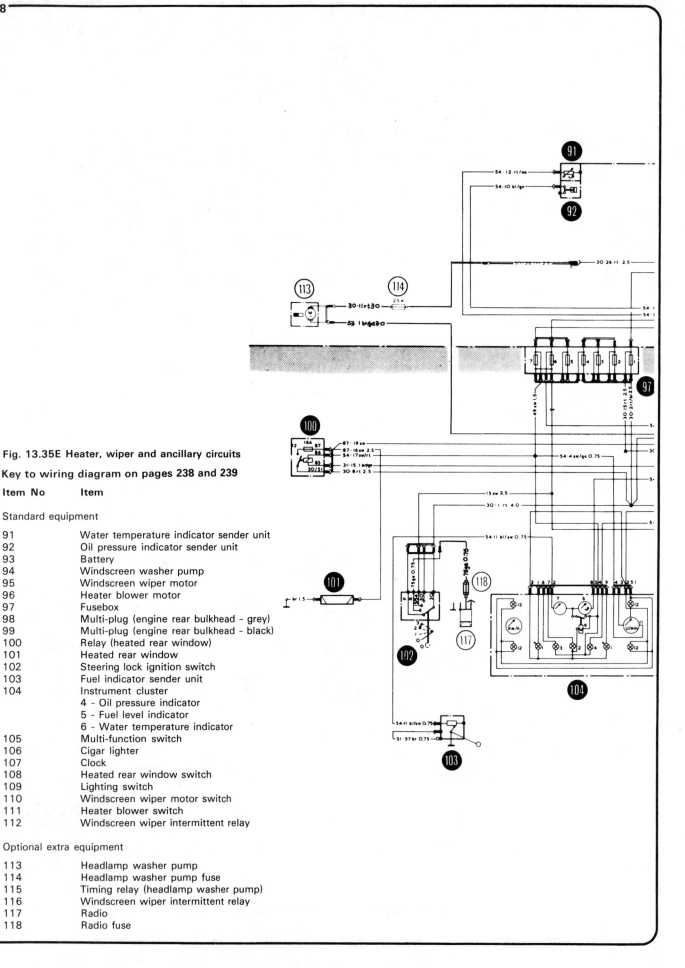

Fig. 13.35E Heater, wiper and ancillary circuits

Key to wiring diagram on pages 238 and 239

Item No	Item

Standard equipment

91	Water temperature indicator sender unit
92	Oil pressure indicator sender unit
93	Battery
94	Windscreen washer pump
95	Windscreen wiper motor
96	Heater blower motor
97	Fusebox
98	Multi-plug (engine rear bulkhead - grey)
99	Multi-plug (engine rear bulkhead - black)
100	Relay (heated rear window)
101	Heated rear window
102	Steering lock ignition switch
103	Fuel indicator sender unit
104	Instrument cluster
	4 - Oil pressure indicator
	5 - Fuel level indicator
	6 - Water temperature indicator
105	Multi-function switch
106	Cigar lighter
107	Clock
108	Heated rear window switch
109	Lighting switch
110	Windscreen wiper motor switch
111	Heater blower switch
112	Windscreen wiper intermittent relay

Optional extra equipment

113	Headlamp washer pump
114	Headlamp washer pump fuse
115	Timing relay (headlamp washer pump)
116	Windscreen wiper intermittent relay
117	Radio
118	Radio fuse

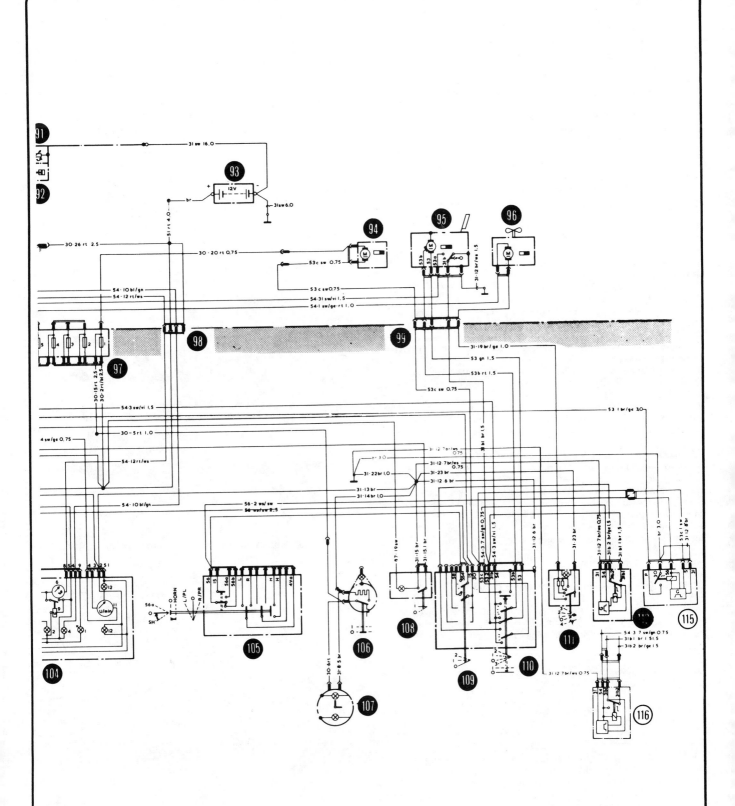

Fig. 13.35E (continued) Heater, wiper and ancillary circuits

11 Suspension and steering

General modifications to the 1980 models

1   A few minor modifications have been made to the suspension system of 1980 Cortinas. The front anti-roll bar is of larger diameter, the spring rates have been changed and the rear shock absorbers on S models are now gas-filled.

2   Vehicles fitted with the 'S-pack', or for Estate models the 'Business-pack', have uprated suspension components and tyres.

3   Removal and refitting of the suspension components are described in Chapter 11. Uprated components are removed and refitted in the same way as their earlier counterparts, but when ordering replacement parts it is important to specify whether the vehicle is fitted with 'S-pack', or 'Business-pack'. Not all the 1980 parts are interchangeable with earlier ones, so it is also necessary to quote the exact model and year.

Inspection and maintenance

4   The suspension and steering components must be checked at 6000 mile intervals for signs of damage and wear. Any item found to be defective must receive immediate attention.

5   Run the vehicle onto ramps, over an inspection pit, or jack it up and support it securely.

6   Check the front and rear suspensions at the points indicated by arrows in Figs. 13.36 and 13.37.

7   Check the front and rear suspension arm bushes for signs of wear and deterioration. Also check the shock absorber mounting bushes and renew as necessary.

8   Clean and inspect the balljoint covers and gaiters. Steering gaiters can be renewed, but if a balljoint cover is damaged, or the joint is worn, a new balljoint must be installed.

9   Check that the nuts and bolts securing the suspension are tightened to the torque settings specified in Chapter 11. Check that all castellated nuts are secured by split pins, and that the pins are in good condition and properly secured.

10 Check the action of the shock absorbers by pressing down each corner of the body in turn. On release the body should return to its normal height without rebounding more than about twice. Shock absorbers which are weak make use of the vehicle dangerous and they must be renewed. Leaking shock absorbers also require renewal; they cannot be repaired.

11 Every 36 000 miles, or 3 years, whichever comes first, the suspension balljoints must be lubricated as shown in Fig. 13.38 using a grease gun with a tapered nozzle. Clean the area around the greasing point, remove the plug and inject the grease. Wipe excess grease from around the joint and reinstall the plug securely.

12 If the tyres show signs of excessive or uneven wear, and no fault can be found in the suspension components, it is likely that the steering geometry is incorrect. The correct settings are given in the Specifications of Chapter 11, but it is recommended that checking is done by a workshop having the necessary special measuring equipment.

Upper and lower swivel balljoints – removal and renewal

Where a swivel balljoint has worn beyond a serviceable limit, a new proprietary brand replacement can be fitted to the stub axle. As replacement units are only supplied as a pair, it is advisable to renew the right- and left-hand upper and lower joints at the same time; if one side is severely worn, it is most probable that its opposite number is in a similar condition. Proceed as follows:

13 Raise the car at the front and support with chassis stands under the chassis frame. Remove the front roadwheels.

14 Disconnect and remove the steering tie-rod ends.

15 Remove the balljoint retaining nuts and, using a balljoint separator, release the tapers.

16 Refer to Section 8 in Chapter 11 and remove the stub axle unit, but have the flexible brake pipe attached to the caliper.

17 Unscrew the retaining bolts and disconnect the anti-roll bar.

18 To remove the swivel joint (upper or lower), centre punch the rivets and then drill them to a depth of $\frac{3}{16}$ in using a $\frac{1}{8}$ in drill. Ensure that this hole is drilled fairly accurately as it is a pilot hole.

19 Now drill out in progressive stages to a diameter of $\frac{3}{8}$ in. Do not drill into the stub axle pressing. Punch the rivets out and remove the old joint/s.

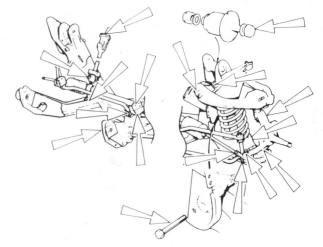

Fig. 13.36 Front suspension and steering check points arrowed (Sec 11)

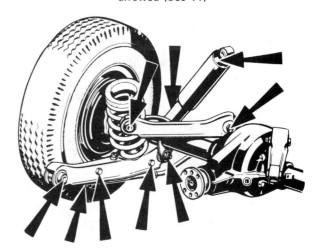

Fig. 13.37 Rear suspension check points (arrowed) (Sec 11)

Fig. 13.38 Suspension balljoint lubrication points (Sec 11)

20 The new joints can now be fitted into position, using the new bolts and self-locking nuts supplied with the replacement kit.

21 Reassemble the stub axle in the reverse order of removal and reconnect the anti-roll bar and tie-rod ends. On completion, refit the roadwheels and check that the steering track is as specified, referring to Chapter 11 for further information.

11.22 Power steering pump

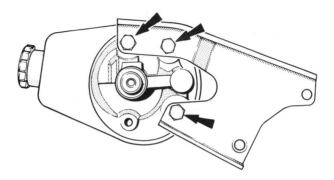
Fig. 13.39 Pump mounting bolts (arrowed) (Sec 11)

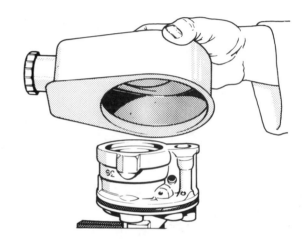
Fig. 13.40 Separating the reservoir from the housing (Sec 11)

11.24 Steering pump pipe connections

Power steering pump – removal and installation

22 A new design of pump is used on the power-assisted steering systems of 1980 models (photo).

23 To remove the pump, lift and prop open the bonnet, and disconnect the battery leads.

24 Remove the pump drivebelt (Chapter 11, Section 32).

25 Disconnect the fluid pipes from the pump (photo), and drain the fluid from the pump and pipes.

26 Remove the rear support bar from the engine and remove the pump with the bracket attached.

27 Installation is the reverse of removal. Top up the power steering reservoir and bleed the system on completion. Tension the belt so that the deflection with hand pressure at the mid-point of the longest span is 0.4 in (10 mm). Do not press on the belt with full body weight when checking belt tension, because this will result in the belt being tightened too much and the pump bearings will wear excessively.

Power steering pump – dismantling and reassembly

28 Remove the three pump mounting bolts (Fig. 13.39) and separate the pump from its bracket. Remove the bolts securing the pulley to the pump and withdraw the pulley.

29 Clean the exterior of the pump thoroughly, taking care to keep the inlet and outlet ports covered so that no dirt can enter.

30 Grip the body of the pump firmly but not tightly in a soft-jawed vice, the pump shaft being downwards, then remove the reservoir by

Fig. 13.41 Removing the endplate retaining ring (Sec 11)

rocking back and forth gently to unseat it from the O-ring on the housing (Fig. 13.40); remove the O-ring from the housing.

31 Insert a thin punch into the hole in the housing opposite the flow control valve. Compress the retaining ring with the punch and remove the ring with a screwdriver (Fig. 13.41). The end plate is spring-loaded and should be pushed out of the housing. If it sticks, remove the plate to release it and then remove the plate and spring (Fig. 13.42).

32 Remove the pump from the vice, invert it and remove the flow control valve and spring (Fig. 13.43).

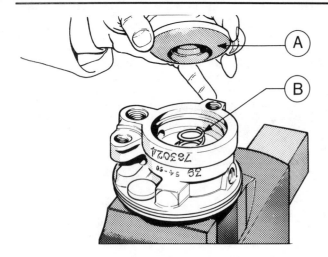

Fig. 13.42 Removing the pump endplate and spring (Sec 11)

A Endplate   B Spring

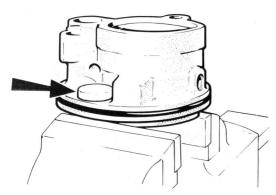

Fig. 13.44 Pump magnet (arrowed) (Sec 11)

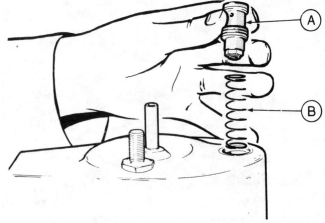

Fig. 13.43 Flow control valve and spring (Sec 11)

A Flow control valve   B Spring

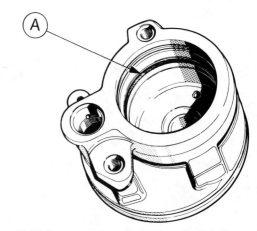

Fig. 13.45 Pressure plate O-ring installation (Sec 11)

A O-ring

33 Use a puller to remove the hub from the shaft and then, while supporting the bottom of the shaft, tap the top of the shaft gently to remove the shaft and pump components.

34 Remove the endplate O-ring from the periphery of the plate, and the pressure plate O-ring from its groove in the pump bore.

35 Dismantle the rotor assembly, pump ring and pressure plate.

36 Remove the shaft seal, taking care not to damage the bore of the housing. Remove and clean the magnet (Fig. 13.44).

37 Clean all metal parts in a non-toxic solvent and then start reassembly by fitting a new pump shaft seal, using a 1 in (25 mm) socket and a hammer, or a press.

38 Lubricate a new pressure plate O-ring with power steering fluid and install the seal in the third groove from the rear of the housing (Fig. 13.45).

39 Fit the thrust plate and rotor onto the shaft with the countersunk side of the rotor towards the thrust plate and then insert the shaft assembly into the housing, ensuring that the thrust plate slides onto the dowel pins (Fig. 13.46).

40 Install the pump ring onto the dowel pins. The arrow on the ring must be uppermost (Fig. 13.47). Install the ten vanes into the rotor slots, ensuring that the rounded end of each vane is outward and that the vanes slide freely.

41 Install the magnet on the housing. Lubricate the pressure plate with power steering fluid and install the plate on the dowel pins, ensuring that the side of the plate having the depression for the spring is uppermost. The plate must be pressed down about 0.06 in (1.6 mm) past the O-ring to seat it.

42 Lubricate a new endplate O-ring with power steering fluid and install it in the second groove from the rear of the housing.

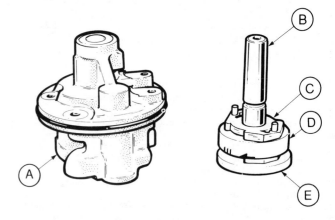

Fig. 13.46 Pump housing and shaft assembly (Sec 11)

A Housing   D Pump ring
B Shaft   E Pressure plate
C Thrust plate

43 Install the endplate spring in its recess in the pressure plate, then lubricate the endplate in power steering fluid; press the endplate just far enough into the housing to be able to install the retaining ring in its groove.

44 Install the endplate retaining ring, ensuring that the gap in the ring is away from the hole in the housing used for removing the ring (see Fig. 13.41).

Fig. 13.47 Installing the pump ring (Sec 11)

A Arrow

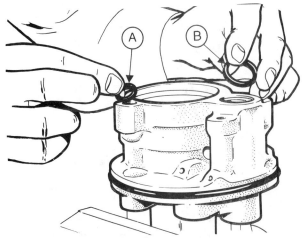

Fig. 13.48 Installing new seals (Sec 11)

A Stud seal   *B Union seal*

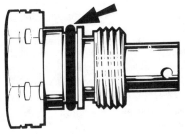

Fig. 13.49 Pump union with O-ring groove arrowed (Sec 11)

45 Insert the flow control valve spring into its hole and insert the valve with its screened end towards the spring.

46 Install a new stud seal and a new union seal into the counterbored holes in the housing (Fig. 13.48).

47 Lubricate the reservoir O-ring and also the inner edge of the reservoir with power steering fluid, and install the reservoir, ensuring that the holes are aligned.

48 Insert and tighten the mounting stud.

49 Fit a new O-ring into the groove next to the hexagon on the union (Fig. 13.49). Insert and tighten the union.

50 Press the hub onto the shaft, bolt on the pulley and the mounting bracket.

Gas-filled rear shock absorbers – removal and installation

51 When gas-filled shock absorbers are not fitted to the vehicle, their internal gas pressure will cause them to extend to their full length.

52 When gas-filled shock absorbers are removed, the car body should be raised relative to the axle until the shock absorber extends to its full length, but is not under tension. When it is in this position, undo the upper and then the lower mounting bolts, and remove the shock absorber.

53 Installation is the reverse of removal, but note that the mounting boss at the lower end of the shock absorber is offset and the boss should be positioned as shown in Fig. 13.50 with the end of the boss which is furthest from the shock absorber centre line being placed closest to the axle mounting point.

Front hub bearings – adjustment (1982 on)

54 Raise and support the front of the vehicle. Remove the wheel centre trim or the wheel itself, as appropriate.

55 Prise off the dust cap, remove the split pin and the adjusting nut retainer.

56 Tighten the adjusting nut to 15 lbf ft (2.1 kgf m) whilst spinning the wheel or hub anti-clockwise.

57 Slacken the nut by half a turn (180°), then retighten it finger tight.

58 Fit the nut retainer in the correct position to accept the split pin without disturbing the adjusting nut. Fit a new split pin and bend over the ends.

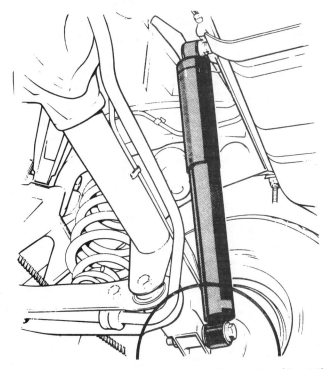

Fig. 13.50 Gas-filled rear shock absorber mounting (Sec 11)

59 Refit the dust cap and the wheel or wheel trim. Lower the car to the ground and (if necessary) tighten the wheel nuts.

12 Bodywork

Modifications to the 1980 range

1 The items listed below are changes which affect the 1980 range of Cortinas. In most instances these items are interchangeable with the corresponding parts of earlier models and it is therefore essential to quote the model and year of the vehicle when ordering replacement parts.

Windscreen and door glass

2 A laminated windscreen is now fitted as standard equipment. It should be noted that the windscreen and rear window weatherstrips on the 1980 models are fitted without using sealer. If leaks occur, first check that the weatherstrip is not distorted and has no foreign body obstructions. Having eliminated these possibilities, sealer can be used

between the weatherstrip and the body, and between the weatherstrip and the glass if the leak persists.

3   A revised design of weatherstrip was introduced on saloon variants in December 1980 (Fig. 13.51). The new design is wider than the old one, and the windscreen and rear windows are correspondingly

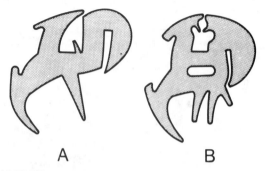

Fig. 13.51 Windscreen and rear window weatherstrip (Sec 12)

A *Section of old weatherstrip*   B *Section of new weatherstrip*

smaller; the new design weatherstrip can only be used with these smaller windscreens and rear windows.

4   The total glass area has been increased to improve forward and rearward vision. Side vision has also been improved by extending the door openings into the roof.

Cable-operated window regulators

5   Starting in October 1980, a cable-operated window regulator was introduced progressively on the front and rear doors of Cortina models (Fig. 13.52). The new type regulator minimises the operating force required to raise and lower the window, but because its installation requires changes to the door inner panel, it is not interchangeable with the previous design.

Cable-operated window regulator – installation

6   In the following installation sequence, the letters A, B, C and D refer to Fig. 13.53 for a front door, or Fig. 13.54 for a rear door.

7   Insert the mechanism into the door and secure it in the area of the handle pivot, using two screws (inset B).

8   Loosely fit the window glass bracket to the regulator mechanism using two screws (inset C).

9   On front doors only, wind the window upwards and, with the aid of a screwdriver, carefully preload slightly the area of the rear corner mitre (Fig. 13.55).

10 Tighten the glass bracket screws (inset C). When tightening the screws of the rear door, ensure that the window is wound up.

11 Wind the window down two turns of the regulator handle.

12 Install and tighten the upper fixing screw(s) (inset A). On the front doors only, push the upper regulator mechanism bracket towards the rear of the door before finally tightening the screw (Fig. 13.56).

13 Wind the window down fully, then insert and tighten the lower fixing screw(s) (inset D).

Sliding roof – adjustment

14 To adjust the sliding roof, first open it about half way, then detach the trim panel at the front of the sliding roof. The trim is secured by clips. When the trim is free, close the roof and slide the trim panel fully rearwards.

15 Keeping the roof closed, loosen the adjusting clamps at the front and rear (Fig. 13.57).

16 To adjust the height of the sliding panel, move the mountings forward, or rearward to achieve the required effect. The heights should be as follows:

Front: *Flush to 0.040 in (1 mm) below main roof front edge*
Rear: *Flush to 0.040 in (1 mm) above main roof rear edge*

17 To adjust the roof winder mechanism, the roof must be closed. Unscrew and remove the two spacer washers and the screw retaining the winder handle. Note the position of the handle and then remove it.

18 Unscrew and remove the winder gear unit (Fig. 13.58).

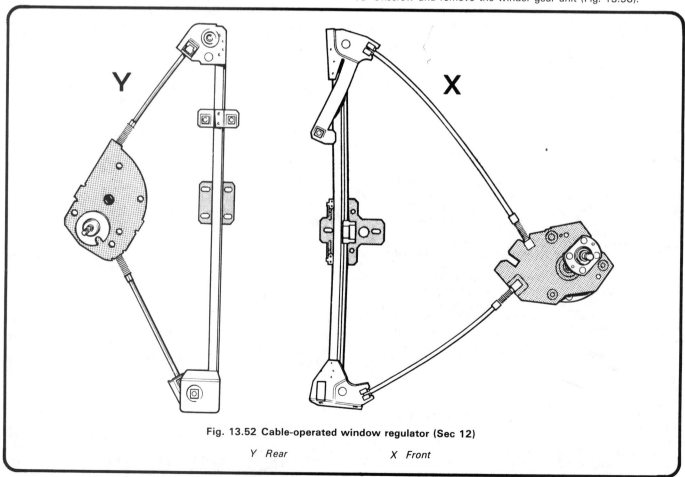

Fig. 13.52 Cable-operated window regulator (Sec 12)

Y Rear   X Front

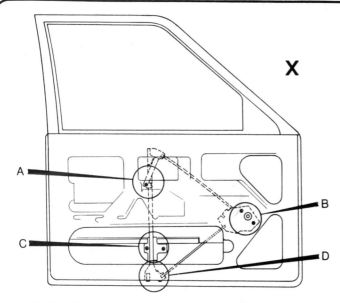

Fig. 13.53 Cable-operated window regulator installation (front door) (Sec 12)

A   Regulator upper fixing
B   Regulator handle fixing
C   Regulator-to-glass bracket fixing
D   Regulator lower fixing

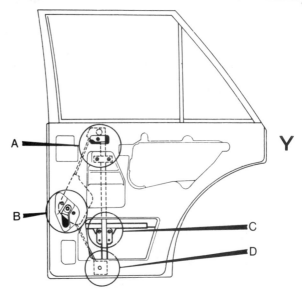

Fig. 13.54 Cable-operated window regulator installation (rear door) (Sec 12)

A   Regulator upper fixing
B   Regulator handle fixing
C   Regulator-to-glass bracket fixing
D   Regulator lower fixing

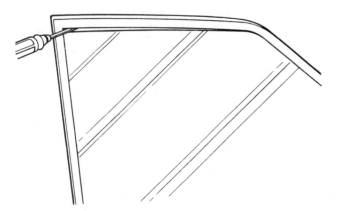

Fig. 13.55 Preloading a front door window (Sec 12)

Fig. 13.56 Pushing the front door regulator upper fixing bracket rearwards (Sec 12)

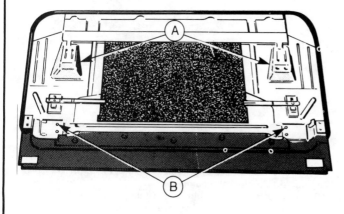

Fig. 13.57 The roof mounting slides (Sec 12)

A   Front   B   Rear

Fig. 13.58 Removing the roof winder mechanism (Sec 12)

19 Wind the gear unit clockwise to its full extent, then wind it back half a turn before installing it.

20 Install the winder handle in the same position as it was before removal, and secure it with its screw and washer. Check the operation of the sliding roof and, if satisfactory, refit the front trim panel. After installing the panel, make sure that it is secure and that no material protrudes onto the front guide rail.

Sliding roof – removal and installation

21 Open the roof panel. Unscrew and remove the four screws which secure the deflector plate to the cable covers. Remove the deflector. Unscrew and remove the front cable cover, noting that the central screws are of the normal metal thread type, while the others are of the self-tapping type.

22 Prise free the upper and lower cable locating clips as shown in Fig. 13.59.

23 Unscrew and remove the guide rail cover screws on each side, then carefully prise free the guide rail covers.

24 Remove the retaining screws of the front guide.

25 Carefully pull the roof along the rails until the roof is almost closed, then lift the guide rails and slide the roof and guide rails free. To avoid damaging the car roof, it is advisable to have an assistant when removing the roof.

26 If the cables and guides are to be removed, detach them from the roof panel. The cables should normally be renewed when the assembly is dismantled, especially if the roof mechanism is known to be faulty.

27 Installation is the reverse of removal, but note the following special points:

(a)   When the roof is back in position, ensure that the rear guide rail pegs engage in the holes in the rear body section

(b)   When installing the cables into the winder unit, make sure that the lower clips are between the guide and the cable. The top clips fit over the complete assembly

(c)   The front cable cover section must be secured loosely when first installed, and only be fully tightened after the roof has been adjusted as described above

Sliding roof weatherstrip – removal and renewal

28 Open the roof halfway, carefully unclip the trim panel at the front of the roof and slide the trim panel rearwards.

29 Remove the four clamp bolts and disconnect the two roof-to-guide rail mounting slides at the front (Fig. 13.60). Swing the two spring arms clear of the rear roof mounting brackets (Fig. 13.61). Unscrew the two rear mounting bracket-to-roof panel bolts and pull off the lockplates. With the help of an assistant, lift the sliding roof panel clear.

30 Unscrew and remove the seven self-tapping screws retaining the rear seal sponge mounting plate and remove the plate. Two of these screws are under the anti-rattle pads.

31 Prise free the two plastic guide peg covers at the rear on each side and then pull the weatherstrip free. The insulator padding from the roof panel lower face can be cut free carefully, for re-use if desired.

32 Clean the insulator pad surface of the roof panel, smear on an even layer of adhesive and carefully press the insulator padding into position.

33 Clean the rear sponge mounting plate, apply some sealer to the weatherstrip location on the plate, then carefully fit the weatherstrip into position.

34 Refit the rear sponge mounting plate and the plastic guide peg covers, then carefully insert the roof panel back into position. Before installing the roof panel, check that the rear mounting brackets are fully forward and against the stops.

35 Refit the rear mounting bracket lockplates and secure the mountings to the roof panel.

36 Relocate the spring arms, then fit the front mounting slides into the guide rail and loosely attach them to the sliding roof.

37 Close the roof and adjust it as described earlier.

38 Check the roof operation before tightening the cover screws. Partially open the roof, slide the trim panel back into position and secure. When fitting, ensure that the material does not snag on the front guide rail, when fitting under it. Clip the panel into position to complete.

Door mirror – removal and installation

39 Prise free the triangular trim panel on the inside of the door, using

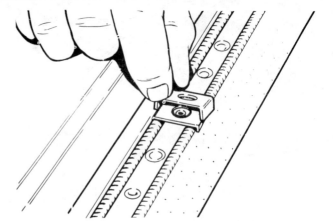

Fig. 13.59 Remove cable locating clips (Sec 12)

Fig. 13.60 Front mounting clamp bolts (Sec 12)

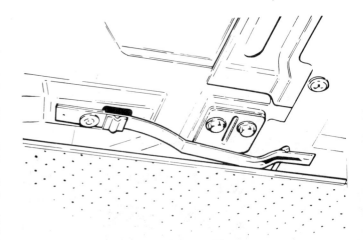

Fig. 13.61 Spring arms clear of rear mounting bracket (Sec 12)

a screwdriver or similar tool. When levering, use a piece of paper, or cardboard to protect the paintwork.

40 On models having a mirror with remote control, it is sometimes difficult to remove the bezel over the control knob using finger pressure only. To remove the bezel, Ford recommend a special tool (Ford number 41-014), shown in Fig. 13.62, but a suitable tool can easily be made from the dimensions given.

41 Unscrew and remove the three retaining screws (photo), and remove the mirror from the door.

42 Installation is the reverse of removal.

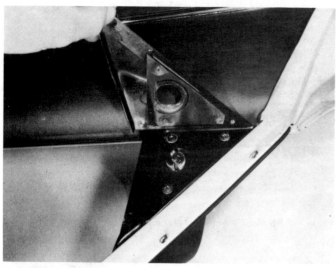

12.41 Door mirror retaining screw

Upper central console – removal and installation

43 Disconnect the battery leads.
44 Unscrew and remove the four console retaining screws shown in Fig. 13.63 then withdraw the console far enough to allow any clock, or radio wiring to be disconnected. When it is free of any attachments, withdraw the console.
45 Installation is the reverse of removal.

Heating and ventilation

46 The heating and ventilating of the Cortina 80 series has been improved and now incorporates central fresh air vents and side window demisting. The heater unit is essentially the same as that used on earlier models and the removal and installation instructions are unchanged from those given in Chapter 12. The heater controls and their adjustment are also unchanged.

Central ventilation panel – removal and installation

47 Disconnect the battery leads.
48 Disconnect and remove the lower left-hand trim panel of the dash, which is retained by either two or three clips and two metal tags.
49 Remove the instrument panel as described in Chapter 10.
50 Unscrew and remove the two vent screws, pull the vent from its location and detach the air supply hose.

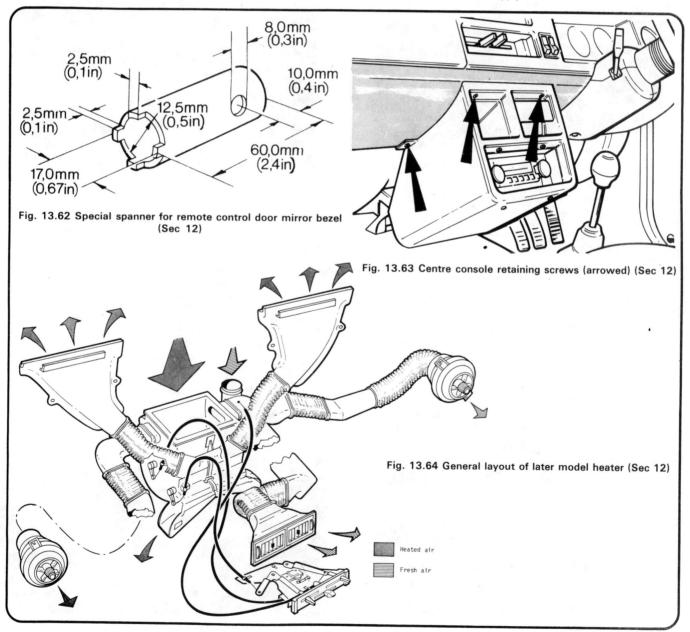

Fig. 13.62 Special spanner for remote control door mirror bezel (Sec 12)

Fig. 13.63 Centre console retaining screws (arrowed) (Sec 12)

Fig. 13.64 General layout of later model heater (Sec 12)

Heated air

Fresh air

51 Installation is the reverse of removal. On completion check the operation of all instruments and controls.

Bumpers

52 The 1980 models have plastic end caps on each side of the bumpers at the front and rear. These give additional side and corner protection to the bodywork.

53 To remove a bumper quarter section, use a block of wood against the edge of the quarter section (photo); use only hand pressure on the wood block. When the bumper end of the quarter section is free, disengage the quarter section from its fixing on the wing by sliding it out of its clip (photo). The clip can be removed from the wing by turning it through 90° and pulling it out.

54 If overriders are fitted, these must be detached before the corner mouldings are removed.

55 To install the corner mouldings, engage the moulding in the clip on the wing and then push the moulding over the end of the bumper. Check for security when fitted.

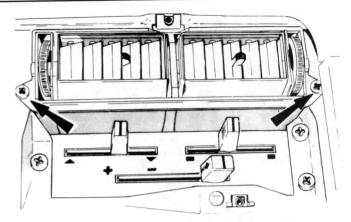

Fig. 13.65 Centre vent attachment screws (arrowed) (Sec 12)

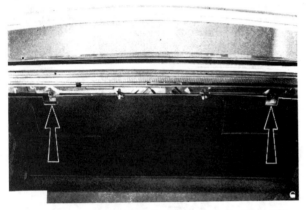

Fig. 13.66 Rear seat back retaining tangs (Sec 12)

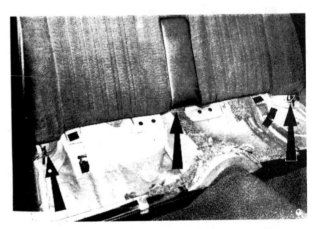

Fig. 13.67 Rear seat back fixing screws (Sec 12)

Rear seat cushion – removal and refitting

56 Locate the flaps in the carpet below the rear seat on either side of the tunnel.

57 Bend back the flaps and remove the screws, one each side, that secure the seat to the floor.

58 Remove the cushion.

59 Refitting is a reversal of the removal procedure.

Rear seat backrest – removal and refitting

60 Remove the rear seat cushion.

61 From inside the passenger compartment locate the tangs that secure the lower edge of the backrest to the floor.

62 Bend back the tangs to free the backrest from the floor.

63 From inside the boot remove the nuts, one each side, from the seat back studs.

64 From inside the passenger compartment pull the backrest from its location and remove it from the vehicle.

65 When refitting, locate the backrest studs through their respective holes and align the lower fixings with the floor tangs.

66 Bend the floor tangs to secure the lower fixings.

67 From inside the luggage compartment, replace and tighten the nuts securing the backrest studs.

68 Replace the rear seat cushion.

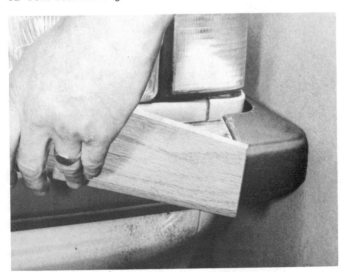

12.53a Removing a quarter bumper

12.53b Quarter bumper retaining clip

Fault diagnosis

Introduction

The car owner who does his or her own maintenance according to the recommended schedules should not have to use this section of the manual very often. Modern component reliability is such that, provided those items subject to wear or deterioration are inspected or renewed at the specified intervals, sudden failure is comparatively rare. Faults do not usually just happen as a result of sudden failure, but develop over a period of time. Major mechanical failures in particular are usually preceded by characteristic symptoms over hundreds or even thousands of miles. Those components which do occasionally fail without warning are often small and easily carried in the car.

With any fault finding, the first step is to decide where to begin investigations. Sometimes this is obvious, but on other occasions a little detective work will be necessary. The owner who makes half a dozen haphazard adjustments or replacements may be successful in curing a fault (or its symptoms), but he will be none the wiser if the fault recurs and he may well have spent more time and money than was necessary. A calm and logical approach will be found to be more satisfactory in the long run. Always take into account any warning signs or abnormalities that may have been noticed in the period preceding the fault – power loss, high or low gauge readings, unusual noises or smells, etc – and remember that failure of components such as fuses or spark plugs may only be pointers to some underlying fault.

The pages which follow here are intended to help in cases of failure to start or breakdown on the road. There is also a Fault Diagnosis Section at the end of each Chapter which should be consulted if the preliminary checks prove unfruitful. Whatever the fault, certain basic principles apply. These are as follows:

Verify the fault. This is simply a matter of being sure that you know what the symptoms are before starting work. This is particularly important if you are investigating a fault for someone else who may not have described it very accurately.

Don't overlook the obvious. For example, if the car won't start, is there petrol in the tank? (Don't take anyone else's word on this particular point, and don't trust the fuel gauge either!) If an electrical fault is indicated, look for loose or broken wires before digging out the test gear.

Cure the disease, not the symptom. Substituting a flat battery with a fully charged one will get you off the hard shoulder, but if the underlying cause is not attended to, the new battery will go the same way. Similarly, changing oil-fouled spark plugs for a new set will get you moving again, but remember that the reason for the fouling (if it wasn't simply an incorrect grade of plug) will have to be established and corrected.

Don't take anything for granted. Particularly, don't forget that a 'new' component may itself be defective (especially if it's been rattling round in the boot for months), and don't leave components out of a fault diagnosis sequence just because they are new or recently fitted. When you do finally diagnose a difficult fault, you'll probably realise that all the evidence was there from the start.

Electrical faults

Electrical faults can be more puzzling than straightforward mechanical failures, but they are no less susceptible to logical analysis if the basic principles of operation are understood. Car electrical wiring exists in extremely unfavourable conditions – heat, vibration and chemical attack – and the first things to look for are loose or corroded connections and broken or chafed wires, especially where the wires pass through holes in the bodywork or are subject to vibration.

All metal-bodied cars in current production have one pole of the battery 'earthed', ie connected to the car bodywork, and in nearly all modern cars it is the negative (–) terminal. The various electrical components' motors, bulb holders etc – are also connected to earth, either by means of a lead or directly by their mountings. Electric current flows through the component and then back to the battery via the car bodywork. If the component mounting is loose or corroded, or if a good path back to the battery is not available, the circuit will be incomplete and malfunction will result. The engine and/or gearbox are also earthed by means of flexible metal straps to the body or subframe; if these straps are loose or missing, starter motor, generator and ignition trouble may result.

Assuming the earth return to be satisfactory, electrical faults will be due either to component malfunction or to defects in the current supply. Individual components are dealt with in Chapter 10. If supply wires are broken or cracked internally this results in an open-circuit, and the easiest way to check for this is to bypass the suspect wire temporarily with a length of wire having a crocodile clip or suitable connector at each end. Alternatively, a 12V test lamp can be used to verify the presence of supply voltage at various points along the wire and the break can be thus isolated.

If a bare portion of a live wire touches the car bodywork or other earthed metal part, the electricity will take the low-resistance path thus formed back to the battery: this is known as a short-circuit. Hopefully a short-circuit will blow a fuse, but otherwise it may cause burning of the insulation (and possibly further short-circuits) or even a fire. This is why it is inadvisable to bypass persistently blowing fuses with silver foil or wire.

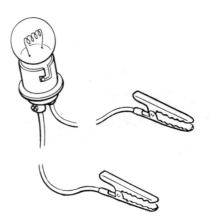

A simple test lamp is useful for investigating electrical faults

Spares and tool kit

Most cars are only supplied with sufficient tools for wheel changing; the *Maintenance and minor repair* tool kit detailed in *Tools and working facilities,* with the addition of a hammer, is probably sufficient for those repairs that most motorists would consider attempting at the roadside. In addition a few items which can be fitted without too much trouble in the event of a breakdown should be carried. Experience and available space will modify the list below, but the following may save having to call on professional assistance:

Spark plugs, clean and correctly gapped
HT lead and plug cap — long enough to reach the plug furthest from the distributor
Distributor rotor, condenser and contact breaker points (where applicable)
Drivebelts — emergency type may suffice
Spare fuses
Set of principal light bulbs
Tin of radiator sealer and hose bandage
Exhaust bandage
Roll of insulating tape
Length of soft iron wire
Length of electrical flex
Torch or inspection lamp (can double as test lamp)
Battery jump leads
Tow-rope
Ignition waterproofing aerosol
Litre of engine oil
Sealed can of hydraulic fluid
Emergency windscreen
Hose clips
Tube of filler paste
Tyre valve core

If spare fuel is carried, a can designed for the purpose should be used to minimise risks of leakage and collision damage. A first aid kit and a warning triangle, whilst not at present compulsory in the UK, are obviously sensible items to carry in addition to the above.

When touring abroad it may be advisable to carry additional spares which, even if you cannot fit them yourself, could save having to wait while parts are obtained. The items below may be worth considering:

Cylinder head gaskets
Alternator brushes
Fuel pump repair kit

One of the motoring organisations will be able to advise on availability of fuel etc in foreign countries.

Engine will not start

Engine fails to turn when starter operated
Flat battery (recharge, use jump leads, or push start)
Battery terminals loose or corroded
Battery earth to body defective
Engine earth strap loose or broken
Starter motor (or solenoid) wiring loose or broken
Automatic transmission selector in wrong position, or inhibitor switch faulty
Ignition/starter switch faulty
Major mechanical failure (seizure) or long disuse (piston rings rusted to bores)
Starter or solenoid internal fault (see Chapter 10)

Starter motor turns engine slowly
Partially discharged battery (recharge, use jump leads, or push start)
Battery terminals loose or corroded
Battery earth to body defective
Engine earth strap loose
Starter motor (or solenoid) wiring loose
Starter motor internal fault (see Chapter 10)

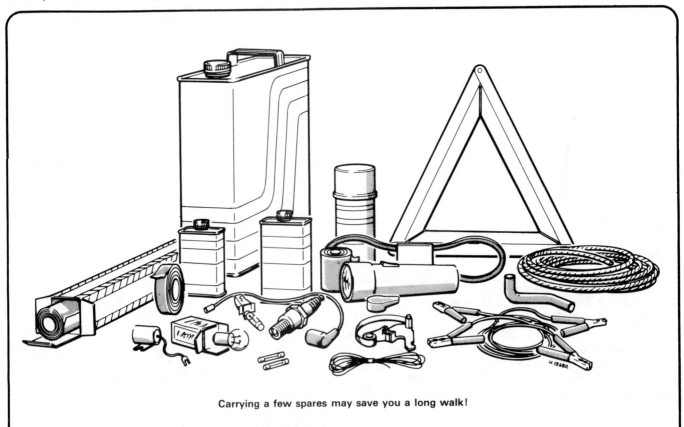

Carrying a few spares may save you a long walk!

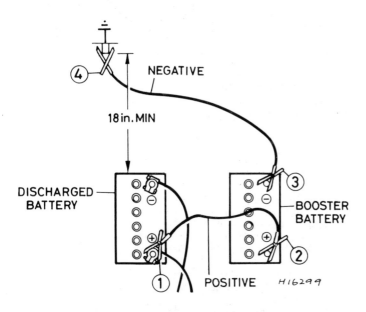

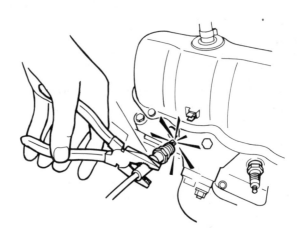

Crank engine and check for a spark. Note use of insulated pliers –
dry cloth or a rubber glove will suffice

Jump start lead connections for negative earth – connect
leads in order shown

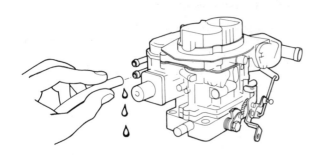

Remove fuel supply pipe from carburettor and check that fuel is
being delivered

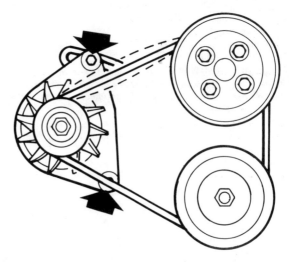

A slack drivebelt may cause overheating and battery charging
problems. Slacken bolts (arrowed) to adjust

Starter motor spins without turning engine
  Flat battery
  Starter motor pinion sticking on sleeve
  Flywheel gear teeth damaged or worn
  Starter motor mounting bolts loose

Engine turns normally but fails to start
  Damp or dirty HT leads and distributor cap (crank engine and
  check for spark) (photo)
  Dirty or incorrectly gapped contact breaker points (if applicable)
  No fuel in tank (check for delivery at carburettor)
  Automatic choke incorrectly adjusted (see Chapter 3)
  Fouled or incorrectly gapped spark plugs (remove, clean and
  regap)
  Other ignition system fault (see Chapter 4 or 13)
  Other fuel system fault (see Chapter 3)
  Poor compression (see Chapter 1)
  Major mechanical failure (eg camshaft drive)

Engine fires but will not run
  Automatic choke incorrectly adjusted (see Chapter 3)
  Air leaks at carburettor or inlet manifold
  Fuel starvation (see Chapter 3)
  Ballast resistor defective (if fitted), or other ignition fault (see
  Chapter 4 or 13)

Engine cuts out and will not restart

Engine cuts out suddenly – ignition fault
  Loose or disconnected LT wires
  Wet HT leads or distributor cap (after traversing water splash)
  Coil or condenser failure (check for spark)
  Other ignition fault (see Chapter 4 or 13)

Engine misfires before cutting out – fuel fault
  Fuel tank empty
  Fuel pump defective or filter blocked (check for delivery)
  Fuel tank filler vent blocked (suction will be evident on releasing
  cap)
  Carburettor needle valve sticking
  Other fuel system fault (see Chapter 3)

Engine cuts out – other causes
  Serious overheating
  Major mechanical failure (eg camshaft drive)

Engine overheats

Ignition (no-charge) warning light illuminated
  Slack or broken drivebelt – retension or renew (Chapter 2)

Ignition warning light not illuminated
Coolant loss due to internal or external leakage (see Chapter 2)
Thermostat defective
Low oil level
Brakes binding
Radiator clogged externally or internally
Electric cooling fan not operating correctly (if fitted)
Engine waterways clogged
Ignition timing incorrect or automatic advance malfunctioning
Mixture too weak

Note: *Do not add cold water to an overheated engine or damage may result*

Low engine oil pressure

Gauge reads low or warning light illuminates with engine running
Oil level low or incorrect grade
Defective gauge or sender unit
Wire to sender unit earthed
Engine overheating
Oil filter clogged or bypass valve defective
Oil pressure relief valve defective
Oil pick-up strainer clogged
Oil pump worn or mountings loose
Worn main or big-end bearings

Note: *Low oil pressure in a high-mileage engine at tickover is not necessarily a cause for concern. Sudden pressure loss at speed is far more significant. In any event, check the gauge or warning light sender before condemning the engine!*

Engine noises

Pre-ignition (pinking) on acceleration
Incorrect grade of fuel
Ignition timing incorrect
Distributor faulty or worn
Worn or maladjusted carburettor
Excessive carbon build-up in engine

Whistling or wheezing noises
Leaking vacuum hose
Leaking carburettor or manifold gasket
Blowing head gasket

Tapping or rattling
Incorrect valve clearances
Worn valve gear
Worn timing chain
Broken piston ring (ticking noise)

Knocking or thumping
Unintentional mechanical contact (eg fan blades)
Worn fanbelt
Peripheral component fault (generator, water pump etc)
Worn big-end bearings (regular heavy knocking, perhaps less under load)
Worn main bearings (rumbling and knocking, perhaps worsening under load)
Piston slap (most noticeable when cold)

General repair procedures

Whenever servicing, repair or overhaul work is carried out on the car or its components, it is necessary to observe the following procedures and instructions. This will assist in carrying out the operation efficiently and to a professional standard of workmanship.

Joint mating faces and gaskets

Where a gasket is used between the mating faces of two components, ensure that it is renewed on reassembly, and fit it dry unless otherwise stated in the repair procedure. Make sure that the mating faces are clean and dry with all traces of old gasket removed. When cleaning a joint face, use a tool which is not likely to score or damage the face, and remove any burrs or nicks with an oilstone or fine file.

Make sure that tapped holes are cleaned with a pipe cleaner, and keep them free of jointing compound if this is being used unless specifically instructed otherwise.

Ensure that all orifices, channels or pipes are clear and blow through them, preferably using compressed air.

Oil seals

Whenever an oil seal is removed from its working location, either individually or as part of an assembly, it should be renewed.

The very fine sealing lip of the seal is easily damaged and will not seal if the surface it contacts is not completely clean and free from scratches, nicks or grooves. If the original sealing surface of the component cannot be restored, the component should be renewed.

Protect the lips of the seal from any surface which may damage them in the course of fitting. Use tape or a conical sleeve where possible. Lubricate the seal lips with oil before fitting and, on dual lipped seals, fill the space between the lips with grease.

Unless otherwise stated, oil seals must be fitted with their sealing lips toward the lubricant to be sealed.

Use a tubular drift or block of wood of the appropriate size to install the seal and, if the seal housing is shouldered, drive the seal down to the shoulder. If the seal housing is unshouldered, the seal should be fitted with its face flush with the housing top face.

Screw threads and fastenings

Always ensure that a blind tapped hole is completely free from oil, grease, water or other fluid before installing the bolt or stud. Failure to do this could cause the housing to crack due to the hydraulic action of the bolt or stud as it is screwed in.

When tightening a castellated nut to accept a split pin, tighten the nut to the specified torque, where applicable, and then tighten further to the next split pin hole. Never slacken the nut to align a split pin hole unless stated in the repair procedure.

When checking or retightening a nut or bolt to a specified torque setting, slacken the nut or bolt by a quarter of a turn, and then retighten to the specified setting.

Locknuts, locktabs and washers

Any fastening which will rotate against a component or housing in the course of tightening should always have a washer between it and the relevant component or housing.

Spring or split washers should always be renewed when they are used to lock a critical component such as a big-end bearing retaining nut or bolt.

Locktabs which are folded over to retain a nut or bolt should always be renewed.

Self-locking nuts can be reused in non-critical areas, providing resistance can be felt when the locking portion passes over the bolt or stud thread.

Split pins must always be replaced with new ones of the correct size for the hole.

Special tools

Some repair procedures in this manual entail the use of special tools such as a press, two or three-legged pullers, spring compressors etc. Wherever possible, suitable readily available alternatives to the manufacturer's special tools are described, and are shown in use. In some instances, where no alternative is possible, it has been necessary to resort to the use of a manufacturer's tool and this has been done for reasons of safety as well as the efficient completion of the repair operation. Unless you are highly skilled and have a thorough understanding of the procedure described, never attempt to bypass the use of any special tool when the procedure described specifies its use. Not only is there a very great risk of personal injury, but expensive damage could be caused to the components involved.

Conversion factors

Length (distance)

	X			X		
Inches (in)	X	25.4	= Millimetres (mm)	X	0.0394	= Inches (in)
Feet (ft)	X	0.305	= Metres (m)	X	3.281	= Feet (ft)
Miles	X	1.609	= Kilometres (km)	X	0.621	= Miles

Volume (capacity)

Cubic inches (cu in; in^3)	X	16.387	= Cubic centimetres (cc; cm^3)	X	0.061	= Cubic inches (cu in; in^3)
Imperial pints (Imp pt)	X	0.568	= Litres (l)	X	1.76	= Imperial pints (Imp pt)
Imperial quarts (Imp qt)	X	1.137	= Litres (l)	X	0.88	= Imperial quarts (Imp qt)
Imperial quarts (Imp qt)	X	1.201	= US quarts (US qt)	X	0.833	= Imperial quarts (Imp qt)
US quarts (US qt)	X	0.946	= Litres (l)	X	1.057	= US quarts (US qt)
Imperial gallons (Imp gal)	X	4.546	= Litres (l)	X	0.22	= Imperial gallons (Imp gal)
Imperial gallons (Imp gal)	X	1.201	= US gallons (US gal)	X	0.833	= Imperial gallons (Imp gal)
US gallons (US gal)	X	3.785	= Litres (l)	X	0.264	= US gallons (US gal)

Mass (weight)

Ounces (oz)	X	28.35	= Grams (g)	X	0.035	= Ounces (oz)
Pounds (lb)	X	0.454	= Kilograms (kg)	X	2.205	= Pounds (lb)

Force

Ounces-force (ozf; oz)	X	0.278	= Newtons (N)	X	3.6	= Ounces-force (ozf; oz)
Pounds-force (lbf; lb)	X	4.448	= Newtons (N)	X	0.225	= Pounds-force (lbf; lb)
Newtons (N)	X	0.1	= Kilograms-force (kgf; kg)	X	9.81	= Newtons (N)

Pressure

Pounds-force per square inch (psi; lbf/in^2; lb/in^2)	X	0.070	= Kilograms-force per square centimetre (kgf/cm^2; kg/cm^2)	X	14.223	= Pounds-force per square inch (psi; lbf/in^2; lb/in^2)
Pounds-force per square inch (psi; lbf/in^2; lb/in^2)	X	0.068	= Atmospheres (atm)	X	14.696	= Pounds-force per square inch (psi; lbf/in^2; lb/in^2)
Pounds-force per square inch (psi; lbf/in^2; lb/in^2)	X	0.069	= Bars	X	14.5	= Pounds-force per square inch (psi; lbf/in^2; lb/in^2)
Pounds-force per square inch (psi; lbf/in^2; lb/in^2)	X	6.895	= Kilopascals (kPa)	X	0.145	= Pounds-force per square inch (psi; lbf/in^2; lb/in^2)
Kilopascals (kPa)	X	0.01	= Kilograms-force per square centimetre (kgf/cm^2; kg/cm^2)	X	98.1	= Kilopascals (kPa)

Torque (moment of force)

Pounds-force inches (lbf in; lb in)	X	1.152	= Kilograms-force centimetre (kgf cm; kg cm)	X	0.868	= Pounds-force inches (lbf in; lb in)
Pounds-force inches (lbf in; lb in)	X	0.113	= Newton metres (Nm)	X	8.85	= Pounds-force inches (lbf in; lb in)
Pounds-force inches (lbf in; lb in)	X	0.083	= Pounds-force feet (lbf ft; lb ft)	X	12	= Pounds-force inches (lbf in; lb in)
Pounds-force feet (lbf ft; lb ft)	X	0.138	= Kilograms-force metres (kgf m; kg m)	X	7.233	= Pounds-force feet (lbf ft; lb ft)
Pounds-force feet (lbf ft; lb ft)	X	1.356	= Newton metres (Nm)	X	0.738	= Pounds-force feet (lbf ft; lb ft)
Newton metres (Nm)	X	0.102	= Kilograms-force metres (kgf m; kg m)	X	9.804	= Newton metres (Nm)

Power

Horsepower (hp)	X	745.7	= Watts (W)	X	0.0013	= Horsepower (hp)

Velocity (speed)

Miles per hour (miles/hr; mph)	X	1.609	= Kilometres per hour (km/hr; kph)	X	0.621	= Miles per hour (miles/hr; mph)

Fuel consumption*

Miles per gallon, Imperial (mpg)	X	0.354	= Kilometres per litre (km/l)	X	2.825	= Miles per gallon, Imperial (mpg)
Miles per gallon, US (mpg)	X	0.425	= Kilometres per litre (km/l)	X	2.352	= Miles per gallon, US (mpg)

Temperature

Degrees Fahrenheit = (°C x 1.8) + 32

Degrees Celsius (Degrees Centigrade; °C) = (°F - 32) x 0.56

*It is common practice to convert from miles per gallon (mpg) to litres/100 kilometres (l/100km),
where mpg (Imperial) x l/100 km = 282 and mpg (US) x l/100 km = 235

Index

Printed by
J H Haynes & Co Ltd
Sparkford Nr Yeovil
Somerset BA22 7JJ England